Also by Tom Wiener

THE BOOK OF VIDEO LISTS

THE *OFF-HOLLYWOOD*
FILM GUIDE

THE DEFINITIVE GUIDE TO INDEPENDENT

AND FOREIGN FILMS ON VIDEO AND DVD

TOM WIENER

THE **OFF-HOLLYWOOD**

FILM GUIDE

RANDOM HOUSE TRADE PAPERBACKS / NEW YORK

RANDOM HOUSE TRADE PAPERBACKS and colophon are trademarks of Random House, Inc.

LIBRARY OF CONGRESS CATALOGING-IN-PUBLICATION DATA
Wiener, Tom.
The off-Hollywood film guide : the definitive guide to independent and foreign
films on video and DVD / Tom Wiener.
p.   cm.
Available also in an electronic format.
Includes indexes.
ISBN 0-8129-9207-5 (alk. paper)
1. Foreign films—United States—Catalogs.   2. Independent filmmakers.
3. Motion pictures—Catalogs.   4. Video recordings—Catalogs.   5. DVD- Video
discs—Catalogs.   I. Title.

PN1995.9.F67 W54 2002
791.43'75—dc21   2002069918

Random House website address:
www.atrandom.com

Printed in the United States of America

9   8   7   6   5   4   3   2

First Trade Paperback Edition

Designed by Gabriel Levine

CONTENTS

ACKNOWLEDGMENTS

*T*his book owes its existence to a number of people, starting with Bob Wilson, a gentleman and fine editor who played matchmaker between me and Random House. Mary Bahr and M. J. Devaney at Random House deserve much praise and credit, not only for their guidance and support, but also for their love of good movies. Special thanks to my copy editor, Evan Camfield, for a splendid job.

I got to watch many old favorites and discover some new ones while researching this book. The lovely Lori Flynn generously offered access to tapes and discs for background.

Evan Geldzahler shared his expertise on war films with me, and I'm always grateful for his insights. Special thanks, too, should go to David Wolford, whose generosity afforded me the opportunity to do this book.

Finally, I cannot begin to thank my wife, Barbara Humphrys, who created the database I needed, offered tech support 24/7, and watched a lot of subtitled films with me. Okay, honey, we can start going to Hollywood movies again.

Tom Wiener
Washington, D.C.

A nd now for something completely different.

Like you, I love movies. And the movies that I love most are the ones that offer something unexpected, something a few feet (or maybe a mile or two) off the beaten track. Movies that weren't created when an agent rounded up three stars and a director and sold a high-concept package to a Hollywood studio, which then went out and spent millions and millions to produce the film and millions more to market, advertise, and promote it.

Some good movies have come out of that process (I'll think of one in a minute), but so have many bad ones (no names, please; we know who they are). So let us now praise less-than-famous men and women filmmakers whose work slipped quietly into movie theaters and now sits on video store shelves begging to be discovered by you.

Off-Hollywood films are what you'll find in this guide—more than 650 of the best foreign and independently produced films of all time. A foreign film is any production principally financed (and usually filmed) outside the United States, including English-language films from Great Britain, Ireland, Canada, New Zealand, and Australia. Defining "independent" is a bit trickier. Any film produced outside the Hollywood studio system is, in effect, an independent movie. Broadly speaking, independent filmmaking has a history as long as that of the movies. Even after the studios rose to power and prominence in the years between the world wars, independent filmmakers managed to find a niche, though a very small one, since the studios also controlled the theater chains.

This guide concentrates on the independent filmmaking movement that began in the 1960s, when talented filmmakers like John Cassavetes (*Shadows, Faces*), Dennis Hopper (*Easy Rider*), and Martin Scorsese (*Who's That Knocking at My Door*) showed the way for dozens of directors to come. Some—Scorsese, Spike Lee, the Coen Brothers, for example— started out as indies but have moved into studio-backed productions, returning to their roots occasionally for special projects. Entries for those who work both sides of the street reflect that split.

I allowed two award-giving organizations—the Sundance Film Festival and the Independent Spirit Awards—to define what was an independent film simply by which films they choose to nominate for their awards. In general, I tried to be inclusive without being exhaustive.

As I mentioned, this is a guide to the best foreign and independent films. If you're looking for an "A list" of titles, consult Essential Movies on page xvii.

All of the films reviewed in this book are available on home video, and many are on DVD. If you're very lucky, your video store carries many of them. But video retailing relies on the latest Hollywood hits to make a profit, and you may have to do some work to find some of these films. Our Resource Directory offers tips on alternative sources for renting and buying.

All of the films are listed in alphabetical order. Titles beginning with foreign articles such as *Le* and *Los* are listed under the first letter of the article, and they are cross-referenced from the next word. Individual entries contain the following information about each film:

- Title
- Country of origin
- Year of release
- Color (C), black and white (B&W), or both (C/B&W)
- Running time
- MPAA rating (G, PG, PG-13, R, X, or NC-17). Unrated films are designated NR.
- Genre
- Director
- Principal cast
- DVD availability (indicated by the icon ⊙ **DVD**)
- DVD special features, if any
- Subgenre categories
- Double-feature suggestion

Films I consider essential are indicated as such; a complete list is on page xvii. Country of origin indicates the countries with a producing interest in the film. The primary country is usually listed first. Year of release is the year a film was released to theaters in its primary country of origin. The cast list offers a generous selection of performers in each film. DVD availability is accurate as of this writing; for more up-to-date information on DVD availability, visit the websites listed in the Resource Directory. DVD special features are those that go beyond the standard add-ons (theatrical trailer, biographies of the cast and crew).

Subgenre categories are my way of cross-referencing every film, to give you a way of connecting to others like it. The genres and their codes are:

Action-Adventure/Westerns (AC)

Comedy (CO)

Documentary (DO)

Drama (DR)

Fantasy/Horror/Science Fiction (FA)

Thriller (TH)

Video Extra (XT)

Each genre contains its own set of numbered categories; you can find them all in the Key to Subgenres on page 444. Every film has a reference to at least one of these lists. For example, *Crouching Tiger, Hidden Dragon* is referenced on five lists: AC3 (Martial Arts), AC7 (Revenge, Getting), AC8 (Swords and Sorcery), DR16 (Life Lessons), and DR18 (Love Stories). Those lists will cross-reference other films in this book that deal with the same subject matter or themes. "Video Extra" offers categories that aren't genre-specific, such as Wide-Screen Delights.

The double-feature suggestion, indicated by "Goes well with," offers another film in this book that is a match for the entry. My matchmaking criteria vary—the two films may have some of the same actors or the same director, they may be companion films in the same series, and/or they may deal with similar material.

Each review contains information on awards the film may have received from the Motion Picture Academy of Arts and Sciences, the New York Film Critics Circle, the Sundance Film Festival (known until the mid-1980s as the U.S. Festival), and the Independent Spirit Awards.

The second part of the book is a series of reference lists. The Subgenre Lists offer you a chance to find films with similar themes and subject matter. The Directors Index lists all of the directors in the book. The Actors Index is a selection of performers of interest; since there are over 2,600 actors referenced in this book, many of them appearing in only one film, listing all of them here isn't practical. The Countries Index breaks down all of the films by the primary producing country. The DVD Index details all films currently available in that format.

If you're using the electronic version of this book, you can search for any title or name or, for that matter, phrase with your Search function keys.

ONLINE

Looking for more information or a second opinion on the films in this book? The Internet can help.

The **Internet Movie Database** (imdb.com) is the first place many film lovers turn for basic information on the movies. It offers thorough credits for any film you can think of, and complete filmographies for anyone listed in their credits. VHS and DVD availability are indexed, with a link to amazon.com for purchases. You can register and enter your own critical rating (on a scale of 1 to 10) for any film, and also see how the ratings break down by age and gender. There are brief reviews, but the site does not offer plot synopses.

All Movie Guide (allmovie.com) does. It's not as strong on the technical credits as imdb.com, but every film in its database is synopsized, reviewed, and cross-referenced with AMG's own subgenres. Plus, it offers a handy daily guide to what's playing on cable and satellite channels. (Full disclosure: I have contributed reviews to this site.)

Movie Review Query Engine (mrqe.com) indexes over twenty-five thousand film titles, offering reviews from a variety of sources. The site is stronger on more recent releases, with reviews from sources like Roger Ebert, *Rolling Stone,* and *The Washington Post.* Dig back farther, and you'll discover lots of critics (and publications) you've never heard of.

Critics.com (critics.com) is oriented to current and recent releases. It compiles reviews from major publications, assigns star ratings (if they're not already given), then averages them out for a critical consensus. You can read the most positive and negative reviews to get an idea of what's right or wrong with any film indexed.

DVD Planet (dvdplanet.com) is a terrific site for locating information on DVDs. You can find out what's available, what's coming out in the next few months, and what special features are offered for each title. They also offer excellent discounts on all of their inventory, allow you to preorder a disc before it's released, and indicate if stock on an item is running low.

Two other sites, **DVD File** (dvdfile.com) and **DVD Review** (dvdreview
.com), offer an enormous amount of information on DVDs: reviews, news,
feature stories and interviews, ordering links, downloads, clips, guides to
those hidden features (insiders call them Easter Eggs), and more. The reviews may provide more information about picture and sound quality than
the casual renter needs, but if you're building a collection of discs, they
can offer a caveat before you buy.

RENTAL SERVICES

The sad fact is that many video stores concentrate their holdings on the
current releases and Hollywood product that reap the biggest profits. If
you're lucky enough to find a store that carries a strong selection of what's
known in the video retailing business as "catalog" product (i.e., any film
released more than five years ago), cherish that store and give it your business, especially if it carries foreign films and independent releases as well.

Renting by mail is an alternative, and in some ways it can be easier than
making those two trips to the video store. I've tried the first two services
listed below, and I have friends who sing the praises of the third.

Movie Library operates out of Philadelphia, and they specialize in just
the kind of films this book carries. They will send free catalogs of their
holdings. As of this writing, their stock is mostly VHS, but they are expanding into DVD. Their web address is vlibrary.com; their phone number
is 1-800-669-7157.

Facets is a Chicago-based company with an immense catalog that runs
the gamut from mainstream fare to the truly obscure. If they don't have it,
it has likely never been on video or is long out of print. They can be found
at facets.org or 1-800-532-2387.

Netflix (netflix.com) specializes in DVDs for rent and sale. They claim
that if a title is available, they will carry it for rent.

As of this writing, Movie Library does not require a membership fee;
Facets and Netflix do. Movie Library and Netflix provide cartons with
postage already affixed to mail back your rentals; Facets does not.

ADDITIONAL REFERENCES

In compiling the basic information for this book, I used several printed
guides: Leonard Maltin's *Movie & Video Guide,* the *Time Out Film Guide,*
and three volumes from the VideoHound kennel of movie references: *The
VideoHound Movie Retriever, VideoHound's World Cinema* by Elliot Wil-
helm, and *VideoHound's DVD Guide.*

ESSENTIAL MOVIES

After Hours
Aguirre: The Wrath of God
Alexander Nevsky
Amarcord
Amelie
American Dream
American Heart
Antonia's Line
Aparajito
The Apostle
Ashes and Diamonds

Babette's Feast
Badlands
The Battle of Algiers
Battleship Potemkin
Beauty and the Beast (1946)
Belle de Jour
The Bicycle Thief
Big Night
Blood Simple
Blowup
The Blue Angel (1930)
Blue Velvet
Boogie Nights
Boys Don't Cry
The Boys of St. Vincent
"Breaker" Morant
Breaking the Waves
Breathless (1959)
The Bridge on the River Kwai

When We Were Kings
Wild Reeds
Wild Strawberries
Wings of Desire
Women in Love
Women on the Verge of a Nervous Breakdown
The World of Apu

Yi Yi (A One and a Two)
Yojimbo
You Can Count on Me

Z
Zero for Conduct

THE *OFF-HOLLYWOOD*
FILM GUIDE

A NOS AMOURS

France 1984 C 102 min. R Drama
Dir: Maurice Pialat
C: Sandrine Bonnaire, Dominique Besnehard, Maurice Pialat

That an actress like Sandrine Bonnaire, with her impressive filmography, is almost totally unknown in this country is a sad commentary on how marginalized foreign films have become; graybeards can recall the days when Jeanne Moreau was known even to people who didn't bother going to films with subtitles. Bonnaire was seventeen when she made her debut here, playing a fifteen-year-old whose sexual activity reflects a fractured home life. Adolescence is tough enough, but throw in a mom who turns every event into a crisis, a dad who's fed up and about to move out, and a brother who's a bit too affectionate, and this girl is using every bit of her resources just to get through the day. *A Nos Amours* won France's César for best film.

DR11, DR41
Goes well with: *Vagabond*

ABSOLUTE BEGINNERS

U.K. 1986 C 107 min. PG-13 Musical
Dir: Julien Temple
C: Eddie O'Connell, Patsy Kensit, David Bowie, James Fox, Ray
  Davies, Mandy Rice-Davies, Sade Adu, Slim Gaillard

Music video directors like Julien Temple get knocked for making films that look like extended videos, but in this case, Temple hit on the perfect excuse—an exploration of the 1958 pop culture scene in Britain, based loosely on Colin MacInnes's novel. From its amazing opening shot (which rivals, at least in technique, the famed openings of Orson Welles's *Touch of Evil* and Robert Altman's *The Player*), Temple establishes that we're in his amusement park, and he's about to take us for a roller-coaster ride. The story, about a naïve photographer (Eddie O'Connell), the fashion designer (Patsy Kensit) he yearns for, and a slick advertising executive (David Bowie), is the usual fluff about breaking in, moving up, and selling out, but the plot is only the clothesline on which to hang a series of gaudy production numbers. O'Connell is forgettably blah, and Kensit is perky as a kind of junior Julie Christie, but the supporting players are the real stars: the ultra-suave James Fox, Bowie and fellow pop stars Ray Davies and Sade (billed under her full name, Sade Adu), jazz veteran Slim Gaillard, and Mandy Rice-Davies of Profumo scandal fame. Gil Evans, one of modern jazz's best arrangers, supervised the score. Best seen in widescreen for maximum impact.

CO10, DR23, MU2, XT7, XT8

Goes well with: *Blowup*

ACCIDENT

U.K.   1967   C   105 min.   PG   Drama
Dir: Joseph Losey
C: Dirk Bogarde, Jacqueline Sassard, Delphine Seyrig, Michael York, Stanley Baker, Vivien Merchant, Harold Pinter, Nicholas Mosley

The second of three collaborations between director Joseph Losey and writer Harold Pinter (following *The Servant,* preceding *The Go-Between*) is one of those Rotting Groves of Academe tales of a professor (Dirk Bogarde), his neglected wife (Vivien Merchant), and their various friends and colleagues. In *The Servant,* Bogarde played the title character, a butler who takes charge of his dissolute boss's life. Here Bogarde is the man whose life is spinning out of control, as he looks to compete with a brash and dashing colleague (Stanley Baker) for the affections of their student (Jacqueline Sassard). Gerry Fisher's camera lingers on the rot behind the characters' faces just long enough for us to notice. The supporting players are all excellent, including Pinter himself as a TV producer and Nicholas Mosley, whose novel Pinter adapted, in a small role.

⊙**DVD:** Available only as part of three-disc Dirk Bogarde Collection, which includes *The Servant* and *The Mind Benders*.

DR19, DR31

Goes well with: *The Servant*

THE ADDICTION

U.S. 1995 B&W 82 min. NR Horror
Dir: Abel Ferrara
C: Lili Taylor, Christopher Walken, Annabella Sciorra, Edie Falco, Michael Imperioli

New York–based director Abel Ferrara offers a reflective take on the vampire film. Lili Taylor plays a dedicated philosophy student who is mugged on the street one night—shades of Ferrara's *Ms. 45*—by a female vampire. She survives the assault, only to begin craving blood, without losing her taste for philosophical arguments. It sounds pretentious, but Ferrara pulls it off, thanks to a snappy running time, artful black-and-white cinematography, and a party scene that tops even the finale of *Ms. 45*. Also of interest: supporting roles for three future players in *The Sopranos:* Michael Imperioli, Edie Falco, and Annabella Sciorra.
FA2, FA9
Goes well with: *Martin*

THE ADVENTURES OF PRISCILLA, QUEEN OF THE DESERT

Australia 1994 C 102 min. R Comedy
Dir: Stephan Elliott
C: Terence Stamp, Hugo Weaving, Guy Pearce

Terence Stamp's first film role was as Billy Budd, and the young actor was perfectly cast in the 1962 film about Herman Melville's seaman whose androgynous beauty and innocence drive another man to murder. Thirty-some years later, Stamp gets to play another beauty, a transsexual who heads a minitroupe of three cross-dressing performers (his mates are played by Hugo Weaving and Guy Pearce). This troupe specializes in mouthing the words to songs by ABBA, whose ongoing popularity down under surely deserves attention from some cultural commentator. The film is a road picture in the spirit of the Crosby-Hope films, and although Bing and Bob never did *The Road to the Outback,* they did wind up in drag in several of their films. The locations offer director Stephan Elliott and cinematographer Brian J. Breheny a magnificent backdrop for the boys on the bus (the bus being the colorfully decorated title character). Lizzy Gardiner and Tom Chappel's outlandish costumes won them an Oscar, and Gardiner, in a dress which seemed to be made up entirely of American Express gold cards, was one of the 1995 Academy Awards show's few memorable winners. Too bad Stamp didn't get to wear that outfit in the film.

⊙**DVD**

CO8, CO10, XT5

Goes well with: *Farewell, My Concubine*

AFFLICTION

U.S. 1997 C 114 min. R Drama

Dir: Paul Schrader

C: Nick Nolte, Sissy Spacek, Willem Dafoe, James Coburn, Mary Beth Hurt, Marian Seldes

Writer-director Paul Schrader's bumpy career hit a high point with this drama adapted from Russell Banks's novel of a small-town screwup (Nick Nolte, winner of the New York Film Critics best actor award) and his abusive father (Oscar winner James Coburn). Grim and unrelenting, yet flashing moments of tenderness and even humor, the story careens toward an ending you know is coming but almost can't bear to watch. Spacek is fine as Nolte's patient lover, but Dafoe, as Nolte's younger brother, seems like an appendix to the action. Schrader seems to be at his best when he's dealing with conflicted loners, as in his script for *Taxi Driver* and his direction of *Mishima* and *Light Sleeper.*

⊙**DVD**

DR11, DR29, DR34

Goes well with: *Character*

AFTER HOURS

ESSENTIAL

U.S. 1985 C 97 min. R Comedy

Dir: Martin Scorsese

C: Griffin Dunne, Rosanna Arquette, Verna Bloom, Thomas Chong, Linda Fiorentino, Teri Garr, John Heard, Cheech Marin, Catherine O'Hara

After Paramount Pictures pulled the plug on his production of *Last Temptation of Christ,* Martin Scorsese decided to get back to his roots: he took to the nighttime streets of New York and made a low-budget, independently produced film. Joe Minion's script, written for a screenwriting class at New York University (Scorsese's alma mater), is a nightmare vision of New York that's leavened by large helpings of dark humor. Griffin Dunne plays a meek computer programmer who lives an uneventful life on the Upper West Side. All that changes in one long night when he ventures into terra incognita—downtown Manhattan—in search of love. He loses his money, finds a corpse, is pursued by a mob that thinks he's a criminal, and winds up encased inside a plaster sculpture. Dunne is perfect as the quintessential New York nebbish, and the crazy-quilt cast (from Linda Fiorentino and Rosanna Arquette as a couple of spooky femme fatales to Cheech Marin and Tommy Chong as a pair of inept burglars) all play their roles with gusto. It's an amusing shaggy-dog story that won Independent Spirit Awards for Best Feature and Director. Scorsese did get to make the more ambitious and artistically risky *Last Temptation* three years later for another studio.

CO2, CO4

Goes well with: *Stranger Than Paradise*

AGUIRRE: THE WRATH OF GOD
ESSENTIAL

West Germany/Peru/Mexico 1972 C 94 min. NR Drama
Dir: Werner Herzog
C: Klaus Kinski, Ruy Guerra, Del Negro, Helena Rojo

Director Werner Herzog and actor Klaus Kinski began their fruitful series of collaborations with this amazing true story of a Spanish conquistador's hapless search through the jungles of Peru for Eldorado. Like Erich von Stroheim obsessing over the underwear his actors wore, Herzog proved to be a filmmaker with an almost pathological need to imitate reality in his art, driving his cast and crew through hazardous conditions on dangerous locations, as if he were a reincarnation of Aguirre. Kinski gave almost as good as he got, as evidenced in the superb documentary, *My Best Fiend,* about the two men and their stormy relationship. *Aguirre* was the breakthrough film for both, establishing Herzog as a leading light of the New German Cinema movement and Kinski as an actor uncommonly gifted at playing obsessives and madmen.

⊙**DVD**

DR1, DR21, DR24

Goes well with: *My Best Fiend*

ALEXANDER NEVSKY
ESSENTIAL

Soviet Union 1938 B&W 107 min. NR Drama
Dir: Sergei Eisenstein
C: Nikolai Cherkasov, Nikolai Okhlopov, Alexander Abrikossov

There are battle scenes, and then there's the battle on the ice in *Alexander Nevsky*. Sergei Eisenstein's epic tale of the thirteenth-century Russian prince who repulsed a Teutonic invasion was commissioned by Joseph Stalin as a not-too-subtle signal to Adolf Hitler that Mother Russia didn't take kindly to invaders of any kind, especially Germans. Making *Alexander Nevsky* proved to be a good political move for Eisenstein; he was coming off a project in Mexico which, because it had nothing to do with singing the praises of the Soviet Union, hadn't endeared him to Stalin. The film's release was temporarily delayed when Stalin and Hitler agreed to a nonaggression pact, but Eisenstein's film eventually proved to be an exceptionally timely piece of propaganda as well as a lasting work of film art. *Nevsky*'s decisive battle, fought in the winter of 1242, is a set piece that displays Eisenstein's eye for grand and small detail and his matchless sense of editing rhythm. And if the visuals aren't enough, the film also boasts one of the greatest scores ever written, by Sergei Prokofiev.

⊙**DVD**

DR24, DR37

Goes well with: *Ivan the Terrible, Part One*

ALL ABOUT MY MOTHER

Spain/France   1999   C   101 min.   R   Drama
Dir: Pedro Almodóvar
C: Cecilia Roth, Marisa Peredes, Penélope Cruz, Antonia San Juan

A New York Film Critics Circle and Academy Award winner for Best Foreign Language Film, *All About My Mother* was Spanish director Pedro Almodóvar's first critical and box office success since his 1988 breakthrough, *Women on the Verge of a Nervous Breakdown*. And like that film, it's a paean to the resiliency of women. Cecilia Roth plays a single mom whose teenage son is killed in a traffic accident. She moves to Barcelona to sort things out with the help of an old friend who, like her estranged husband, is a transvestite. Don't rent *Mother* expecting the wackiness of *Women;* it's a straight (give or take a few characters) story about acting (on stage and in film) and role-playing (in everyday life). Roth also becomes involved with an aging stage actress whom her late son idolized, and with a pregnant nun, played with unusual demureness by Penélope Cruz. Well, it wouldn't be Almodóvar if the film didn't pile on the subplots.

⊙**DVD:** Includes "making of" featurette.
DR4, DR11, DR39
Goes well with: *Lola Montès*

AMARCORD

ESSENTIAL

Italy/France   1974   C   127 min.   R   Comedy-Drama
Dir: Federico Fellini
C: Magali Noël, Bruno Zanin, Pupella Maggio, Armando Brancia, Giuseppe Iangiro

Federico Fellini's most ingratiating film, a well-deserving Oscar and New York Film Critics Circle winner, is a series of sketches about his youth in a seaside town in the 1930s. No Fellini picture would be complete without a gallery of grotesques, but here, those faces serve material that is generally lighthearted and playful. An uncle with a predilection for climbing trees and refusing to come down, a buxom tobacconist who inspires adolescent fantasies, an ocean liner that is greeted by a flotilla of townspeople, a peacock that spreads its plumage in the midst of a snowstorm: *Amarcord* contains more memorable scenes and images than any Fellini movie outside of *8½*. Not everything Fellini recalls is sweetness and light, though, as a new fascist regime threatens the town's sense of tranquility and, more important, its tolerance for diverse political opinions.

⊙**DVD:** Includes restoration demonstration.
DR3, DR11, DR34, DR41
Goes well with: *Au Revoir, Les Enfants*

AMELIE

ESSENTIAL

France/Germany   2001   C   121 min.   R   Comedy
Dir: Jean-Pierre Jeunet
C: Audrey Tautou, Mathieu Kassovitz, Rufus, Yolande Moreau, Urbain Cancelier, Dominique Pinon, André Dussollier (narrator)

The codirector of the dark fantasies *Delicatessen* and *City of Lost Children* turns to the light with this ingenious comedy about a Parisian woman whose rather odd upbringing (detailed in an amusing prologue) has left her acutely aware of the physical world and the needs of people in her Montmartre neighborhood. The film is set in the summer and early fall of 1997. When Amelie learns of the death of Princess Diana, her reaction is to dedicate herself to making the people she sees every day happy, without them learning their benefactor's identity. It sounds like a sappy feel-good story, but that's only half right. Jeunet loves nearly all of his characters, but it's a warts-and-all kind of love. He's clearly fascinated by the way people who live in a community interact, either by chance or choice, and in some cases the two are impossibly intertwined. Of course, Amelie needs to do herself a favor, too, and there is the matter of an attractive young man who holds down two jobs, in a porn shop and an amusement park. This is the kind of film you'll find yourself flashing back on at odd moments, in part because of its rich bounty of visual tricks and allusions and in part because the people in it, beginning with Amelie, are just so darn engaging.

⊙**DVD**

CO9, DR16, DR36

Goes well with: *Comfort and Joy*

AMERICAN DREAM

ESSENTIAL

U.S./U.K.   1989   C   100 min.   NR   Documentary
Dir: Barbara Kopple

If Barbara Kopple hadn't already made the Oscar-winning *Harlan County, U.S.A.,* it would be tempting to call *American Dream* the great American documentary about labor strife. In fact, *Dream* won Kopple her second Oscar in a category that has become more notorious in recent years for excluding films (*The Thin Blue Line, Hoop Dreams*) than for recognizing deserving efforts. *American Dream* (somehow the title doesn't seem pretentious in Kopple's hands) follows the travails of a group of workers at the Hormel meat plant in Austin, Minnesota, who are battling company hostility to their jobs and hard-earned benefits, as well as strife within their own union. Kopple is clearly on the workers' side, but the film never feels like it's proselytizing. She's a patient observer and her persistence pays in scene after telling scene. *American Dream* also won three awards at Sundance: the Filmmaker's Trophy, the Audience Award and the Grand Jury Prize.

DO1

Goes well with: *Matewan*

THE AMERICAN FRIEND
France/West Germany   1977   C   127 min.   NR   Thriller
Dir: Wim Wenders
C: Dennis Hopper, Bruno Ganz, Lisa Kreuzer, Gérard Blain, Jean Eustache, Samuel Fuller, Nicholas Ray

Who would guess that Matt Damon and Dennis Hopper might wind up playing the same fictional character? Damon starred as mystery writer Patricia Highsmith's clever con man Tom Ripley in 1999's *The Talented Mr. Ripley,* and Hopper plays an older incarnation in this adaptation of *Ripley's Game.* The story involves a terminally ill picture framer (Bruno Ganz) who agrees to assassinate a mobster at the behest of the well-connected Mr. R, now making his living as an art dealer. Director Wim Wenders seems less interested in narrative than mood, and he has the superb cinematographer Robby Müller on hand to create plenty of the latter. After a while, the film feels like a lesson in Film Noir 101, with cameos by French film director Jean Eustache and American filmmaker icons Samuel Fuller and Nicholas Ray.

TH9, TH13, XT3
Goes well with: *Purple Noon*

AMERICAN HEART
ESSENTIAL

U.S.   1992   C   113 min.   R   Drama
Dir: Martin Bell
C: Jeff Bridges, Edward Furlong, Lucinda Jenney

A companion to *Streetwise,* Martin Bell's 1984 documentary about homeless kids in Seattle, *American Heart* shares the same setting, focusing on a teenager who's just one slip away from those same mean streets. Edward Furlong plays him, and *Heart* tells the story of his relationship with his father, just released from prison. Jeff Bridges is all tattoos and swagger as the ex-con; his attitude toward the son he barely knows is a mixture of affection and disdain. The push and pull between the two, one nearly a man and the other trying to learn how to be one, makes for affecting confrontations, and Peter Silverman's script doesn't take any easy outs. Bridges earned a well-deserved Best Male Lead trophy at the Independent Spirit Awards; sadly, Academy voters ignored what is arguably his most commanding and moving performance.

DR11, DR36, DR41
Goes well with: *Streetwise*

AMERICAN PSYCHO

U.S./Canada 2000 C 97 min. R Drama
Dir: Mary Harron
C: Christian Bale, Willem Dafoe, Jared Leto, Reese Witherspoon, Samantha Mathis, Chloë Sevigny

Bret Easton Ellis's 1991 novel about a Wall Street yuppie turned serial killer was a reviled book that also seemed virtually unfilmable, with its detailed descriptions of chainsaw murders and eviscerations. Director and cowriter Mary Harron wisely cut down on the violence and sex and pumped up the volume on the satire of late 1980s greedheads. This is the film, at least in part, that Brian DePalma's woebegone *Bonfire of the Vanities* wanted to be: a smart send-up of the New York Material Boy ego run rampant. The time frame is ultimately incidental: Patrick Bateman (Christian Bale) and his ilk still walk the streets of Manhattan today. Chloë Sevigny (as Patrick's naïve secretary), Reese Witherspoon (as his mud-puddle-deep fiancée), and Samantha Mathis (as his drug-addled mistress) are good in essentially one-note performances, but it's Bale's show all the way, and he delivers, with his reptilian eyes and buffed bod and snarky voice. The funniest scene of a surprisingly funny movie: the war of the business cards.

⊙**DVD:** Two editions, R-rated and unrated. Both contain "making of" featurette and interview with Christian Bale.

DR6, DR20, DR29, TH3, TH15
Goes well with: *Pi*

AMORES PERROS

Mexico 2000 C 153 min. R Drama
Dir: Alejandro González Iñárritu
C: Emilio Echevarría, Gael García Bernal, Goya Toledo, Álvaro Guerrero, Vanessa Bauche

The only film whose disclaimer about animal mistreatment comes in the opening credits, *Amores Perros* earns that warning in the very first scene, a harrowing illegal dog fight in Mexico City. *Amores Perros* is translated as *Love's a Bitch,* a clever pun given that dogs are a common denominator among its three linked stories. Writer Guillermo Arriaga and director Alejandro González Iñárritu have fashioned an engrossing and moving story of lost urban souls. Octavio (Gael García Bernal) is a young layabout who uses his brother's tough dog to gain access to the world of illegal fighting; he thinks the money he earns will help him woo his neglected sister-in-law, Susana (Vanessa Bauche). In the middle story, Daniel (Álvaro Guerrero), a successful editor, deserts his wife and children for a young model, Valeria (Goya Toledo), but a horrific traffic accident and the disappearance of her small, beloved dog nearly prove to be deal breakers on their new relationship. The third and strongest story concerns El Chivo (Emilio Echevarría), a street person with a pack of stray dogs and a mysterious past. He's seen as a background character in the other two stories, but *Amores Perros* saves its best writing and direction to flesh out his story in the film's concluding half hour. As details of El Chivo's past are revealed, the film surges strongly toward a hopeful conclusion.

⊙**DVD:** Includes "making of" featurette; music video; audio commentary.

DR6, DR36, XT4

Goes well with: *Los Olvidados*

AND NOW FOR SOMETHING COMPLETELY DIFFERENT

U.K.   1971   C   89 min.   PG   Comedy

Dir: Ian McNaughton

C: Graham Chapman, John Cleese, Eric Idle, Terry Gilliam, Terry Jones, Michael Palin

Anyone reading this book who is not familiar with *Monty Python's Flying Circus:* This is your wake-up call for being oblivious to British comedy of the last thirty years. This collection of Python sketches, featuring the inimitable Graham Chapman, John Cleese, Terry Gilliam, Eric Idle, Terry Jones, and Michael Palin, is an essential document for those who would wish to discuss such events as the Upper Class Twit of the Year Race, or the invasion of our fair cities by the evil gang known as Hell's Grannies, or to learn the fine art of trying to return a dead parrot to a pet shop. It should be mentioned, for the record, that Mr. Gilliam, the only American in the group, generally does not appear in the film but contributes splendid and somewhat surreal animated sequences between the sketches.

⊙**DVD**

CO12, XT1

Goes well with: *Monty Python's The Meaning of Life*

ANDROID

U.S.   1982   C   80 min.   PG   Science Fiction

Dir: Aaron Lipstadt

C: Klaus Kinski, Don Opper

Proving that there is life without Werner Herzog (his most frequent and successful director), Klaus Kinski plays a mad scientist in this enjoyable science-fiction fable. It's no accident that Kinski's wild-eyed appearance apes that of Rudolf Klein-Rogge in Fritz Lang's blueprint mad-scientist movie, *Metropolis*. As in that film, the story involves a creator's relationship with his mechanical android; Dan Opper plays an engineered marvel, Max 404, who resolves to thwart plans to dump him in the recycle bin. There are also sly references to *Blade Runner*'s story of the mechanical man longing for a human life. Any sci-fi film whose budget is so low that it has to borrow sets left over from another film (as *Android* did, from a big-budget fiasco called *Battle Beyond the Stars*) better have something on its mind; director Aaron Lipstadt and his writers (Opper and James Reigle) do, and the result is a witty sleeper.

FA8

Goes well with: *Metropolis*

AN ANGEL AT MY TABLE

New Zealand/Australia/U.K.   1990   C   158 min.   NR   Drama
Dir: Jane Campion
C: Kerry Fox, Alexia Keogh, Karen Fergusson

New Zealander Janet Frame built a solid reputation, starting with her debut in 1951 at the age of twenty-seven, as one of her country's leading poets and short-story writers. But it is her trio of memoirs, published between 1982 and 1985, by which most Americans know her, thanks to Jane Campion's adaptation. Originally shown in three parts on New Zealand television, the film follows Frame from her impoverished childhood to her beginnings as a writer. The central event of her youth was her confinement for eight years in a mental hospital (where she was treated with shock therapy) after a misdiagnosis of schizophrenia. The gifted Campion could have turned this material into a soppy story of a misunderstood artist, but she chooses to portray Frame as a prickly but hardly impossible young woman. Kerry Fox plays Frame as an adult, and she's mesmerizing, refusing to ingratiate her character to us and yet winning our sympathy. *Angel* is consistent with Campion's unsentimental view of women outsiders in such films as *The Piano* and *The Portrait of a Lady*. The Independent Spirit Awards gave it their Best Foreign Film prize.

DR2, DR17, DR29, DR39

Goes well with: *My Brilliant Career*

ANGELS AND INSECTS

U.S./U.K. 1995 C 116 min. R Drama
Dir: Philip Haas
C: Mark Rylance, Kristin Scott Thomas, Patsy Kensit, Jeremy Kemp

The suffocating strictures of Victorian society are on full display in this adaptation of A. S. Byatt's novel *Morpho Eugenia*. Mark Rylance is a naturalist whose research at the country estate of his patron, a wealthy insect collector, lands him squarely in the sights of Eugenia (Patsy Kensit), the family's spoiled daughter. But as Rylance becomes more involved in his work, Kensit looks elsewhere for sexual comfort. Kristin Scott Thomas plays a poor family relation who assists Rylance in his research and to whom he turns for comfort. Director Philip Haas and his cowriter and wife, Belinda, suggest that their rational man of science might as well have turned to the strange behavior of his fellow humans for study; the film's stylized costumes, created to make people resemble insects, were nominated for an Academy Award. The film was originally made for PBS's *American Playhouse* series, though it's more sexually explicit than what you may be used to seeing on public TV.

⊙**DVD**

DR5, DR11, DR18, DR24, DR29

Goes well with: *Cousin Bette*

ANTONIA'S LINE

ESSENTIAL

Netherlands/Belgium/U.K. 1995 C 105 min. R Drama
Dir: Marleen Gorris
C: Willeke van Ammelrooy, Els Dottermans, Jan Decleir, Mil Seghers

A ninety-year-old woman looks back on her most unusual life on the day she decides to die. Marleen Gorris's Oscar winner (for Best Foreign Language Film) is about independent women of all types and ages, starting with its lead character. Antonia is widowed by World War II but decides to create an extended family, starting with her daughter, who is determined to have a child of her own, in spite of the fact that she's a lesbian. The story unfolds like something told by Gabriel García Marquez: it's magic realism, Dutch-style, and totally charming. Gorris's next film, in English, was about another woman examining her past, Virginia Woolf's *Mrs. Dalloway*.

⊙**DVD**

DR11, DR16, DR21, DR39, XT4

Goes well with: *Household Saints*

APARAJITO

ESSENTIAL

India 1956 B&W 108 min. NR Drama

Dir: Satyajit Ray

C: Pinaki Sen Gupta, Smaran Ghosal, Karuna Banerjee, Kanu Banerjee, Ramani Sen Gupta

The second film in Satyajit Ray's masterful Apu Trilogy (bracketed
by *Pather Panchali* and *The World of Apu*) takes Apu (Pinaki Sen Gupta)
away from home for the first time. The family's struggles with poverty,
dramatized in *Pather Panchali,* are now Apu's struggles to become educated at the university in Calcutta. Working a full-time job with a printer
leaves him little time to sleep, but even after he's caught dozing and
thrown out of one of his classes, he remains determined to better himself. The film's best sequence is a visit home; when he decides to miss
the return train on purpose to spend one more day with his mother (the
remarkable Karuna Banerjee), the joy on her face is eloquent beyond
words. All three films deal with Apu's ability to weather the emotional
storms created by the death of someone close to him; Ray's directorial
touch in these scenes is especially skillful. Try, if you can, to see these
films in order; they are available for purchase as a boxed set.

DR11, DR31, DR41

Goes well with: *The World of Apu*

APARTMENT ZERO

U.K./Argentina 1988 C 124 min. R Drama

Dir: Martin Donovan

C: Colin Firth, Hart Bochner, Dora Bryan

The great Roommate from Hell movie, though *Apartment Zero* is a
lot less gory than most other films in the "From Hell" subgenre. Martin
Donovan directed and cowrote this creepy story set in Buenos Aires. A
British movie buff (Colin Firth) with a dream job as a movie theater
projectionist needs a roomie, and a handsome American (Hart Bochner)
seems to fit the bill. Bochner plays off his pretty-boy looks to suggest a
man who might literally charm you to death, and Firth's expressions al-

ternate between rapture over and suspicion of his new pal. The movie's loaded with references and allusions to old films, but you don't have to be in on those jokes to get the central one: Be careful what you wish for.

DR19, DR21, DR27

Goes well with: *Proof*

THE APOSTLE

ESSENTIAL

U.S. 1997 C 134 min. PG-13 Drama
Dir: Robert Duvall
C: Robert Duvall, Farrah Fawcett, Miranda Richardson, Billy Bob Thornton, June Carter Cash, Todd Allen, Billy Joe Shaver

A personal project for actor Robert Duvall, who wrote it, directed it, starred in it, and, for all we know, helped with the catering, *The Apostle* is an honest attempt to deal with issues of faith and redemption. Duvall plays a preacher gone bad, in the American tradition of Henry Ward Beecher and Jimmy Swaggert. On the run from a sticky situation involving his use of a baseball bat on someone's skull, Duvall searches for a new congregation and, more important, a reconciliation with God. The film makes its points in a leisurely kind of way, with director Duvall letting actor Duvall and his colleagues carry on a bit too much at times. Among the supporting cast, the most surprising name may be that of country singer June Carter Cash, unless you know that in the 1950s she lived in New York and took acting lessons. Duvall dominated the 1998 Independent Spirit Awards, walking off with Best Picture, Best Male Lead, and Best Director.

⊙**DVD:** Includes "making of" featurette and audio commentary by Duvall.

DR21, DR30

Goes well with: *Priest*

ASHES AND DIAMONDS

ESSENTIAL

Poland 1958 B&W 105 min. NR Drama
Dir: Andrzej Wajda
C: Zbigniew Cybulski, Ewa Krzyzanowska, Adam Pawlikowski

The concluding film in Andrjez Wajda's trilogy of World War II Poland (which began with *A Generation* and *Kanal*), *Ashes and Dia-*

monds takes place on the final day of the war in a small town. A resistance fighter, played by the charismatic Zbigniew Cybulski, is ordered to assassinate a local Communist Party official. Whose side are you on, the film's characters keep asking each other, and allegiances seem to shift almost by the minute. It's clear that the Russians are ready to replace the Germans as Poland's masters. Is resistance to them futile? Is there no end to this fighting? Cybulski, touted as the Polish James Dean, also has a touch of John Lennon about him—maybe it's those wire-rimmed glasses. Cybulski was killed in a railway accident, and, like Lennon, he died at age forty.

DR25, DR38

Goes well with: *Kanal*

ATALANTE, L'.

See *L'Atalante*

AU REVOIR, LES ENFANTS

France/West Germany 1987 C 103 min. PG Drama
Dir: Louis Malle
C: Gaspard Manesse, Raphael Fejtö, Francine Racette

As a youth at a Catholic boarding school in Occupied France, future director Louis Malle watched as three Jewish boys were concealed from the Nazis. It was an act of courage that he celebrated forty-some years later in one of his best films. The preadolescent boys in *Au Revoir* are more fascinated with their new classmates than fearful of the consequences of hiding them, but the film makes it clear how easily some youngsters will let the truth slip out to the wrong person. (As *The Sorrow and the Pity* demonstrated, collaborators were all too common in France.) *Au Revoir* isn't good just because it's such a personal work or because its heart is in the right place. Malle understands that overplaying his hand will cheapen the genuine emotion. The film won several Césars, France's equivalent of the Oscar.

DR3, DR28, DR31, DR38, DR41

Goes well with: *Europa Europa*

AN AUTUMN AFTERNOON

Japan 1962 C 115 min. NR Drama
Dir: Yasujiro Ozu
C: Chishu Ryu, Shima Iwashita, Shinichiro Mikami, Keiji Sada

Most great directors wrap up their careers with a film that has critics sighing with regret over their diminished skills. Then there's Yasujiro Ozu. Though he never gained the fame of his more eclectic and accessible colleague Akira Kurosawa, Ozu's quietly observed films about family life in contemporary Japan deserve wider attention. His 1962 swan song, a rare outing in color, is among his strongest works. It stars Ozu regular Chishu Ryu as an aging widower with three children: a married son with money problems, an unmarried daughter still living at home though she's twenty-seven, and a son hung up between late adolescence and early adulthood. Their problems may not seem to amount to a hill of beans, but Ozu's careful and sympathetic observations draw you right into their world. The final scene, with Ryu having finally persuaded his daughter to marry and leave the house, is a heartbreaker.

DR11, DR14

Goes well with: *Eat Drink Man Woman*

AVVENTURA, L'.

See *L'Avventura*

B

BABETTE'S FEAST

Denmark 1987 C 102 min. G Drama
Dir: Gabriel Axel
C: Stéphane Audran, Jean-Philippe Lafont, Gudmar Wivesson, Jarl Kulle, Bibi Andersson

You don't have to love good food or know anything about gourmet cooking to enjoy *Babette's Feast,* because the title event, which takes up most of the second half of the film, is symbolic of something deeper. Stephane Audran, one of the great French actresses, plays a housekeeper working for two elderly sisters in a Danish seaside village in the late nineteenth century. Babette serves their modest needs and manages to keep secret the details of why she fled France for Denmark. After years of service, Babette decides to cut loose for a special meal, and in so doing lets at least one secret from her past leak out. Based on a short story by Isak Dinesen, *Babette's Feast* understands that expressions of love can take many forms. It won a richly deserved Oscar for Best Foreign Language Film.

⊙**DVD**
DR16, XT2
Goes well with: *Like Water for Chocolate*

BACKBEAT

U.K./Germany 1993 C 100 min. R Drama
Dir: Iain Softley
C: Stephen Dorff, Sheryl Lee, Ian Hart, Gary Bakewell

The Beatles have inspired two first-rate films dealing with the peripheries of their careers: *The Hours and Times,* about the relationship between John Lennon and the group's first manager, Brian Epstein, and this engaging drama centering on the band's first bass player, Stu Sutcliffe. American actor Stephen Dorff plays Sutcliffe, an aspiring artist who went along with the band in 1960 to Hamburg, Germany, for a series of gigs largely out of loyalty to his pal John (played by Ian Hart, who also was Lennon in *Hours*). When the band returned to England, he stayed behind with his girlfriend, Astrid Kirchherr (Sheryl Lee), to pursue a career in painting. Sutcliffe's main contribution to the Beatles was to shape their look, especially the famed haircuts; he pulled away from music at the urging of Astrid (whom Lennon saw as a rival, the film suggests). Music producer Don Was used crack contemporary musicians to faithfully recreate the Fab Four's energetic early sound, which was largely cover versions of American rock and rhythm-and-blues tunes.

DR17, DR23

Goes well with: *The Hours and Times*

BADLANDS

ESSENTIAL

U.S. 1973 C 95 min. PG Drama
Dir: Terrence Malick
C: Martin Sheen, Sissy Spacek, Warren Oates, Ramon Bieri, Alan Vint, Terrence Malick

Writer-director Terrence Malick hit on a unique way to dramatize the infamous Charles Starkweather killing spree of 1958: through the eyes of his young traveling companion, Caril Fugate. Martin Sheen is Kit Caruthers, a young man who rattles the garbage cans he empties with a sullen defiance, and Sissy Spacek is Holly Stargis, a fifteen-year-old baton twirler who dreams of something more thrilling than life with a stern single father (Warren Oates). Spacek's voice-over narration, read in tones as flat as the highway she and Sheen hit as soon as her father becomes Victim No. 1, lifts this film above the ordinary crime scene re-creation. Holly sees poetry in almost everything Kit does, and she's convinced that he has no choice but to kill the people who stand in the way of their idyllic life together. (Narration by an innocent character who forces us to see events and images in a certain light also informed

Malick's next two films, *Days of Heaven* and *The Thin Red Line.*) The generally reclusive Malick plays a door-to-door salesman.

⊙**DVD**

DR6, XT5

Goes well with: *Pierrot le Fou*

THE BALLAD OF GREGORIO CORTEZ

U.S. 1982 C 104 min. PG Drama

Dir: Robert M. Young

C: Edward James Olmos, James Gammon, Tom Bower, Bruce McGill, Brion James

In 1901 Texas, a Mexican cowhand shoots a sheriff and flees with a mammoth posse in pursuit. Is the killing a simple misunderstanding exacerbated by a language problem, or retaliation for racial abuse? Robert M. Young's film chooses the former explanation for his account of this true story, but he also shows that the reason Cortez became a folk hero to Mexican immigrants living in Texas was because they chose the second motive. As Cortez, Edward James Olmos is sensational in a film originally produced for PBS's *American Playhouse* series. This unabashedly liberal film won a Special Jury Prize at the U.S. Film Festival, the forerunner of the Sundance Film Festival.

DR7, DR17, DR28

Goes well with: *Lone Star*

THE BALLAD OF RAMBLIN' JACK

U.S. 2000 C/B&W 112 min. PG-13 Documentary

Dir: Aiyana Elliott

A father who leaves a birthday phone message to his daughter six days after the big day because "this was the first time I could get to a phone" might have a built-in excuse if his name is Ramblin' Jack Elliott, and he's a cowboy folksinger who has been on the road for fifty years of his life. Actually, Jack's name is Elliott Adnopoz and he's from Brooklyn, New York. Aiyana Elliott, Jack's daughter from his fourth marriage, made this marvelous film about her old man partly out of love for his accomplishments and partly as an excuse to hang out with him and figure out what went wrong between him and her mom, Martha. Elliott is rightly positioned as the missing link between Woody Guthrie (whom he befriended and rambled with before Guthrie's fatal illness debilitated him) and Bob Dylan (who borrowed some of Elliott's licks). Though the elusive Dylan is present here only in clips, we do get perspective from two of Jack's wives, two of Woody's offspring (Arlo and Nora), Kris Kristofferson, and a collection of club owners and talent managers who answer Aiyana's question from a different angle: Jack was too irresponsible to be trusted to show up for a gig or recording session. The film won a Special Jury Prize for artistic achievement at Sundance.

⊙**DVD:** Includes audio commentary by Ramblin' Jack Elliott; excerpts from the short "Ramblin' Jack in Texas"; discography.

DO4, DO5, DO7

Goes well with: *The Weavers: Wasn't That a Time!*

BANDIT QUEEN

India 1994 C 119 min. NR Drama
Dir: Shekhar Kapur
C: Seema Biswas, Nirmal Pandey, Manoj Bajpai

The true-life account of one of contemporary India's most controversial figures, Phoolan Devi, *Bandit Queen* is relentlessly violent, which may put off some viewers hungry to see a film about a woman of heroic stature. A woman from the lower caste, Devi (Seema Biswas) was sold into marriage at the age of eleven and suffered sexual abuse for much of her life before (and even after) devoting herself to avenging official oppression of woman and her caste. Not satisfied that the legal system would recognize her claims, Devi rallied the masses behind her with a series of daring robberies, kidnappings, and murders aimed at upper-caste men. Screenwriter Maia Seri based her script on her own biography of Devi and on diaries that Devi kept during an eleven-year prison stint, though the Bandit Queen repudiated some of the material when the film was released. Shekhar Kapur followed this with another film about a very different queen, *Elizabeth.*

⊙**DVD**

DR5, DR6, DR17, DR25, DR26, DR39

Goes well with: *Kama Sutra: A Tale of Love*

BARCELONA

U.S. 1994 C 100 min. PG Comedy
Dir: Whit Stillman
C: Taylor Nichols, Chris Eigeman, Tushka Bergen, Mira Sorvino, Thomas Gibson

If there is one director currently making what could be called comedies of manners, it's Whit Stillman, whose best film to date is set during the 1980s in Spain's most charming city. *Barcelona* details the daily comings and goings of two Americans: an uptight salesman (Taylor Nichols) and his cousin (Chris Eigeman), a Naval officer who defines "ugly American." Both stars appeared in Stillman's impressive debut, *Metropolitan,* and they're a wonderful comedy team: Nichols the fumbling but well-meaning outsider, Eigeman the know-it-all but truly clueless "insider." Stillman sets his story at the end of the cold war, which allows him to cleverly layer dramatic points about the ongoing need for America to have such a strong military presence in Europe. The cinematography by John Thomas won an Independent Spirit Award.

⊙**DVD:** Includes audio commentary by Whit Stillman, Chris Eigeman, and Taylor Nichols; alternate ending; interview with Mira Sorvino.

CO4, CO7

Goes well with: *Metropolitan*

BASQUIAT

U.S.   1996   C   108 min.   R   Drama

Dir: Julian Schnabel

C: Jeffrey Wright, David Bowie, Dennis Hopper, Gary Oldman, Willem Dafoe, Michael Wincott, Claire Forlani, Benicio Del Toro, Parker Posey, Christopher Walken, Courtney Love, Tatum O'Neal, Paul Bartel

Painter-turned-filmmaker Julian Schnabel's film about artist Jean-Michel Basquiat is less a portrait of the artist as a young man than an exploration of how the New York art world discovers and nurtures new talent. It's a process routinely explored in the pages of the *New York Times* and art publications but almost never seen on film. Jeffrey Wright makes Basquiat, whose run lasted only seven years before he died of drug-related causes in 1987 at the age of twenty-eight, a curious blend of diffidence and ambition. And check out that supporting cast, a roll call of familiar character actors, starting with David Bowie as a most convincing Andy Warhol (who was an early champion of Basquiat's work), plus a few ringers (when was the last time you saw Tatum O'Neal in a movie?). Schnabel's approach to the material is more straightforward here than in his next film, *Before Night Falls;* both are better at context than characterization. Four years before his Oscar win for *Traffic,* Benicio Del Toro walked off with an Independent Spirit Award for his performance as Benny Dalmau, Basquiat's basketball-playing pal and romantic rival.

DR2, DR17, DR36, XT7

Goes well with: *Before Night Falls*

THE BATTLE OF ALGIERS

ESSENTIAL

Italy/Algeria 1965 B&W 123 min. NR Drama
Dir: Gillo Pontecorvo
C: Yacef Saadi, Jean Martin

The filmmaking in *The Battle of Algiers* is so raw and unprocessed, you can't tell where the documentary footage stops and the dramatic re-creation begins. Subsidized by the Algerian government, *Battle* is a riveting account of the uprisings against French colonial rule between 1954 and 1962. Italian director Gillo Pontecorvo (who wrote the script with Franco Solinas) was a former journalist and World War II resistance fighter with a strong commitment to leftist causes. He clearly admired the Algerian resistance fighters who relied on guerrilla tactics to force France into an untenable situation. Their urban bombing campaigns may strike some viewers as uncomfortably close to the tactics employed by Palestinians protesting their treatment by Israel. The timing of the film's release, at the beginning of protests against American involvement in Vietnam, gave the film enormous cachet in certain political and social circles, and *Battle* captured Oscar nominations for foreign film, original screenplay, and direction. Pontecorvo's follow-up, *Burn!,* also dealt with colonialism, this time in the New World.

DR25, DR37

Goes well with: *Burn!*

BATTLESHIP POTEMKIN

ESSENTIAL

Soviet Union 1925 B&W 65 min. NR Drama
Dir: Sergei Eisenstein
C: Alexander Antonov, Vladimir Barsky, Grigori Alexandrov, Mikhail Gomonov

Among the most celebrated films ever made, *Potemkin* (its often-used shorthand title) is a dynamic exercise in filmmaking that also served a Soviet régime looking for its country's art to reflect the aims of the Communist revolution. The story dramatizes a 1905 mutiny aboard the title ship, a rebellion which spread to the port city of Odessa, where Czarist troops massacred civilians in a show of force that only temporarily delayed a more widespread revolt. Sergei Eisenstein understood the power of strong imagery and how editing those images with a dynamic sense of rhythm could stir viewers, and his massacre scene, set on a broad outdoor set of stairs, is a set piece that directors as varied as Woody Allen and Brian DePalma have quoted from.

⊙**DVD**

DR24, DR38

Goes well with: *The Battle of Algiers*

BEAUTY AND THE BEAST

ESSENTIAL

France   1946   B&W   95 min.   NR   Fantasy

Dir: Jean Cocteau

C: Jean Marais, Josette Day, Marcel André

With all due respect to Disney's lovely 1991 animated film, the real deal when it comes to screen versions of the *Beauty and the Beast* fable is Jean Cocteau's 1946 film. Josette Day is Beauty, the young woman who would sacrifice herself to the wicked but lovestruck Beast to save her imprisoned father. Jean Marais gets three roles here, and if he's less expressive as an actor than Day, he's so damned magnetic, even under all that Beast makeup, that you can't take your eyes off him. Cocteau's surreal effects create the dreamlike atmosphere of a classic fairy tale, and Henri Alekan's shimmering black-and-white cinematography makes you understand why some filmmakers never wanted to work in color.

⊙**DVD:** Includes documentary about origins of film's fable; audio commentary by historian Arthur Knight; restoration demonstration.

DR18, FA4

Goes well with: *Orpheus*

BEFORE NIGHT FALLS

U.S.   2000   C   125 min.   R   Drama

Dir: Julian Schnabel

C: Javier Bardem, Olivier Martínez, Andrea Di Stefano, Sean Penn, Johnny Depp, Jerzy Skolimowski

Javier Bardem's riveting performance (which won an Independent Spirit Award) is the best reason to see this diffuse but generally informative biography of Cuban writer Reinaldo Arenas. As an adolescent growing up in dire poverty, Arenas eagerly dreamed of being part of Fidel Castro's new Cuba, but Arenas soon discovered that, in his words, "the revolution was not for everybody." He was a two-time loser: an artist uninterested in supporting the state's aims, and a homosexual. Persecuted, forced to publish his writings abroad, and finally imprisoned, Arenas was finally able to escape his homeland when Castro opened his jails and asylums and exported over one hundred thousand "undesirables" to the U.S. Note to stargazers: Sean Penn has only one brief scene, and though Johnny Depp plays two roles, both are relatively brief.

⊙**DVD:** Includes audio commentaries by Julian Schnabel, Javier Bardem, writer Lazaro Gomez-Carilles, composer Carter Burwell, and codirector of photography Xavier Perez Grobet; excerpts from *Improper Conduct,* documentary about persecution of homosexuals in Cuba; 1983 interview with Reinaldo Arenas; behind-the-scenes documentary.

DR2, DR17, DR19

Goes well with: *The Buena Vista Social Club*

BELLE DE JOUR

ESSENTIAL

France/Italy   1967   C   100 min.   R   Drama
Dir: Luis Buñuel
C: Catherine Deneuve, Jean Sorel, Michel Piccoli, Geneviève Page, Francisco Rabal, Pierre Clementi

Luis Buñuel used Catherine Deneuve in this film in a role familiar to fans of Alfred Hitchcock's work with Grace Kelly, Kim Novak, and Tippi Hedren. She's the cool, elegant blonde with hidden reserves of sensuality. Deneuve plays Sevèrine, a newlywed who's clearly bored with her young husband's lovemaking, so she takes a day job in a high-class brothel under the name "Belle." At least, we *think* she takes that day job. Are Belle's erotic adventures real or just a product of Sevèrine's very active dream life? The sly Buñuel won't let on, and it's possible to view *Belle de Jour* differently each time you watch it. After years of scuffling in Mexico and his native Spain with modest budgets and less than magnetic actors, Belle marked Buñuel's major-league filmmaking debut, kicking off a great run of late-career classics that included *The Discreet Charm of the Bourgeoisie.*

⊙**DVD:** Includes audio commentary by Buñuel scholar Julie Jones.
DR19, DR33, DR39
Goes well with: *Viridiana*

BELLE EPOQUE

Spain/Portugal/France   1992   C   108 min.   R   Comedy
Dir: Fernando Trueba
C: Fernando Fernán Gómez, Jorge Sanz, Maribel Verdú, Ariadna Gil, Miriam Diaz Aroca, Penélope Cruz, Mary Carmen Ramírez

A former colleague of mine who programmed films for the American Film Institute Theater used to refer to certain movies as "soufflé-light comedies," and *Belle Epoque* fits that description perfectly. In 1931 Spain, a young soldier deserts from the army and takes refuge in a village with a friendly artist. That the man also has four lovely daughters keeps the soldier from deserting any farther, and the delightful question is, which girl should he choose? Fernando Trueba turns the makings of an exploitation film into something better: a sexy comedy that hearkens back to pre-Franco Spain, an age of relative innocence. It was a surprise winner at the 1994 Academy Awards, beating out *Farewell, My Concubine* and *The Wedding Banquet* for Best Foreign Language Film.

CO6, CO9
Goes well with: *Tom Jones*

BELLE NOISEUSE, LA.

See *La Belle Noiseuse*

BERKELEY IN THE SIXTIES

U.S.   1990   C/B&W   117 min.   NR   Documentary
Dir: Mark Kitchell

If those of us who love historical documentaries wait long enough, the good subjects have a way of finding a filmmaker who understands how to record them and offer some perspective as well. Kudos to producer-director Mark Kitchell for capturing a time and a place, as plainly stated in the title, that is key to understanding contemporary

American culture. The University of California was the scene of some of the decade's most intense clashes between idealistic students and activists on the one side and official authority, from the statehouse on down, on the other. Kitchell skillfully combines archival footage with current-day interviews with many key players, most of them on the activist side. The footage of then-governor Ronald Reagan taking on the activists helps explain his rise to national prominence as the man who would hold the tide against the unwashed mass of antiestablishment punks. And Kitchell managed to obtain the rights to a number of key 1960s rock anthems that provided the soundtrack to a heady age of tumult. Winner of the Audience Award at Sundance, and a nominee for an Academy Award.

DO1, DO8, DO9, DO11

Goes well with: *Between the Lines*

BEST IN SHOW

U.S.   2000   C   90 min.   PG-13   Comedy

Dir: Christopher Guest

C: Christopher Guest, Eugene Levy, Catherine O'Hara, Michael McKean, Parker Posey, Fred Willard, Larry Miller, Bob Balaban, Jennifer Coolidge, John Michael Higgins, Michael Hitchcock, Jane Lynch

Christopher Guest's follow-up to his brilliant backstage comedy *Waiting for Guffman* is another film about the business of show—in this case, showing dogs in competition. Guest's troupe of actors (which includes himself, as a North Carolina–based bloodhound owner) are brilliant at creating characters with unexpected dimensions. Though much of the dialogue was improvised, every actor is able to sustain running gags far beyond the statute of comic limitations. Eugene Levy and Catherine O'Hara are at the center of the film; he's a guy with two left feet (literally) and a truly amazing overbite, and she's a woman who can't help running into her ex-boyfriends, all of them ready to recall in excruciating detail their past sexual encounters. The DVD's outtakes are a true bonus, especially the tour of the Guest character's beach ball collection.

⊙**DVD:** Includes deleted scenes.

CO10, CO12

Goes well with: *Waiting for Guffman*

BETWEEN THE LINES

U.S. 1977 C 101 min. R Comedy-Drama

Dir: Joan Micklin Silver

C: John Heard, Lindsay Crouse, Jeff Goldblum, Jill Eikenberry, Gwen Welles, Bruno Kirby, Stephen Collins, Michael J. Pollard, Lane Smith, Marilu Henner

Alternative newspapers like Boston's *Phoenix* grew out of the anti-war, antiestablishment protests of the 1960s, and they soon became profit centers for advertisers eager to target a youthful audience of readers and consumers. *Between the Lines* is an engaging comedy-drama that shows how the success of one such paper is also the undoing of its staff of idealistic writers and editors when a new owner takes over. Joan Micklin Silver had a dream cast of young performers to work with here; if you've been a longtime fan of John Heard, Jeff Goldblum, Lindsay Crouse, and Jill Eikenberry, it's likely that this is the first film you saw them in. Fred Barron's screenplay adroitly juggles its characters' personal problems and the larger issues of their day jobs.

CO5, CO8, DR12

Goes well with: *Return of the Secaucus 7*

THE BICYCLE THIEF

ESSENTIAL

Italy 1947 B&W 90 min. NR Drama

Dir: Vittorio De Sica

C: Lamberto Maggiorani, Lianella Carell, Enzo Staiola

Long regarded not only as a milestone in Italian postwar cinema but as one of the greatest films ever made, *The Bicycle Thief* wears its reputation well. The story is simplicity itself: Antonio (Lamberto Maggiorani), a laborer long out of work, finally gets a job, but it requires him to have a bicycle, and on his first day at work, the bike is stolen. (He and his wife are so poor that they had to sell their bedsheets to reclaim his old bike from the pawnshop.) Antonio spends the next day, a Sunday, wandering around Rome with his son, Bruno (Enzo Staiola), looking for the bike. The film is both specific—a stunningly detailed portrait of Rome, still recovering after the devastation of World War II—and universal. Antonio's search for his bicycle is really a search for some measure of comfort in a city indifferent to his needs. His frustration and humiliation are so palpable that when he's driven to desperation in the film's final scenes, it's impossible not to root for him. Director Vittorio De Sica and screenwriter Cesare Zavattini created a stunning portrait of urban life. The film won a special Academy Award, the first ever given to a foreign-language film, before the formal category was introduced, and the New York Film Critics Circle prize for Best Foreign Language Film.

⊙**DVD:** Includes liner notes by playwright Arthur Miller.

DR11, DR16, DR36, DR40, XT7

Goes well with: *Open City*

THE BIG BANG

France 1990 C 81 min. R Documentary

Dir: James Toback

Among all the films in this book that deal with the really big questions—why are we here, is there a higher power, is there an afterlife—only one asks those questions outright. For this thoroughly engaging documentary, filmmaker James Toback allows a diverse group of people, both celebrities and civilians, to offer their thoughts on weighty matters. Among the recognizable names and faces: the late film producer Don Simpson, basketball player Darryl Dawkins, boxer-author José Torres, New York restaurateur Elaine Kaufman, violinist Eugene Fodor, humorist Veronica Geng, and mobster-turned-actor Tony Sirico (he plays Paulie Walnuts on *The Sopranos*). Also included are a young girl and boy, a medical student, an astronomer, and a Holocaust survivor. Toback tosses in scenes of himself trying to persuade his producer to back the project, and they serve as a clever commentary on the difficulty of getting any documentary film made.

DO7, DR30

Goes well with: *Slacker*

BIG DEAL ON MADONNA STREET

Italy 1958 B&W 106 min. NR Comedy

Dir: Mario Monicelli

C: Vittorio Gassman, Renato Salvatori, Memmo Carotenuto, Rossana Rory, Carla Gravina, Claudia Cardinale, Carlo Pisacane, Tiberio Murgia, Marcello Mastroianni, Totò

Released only four years after *Rififi, Big Deal on Madonna Street* effectively spoofed the heist genre that earlier film had defined. Its gang of crooks, led by a glass-jawed fighter named Peppe (Vittorio Gassman) who steals the idea for their "big deal" from a fellow prisoner in jail, are the Ralph Kramdens of crime: big thinkers, small doers. In fact, two of the gang drop out on the big night, leaving Peppe with Tiberio (Marcello Mastroianni), a photographer with one arm in a cast; Ferribotte (Tiberio Murgia), a dapper but hapless man who spends most of his time chasing men away from his lovely sister (Claudia Cardinale); and Cruciani (Totò), a toothless runt who's always mooching food. A noisy bag of tools, a lover's quarrel that traps the quartet on a skylight for hours, several pesky cats, and a mistaken sense of direction are but a few of the problems they encounter as they work their way from an apartment into a neighboring store. Piero Umiliani's jazz score offers a witty counterpoint to the ineptitude onscreen.

⊙**DVD**

CO1, CO12

Goes well with: *Rififi*

BIG NIGHT

ESSENTIAL

U.S. 1996 C 107 min. R Comedy

Dir: Stanley Tucci and Campbell Scott

C: Stanley Tucci, Minnie Driver, Tony Shalhoub, Ian Holm, Isabella Rossellini, Campbell Scott, Allison Janney

Or, *Waiting for Louis Prima*. In a small New Jersey town in the 1950s, rival Italian restaurants square off. The popular one serves the basic red-sauce dishes that unsophisticated American palates then thought was authentic Italian cooking, while the other, run by a pair of brothers from the old country, is the purist operation struggling to entice the taste buds of the locals. Then comes word that pop singer Louis Prima is coming to town, and the owner of the popular joint offers to host a special meal at his rivals' operation, just to show there's no hard feelings. You won't find a funnier movie about food, both as a business and as a source of pure sensual enjoyment, than *Big Night*. The cast is perfection: Ian Holm as the successful restaurateur, Stanley Tucci and Tony Shalhoub as his rivals, Minnie Driver, Isabella Rossellini, and Allison Janney as the women in their lives, and Campbell Scott as a bumbling car salesman. *Big Night* walked off with screenwriting awards at the Independent Spirit ceremony and the Sundance festival, and won the New Director Award from the New York Film Critics Circle.

⊙**DVD**

CO3, CO11, XT2

Goes well with: *Tampopo*

THE BIG PICTURE

U.S. 1989 C 100 min. PG-13 Comedy
Dir: Christopher Guest
C: Kevin Bacon, Emily Longstreth, J. T. Walsh, Jennifer Jason Leigh, Kim Miyori, Michael McKean, Teri Hatcher, Martin Short, John Cleese

Watching moviemakers make fun of Hollywood is one of America's great indoor sports, and Christopher Guest's directorial debut is an engaging snapshot of the new Hollywood, which seems to pride itself on never making a decision. Kevin Bacon plays a naïve young filmmaker who spends much more time taking meetings than he does working on his debut film; after a while, you get the feeling that he's running on a very fast treadmill to oblivion. The self-absorbed, the insecure, the obnoxious, and the just plain nutty—they're all here in profusion, most of them out to frustrate our Candide. *The Big Picture* is a view of Hollywood from its entry points, as opposed to Robert Altman's *The Player,* a view from a higher, if unsteadier, perch.

CO10

Goes well with: *The Player*

BILLY LIAR

U.K. 1963 B&W 98 min. NR Comedy
Dir: John Schlesinger
C: Tom Courtenay, Julie Christie, Wilfred Pickles, Mona Washbourne, Finlay Currie

The world of Ambrosia is a mythical kingdom founded by Billy Fisher, an undertaker's assistant in a northern English town. When his dead-end job, complicated love life (he's engaged to two women but loves a third), and stultifying family start to wear on him, Billy is off to Ambrosia, where he can be whatever he wants. Tom Courtenay followed his smashing debut in *The Loneliness of the Long Distance Runner* with this amusing and tender comedy that also served to introduce many filmgoers to Julie Christie, as Billy's true love.

⊙**DVD:** Includes commentaries by John Schlesinger, Tom Courtenay, and Julie Christie, and excerpts from a BBC documentary on British cinema in the 1960s.

CO5

Goes well with: *The Young Poisoner's Handbook*

BLACK MASK

Hong Kong   1997   C   96 min.   R   Action-Adventure
Dir: Daniel Lee
C: Jet Li, Karen Mok, Françoise Yip, Lau Ching Wan

Martial arts star Jet Li is the real deal: a tremendous athlete with a winning screen personality. In his breakthrough film, re-edited from its original 1996 version and dubbed into English, he plays a genetically engineered soldier who's called out of retirement (he has been working in a library!) when his cyborg colleagues, who've gone a little haywire, conspire to take over Hong Kong's drug trade. He dons a mask that makes him like a cross between the Green Hornet and Kato, and quickly establishes himself as the scourge of all artificial men who would replace their human counterparts in illegal business operations. Li's leaps and bounds are like something out of a Michael Jordan highlight reel. Unlike Jackie Chan, he plays it straight—you won't find any blooper outtakes at the end of a Jet Li movie.

⊙**DVD**
AC3, AC5
Goes well with: *La Femme Nikita*

BLACK NARCISSUS

U.K.   1947   C   99 min.   NR   Drama
Dir: Michael Powell and Emeric Pressburger
C: Deborah Kerr, David Farrar, Sabu, Jean Simmons, Kathleen Byron, Flora Robson

Cinematographer Jack Cardiff, honored in March 2001 at the Academy Awards for his peerless work, won his first Oscar in competition for this drama set in the Himalayas. A British sister superior (Deborah Kerr, named Best Actress by the New York Film Critics Circle) and four nuns attempt to establish a mission in a deserted castle perched on the edge of a sheer cliff. But so many factors conspire against them—the appearance of a dashing young British agent, the sense that their building is haunted, the reminders of a very sensual culture that they've more or less invaded—that the women each begin to crack. The writing-directing team of Michael Powell and Emeric Pressburger adapted Rumer Godden's novel, and with Cardiff and art director Alfred Junge (also an Oscar winner) they create an atmosphere that's both breathtakingly beautiful and neurotically claustrophobic. Amazingly, most of the film was shot in a studio. A DVD must, especially for its enticing extra features.

⊙**DVD:** Includes commentary by Michael Powell and Martin Scorsese; plus documentary on Jack Cardiff.

DR7, DR27, DR30, DR39

Goes well with: *The Mission*

BLACK ROBE

Canada/Australia 1991 C 101 min. R Drama

Dir: Bruce Beresford

C: Lothaire Bluteau, August Schellenberg, Aden Young, Sandrine Holt, Tantoo Cardinal

Not far behind the first wave of European explorers of the New World came the missionaries, eager to establish a beachhead for Christianity in this strange and beautiful land. Canadian actor Lothaire Bluteau plays a seventeenth-century Jesuit priest assigned to work in Quebec, where he faces all the expected obstacles (including the temptation to surrender his vows of chastity) in this intelligent and uncompromising adaptation of Brian Moore's novel. (Moore wrote the screenplay.) Australian director Bruce Beresford worked with his frequent cinematographer Peter James to capture the majesty of a land spoiled only by the arrival of well-meaning invaders hungry to bring heathens to a better understanding of the spiritual side of life.

⊙**DVD**

DR7, DR24, DR30

Goes well with: *The Mission*

BLOOD AND WINE

U.S./U.K. 1997 C 98 min. R Thriller

Dir: Bob Rafelson

C: Jack Nicholson, Judy Davis, Michael Caine, Stephen Dorff, Jennifer Lopez

Jack Nicholson and Bob Rafelson go way back, all the way to the Monkees' big-screen debut, *Head,* which Rafelson directed and Nicholson wrote. Their best collaboration came two years later, in 1970, with *Five Easy Pieces,* in which Nicholson acted up a storm that could capsize a flotilla of fishing boats. After mixed success in three more films, they returned to form in this nasty little thriller. Nicholson's Florida-based wine distribution business is drying up, and he calls on an old buddy, a wheezing ex-con played by Michael Caine, to help him pull off a jewelry heist to help balance the books. *Blood and Wine* is rich with characters, well fleshed out by actors as diverse as Judy Davis (as Nicholson's resentful wife), Stephen Dorff (as his even more resentful son) and Jennifer Lopez (as his mistress).

DR6, DR11, TH8, TH13

Goes well with: *The Underneath*

THE BLOOD OF A POET

France   1930   B&W   53 min.   NR   Fantasy

Dir: Jean Cocteau

C: Lee Miller, Pauline Carton, Odette Talazac, Enrique Rivero, Jean Cocteau (narrator)

Poet, writer, and painter Jean Cocteau's first film is a witty, sometimes obscure, and always provocative look at the life of an artist. There is no story line; the film is divided into two halves. In the first, the artist (Enrique Rivero) becomes a bit too involved in a painting and winds up merging with a portion of it. In the second half, the artist seeks inspiration at a hotel by peeping through various keyholes at tableaux, after which he repairs to a public room for a game of cards with a living statue (Lee Miller, the American model who later became a famous wartime photographer). It's self-referential but hardly self-indulgent stuff, though it's better to know something about Cocteau's art and life going in than to use this as a cold introduction. The Criterion edition DVD provides some helpful supporting material.

⊙**DVD:** Includes behind-the-scenes photos; 1984 documentary on Jean Cocteau; transcript of Cocteau lecture presented at a 1932 screening; Cocteau essay from 1946.

DR2, XT6

Goes well with: *Orpheus*

BLOOD SIMPLE

ESSENTIAL

U.S.   1984   C   97 min.   R   Thriller

Dir: Joel Coen

C: John Getz, Frances McDormand, Dan Hedaya, Samm-Art Williams, M. Emmet Walsh

The film noir purists—the people who think that no film shot in color is worthy of the noir label—didn't much cotton to the debut of Joel and Ethan Coen, the filmmaking brothers (Joel directs, Ethan produces, both write). So call it something else, but *Blood Simple* delivers the goods for people who like thrillers in which nothing is as it seems and no one is above suspicion or a dirty deed done cheap. The set-up: Texas slob (Dan Hedaya) hires slimeball (M. Emmet Walsh) to murder the slob's cheatin' wife (Frances McDormand) and her lover (John Getz). Citizens of the Lone Star State will argue in vain that this kind of stuff rarely happens down there, but all of us who live elsewhere know better, and so do the Coens, who start piling on the reversals and double-crosses with gusto. Calling the Coens cold-hearted toward their characters misses the point; if you want warm-hearted humanism, you're in the wrong aisle of the video store anyway. *Blood Simple* was awarded Best Director and Best Male Lead (for M. Emmet Walsh's effectively creepy performance) at the Independent Spirit ceremony; the film also won a Grand Jury Prize at Sundance.

⊙**DVD:** Includes audio commentary by Kenneth Loring of Forever Young Films.

TH5, TH10, TH13

Goes well with: *One False Move*

BLOWUP

ESSENTIAL

U.K./Italy 1966 C 111 min. NR Drama
Dir: Michelangelo Antonioni
C: Vanessa Redgrave, David Hemmings, Sarah Miles, Verushka, Jill
    Kennington, Jane Birkin, Gillian Hills

Talk about a party pooper: London in the 1960s was just about the swingingest, most happening place on the planet, but here comes that dour Italian director Michelangelo Antonioni to show us how shallow it all really was. Thomas (David Hemmings) is a photographer who is a study in passivity; he only observes but never participates or reaches out, whether he's shooting indigent men in a flophouse or lithe fashion models in his studio. But a series of pictures he impulsively snaps one day in a park lead him to suspect he has witnessed a murder, especially after he enlarges the prints. Even after the woman (Vanessa Redgrave) from the pictures shows up at his studio, offering him sex in exchange for the negatives, Thomas is paralyzed with indecision. The almost baby-faced Hemmings is perfectly cast as a man with no convictions; not even a trip to a nightclub where the Yardbirds whip the crowd into a frenzy by smashing their instruments can move him. The wonderfully rich color schemes were achieved by ace cinematographer Carlo di Palma, who also shot Antonioni's first color film, *Red Desert.*

DR20, XT7

Goes well with: *Light Sleeper*

THE BLUE ANGEL

ESSENTIAL

Germany/U.S.   1930   B&W   104 min.   NR   Drama
Dir: Josef von Sternberg
C: Marlene Dietrich, Emil Jannings, Kurt Gerron, Rosa Valetti

No European actress made a bigger first impression on American filmgoers than Marlene Dietrich did in Josef von Sternberg's drama of lust and corruption. (The film was shot in both German and English versions, in anticipation of its crossover success.) *Angel* also marked the first film in what would become the most fruitful collaboration between a director and actress in the history of film. (It continued in Hollywood with six films for Paramount Pictures including *Morocco, Shanghai Express, Blonde Venus,* and *The Scarlet Empress.*) As Lola-Lola, Dietrich played a cabaret performer who's understandably indifferent to the attentions of her biggest fan, a portly professor played with almost masochistic fervor by Emil Jannings. The professor is obsessed with the *idea* of Lola-Lola; it's almost as though he intellectualizes a relationship with her, knowing that they can never truly be lovers. Dietrich's rendition of "Falling in Love Again" expresses all the world-weariness of a woman with too many admirers and not enough friends.

⊙**DVD:** Includes two discs with German- and English-language versions (latter runs 100 min.); Dietrich screen test; 1971 interview with Dietrich; three numbers from a late-career concert.

DR4, DR19, TH7

Goes well with: *Pandora's Box*

BLUE VELVET

ESSENTIAL

U.S.   1986   C   120 min.   R   Drama
Dir: David Lynch
C: Kyle MacLachlan, Isabella Rossellini, Dennis Hopper, Laura Dern, Hope Lange, Dean Stockwell, Jack Nance, Brad Dourif

Nearly every project that director David Lynch has been involved with since *Blue Velvet* has been a variation on the theme of corruption of innocence stated in that groundbreaking film. Kyle MacLachlan and Laura Dern are the innocents here, the well-scrubbed small-town kids who run afoul of the gangster Frank (Dennis Hopper) and the masochistic singer Dorothy (Isabella Rossellini, in a performance that won her the Best Female Lead prize from the Independent Spirit Awards). As in his TV series *Twin Peaks,* Lynch loves to imagine the ripe rot behind the picket fences and beneath the manicured lawns of small-town America, and by God, he's determined not only to uncover that rot but to shove it in our faces. You can flinch, you can turn away, you can choose to rent another film, but the achievement of *Blue Velvet* remains as a singularly disturbing vision of the heart of darkness.

⊙**DVD**

DR19, DR27, DR34

Goes well with: *Eye of God*

BOB LE FLAMBEUR

France 1955 B&W 102 min. PG Thriller

Dir: Jean-Pierre Melville

C: Roger Duchesne, Isabel Corey, Daniel Cauchy, Guy Decomble

Gamblers are everywhere we look these days, playing the slots in Indian-run casinos, scratching lottery tickets in convenience stores, on cell phones to their brokers looking for the latest stock tips. Somehow the romance has gone out of the gambling game, and Jean-Pierre Melville's studied and evocative thriller is a reminder of another time, when the betting population was much smaller and more likely to verge on the criminal. Roger Duchesne plays the coolest Bob who ever inhabited a movie, an elegant loser at the tables in Deauville's swank casinos who has decided on a game with much bigger stakes: a heist of a casino's cash reserves, with a hand-picked gang. You might assume that Bob and his pals inspired Frank Sinatra and the Rat Pack's classic *Ocean's 11,* except that *Bob le Flambeur* didn't get a real U.S. release until 1982, when it became an instant cult hit, nine years after director Melville's death.

⊙**DVD**

DR13, TH8, TH13

Goes well with: *Rififi*

BOOGIE NIGHTS

ESSENTIAL

U.S. 1997 C 152 min. R Drama

Dir: Paul Thomas Anderson

C: Mark Wahlberg, Burt Reynolds, Julianne Moore, John C. Reilly, Don Cheadle, Heather Graham, Luis Guzman, Philip Seymour Hoffman, William H. Macy, Alfred Molina, Philip Baker Hall, Robert Ridgley, Ricky Jay

Paul Thomas Anderson's brilliant peep show about the adult film industry, which spans several years and ends in the early 1980s, when home video began to change the way films were made and distributed, may strike some viewers as an excuse to wallow in the lives of less-than-admirable people. But Anderson sees filmmaking on any level as composed of serial sets of families: you work on a production for long hours with the same people and then move on. On adult films, the families were closer, because the filmmakers knew they were working outside accepted society. Playing Jack, the director/paterfamilias, Burt Reynolds makes it clear that, given the right role, he's a first-rate actor and not just a by-the-numbers star; he won the New York Film Critics Circle prize for Best Supporting Actor. Everyone else in the large cast is as good as they've ever been. *Boogie Nights* is sympathetic to all of its characters, though Anderson is also painfully honest about their delusions.

⊙**DVD:** Includes commentary by Paul Thomas Anderson and deleted scenes.

DR11, DR12, DR22

Goes well with: *Day for Night*

BOTTLE ROCKET

U.S. 1996 C 95 min. R Comedy

Dir: Wes Anderson

C: Owen Wilson, Luke Wilson, Robert Musgrave, Andrew Wilson, Lumi Cavazos, James Caan

Heist movies generally come in two varieties: the straight-faced type (*Bob le Flambeur*) and the ones whose screwup characters guarantee that the suspense lies in guessing how far they'll get before they're caught. Wes Anderson's oddball directorial debut is definitely in the second category. Dignan (Owen Wilson, who wrote the script with Anderson) is a young man whose brazenness is outweighed by his lack of sense—which doesn't stop him from pursuing a life of crime. Dignan is a comic creation for the ages, spouting idiotic philosophy, hatching dead-end schemes, and, worst of all, throwing in with Mr. Henry, a mentor (James Caan at his cockeyed best) who clearly is going to leave him hanging out to dry. Dignan's confederacy of dunces also includes Anthony Adams (played by Luke Wilson, Owen's real-life brother) and Robert Maplethorpe (Robert Musgrave), whose parents' large and well-appointed home also plays a key role in the story. Andrew Wilson, a third brother in the clan, has a small role as Robert's obnoxious older brother.

⊙**DVD**

CO1

Goes well with: *Fargo*

BOUND

U.S.   1996   C   109 min.   R   Thriller
Dir: Larry Wachowski and Andy Wachowski
C: Jennifer Tilly, Gina Gershon, Joe Pantoliano, John Ryan, Christopher Meloni

In the fine tradition of the Coen brothers and their neonoir debut, *Blood Simple,* the Wachowski brothers stepped up from being just writers (on the forgettable Sylvester Stallone film *Assassins*) to directing a stylishly told tale of greed and double-crosses. Jennifer Tilly is Violet, girlfriend to a dim bulb named Caesar (Joe Pantoliano), whose main profession is laundering money, large sums of it, in their apartment. Enter a new neighbor, Corky (Gina Gershon), with eyes for Violet, and soon enough, the women are not only making love, they're also making plans to snatch Caesar's stash. The Wachowskis show even more flair for flashy camerawork and editing tricks than the Coens did on their first outing, although their follow-up, the megabudgeted *The Matrix,* suggests the world of independent, low-budget films is receding quickly in their rearview mirror.

⊙**DVD:** Includes commentary by the Wachowski brothers.

DR19, TH5, TH7, TH13

Goes well with: *Blood Simple*

BOX OF MOONLIGHT

U.S./Japan   1997   C   111 min.   R   Drama
Dir: Tom DiCillo
C: John Turturro, Sam Rockwell, Catherine Keener, Lisa Blount, Dermot Mulroney

Box of Moonlight is a rare example of film whimsy that works beyond all expectations. John Turturro is Al Fountain, an electrical engineer on assignment several states away from his family. Car trouble on a rural back road delivers him to the hospitality of a young man who calls himself the

Kid (Sam Rockwell). This dropout lives in a rambling double-wide far enough off the beaten track that Al cannot make an honest attempt to escape while his car is being repaired. The Kid spends most of his time hanging out behind the trailer (where he's collected an assortment of paraphernalia that resembles a yard sale), barbecuing and ruminating on a life well spent away from the rest of the world. The eventual arrival of the lovely DuPre sisters (Catherine Keener and Lisa Blount) is another enticement for Al to linger. Writer-director Tom DiCillo knows just how far to push this material before it becomes precious or too obvious.

⊙**DVD**

DR12, DR16, DR21

Goes well with: *Lawn Dogs*

BOYS DON'T CRY

ESSENTIAL

U.S.   1999   C   119 min.   R   Drama

Dir: Kimberly Peirce

C: Hilary Swank, Chloë Sevigny, Peter Sarsgaard, Brendan Sexton III, Alison Folland, Alicia Goranson

Confusion over sexual identity has never been more poignantly portrayed on film than in this real-life drama about Teena Brandon, a young Nebraska woman who decides to "become" a young man. Reversing names, binding her breasts, cutting her hair and lowering her voice seem to do the trick. But Brandon's success with the ladies leads to a collision of frustrated souls—an individual in search of his/her true sexuality and two men bored with their dead-end lives and filled with rage. Hilary Swank, Oscar and New York Film Critics Circle winner for Best Actress, may never get a better role in her career, and as her antagonists, Peter Sarsgaard and Brendan Sexton III are credibly drawn characters who don't come off as cartoonish rednecks. Also amazing is Chloë Sevigny as Brendan's last girlfriend, a woman with her own confusion over sexual identity. Swank and Sevigny both won Independent Spirit Awards.

⊙**DVD:** Includes audio commentary by Kimberly Peirce.

DR17, DR19, DR21, DR39

Goes well with: *Before Night Falls*

THE BOYS OF ST. VINCENT

ESSENTIAL

Canada   1993   C   186 min.   NR   Drama

Dir: John N. Smith
C: Henry Czerny, Johnny Morina, Sebastian Spence, Brian Dodd

Originally shown on Canadian television as a two-part film, *The Boys of St. Vincent* is a devastating docudrama about a real case of extensive child molestation by Catholic clergy in an orphanage. Part One takes place in 1975 and centers on the arrival of a young boy, Kevin, who is taken under the wing of the stern Brother Lavin. Part Two flashes ahead to 1990, when the long-suppressed scandal breaks and Brother Lavin, who has left the order and is now married with two children, is brought to account for his crimes. Henry Czerny is persuasive at portraying a man with a grotesquely twisted sense of morality. Acclaim in Canada for this film was so great, and its subject matter so timely, that it earned a limited theatrical release in the U.S. before becoming available on video.

DR6, DR31

Goes well with: *The Devil's Playground*

"BREAKER" MORANT
ESSENTIAL

Australia   1980   C   107 min.   PG   Drama
Dir: Bruce Beresford
C: Edward Woodward, Jack Thompson, John Waters, Bryan Brown

Among the first wave of Australian films to break on U.S. shores in the late 1970s was this true-life drama set during the Boer War. Never let it be said that the Aussies will give the Brits any slack when it comes to portraying the British military. Down under, passions still run deep over Gallipoli, the World War I battle in which thousands of Australian troops died, some would say needlessly at the bloody hands of British incompetence. Here, the British Empire's image must be preserved by a court-martial of a trio of Australian soldiers, who bravely face a firing squad for their tenuous-at-best involvement in the murder of prisoners. *"Breaker" Morant* is also notable as the film that introduced director Bruce Beresford and stalwart actors Edward Woodward and Bryan Brown to American audiences. (Note: The actor John Waters listed here is not the independent film chronicler of Baltimore.)

⊙**DVD**

DR24, DR26, DR37

Goes well with: *Gallipoli*

BREAKING THE WAVES
ESSENTIAL

Denmark   1996   C   156 min.   R   Drama
Dir: Lars von Trier
C: Emily Watson, Stellan Skarsgård, Adrian Rawlins, Katrin Cartlidge, Jean-Marc Barr

Religious faith can be tested in many ways, but never more strangely than in Danish director Lars von Trier's drama about a young wife from a fundamentalist family. When her husband, a religious skeptic, is crippled in a workplace accident, he makes an unusual request of her: He can only enjoy sexual satisfaction (and, he implies, have any hope to go on living) if she has sex with other men and then tells him about it. Yes, it does sound like a premise for a late-night film on an adults-only channel, but von Trier is not interested in turning us into the sexual voyeurs the husband has clearly become. He's using this setup as a means of exploring the limits of faith. Emily Watson's performance is key to this long but ultimately rewarding drama. She makes sense out of a woman who has chosen to obey two masters, her husband and her own custom-made version of an understanding God. Robby Müller's stylized cinematography, favoring a bumpy, handheld look with the primary colors bleached out, contributes to the character's sense of dislocation. The New York Film Critics Circle showered the film with its Best Director, Best Actress, and Best Cinematography Awards.

⊙**DVD**
DR19, DR30, DR39
Goes well with: *The Rapture*

BREATHLESS
ESSENTIAL

France   1959   B&W   89 min.   NR   Drama
Dir: Jean-Luc Godard
C: Jean Seberg, Jean-Paul Belmondo, Daniel Boulanger, Liliane David, Jean-Pierre Melville

Breathless was the first foreign-language rock-and-roll movie. It was not about rock, it did not contain any rock on its soundtrack, but American filmgoers who saw it in 1959 likely felt the same way pop music listeners did when Elvis Presley broke through in 1956: The rules have changed. Jean-Luc Godard's story of a common crook and his free-spirited American girlfriend was jagged, ragged, self-aware, and indifferent to any form of politeness. Jean-Paul Belmondo wasn't your commonly handsome leading man, but he carried himself with such panache that audiences connected with him immediately. (His character's fascination with Humphrey Bogart, another unconventionally attractive leading man, was no accident.) Jean Seberg recovered from her awful notices in the misbegotten *Saint Joan* to play a new kind of young woman: freshly minted, uninhibited, and less interested in a life of quiet domesticity than in life of the moment. The handheld camera, the jarring editing, the sense that we are eavesdropping on street life rather than watching a series of carefully composed dramatic tableaux, all mark a serious break from French cinema of the past. The New Wave that in essence began with *Breathless* had far-reaching effects, even on Hollywood filmmakers such as Warren Beatty, who considered Godard to direct *Bonnie and Clyde*.

⊙**DVD**

DR6, DR18, XT3, XT7

Goes well with: *Pierrot le Fou*

THE BRIDGE ON THE RIVER KWAI

ESSENTIAL

U.K. 1957 C 161 min. PG Drama

Dir: David Lean

C: William Holden, Alec Guinness, Jack Hawkins, Sessue Hayakawa, Geoffrey Horne, James Donald

David Lean began his directorial career with *In Which We Serve,* a 1942 World War II drama whose midconflict release dictated an uncomplicated approach to British heroism. But when he returned to the genre fifteen years later, it was to inject a much-needed dose of moral ambiguity. Carl Foreman and Michael Wilson's adaptation of Frenchman Pierre Boulle's novel (the film's screenwriting Oscar initially went to Boulle, because Foreman and Wilson were blacklisted) is a story that runs on two parallel tracks: the building by British POWs of a bridge key to the Japanese war effort in Southeast Asia, and the efforts by a team of American and British commandos to sabotage the project. Alec Guinness, Lean's favorite actor, won his only Oscar for his portrayal of the British officer forced to serve the Japanese and attempting to rationalize his aid of the enemy. Sessue Hayakawa plays his memorable adversary, the commandant of the POW camp. Their seesaw struggles are ultimately more interesting that the conventional story line involving William Holden and Jack Hawkins's commando mission. The film will lose much of its impact if you can't see it in a widescreen version, especially for the exciting climax. Winner of seven Oscars—including Best Picture, Director, Cinematography (by Jack Hildyard), Film Editing, and Musical Score—*Bridge* also picked up picture, director, and actor awards from the New York Film Critics Circle.

⊙**DVD**

DR26, DR37

Goes well with: *Merry Christmas, Mr. Lawrence*

BRIDGET JONES'S DIARY
U.K./France   2001   C   94 min.   R   Comedy
Dir: Sharon Maguire
C: Renée Zellweger, Hugh Grant, Colin Firth, Gemma Jones, Jim Broadbent, Sally Phillips

In a rare instance of a movie improving on a book, this adaptation of Helen Fielding's bestselling comic novel about a thirty-two-year-old single woman's year of agony and occasional ecstasy compresses a somewhat attenuated story into a more economically satisfying narrative. Fielding shared screenwriting credit with Andrew Davies and Richard Curtis; the latter's participation is key, as several elements of his successful work on *Four Weddings and a Funeral* and *Notting Hill* carry over here. Like the Hugh Grant characters in those films, Bridget has a lonelyhearts-club band of friends to keep her spirits up in tough times, and she is embarrassed several times in public situations. In fact, the film is a first-rate comedy of humiliation, with brave Renée Zellweger putting on pounds and an acceptable-sounding British accent to play the hapless but lovable Bridget. In her first lead role, Zellweger carries the film effortlessly, playing nicely off both Grant (as her rakish boss) and Colin Firth (playing Mark Darcy, one of the novel and film's references to Jane Austen).

⊙**DVD:** Includes audio commentary by Maguire; "making-of" featurette; music video.

CO9

Goes well with: *Party Girl*

BRIEF ENCOUNTER
U.K.   1945   B&W   85 min.   NR   Drama
Dir: David Lean
C: Celia Johnson, Trevor Howard, Stanley Holloway

A film that has come full circle in its reputation, *Brief Encounter* was for years revered as an uncommonly beautiful "little" film. It's a Noel Coward story of a one-day meeting by two souls in a British railroad station that ends with the realization that they can never make a life together. In the 1960s it became fashionable to dismiss the film as mawkish and hardly worthy of classic status. Now *Brief Encounter* is back on the A-list again, its modest charms still intact, like a lovely woman who has aged gracefully without anyone noticing. David Lean and Ronald Neame sensitively adapted Coward's play; the performances by the two leads, Celia Johnson and Trevor Howard, are impeccable; and most important, *Encounter* evokes a time and place, postwar Britain, where the rules were suddenly changed or at least up for questioning.

⊙**DVD:** Includes audio essay by film historian Bruce Eder and restoration demonstration.

DR18

Goes well with: *Chungking Express*

BROKEN ENGLISH

New Zealand   1996   C   92 min.   NC-17   Drama
Dir: Gregor Nicholas
C: Aleksandra Vujcic, Julian Arahanga, Rade Serbedzija, Marton Csokas

The English spoken here is by two groups of people for whom it's not a first language. Set in New Zealand, *Broken English* is about ethnic conflict of a very personal nature. The willful daughter (Aleksandra Vujcic) of a Croatian family living in exile from the horror of the conflict in the former Yugoslavia makes the mistake of falling in love with a Maori cook (Julian Arahanga). It's a mistake as defined by one person: her embittered and dictatorial father (Rade Serbedzija), for whom TV news reports of atrocities in his homeland shape a mounting rage against anyone in his new country who isn't "one of ours." Serbedzija is convincingly scary as a man whose frustration has so deeply poisoned his soul that he can't stand for anyone else to be happy. The movie earned an NC-17 for one lusty (and funny) scene of lovemaking; R-rated versions of the film are available.

DR7, DR11, DR19, DR28

Goes well with: *Once Were Warriors*

BROTHER'S KEEPER

ESSENTIAL

U.S.   1992   C   104 min.   NR   Documentary

Dir: Joe Berlinger and Bruce Sinofsky

A documentary that tries to deal with as many issues as this one usually winds up running three or four times as long. So give *Brother's Keeper* extra credit for managing to explore aging, mercy killing, small-town life, and the role of media in shaping news stories, all in well under two hours. Delbert Ward, an elderly farmer with limited mental resources, is accused of murdering his sick brother Bill on their homestead outside a small town in upstate New York, though most of the townspeople offer a generous interpretation of Bill's death. Delbert, Bill, and their two brothers all lived as bachelors on the family farm, and the consensus among their neighbors is to cut them a wide amount of slack, even when pesky media types start tossing around charges of incest. Filmmakers Berlinger and Sinofsky subtly steer the debate in certain directions without laying heavy hands on the material. The film won awards from both the New York Film Critics Circle (Best Documentary) and the Sundance Film Festival (Audience Award).

DO2

Goes well with: *Paradise Lost: The Child Murders at Robin Hood Hills*

THE BROTHERS MCMULLEN

ESSENTIAL

U.S.   1995   C   97 min.   R   Drama

Dir: Edward Burns

C: Jack Mulcahy, Mike McGlone, Edward Burns, Shari Albert, Maxine Bahns, Connie Britton

Writer-director-actor Edward Burns's breakthrough film, made on a shoestring budget, was 1994's poster child for quality independent film-making, winning awards from the Independent Spirits (for Best First Feature) and at the Sundance festival (Grand Jury Prize for Dramatic Film). That his subsequent work hasn't met with the same kind of adoration doesn't diminish the accomplishments of *The Brothers M.* (And any comparison to Dostoyevsky will have to be made by Russian Lit majors who are better read than I.) Burns, Jack Mulcahy, and Mike McGlone play Exhibits A, B, and C on why women who want just a hint of real commitment from their men get peeved at every man who ever lived, Long Island Irish Catholic or not. Some reviewers knocked Burns's film for seeming to endorse its perpetually adolescent males' behavior. But to these eyes, *The Brothers McMullen* is, like *Diner,* an alleged comedy about men that gets less funny every time you see it or think about how self-deception dominates these characters' lives.

⊙**DVD:** Available in two editions. The Special Edition contains audio commentary by Edward Burns. An Ed Burns box set, *Stories from Long Island,* contains this film, *She's the One,* and *No Looking Back,* with audio commentary by Burns and a "making of" featurette.

DR11, DR18

Goes well with: *In the Company of Men*

THE BUENA VISTA SOCIAL CLUB

ESSENTIAL

U.S./U.K./Germany/France/Cuba   1999   C   105 min.   G   Documentary

Dir: Wim Wenders

It's not every documentary film that can be held happily responsible for stirring worldwide interest in an entire genre of music, but welcome to the *Club.* And give musician Ry Cooder a lot of credit; his trip to Havana to track down a group of aging musicians whose careers had been interrupted by Castro's revolution resulted in a recording session and a return trip with filmmaker Wim Wenders (with whom Cooder had collaborated on *Paris, Texas*) in tow. The album of the original recording sessions is now the biggest-selling recording of world music ever, and the movie enjoyed its own modest success at the box office. The shots of a desolate Havana contrast with the joyous expressions of the musicians, many in their eighties, whose careers and lives were given a second chance by the BVSC phenomenon. A trip to New York to play at Carnegie Hall is the film's poignant capper; the frail but still vibrant Cubans are nearly overwhelmed, first by the towering skyscrapers and then by the emotional audience reaction to their playing. The New York Film Critics Circle bestowed on it their Best Nonfiction Film award.

⊙**DVD:** Includes audio commentary by Wim Wenders and deleted scenes.

DO5

Goes well with: *Before Night Falls*

BURDEN OF DREAMS

U.S. 1982 C 94 min. NR Documentary
Dir: Les Blank

California independent filmmaker Les Blank has been making lovely documentaries for over twenty-five years, usually on subjects related to popular music. His big breakthrough to a larger audience came with a stunningly lucky break: Director and friend Werner Herzog allowed Blank to accompany him to the jungles of South America on location for his ambitious epic, *Fitzcarraldo*. The production was fraught with difficulties—some of them self-inflicted by Herzog (see the *Fitzcarraldo* entry) and some the result of unforeseen circumstances (the original star, Jason Robards, took ill during production and was replaced by Klaus Kinski). As a document of a troubled film shoot that resulted in a miraculously wonderful film, it's invaluable.

DO5

Goes well with: *Fitzcarraldo*

BURKE AND WILLS

Australia 1985 C 140 min. PG-13 Action-Adventure
Dir: Graeme Clifford
C: Jack Thompson, Nigel Havers, Greta Scacchi, Matthew Fargher

Robert Burke and William Wills could have been the Lewis and Clark of Australia, but their 1860–61 expedition to map the vast center of the continent ended in death for both. Since no white man had ventured very far into the interior, there was plenty of room for speculation that it might contain a vast sea or rich mineral deposits or even a forest suitable for creating new cities. Burke and Wills found none of the above, though they did become the first white men to traverse the continent (starting from the south, near Melbourne). Alienating the aborigines who might have helped them and mismanaging their supplies, the two men didn't survive the arduous return trip. (The film also suggests that some political shenanigans by their supporters back in Melbourne contributed to their demise.) Only one man from the expedition did make it back: John King, who was befriended by the aborigines ("They looked upon me as one of themselves," he testified to a royal commission investigating the tragedy). Jack Thompson plays the bullheaded Burke and Nigel Havers is the more reflective Wills in this solid account, which neither lionizes nor demonizes two fascinating historical characters.

AC2, DR17, DR24
Goes well with: *Mountains of the Moon*

THE BURMESE HARP
Japan   1956   B&W   116 min.   NR   Drama
Dir: Kon Ichikawa
C: Rentaro Mikuni, Shoji Yasui, Tatsuya Mihashi

Japanese director Kon Ichikawa made two great antiwar films in the 1950s, this one and *Fires on the Plain. Harp* takes place in the closing days of the war, as a ragtag band of soldiers tries to make its way through the jungles of Burma. Stopping in a village for the night, they are confronted by a force of British soldiers, but before hostilities break out, word comes that peace has been declared. One Japanese soldier, Mizushima (Shoji Yasui), volunteers to warn guerrillas hiding out in nearby mountain caves that they should surrender or face annihilation by Allied troops. The guerrillas decide to fight to the end, and they're wiped out; Mizushima survives the assault and decides on his own to become a Buddhist priest, dedicating his life to burying the mounds of corpses he finds while wandering the countryside. His comrades know nothing of this; they are confined to a POW camp but remain hopeful that he survived the mountain assault. There is a brief reunion just before they are repatriated to Japan, but Mizushima makes clear what his new mission is. The film makes wonderful (and surprising) use of the song "No Place Like Home" at key moments in the story.

DR8, DR16, DR37
Goes well with: *Fires on the Plain*

BURN!
Italy/France   1969   C   112 min.   PG   Drama
Dir: Gillo Pontecorvo
C: Marlon Brando, Evaristo Márquez, Renato Salvatori, Tom Lyons, Norman Hill

Gillo Pontecorvo's background as a left-leaning political activist served him well in his breakthrough feature, *The Battle of Algiers,* and its follow-up, *Burn!* This story plays faster and looser with its historical facts. Marlon Brando plays William Walker, a British agent provocateur sent in 1845 to a Portuguese island colony in the Caribbean. His mission is to incite a revolt by the black slave peasants against their colonial masters; once the regime is overthrown, a puppet governor is installed to give the British free access to the island's rich sugar crop. That Brando and Pontecorvo didn't get along during filming had no effect on the result, a powerful condemnation of colonialism that's only a notch below the masterful *Battle of Algiers*. (Brando's character is not the same man played by Ed Harris in the 1988 historical drama *Walker,* though they share the same name and penchant for meddling in foreign affairs.)

DR24, DR25, DR28

Goes well with: *The Mission*

BURNT BY THE SUN

ESSENTIAL

Russia 1994 C 135 min. NR Drama

Dir: Nikita Mikhalkov

C: Nikita Mikhalkov, Ingeborga Dapkounaite, Oleg Menchikov, Nadia Mikhalkov

A Soviet scientist once wrote, referring to the mid-1930s, when Stalinist purges turned former heroes of the state into outcasts, "In those days a knock on the door could mean death." That black historical hole is illuminated in this stunning and stirring drama from director-actor Nikita Mikhalkov. He plays a retired hero of the 1917 revolution whose sojourn in the summer of 1936 with his younger wife (Ingeborga Dapkounaite) and little daughter is interrupted by the arrival of an unwelcome visitor: a government official who also happens to be his wife's ex-lover. The story builds slowly to reveal the callous disregard of so-called progressive political régimes for the dignity of the individual citizen. The seeds of Stalin's poisonous legacy, which began with his consolidation of power in the 1920s, were sown in millions of incidents like this one. Mikhalkov's daughter Nadia plays his daughter in the film; their appearance together at the Academy Awards to accept the film's Oscar for Best Foreign Language Film was a highlight of the March 1995 ceremony.

DR11, DR24, DR25

Goes well with: *Sunshine*

THE BUTCHER BOY

U.S./Ireland 1997 C 106 min. R Drama

Dir: Neil Jordan

C: Stephen Rea, Fiona Shaw, Eamonn Owens, Alan Boyle, Ian Hart, Sinéad O'Connor, Milo O'Shea, Patrick McCabe

Seldom does a literary work employing a stylized first-person narrative make a successful transition to the screen, but *The Butcher Boy* is a happy exception. Patrick McCabe's amazing novel was adapted by the author and director Neil Jordan; it tells the story of Francie Brady (Eamonn Owens), a boy whose boundless energy and sense of mischief masks the soul of a true psychotic. Francie's mom suffers from mental breakdowns and his dad (Stephen Rea) can barely stay sober, so he's off on his own much of the time, roaming the streets of his village, playing pranks and staying one step ahead of the law. The story is set in the early 1960s, and Francie's obsession with the Cuban Missile Crisis and a nuclear holocaust contribute to his pathology. So does his fascination with the Virgin Mary, who is played in one of his frequent visions by singer Sinéad O'Connor. McCabe can also be glimpsed as the town drunk. It's a disturbing but exhilarating piece of filmmaking, likely the best film Jordan has made to date.

DR21, DR29, DR41

Goes well with: *The Young Poisoner's Handbook*

C

THE CABINET OF DR. CALIGARI

ESSENTIAL

Germany 1919 B&W 69 min. NR Horror

Dir: Robert Wiene

C: Werner Krauss, Conrad Veidt, Lil Dagover

Creaky but still creepy, *Caligari* is the German film that started that country's first great film movement. With its expressionist sets and unsettling tale of an evil scientist (Werner Krauss) ordering his accomplice, a somnambulist named Cesare (Conrad Veidt), to commit seemingly random murders, it inspired many horror films to come. It's also the first great film related from a subjective point of view: the tale is told by the mad Caligari, complete with the skewed perspectives of a nightmare. Caligari's vision expressed Germany's turbulent postwar frame of mind, and its suggestion of a charismatic leader turning his subjects into mindless zombies gave the film a second life fifteen years later, with the rise of Hitler and his Nazi thugs. Don't expect subtle acting or brilliant dialogue, but do expect an utterly disturbing experience.

⊙**DVD:** Includes audio essay by Mike Budd.

FA5, FA8, FA9

Goes well with: *Metropolis*

CAL

U.K. 1984 C 102 min. R Drama

Dir: Pat O'Connor

C: Helen Mirren, John Lynch, Donal McCann, John Kavanagh, Ray McAnally

If Helen Mirren weren't one of the most persuasive actresses in movies of the last twenty years, *Cal* wouldn't stand a chance. The story is meant to dramatize the ongoing tensions in Northern Ireland, but its premise is precariously thin. Believing that the thirtysomething widow of a Protestant policeman slain by the IRA would have an affair with a nineteen-year-old who's no ball of fire is asking a lot of us, but for the teenager to realize that he drove the murderer's getaway car demands a major suspension of disbelief. Mirren's performance as a woman resigned to finding some peace and happiness in the wake of shattering tragedy is the best reason to see this film. Another is the lovely score by Mark Knopfler.

DR19, DR25, DR41

Goes well with: *The Crying Game*

CALLE 54

Spain/France/Italy   2000   C   106 min.   G   Documentary
Dir: Fernando Trueba

A labor of love by director Fernando Trueba, an unabashed fan of Latin jazz music, *Calle 54* is like having an all-star concert right in your home. Trueba filmed performances by the late Tito Puente, the father and son piano duo Bebe and Chucho Valdés, tenor sax legend Gato Barbieri, and nine other musicians at Sony's 54th Street studios in Manhattan (thus, the title). Trueba's cameras prowl around the performers, with shots clearly worked out ahead of time to catch each soloist at the right moment. In its theatrical version, this was largely a performance film, with snippets of each musician talking briefly about his or her background. But on the DVD, there's plenty of additional material on the history of the genre, with expanded interview material and handy discographies of each player to help you build your CD collection.

⊙**DVD:** Includes audio commentary by jazz historian Nat Chediak; documentary on the history of Latin jazz; musician bios; discographies.

DO5, DO6

Goes well with: *The Buena Vista Social Club*

CAREFUL, HE MIGHT HEAR YOU

Australia   1983   C   116 min.   PG   Drama
Dir: Carl Schultz
C: Wendy Hughes, Robyn Nevin, Nicholas Gledhill, John Hargreaves

Among the best films told from a child's point of view is this Australian adaptation of Sumner Locke Elliott's novel. P.S., so named by his mother, who died shortly after he was born, grows up in the loving household of his aunt and uncle, while his wastrel father is off searching for gold. A second aunt, a severe woman who has never married, obtains a court order giving her partial custody of the six-year-old boy, and the tug-of-war between the two households for the heart and soul of P.S. is on. Nicholas Gledhill plays P.S. as a normal child who just wants some stability in his life; you have to wonder how child actors can play intense parts like this one without being affected in some way. Wendy Hughes is the maiden aunt, a woman who thinks she needs someone to love but has no idea what to do when she's presented with the opportunity.

⊙**DVD**

DR11, DR29, DR41

Goes well with: *My Life as a Dog*

CARMEN

Spain   1983   C   102 min.   R   Musical

Dir: Carlos Saura

C: Antonio Gades, Laura Del Sol, Paco de Lucia, Cristina Hoyos, Juan Antonio Jiménez

Not a straight version of Bizet's opera, but something almost as good. Antonio Gades and Carlos Saura's script has a choreographer (Gades) casting a dance version of the opera, and his selection of the lead (Laura Del Sol) proves that life can imitate art. On its most basic level, the film is no different than any other backstage drama in which the director and his lead actress can't keep their hands off each other, with potentially disastrous consequences for themselves and their colleagues. But it has the added virtues of Bizet's fabulous music, riveting flamenco dancing, and two gorgeous leads.

DR5, DR19, MU1

Goes well with: *La Traviata*

CARNIVAL OF SOULS

U.S.   1962   B&W   83 min.   PG   Horror

Dir: Herk Harvey

C: Candace Hilligoss, Sidney Berger, Frances Feist, Herk Harvey

The only feature directed by industrial filmmaker Herk Harvey, *Carnival of Souls* is a horror film that operates on a level somewhere south of consciousness. A young woman (Candace Hilligoss) survives a car accident, but her life can't be the same. She becomes a church organist, but the parishioners barely acknowledge her existence. And then there's this strange man (played with real menace by the director himself) who follows her everywhere. Shot in and around Lawrence, Kansas, *Carnival* turns the plains of the Midwest into eerie landscapes. Harvey's limited budget is a virtue; elaborate special effects aren't required to create a genuine aura of terror and uncertainty. Don't confuse this with the inferior 1998 remake.

⊙**DVD:** Two disc package includes original version and extended director's cut; documentary, "The Movie That Wouldn't Die!," about 1989 reunion of cast and crew; outtakes; video update on the film's locations; audio commentary by writer John Clifford and Herk Harvey; excerpts from industrial films made by Harvey.

DR8, FA9

Goes well with: *The Addiction*

CARRIED AWAY

U.S.   1996   C   107 min.   R   Drama

Dir: Bruno Barreto

C: Dennis Hopper, Amy Irving, Amy Locane, Julie Harris, Gary Busey, Hal Holbrook, Priscilla Pointer

Carried Away, adapted from the Jim Harrison novella *Farmer,* is about an indecisive man who makes a bad decision. Farmer-turned-schoolteacher Joseph Svenden (Dennis Hopper) has two women in his life, his ailing mother (Julie Harris) and his longtime fiancée, Rosealee Hensen (Amy Irving), also a teaching colleague. His mother is clinging to life and their family farm, and his fiancée is waiting patiently for him. Salvation, or at least no-strings-attached sex, enters his life in the form of Catherine Wheeler (Amy Locane), a troubled student who seduces him. One of the film's strengths is in fleshing out Catherine's character, as when we meet her father (Gary Busey), a military officer and control freak who's watching his daughter and family spin out of control. This may be Dennis Hopper's best "straight" performance in a résumé full of psychos and stoners. Irving, Locane, and Busey are all terrific, too. Director Bruno Barreto and Irving are married; Irving's mother, actress Priscilla Pointer, plays her mother here.

DR19, DR33, DR34

Goes well with: *Last Tango in Paris*

CARRINGTON

U.K./France 1995 C 122 min. R Drama

Dir: Christopher Hampton

C: Emma Thompson, Jonathan Pryce, Steven Waddington, Rufus Sewell, Samuel West, Penelope Wilton, Janet McTeer

British painter Dora Carrington and biographer Lytton Strachey were in love. Deeply in love. There was just this little problem; Strachey was gay. Writer-director Christopher Hampton's study of a two-career relationship shows how both partners were able to pursue their work and conduct affairs that weren't exactly extramarital, since Dora and Lytton never married. (Dora did marry Ralph Partridge, and Lytton was smitten with him, but we don't want to give too much away here.) Both were associated with the Bloomsbury group, so we get glimpses of Clive and Vanessa Bell (Richard Clifford and Janet McTeer), but not, alas, Virginia Woolf, to whom Strachey was once engaged. Emma Thompson and Jonathan Pryce infuse these real-life artists with an immense amount of detail. After watching *Carrington,* you'll be rushing off to read one of Strachey's books (start with *Eminent Victorians*) or to find a volume of Carrington's paintings (a bit tougher mission).

⊙**DVD:** Includes behind-the-scenes featurette.

DR2, DR17, DR18, DR21

Goes well with: *The Whole Wide World*

THE CELEBRATION

ESSENTIAL

Denmark 1998 C 101 min. R Drama

Dir: Thomas Vinterberg

C: Ulrich Thomsen, Henning Moritzen, Thomas Bo Larsen, Paprika Steen

The Dogma 95 manifesto that certain European filmmakers have tried to follow (it bans certain editing techniques as unfairly manipulative and insists on natural light only, among other guidelines) gained worldwide attention through this Danish drama about a birthday party from hell. The prosperous head of a clan is turning sixty, and he has invited all his offspring and friends to his country estate for a real wingding. Writer-director Thomas Vinterberg takes elements from virtually every horrid family gathering you've ever attended, then pulls a major skeleton out of the patriarch's closet for good measure. It's not all domestic psychodrama; Vinterberg knows how to get a laugh out of his characters' predicaments. Winner of Best Foreign Language Film from the New York Film Critics Circle.

⊙**DVD**

DR11

Goes well with: *A Sunday in the Country*

THE CELLULOID CLOSET

U.S./France/Germany/U.K. 1995 C/B&W 102 min. R Documentary

Dir: Robert Epstein and Jeffrey Friedman

The quality of any documentary about film history is in large part determined by the access filmmakers are allowed to relevant clips. Just for gaining access to scenes from over one hundred films for their study of gay text and subtext in Hollywood, directors Rob Epstein and Jeffrey Friedman should be awarded gold medals. Based on Vito Russo's superb study, one of the first of its kind, *Closet* is not about dishing over who's gay in the movies, rather, it's a largely serious examination of the way Hollywood films have dealt with homosexual themes and characters, both directly and indirectly. All of the interview subjects (including Tom Hanks, Shirley MacLaine, Gore Vidal, Harvey Fierstein, and Susan Sarandon) add relevant observations about their own films. The Sundance festival awarded the film its Freedom of Expression prize.

⊙**DVD**

DO5

Goes well with: *Apartment Zero*

CÉRÉMONIE, LA.

See *La Cérémonie*

CESAR AND ROSALIE

France/Italy/West Germany 1972 C 104 min. R Drama

Dir: Claude Sautet

C: Yves Montand, Romy Schneider, Sami Frey, Umberto Orsini, Isabelle Huppert

The late Romy Schneider was never greater than in this amiable romantic drama, in which she plays a divorced woman living with an older man, a successful industrialist. Enter an old flame of Rosalie's, and the dramatic wheels begin to spin. Yves Montand and Sami Frey play the men in Rosalie's life, but it's Schneider's wonderfully nuanced performance that holds our attention. She had graduated from child actress to adult star, working in both Europe and occasionally in Holly-wood before dying of a heart attack in 1982 at the age of forty-three.

DR18

Goes well with: *Un Coeur en Hiver*

CHAPLIN

France/Italy/U.K./U.S.   1992   C   144 min.   PG-13   Drama
Dir: Richard Attenborough
C: Robert Downey, Jr., Dan Aykroyd, Geraldine Chaplin, Kevin Dunn, Anthony Hopkins, Milla Jovovich, Moira Kelly, Kevin Kline, Diane Lane, Penelope Ann Miller, Paul Rhys, Marisa Tomei, James Woods, David Duchovny

Richard Attenborough's film about one of the few indisputable ge-niuses ever to make movies tries to cover too much ground. Charlie Chaplin's life was far too rich, even for a movie running almost two and a half hours. His offscreen life alone, with four marriages, countless af-fairs, and at least one major paternity suit, as well as his status as the most prominent victim of the red scare of the 1950s, would make for a 144-minute movie all on its own. Yet even when it's gliding by moments where we want to it linger, *Chaplin* is never less than fascinating, thanks in large part to Robert Downey, Jr.'s amazing performance. (Commen-tators who dismissed his career as second-rate during his well publi-cized drug problems obviously never saw this film.) Downey masters the physical side of Chaplin's comedy and provides a sympathetic un-derstanding of a man whose impoverished childhood drove him all his life toward acceptance. Also outstanding in the cast are Geraldine Chaplin—Charlie's daughter—here playing his mentally fragile mother; Dan Aykroyd as silent-film producer Mack Sennett; and Moira Kelly as two women in Chaplin's life, one of them his fourth and final wife, Oona O'Neill.

⊙**DVD:** Includes "making of" featurette.

DR2, DR17, DR22

Goes well with: *Life Is Beautiful*

CHARACTER
ESSENTIAL

Netherlands   1997   C   125 min.   R   Drama
Dir: Mike van Diem
C: Fedja van Huêt, Jan Decleir, Betty Schuurman, Victor Löw

The setting is 1920s Rotterdam, but it could be 1840s London for the Dickensian vibes this Oscar-winning Dutch drama gives off. The story begins with the murder of a forbidding-looking man and the arrest of a much younger suspect, whose flashback confession reveals everything. The victim was Dreverhaven, a prominent and widely feared business-man whose ruthlessness in matters both personal and professional drove his son to revenge, and that's all you need to know about this grip-ping story. Debut director Mike van Diem and his production team cre-ate a stylized view of the past, shot in muddy browns and grays, filled with deep shadows and murky pools of light; at times, the setting almost overwhelms the characters, who always seem to be bustling in and out of hulking buildings (the film was shot in several European cities; the location scouts should have been given their own Academy Awards). Belgian actor Jan Decleir is magnificently evil as Dreverhaven. It's the kind of role that Orson Welles in his prime would have killed to play.

DR11, DR24, XT4

Goes well with: *Affliction*

CHASING AMY

U.S.   1997   C   111 min.   R   Comedy
Dir: Kevin Smith
C: Ben Affleck, Joey Lauren Adams, Jason Lee, Jason Mewes, Kevin
   Smith, Matt Damon, Casey Affleck

The two male leads in Kevin Smith's engaging comedy have a mini-universe they can control: the comic strip they draw and write. But like the dudes in Smith's first feature, *Clerks,* they're less adept at handling the world beyond their self-created realm. Smith loves to cozy up to guys seriously disconnected from reality, and Ben Affleck and Jason Lee make a much more engaging pair than Brian O'Halloran and Jeff Anderson in *Clerks.* (Smith's script this time out is a lot more sophisti-cated, too.) Affleck is understandably smitten by an attractive and smart artist (Joey Lauren Adams) whom he meets at a comic book convention, and his pursuit of her, complicated just a bit by the fact that she is a les-bian, also upsets the inkwell of his artist partner. As in all of Smith's first four films, he and his acting partner, Jason Mewes, appear as Silent Bob and Jay, a sort of Greek chorus; they got their own starring roles in *Jay and Silent Bob Strike Back. Chasing Amy* picked up two awards at the Independent Spirit ceremony, for Lee's performance and Smith's script.

⊙**DVD:** Includes audio commentary by Kevin Smith; deleted scenes; outtakes; and "The Askewniverse Legend," a guide to the characters in Smith's New Jersey trilogy.

CO9

Goes well with: *Party Girl*

CHILDREN OF PARADISE

ESSENTIAL

France 1945 B&W 195 min. NR Drama

Dir: Marcel Carné

C: Jean-Louis Barrault, Arletty, Pierre Brasseur, Albert Rémy, Maria Câsarés, Marcel Herrand

It is almost underrating this magnificent epic to call it the greatest backstage romance of all time, because it offers more dimensions on each viewing. Made in Paris during the Nazi Occupation under immensely difficult circumstances (you can imagine that there wasn't too much time or money for retakes), *Children of Paradise* tells the story of a nineteenth-century Parisian courtesan, Garance (Arletty), and the three men who love her: the married mime Baptiste Debureau (Jean-Louis Barrault), the actor Frederick Lemaître (Pierre Brasseur), and the criminal Pierre-François Lacenaire (Marcel Herrand). The setting is Paris's Boulevard of Crime, and the title refers to the upper balconies of the local theater, where the poor people from the Boulevard gather to watch (and loudly comment on) the productions of the day. Amazingly, although people are stealing from one another and miserable conditions abound, all the characters seem to be having a rollicking time of it; there is a joyous sense of democracy at work here that is found in few American films. Director Marcel Carné and writer Jacques Prévert don't just re-create the physical past, they fill it with gloriously three-dimensional characters. If you ever find yourself despairing of the cinema's power to move and engage you, rent this film.

⊙**DVD:** Two disc set. One includes audio commentary by scholar Brian Stonehill; introduction by Terry Gilliam; restoration demonstration. Second includes audio commentary by scholar Charles Affron; Prévert's film treatment.

DR4, DR18, DR24, DR36

Goes well with: *Farewell, My Concubine*

CHILDREN OF THE REVOLUTION

Australia   1996   C   101 min.   R   Comedy
Dir: Peter Duncan
C: Judy Davis, Sam Neill, F. Murray Abraham, Geoffrey Rush, Richard
  Roxburgh, Rachel Griffiths

The premise of this audacious and very smart black comedy can be summed up in one tabloid headline: I HAD JOSEPH STALIN'S LOVE CHILD! Judy Davis plays the mom in question, Joan Fraser. As a young, committed, and not terribly sophisticated Communist living in postwar Australia, Joan gets the chance of a lifetime when she journeys to Moscow to meet the great man. The Soviet dictator (played with gusto by F. Murray Abraham) takes a real shine to this young idealist, and the film offers a new interpretation of the cause of his death. Back in Australia, Joan eventually marries Zachary Welsh (Geoffrey Rush), who's also a leftist, and gives her little baby the name Joseph Welsh. (See *Point of Order!* if you don't get the joke.) Little Joe grows up to be a committed activist, though not quite in the way Mom intended. Davis carries the film over its rough patches; her intensity as an actress is almost frightening. Also of note is a witty performance by Rachel Griffiths as Constable Anna, who becomes an unlikely love match for Joe (they meet at a political demonstration). Director Peter Duncan worked from his original screenplay.

   CO2, CO3, CO8
Goes well with: *A World Apart*

THE CHOCOLATE WAR

U.S.   1988   C   103 min.   R   Drama
Dir: Keith Gordon
C: John Glover, Ilan Mitchell-Smith, Wally Ward, Bud Cort, Adam
  Baldwin, Jenny Wright

Actor Keith Gordon made an impressive directing debut with this drama set in a private Catholic school. (And he followed it up with two excellent films, *A Midnight Clear* and *Mother Night*.) The three-way struggle in this hothouse involves a rebellious student (Ilan Mitchell-Smith), a dictatorial teacher (John Glover), and a secret society called the Vigils, who are interested only in gaining and keeping power. The title refers to a candy-selling contest, the kind of event that at some schools becomes more than a fundraiser—the sales figures become a reflection of the character of each student. Gordon adapted Robert Cormier's young adult novel. Not as well known as *Dead Poet's Society,* which covers some of the same ground, it's a superior film, eschewing sentiment for an honest portrayal of the corruption of youth.

DR31, DR41

Goes well with: *The Devil's Playground*

CHOOSE ME

U.S.   1984   C   106 min.   R   Drama
Dir: Alan Rudolph
C: Geneviève Bujold, Keith Carradine, Lesley Ann Warren, Rae Dawn Chong, Patrick Bauchau, John Laroquette

No one ever gets seriously drunk or combative in the bar that's the main setting for this rumination on urban love and loss. But it's not like writer-director Alan Rudolph is trying to create a film version of *Cheers.* After all, the owner of the bar (Lesley Ann Warren) sleeps around and is miserable for it; one of her regulars (Geneviève Bujold) is a radio romance therapist whose private life is a shambles, another is a woman (Rae Dawn Chong) spying on her faithless lover (Patrick Bauchau). And then there's the new guy (Keith Carradine), a drifter with a lot of fancy stories about his past and an irresistible way with the women. *Choose Me* feels like an American version of an Eric Rohmer movie—people talk endlessly about romance—but Rudolph's characters are edgier and not as smart as Rohmer's. Both Warren and Bujold, as women coming at love from different directions, are as good as they have ever been.

DR18, DR36

Goes well with: *Trouble in Mind*

CHUNGKING EXPRESS

Hong Kong   1994   C   103 min.   PG-13   Drama
Dir: Wong Kar-Wai
C: Brigitte Lin, Takeshi Kaneshiro, Tony Leung, Faye Wang

Some urban newspapers offer a different kind of personal ad in their pages, through which you can try to contact that specific man or woman who gave you a knowing glance yesterday on the subway or at Starbuck's. Wong Kar-Wai's drama, set in Hong Kong, feels like it grew out of reading those columns. It involves two policemen looking for love in and around a fast-food stand. One is attracted to a woman in a blond wig whose profession may compromise the cop's own job, and the other guy is unwittingly "investigated" by a counter worker with California on her mind. Shot in twenty-three days, the film has an off-the-cuff quality that makes *Chungking Express* much more engaging than many a tightly scripted, by-the-numbers film.

⊙**DVD**

DR18, DR36, XT7

Goes well with: *Choose Me*

CINEMA PARADISO

ESSENTIAL

Italy/France 1988 C 123 min. PG Drama
Dir: Giuseppe Tornatore
C: Philippe Noiret, Jacques Perrin, Salvatore Cascio, Marco Leonardi

A loving tribute to the power of movies to heal and soothe us, *Cinema Paradiso* is about the friendship between a projectionist (Philippe Noiret) in a postwar Italian village and the little boy (Salvatore Cascio) he befriends. The boy, Salvatore, gets to watch as the man in the booth tries to resist pressure from the local priest to literally cut out offending shots and scenes involving any intimations of sex. It's clear almost from the start of the story that Salvatore's obsession with film is going to turn into a lifelong love affair with the movies. Clips from dozens of films, both familiar classics of the era and more obscure Italian releases, pepper the story, which was a no-surprise Oscar winner for Best Foreign Language Film.

⊙**DVD**

DR12, DR16, DR34

Goes well with: *Amarcord*

THE CIRCLE

Iran/Italy 2000 C 91 min. NR Drama
Dir: Jafar Panahi
C: Nargess Mamizadeh, Maryiam Palvin Almani, Mojgan Faramarzi, Elham Saboktakin

The rights, privileges, and freedom that women in Western societies take for granted are hard to come by in countries like Iran, the setting for Jafar Panahi's devastating drama. Filmed like a documentary—with handheld cameras filming many scenes in real time—the series of overlapping vignettes illustrates the myriad shackles placed on Iranian women, who can't travel on public transportation alone, can't smoke in public, can't seek certain medical procedures without permission from a husband, and are often jailed for petty offenses. In fact, most of the characters depicted here are ex-cons or escapees, furtively making their way through the streets of an unforgiving city. Panahi captures the resourcefulness and desperation of life in a country stubbornly clinging to a narrow view of humanity.

⊙**DVD**

DR36, DR39

Goes well with: *Kandahar*

CITIZEN RUTH

ESSENTIAL

U.S.   1996   C   109 min.   R   Comedy

Dir: Alexander Payne

C: Laura Dern, Swoosie Kurtz, Mary Kay Place, Kurtwood Smith, Kelly Preston, Burt Reynolds, Alicia Witt, Diane Ladd

It's rare to see an equal opportunity satire, but *Citizen Ruth* is the film with something to offend everyone on both sides of the abortion debate. Laura Dern plays the title character, a lost soul whose addiction to substance abuse (mostly glue-sniffing) is matched by her fertility: she is pregnant with her fifth child, and the first four have all been put up for adoption. When a judge orders her to have an abortion, in step two groups who would be either Ruth's "rescuers" (the pro-life folks) or "protectors" (the pro-choice forces). Director Alexander Payne and his writing partner, Jim Taylor, won't take sides here, though you can say that the pro-life characters (led by a wonderfully flamboyant Burt Reynolds) are funnier. Look for Diane Ladd, Dern's real-life mom, playing Ruth's mother in a stunningly hilarious scene near the end of the film. Dern should have at least been nominated for an Oscar for this performance, the best of her career. Taylor and Payne went on to make the equally ruthless satire on high school politics, *Election*.

CO2, CO8

Goes well with: *Rambling Rose*

THE CITY OF LOST CHILDREN

France/Spain/Germany   1995   C   112 min.   R   Fantasy

Dir: Jean-Pierre Jeunet and Marc Caro

C: Ron Perlman, Joseph Lucien, Daniel Emilfork, Mireille Mossé

The truly nightmarish world of fairy tales such as those of the Grimm Brothers is captured in this unsettling fantasy by the filmmaking team of Jean-Pierre Jeunet and Marc Caro. In their mythical city, a madman kidnaps children to be able to inhabit their dreams. Horror fans will recognize the premise from the *Nightmare on Elm Street* series, but Jeunet and Caro are much more interested in creating an entire world of creepy creatures, including the villain's cloned minions, than in presenting state-of-the-art gore effects. As in their previous film, *Delicatessen,* Jeunet and Caro's set designs are the real stars; you don't recall the performances from their films as much as you do their claustrophobic, cluttered rooms and labyrinthine streets. The musical score is by Angelo Badalamenti, David Lynch's favorite composer.

⊙**DVD:** Includes commentary audio track; production and costume design galleries.

FA3, FA5, FA6, FA8, XT6
Goes well with: *Delicatessen*

CLERKS
ESSENTIAL

U.S.   1994   B&W   89 min.   R   Comedy
Dir: Kevin Smith
C: Brian O'Halloran, Jeff Anderson, Marilyn Ghigliotti, Lisa Spoon-
    hauer, Jason Mewes, Kevin Smith

If Kevin Smith's debut feature really did cost $27,000 to make, surely everyone on the film worked pro bono—and indeed it turned out to be for the good, because this profane, hipper-than-thou, too-cool-to-fool comedy ought to be buried in a time capsule. Centuries from now, archaeologists will get a big-gulp helping of Dude Culture of the late twentieth century when they access *Clerks* (assuming there are still VHS or DVD players in operation then). Mr. Smith, an anthropologist disguised as a filmmaker, explores a subculture that thrives on the edges of our daily radar: those seen-it-all guys who check out your films at the video store or your six-pack at the convenience store. This also marked the film debut of the loquacious Jay (Jason Mewes) and Silent Bob (Smith), a team of comic characters that are Smith's homage to Laurel and Hardy filtered through Cheech and Chong by way of Penn and Teller. The folks at the 1994 Sundance festival were impressed; they gave Smith their Filmmaker's Trophy.

⊙**DVD:** Includes alternate ending; audio commentary by Kevin Smith and cast members; deleted scenes.

CO5

Goes well with: *Chasing Amy*

THE COCA-COLA KID

Australia   1985   C   94 min.   R   Comedy
Dir: Dušan Makavejev
C: Eric Roberts, Greta Scacchi, Bill Kerr, Chris Haywood

The story of a brash American abroad getting his or her comeuppance gets a gently satiric spin in this comedy by a filmmaker from Yugoslavia working in Australia. Dušan Makavejev directs Eric Roberts as Becker, the cola salesman who is convinced that fifteen million thirsty Australians need and want his product. The no-worries Aussies can't see what the big deal is about a bottle of soda, especially since there's plenty of beer available. Becker is so focused on pitching the real thing that he almost misses the romantic signal flares sent up by his sexy secretary (Greta Scacchi). 1985 was a big year for Roberts, with this performance and an equally riveting one in the adventure film *Runaway Train;* his roles since then have mostly been supporting parts in largely forgettable films.

⊙**DVD**

CO4

Goes well with: *Local Hero*

COCKFIGHTER

U.S.   1974   C   83 min.   R   Drama
Dir: Monte Hellman
C: Warren Oates, Richard B. Shull, Harry Dean Stanton, Troy Donahue, Millie Perkins, Robert Earl Jones, Charles Willeford

Character actor Warren Oates didn't get many chances to play leads in his career, and he must have had mixed feelings about being the title character in this drama—he speaks no lines until the final scene. (He does provide voice-over narration.) Charles Willeford (best known for *Miami Blues* and other Florida-based crime novels) adapted the script from his novel, a brooding character study of a man immersed in the netherworld of pitting birds against each other for sport. The eye-opening supporting cast includes another largely unsung character actor, Harry Dean Stanton, plus early 1960s teen icons Troy Donahue and Millie Perkins, Robert Earl Jones (James's father), and Willeford in a small part. Director Monte

Hellman and cinematographer Néstor Almendros (a long-time associate of François Truffaut) don't flinch from the worst kind of human behavior, but the film never feels like it's wallowing in violence. Oates fans will want to get the DVD, which includes a documentary on their man.

⊙**DVD:** Includes audio commentary by Monte Hellman and production assistant Steven Gaydos; documentary feature, "Warren Oates: Across the Border."

DR21, DR35

Goes well with: *Ghost Dog: The Way of the Samurai*

COEUR EN HIVER, UN.

See *Un Coeur en Hiver*

COLD COMFORT FARM

U.K.   1995   C   95 min.   PG   Comedy
Dir: John Schlesinger
C: Kate Beckinsale, Sheila Burrell, Stephen Fry, Freddie Jones, Joanna
    Lumley, Ian McKellen, Miriam Margolyes, Rufus Sewell

This adaptation of Stella Gibbon's acclaimed satirical novel features a smashing performance by Kate Beckinsale as Flora Poste, erstwhile novelist and do-gooder. In need of lodgings, subject matter for her first book, and objects to manipulate for her sense of a well-ordered universe, Flora moves into a dilapidated country house full of country cousins. They provide her with plenty of material for her book and her charitable impulses; the unintended consequence of her sojourn is a new-found sense of proportion about her own relatively privileged life. As the wackiest of Flora's relatives, a lay preacher with an unusual sense of sin and retribution, Ian McKellen chews whatever scenery is within reach. Malcolm Bradbury did the superb adaptation, with veteran director John Schlesinger rising to the occasion for one of his strongest late-career efforts.

CO3, CO4

Goes well with: *Slums of Beverly Hills*

COME AND SEE

ESSENTIAL

Soviet Union   1985   C   142 min.   NR   Drama
Dir: Elem Klimov
C: Alexei Kravchenko, Olga Mironova, Liubomiras Lauciavicius

Ales Adamovich, the cowriter of this powerful World War II drama, fought with Russian partisans in Belarus in 1943, when the Nazis were systematically torching villages (over six hundred in all) and slaughtering their inhabitants. He and director Elem Klimov adapted his story about his experiences, telling of the horrors through the eyes of a thirteen-year-old peasant boy named Florya. After he finds a rifle left buried near his farm, Florya insists on joining the partisans, despite his mother's protest. He's separated from his unit and left behind with Glascha, a lovely young girl, but then his troubles begin. Left nearly deaf by exploding bombs, he and Glascha find that his home village has been decimated, and they wade through a swamp to locate the survivors. Florya returns to the front hoping for vengeance, only to find himself in a village that's right in the path of the Nazi firestorm. Alexei Kravchenko, the young actor who plays Florya, seems to age about forty years in the space of the film's two-and-a-half hours; reportedly, the director had him hypnotized to be able to get through some of the horrific scenes. *Come and See* ranks with the best war films, especially those that unflinchingly document the monumental barbarism of soldiers attacking defenseless civilians.

⊙**DVD:** Two-disc set includes menus and soundtrack in three languages, subtitles in thirteen languages; interviews with Elem Klimov and Alexei Kravchenko; archival films on Nazi brutalities and partisans in Belarus.

DR24, DR37, DR38, DR41

Goes well with: *Night of the Shooting Stars*

COMFORT AND JOY

U.K.   1984   C   105 min.   PG   Comedy
Dir: Bill Forsyth
C: Bill Paterson, Eleanor David, C. P. Grogan, Alex Norton, Patrick Malahide

If Bill Forsyth's follow-up to the sublime *Local Hero* falls a wee bit short of that film's delirious comic heights, it retains a large helping of Forsyth's droll wit. Bill Paterson plays Alan, a Glasgow disc jockey whose life is a shambles: his girlfriend Maddy (Eleanor David) is a compulsive thief (their apartment is filled with the spoils of her shoplifting trips) who suddenly announces she's moving in with another bloke, leaving Alan to yearn for a little romance and a job that entails something more substantial than spinning easy-listening music for the Geritol crowd. On top of that, it's Christmas, that magical season that always gives the downhearted a real kick in the head. Alan persuades his station to let him do a radio documentary, and he stumbles onto a war— of local ice cream vendors. Covering the tit-for-tat spats between Mr. McCool and Mr. Bunny isn't exactly reporting from the streets of Belfast, but there is compensation: Charlotte (C. P. Grogan), the loveli- est of the combatants. Guitarist Mark Knopfler, who did the sensational score for *Local Hero,* offers a lovely encore for this film.

CO8, CO10

Goes well with: *Local Hero*

THE COMMITMENTS

Ireland/U.K./U.S.   1991   C   117 min.   R   Comedy

Dir: Alan Parker

C: Robert Arkins, Michael Aherne, Angeline Ball, Maria Doyle, Dave Finnegan, Bronagh Gallagher, Felim Gormley, Glen Hansard, Dick Massey, Kenneth McCluskey, Johnny Murphy, Andrew Strong, Colm Meaney

No filmmaker has ever done a serious exploration of the attraction that American blues and soul music has for young people in the British Isles, but Alan Parker's beguiling comedy will do as an opening set. A group of young working-class Dubliners who are crazy about Wilson Pickett, Otis Redding, and Aretha Franklin decide to form a soul band and share their passion with the pub crawlers of their fair city. Their band does such an amazing job of covering soul classics from "Mustang Sally" to "I Never Loved a Man" and "Try a Little Tenderness" that the record company man comes calling—and of course, the whole enter- prise begins to flounder. Among the actors who do their own perform- ing, the standout is seventeen-year-old Andrew Strong, who is as influenced by Joe Cocker as by the Wicked Mr. Pickett. Dick Clement, Ian La Frenais and Roddy Doyle adapted Doyle's novel, the first in his Barrytown trilogy (named for the Dublin working-class neighborhood); its successors, *The Van* and *The Snapper,* were both fine movies, but they lacked the real spark of this one. The film's best shot: of Colm Meaney (who plays the main character in the two sequels) in his living room, sitting beneath two pictures—one of the Pope and one of Elvis Presley.

⊙**DVD:** Includes "making of" featurette; "Treat Her Right" video; soundtrack sampler.

CO10

Goes well with: *Telling Lies in America*

THE CONFORMIST

ESSENTIAL

Italy/France/West Germany   1971   C   115 min.   R   Drama
Dir: Bernardo Bertolucci
C: Jean-Louis Trintignant, Stefania Sandrelli, Dominique Sanda, Pierre
    Clémenti, Pasquale Fortunato

It's a story about collaboration, but as the title suggests, it's also about the compromises any of us can make to fit in, to go along, to keep our heads down. Jean-Louis Trintignant plays Marcello, an Italian desperate to ingratiate himself with the Fascist government of the 1930s. His marriage is a sham (he's a closeted homosexual), but as in all other things, he has to keep up appearances. The Fascists ask him to assassinate a former professor whose politics are too liberal for their comfort, and Marcello takes the job with both fear and loathing. Trintignant looks furtive in almost every scene, as though he is sure that at any moment someone will jump out from behind a curtain or lamppost and expose his shallow opportunism. The cinematography is by Vittorio Storaro (who also shot *The Last Emperor* and *Last Tango in Paris* for director Bernardo Bertolucci), and it's so stunning, with rich colors, deep shadows, and almost blinding shafts of light pouring in from enormous windows, that you could watch this film with the sound on MUTE and still enjoy it. Bertolucci adapted Alberto Moravia's novel.

DR24, DR25

Goes well with: *Mephisto*

CONTEMPT

ESSENTIAL

France/Italy   1963   C   103 min.   NR   Drama
Dir: Jean-Luc Godard
C: Brigitte Bardot, Jack Palance, Michel Piccoli, Giorgia Moll, Fritz
    Lang, Jean-Luc Godard, Raoul Coutard

Only a handful of film directors have the financial resources (as with George Lucas) or the stature that draws an ongoing patron (as with Stanley Kubrick and Warner Bros.) to fully control motion pictures with budgets into seven figures. The rest of the filmmaking community has to go begging for support and deal with the inevitable compromises of the money men. *Contempt* is Jean-Luc Godard's acidulous portrait of that process. Michel Piccoli plays Paul Javal, a writer who's hired by Jeremy Prokosch (Jack Palance), a crass Hollywood producer, to script *The Odyssey* for none other than esteemed German director Fritz Lang, who plays himself. It doesn't matter that Lang's career as a film director was behind him at the time *Contempt* was made; Godard, who also plays Lang's assistant, wanted to show how even a film artist like the man who gave the world *M* and *Metropolis* wasn't above the humiliation of dancing to the music of a world-class vulgarian like Prokosch. *Contempt* was produced by Joseph E. Levine, a man who bore no small resemblance to Prokosch; either he didn't mind being lampooned or he couldn't conceive that Godard was biting the hand that was feeding him. Also worth noting: Raoul Coutard's wide-screen cinematography (Coutard plays the cinematographer of the film within the film) and Brigitte Bardot's performance as Camille, Paul's wife, who's disgusted with their life.

DR20, DR22

Goes well with: *The Player*

THE COOK, THE THIEF, HIS WIFE AND HER LOVER
ESSENTIAL

France/Netherlands   1989   C   124 min.   NC-17   Drama
Dir: Peter Greenaway
C: Helen Mirren, Michael Gambon, Tim Roth, Richard Bohringer, Alan Howard

In the love-it-or-hate-it corner of the film world, Peter Greenaway's tale of adultery, crass cruelty, torture, and cannibalism (among other pleasant topics) occupies a special niche. Most of the story is set in a swank restaurant owned by a gangster (Michael Gambon) who frequents it along with his collection of sycophants and his abused wife (Helen Mirren). She's attracted to a lone diner (Alan Howard) at a nearby table; they commence a clandestine affair in the establishment's restrooms and continue it, with the help of the cook (Richard Bohringer), in the restaurant's back rooms. The thief finds out about the affair and devises an exquisitely grisly means of revenge on his wife, who then turns the tables on him, again with the help of the cook. As the title suggests, these aren't individuals, but archetypes: the gangster representing unchecked violence, his wife suppressed sexuality, the writer intellectual curiosity, the cook artistry. Sacha Vierney's magnificent wide-screen photography, with the camera gliding from one room of the restaurant to another, is reason enough to see the film. In spite of the oppressive atmosphere and random acts of cruelty (the opening scene may determine your ability to last through the entire film), it's the most accessible work of a director who seems determined to make densely allusive works of limited appeal.

⊙**DVD**

DR6, DR19, XT2, XT8

Goes well with: *Mona Lisa*

COOKIE'S FORTUNE

U.S.   1999   C   118 min.   PG-13   Comedy

Dir: Robert Altman

C: Glenn Close, Julianne Moore, Liv Tyler, Chris O'Donnell, Charles
  S. Dutton, Patricia Neal, Ned Beatty, Courtney B. Vance, Donald
  Moffat, Lyle Lovett

Robert Altman and writer Anne Rapp nicely capture the amiable eccentricities of a small Southern town in this genial comedy. Cookie (Patricia Neal) is a much-beloved widow whose unexpected death brings out the worst in her rapacious sister (played with great gusto by Glenn Close) and the best in everyone else in town. Circumstantial evidence suggests that that Cookie's handyman (Charles S. Dutton) murdered his boss, but even after he's arrested, no one believes he really committed the crime. The film's sliest conceit is that a black man accused of killing his white employer in the Deep South would find his jail cell filled with well-wishers rather than a lynch mob. Liv Tyler (as Cookie's granddaughter) and Julianne Moore (as a third, dim-witted sister) head the typically strong Altman ensemble cast.

⊙**DVD:** Includes audio commentary by Robert Altman.

CO11

Goes well with: *State and Main*

COUP DE TORCHON

France   1981   C   128 min.   NR   Comedy

Dir: Bertrand Tavernier

C: Philippe Noiret, Isabelle Huppert, Stéphane Audran, Irène Skobline,
  Eddy Mitchell, Jean-Pierre Marielle

Pulp writer Jim Thompson (1907–77) lived long enough to see several of his novels adapted for film, although when he died none of his work was in print. He even worked on Stanley Kubrick's 1956 version of *The Killing,* at the top of any Thompson film list. (Another first-rate Thompson film is *The Grifters.*) All Thompson's seamy tales of greed, lust, betrayal, and virtually every other vice you could name have distinctly American settings, but Bertrand Tavernier and cowriter Jean Aurenche boldly transposed the Thompson novel *Pop. 1280,* set in a tiny Texas town, to late 1930s French Equatorial Africa, and the change of scenery does the story good. Philippe Noiret is the village police chief who's growing tired of his wife's casual infidelities (even though he has a mistress of his own) and the lack of respect he's shown by the locals. He sets out to accentuate the positive by eliminating the negative. And, since he's the top cop in town, his job is to investigate the murders he's committed. Tavernier and his top-notch cast (with Stéphane Audran as the wife and Isabelle Huppert as the mistress) effortlessly capture the comic irony that's the best feature of Thompson's writing.

⊙**DVD:** Includes deleted footage; interview with Bertrand Tavernier; alternate ending.

CO2, DR29

Goes well with: *Kind Hearts and Coronets*

COUSIN BETTE

U.S./U.K.   1998   C   108 min.   R   Drama

Dir: Des McAnuff

C: Jessica Lange, Bob Hoskins, Elisabeth Shue, Hugh Laurie, Aden Young, Geraldine Chaplin, Laura Fraser

Playing the poor relation to a family of vipers, Jessica Lange is the best reason to see this unflinching adaptation of Honoré de Balzac's novel of 1846 Paris. Bette's attempts to keep her honor and dignity intact in the face of a failed relationship with a young artist (Aden Young), topped by her family's rejection, are poignantly believable. Elisabeth Shue is terrific as Bette's cousin and worst enemy, an aspiring chanteuse with a heart as big as a shriveled pea. Director Des McAnuff adroitly choreographs the petty power plays that only the combination of family infighting and social pretensions can produce.

⊙**DVD**

DR5, DR11, DR29, DR39

Goes well with: *The House of Mirth*

COUSIN BOBBY

U.S. 1991 C 70 min. NR Documentary
Dir: Jonathan Demme

Jonathan Demme's other 1991 film (the one you might have heard of was *The Silence of the Lambs*) is the kind of personal project you wish every talented director would take the time to make. After thirty years of being out of touch with the title character, Demme looks up Robert Castle, the pastor of St. Mary's Episcopal Church in Harlem. Castle's progressive views on racism endear him to his parishioners, but not necessarily to the church bureaucracy. During Castle's first assignment, in 1960s Jersey City, where he was born and raised, he befriended Black Panther activists and wound up being blackballed from the church for several years, during which time he lived on a farm in Vermont, raising four children. Demme and his cameramen follow Castle into tenement buildings, to a demonstration to shame the city into repairing an enormous pothole on 125th Street, to another demonstration at which he gives a fiery speech about the scourge of drugs in the neighborhood and the indifference of the city fathers. The film is also Demme's way of filling in missing gaps of family history and passing on lore. The overall effect is like looking through a scrapbook whose pages alternate between personal photos and clippings of news stories about inner-city problems.
DO7

Goes well with: *Priest*

CRADLE WILL ROCK

U.S. 1999 C 134 min. R Drama
Dir: Tim Robbins
C: Hank Azaria, Rubén Blades, Joan Cusack, John Cusack, Cary Elwes, Philip Baker Hall, Cherry Jones, Angus Macfayden, Bill Murray, Vanessa Redgrave, Susan Sarandon, Jamey Sheridan, John Turturro, Emily Watson

As a re-creation of New York's arts scene of the late 1930s, *Cradle Will Rock* is that rare historical film that gets both the letter and the spirit of an era down pat. If its casting choices occasionally have you shaking your head (John Cusack as Nelson Rockefeller?), the movie is at least upfront about its leftist politics, wearing them on a very large sleeve. Most of the stories in the film revolve around the production of Marc Blitzstein's anticapitalist musical *The Cradle Will Rock,* which was scheduled to be produced under the auspices of the New Deal's Works Progress Administration but ran afoul of conservative Washington politicians. Orson Welles (Angus Macfayden), John Houseman (Carey Elwes), and Diego Rivera (Rubén Blades) are players in this and other semirelated plots, but holding the film's center stage are three performances: Cherry Jones as Hannie Flanagan, the WPA official who sided with Welles and Houseman against the Washington busybodies; Hank Azaria as the idealistic Blitzstein; and Emily Watson as a fictional down-and-out actress who becomes the star of his show. Whatever stumbles *Cradle* takes, it ends on a high note, a final shot that's among the best of any film in the last decade.

⊙**DVD:** Includes "making-of" featurette.

DR2, DR4, DR17, DR24, DR36, DR40

Goes well with: *Topsy-Turvy*

CREATOR

U.S.   1985   C   107 min.   R   Drama

Dir: Ivan Passer

C: Peter O'Toole, Mariel Hemingway, Vincent Spano, Virginia Madsen, David Ogden Stiers

In this engagingly offbeat drama, Peter O'Toole plays a California scientist mourning the death of his wife. He's not looking to achieve closure but to re-create the past in his laboratory. (It's *The Bride of Dr. Frankenstein.*) Only in California are people optimistic and arrogant enough to think that life should (and can) never end: Hey, man, who'd ever wanna die and leave this place? O'Toole is harmlessly eccentric; as his assistant, Vincent Spano strikes sparks with Virginia Madsen, the model for O'Toole's re-creation. Director Ivan Passer began his career in Czechoslovakia with several well-regarded films, but his best work came after he emigrated to the U.S. and made two little-seen dramas about life in California, this film and *Cutter's Way.*

⊙**DVD**

DR8, DR21

Goes well with: *Metropolis*

CRIES AND WHISPERS

ESSENTIAL

Sweden   1972   C   106 min.   R   Drama

Dir: Ingmar Bergman

C: Harriet Andersson, Liv Ullmann, Ingrid Thulin, Kari Sylwan, Erland Josephson

Has any filmmaker directed more great female performances than Ingmar Bergman? A short list of Bergman's best work reveals the simple reason: He seems to be more interested in the complexities of women than men. *Cries and Whispers,* made in the midst of an incomparably strong run for Bergman (following *Persona, Shame,* and *The Passion of Anna* and preceding *Scenes from a Marriage*) is almost maleless, delving into the lives of three sisters (Liv Ullmann, Harriett Andersson, Ingrid Thulin) and their servant (Kari Sylwan) in a chamber drama that could be arguably the greatest film of arguably the greatest director. The colors in Oscar-winning cinematographer Sven Nykvist's palette seem to be confined to white and red, and the film is all the more expressive for this limitation. The film almost swept the major awards from the New York Film Critics Circle, winning Best Film, Director, Actress (Ullmann), and Screenplay.

⊙**DVD**

DR11, DR39

Goes well with: *Dancing at Lughnasa*

CROSSING DELANCEY

U.S.   1988   C   97 min.   PG   Drama

Dir: Joan Micklin Silver

C: Amy Irving, Reizl Bozyk, Peter Riegert, Jeroen Krabbé, Sylvia Miles, Suzzy Roche, Rosemary Harris, David Hyde Pierce

With personal ads in the newspaper, singles-only nights at bars, and health clubs that allow you to check out the physique before you make your move, who needs matchmakers anymore? The charm of director Joan Micklin Silver's romantic comedy (adapted by Susan Sandler from her play) is that it's oblivious to its era. Amy Irving is a young and single Jewish woman living in New York, where, of all places, you would think there would be enough eligible men to go around. Not so fast, bubbeleh. Eligible maybe, but good enough for our heroine? Now that's another matter. Enter the Pickle Man, played by Peter Riegert. He seems right, but is a man who sloshes around in brine all day the kind of guy to hold hands with on a regular basis? The matchmaker (played with sly charm by Reizl Bozyk) thinks so, and this smart little film doesn't ever insult your intelligence, even as it heads to the predictable conclusion.

DR18, DR28, DR36, DR39, XT7

Goes well with: *Hester Street*

THE CROSSING GUARD

U.S. 1995 C 114 min. R Drama

Dir: Sean Penn

C: Jack Nicholson, David Morse, Anjelica Huston, Robin Wright Penn, Piper Laurie, Richard Bradford, Robbie Robertson, John Savage

Jack Nicholson, whose career has been stuffed with show-stopping scenes and lines, is like the baseball slugger whom the fans pay money to see hit a home run at least once a game. Don't rent *The Crossing Guard* expecting "I want you to hold it between your knees" or "Heeere's Johnny" or "You can't handle the truth." But consider Nicholson's performance here as the equivalent of Sammy Sosa getting two doubles and two singles—and the Cubs winning the game. *The Crossing Guard* is about a man in pain, still brooding over the death of his young daughter at the hands of a drunk driver (David Morse). After a relatively brief prison term, the killer is about to be released into the hands of a vengeful Nicholson. Writer-director Sean Penn makes Morse's character, still carrying his own pain after all these years, in some ways more sympathetic than Nicholson's, whose obsession has destroyed his marriage.

ⓒ**DVD:** Includes audio commentary by Sean Penn, Anjelica Huston, David Morse, and cinematographer Vilmos Zsigmond.

DR8, DR27

Goes well with: *The Sweet Hereafter*

CROUCHING TIGER, HIDDEN DRAGON

ESSENTIAL

Hong Kong/Taiwan/China/U.S. 2000 C 119 min. PG-13 Action-Adventure

Dir: Ang Lee

C: Chow Yun-Fat, Michelle Yeoh, Zhang Ziyi, Chang Chen, Lung Si-hung, Cheng Pei-Pei

The unexpected success of this film, which has become the most popular foreign-language film ever released in the U.S., shouldn't be held against it. The initial ecstatic reviews were inevitably followed by a small backlash that seemed to be more about *Crouching Tiger's* concessions to popular conventions than its real achievement. Aside from a musical production number (and the film does have a terrific Oscar-winning score by Tan Dun), this film has everything—romance (two love stories), action, political intrigue, suspense, fantasy, and more than a little mysticism—and it juggles all these balls as deftly as any polyglot film ever has. Ang Lee is like those TV chefs tossing around the most amazing array of ingredients and producing a dish that's sublime. The story involves the quest by a famed swordsman (Chow Yun-Fat) for a weapon owned by his master, and his romance with a rival swordswoman (Michelle Yeoh); a second, parallel tale traces the love between the pampered but athletic daughter (Zhang Ziyi) of a local official and a dashing bandit (Chang Chen). And just as in another blockbuster hit, about a certain ocean liner, both love stories have bittersweet but wholly satisfying endings. *Crouching Tiger* was one of its year's most awarded films, winning four Oscars (Best Foreign Language Film, Art Direction, Cinematography, and Original Score), three Independent Spirits (Best Feature, Director, Supporting Female), and one award from the New York Film Critics Circle, for its cinematography by Peter Pau.

⊙**DVD:** Includes dubbed soundtrack and audio commentary by Ang Lee.

AC3, AC7, AC8, DR16, DR18

Goes well with: *Excalibur*

CROUPIER

ESSENTIAL

U.K./France/Germany/Ireland   1999   C   91 min.   R   Drama
Dir: Mike Hodges
C: Clive Owen, Gina McKee, Alex Kingston, Alexander Morton, Kate Hardie, Paul Reynolds, Nick Reding

Although gambling is on its way to becoming a pastime in this country second to none, few filmmakers seem interested in exploring the psychology of the individual gambler or the world of casinos. (Paul Thomas Anderson's *Hard Eight* is a rare exception.) What's most attractive about Paul Mayersburg's script about a man (Clive Owen) who revives his career as a croupier (blackjack dealer) is the man's motivation: He's an aspiring novelist who needs money, and as a writer, he's also interested in getting out in the real world and collecting material for his book. Rarely does a voice-over narrator work as well as it does here, with Owen telling us not just what we're seeing (a convenient way to explain how casinos work, a device Martin Scorsese used with Robert De Niro's character in *Casino*), but also what he's thinking about what we're seeing. *Croupier* follows the conventions of film noir—the man with a loyal girlfriend (Gina McKee), but he's drawn to a shady lady (Alex Kingston) who then involves him in a scheme that seems foolproof. Anyone who has seen a handful of movies where the guy is being played for a sap knows better. But the wrap-up of *Croupier* is so ingeniously ambiguous that even a repeat viewing may only raise more questions about who knew what and when and how.

⊙**DVD**

DR2, DR6, DR13, TH8

Goes well with: *Bob le Flambeur*

CRUMB

ESSENTIAL

U.S. 1994 C 119 min. R Documentary

Dir: Terry Zwigoff

Forever identified with the counterculture of the late 1960s and early 1970s through his Fritz the Cat and Mr. Natural characters and his legendary cover art for Big Brother and the Holding Company's *Cheap Thrills,* artist Robert Crumb is a man of contradictions. He doesn't care for rock and roll, preferring to delve into his collection of old 78 rpm blues records. He seems quite happily married, but he has no compunction about discussing (and illustrating) his sexual obsessions. And as squirrelly as he might seem, when you hear his two brothers talk about their upbringing, you have to admire Robert for coming through it all relatively unscathed. (Sadly, the brothers come off more like casualties; two Crumb sisters declined to talk to director Terry Zwigoff's cameras.) And ultimately Crumb comes off as more than just a chronicler of a certain zeitgeist; he's an artist who wants to be taken more seriously, and this film provides ample reason to do just that. Both the Sundance judges and the New York Film Critics Circle named it best documentary of the year.

⊙**DVD**

DO4

Goes well with: *Ghost World*

A CRY IN THE DARK

U.S./Australia 1988 C 121 min. PG-13 Drama

Dir: Fred Schepisi

C: Meryl Streep, Sam Neill, Bruce Myles, Charles Tingwell

Released in Australia under the more evocative title *Evil Angels,*
A Cry in the Dark documents the true case of Lindy Chamberlain, a religious woman whose composure in the face of unspeakable tragedy
was her downfall, at least in the court of public opinion. The angels that
Chamberlain and her husband might have believed were watching over
them and their infant as they camped near Ayers Rock (now known as
Mount Uluru), the most familiar symbol of Australia's Outback, deserted them one night when their baby disappeared. Lindy was convinced that a wild dog had made off with the baby, but her nearly
emotionless public appearances inflamed a public who preferred to
think the worst of her. Meryl Streep and Sam Neill are sensationally
good as the Chamberlains, and director Fred Schepisi spares his native
Aussies nothing in portraying so many of them as scandalmongers de-
void of sympathy for a woman of principle and reserve.

⊙**DVD**

DR17, DR39

Goes well with: *The Passion of Joan of Arc*

CRY-BABY

U.S.   1990   C   85 min.   PG-13   Comedy

Dir: John Waters

C: Johnny Depp, Amy Locane, Susan Tyrrell, Polly Bergen, Iggy Pop,
    Ricki Lake, Traci Lords, Troy Donahue, Mink Stole, Joe Dallesan-
    dro, Joey Heatherton, David Nelson, Patricia Hearst, Willem Dafoe

John Waters's follow-up to his commercial breakthrough, *Hairspray,*
isn't as gloriously over the top as that film, but it's still an entertaining
pastiche of the pop culture motifs Waters cherishes. In 1954 Baltimore,
a straight-arrow high school student (Amy Locane) who should know
better is smitten with the school's top hoodlum (Johnny Depp). Beneath
all that black leather he's truly a sensitive guy, able to shed tears at the
drop of a charm bracelet. Waters clearly loves the exploitation films of
the era, the ones that purportedly condemned juvenile delinquents while
making them much more attractive than their straight counterparts. The
usual Waters crazy-quilt cast is on hand—what other filmmaker gives
you Polly Bergen and Iggy Pop in the same eighty-five-minute experience? But sorely missed is Waters's longtime collaborator, Divine, who
died of a heart attack before the film was made.

CO5, CO12

Goes well with: *Hairspray*

THE CRYING GAME

ESSENTIAL

U.K. 1992 C 112 min. R Drama

Dir: Neil Jordan

C: Stephen Rea, Miranda Richardson, Forest Whitaker, Jim Broadbent, Ralph Brown, Adrian Dunbar, Jaye Davidson

The so-called "secret" of *The Crying Game*—that one character is not what he or she seems to be—shouldn't distract from its soundness as a psychological portrait of a man caught between the demands of his employers (a gang of IRA thugs) and the tug of his conscience. Stephen Rea, who possesses as sad a pair of eyes as any film actor ever, is the man in the middle. He's guarding a kidnapped British soldier (Forest Whitaker) when something quite unexpected occurs, which leads him to contact the soldier's lover (Jaye Davidson). Meanwhile, his IRA mates are keeping an eye on him, worried that this weak link might wind up jeopardizing their operations. Writer-director Neil Jordan, who won an Oscar and an award from the New York Film Critics Circle for his screenplay, draws the tension even tighter with the Big Revelation, because it puts Rea's character into even more turmoil about who *he* is. The film also picked up a Best Foreign Film award from the Independent Spirit Awards and a Supporting Actress prize (for Miranda Richardson, as an icy IRA operative) from the New York critics.

⊙**DVD**

DR6, DR19

Goes well with: *Cal*

CUTTER'S WAY

ESSENTIAL

U.S. 1981 C 105 min. R Drama

Dir: Ivan Passer

C: Jeff Bridges, John Heard, Lisa Eichhorn, Stephen Elliott, Ann Dusenberry, Nina Van Pallandt, Julia Duffy

Newton Thornburgh's novel *Cutter and Bone* falls firmly in the tradition of Raymond Chandler and Ross MacDonald, the great crime novelists who exposed the darker recesses of sunny Southern California. Set in the spectacularly beautiful town of Santa Barbara (where MacDonald lived for many years), the film tells the story of Cutter, a crippled Vietnam veteran, and Bone, his chronically unemployed pal, who live on the margins of society, scraping by on government checks, smoking too much grass, and drinking too much of anything alcoholic. When Bone spots one of Santa Barbara's elite citizens committing a murder, Cutter devises a plan to take the man down as a symbol of everything they hate about the smugness of a community that worships conservative values. Czech émigré Ivan Passer has an outsider's eye for the telling details of his adopted country. As Cutter, John Heard looks like a stoned Long John Silver with his eyepatch and crutch, and Jeff Bridges as Bone is a beach boy gone bad. They're both superb, with Lisa Eichhorn strong in support as Bone's cynical girlfriend. Jeffrey Alan Fiskin did the excellent adaptation, and Jordan Cronenweth's camera captures the beauty of Santa Barbara as well as the rot not far beneath the surface.

⊙**DVD**

DR20, DR21, DR34, TH4

Goes well with: *Short Cuts*

D

DANCE WITH A STRANGER
U.K.   1985   C   101 min.   R   Drama
Dir: Mike Newell
C: Miranda Richardson, Rupert Everett, Ian Holm, Matthew Carroll,
Joanne Whalley

The Ruth Ellis case is famous in Britain as the last instance (1955) in
which a woman in that country was hanged for her crime. The story
could have been written by James M. Cain: a wayward blonde and her
young lover conspire to murder the older man who's hopelessly in love
with her. Miranda Richardson and Rupert Everett are the conspirators,
but it's Ian Holm's nicely shaded performance as the duped gentleman
that's the real heart of the film. Ellis's coldhearted lack of remorse for
her crime contributed to the public's revulsion toward her, and director
Mike Newell neatly captures the tabloidish coverage of Ellis's crime
and the suffocating atmosphere of the era, when blondes who had too
much fun were expected to pay for their sins.

⊙**DVD:** Includes an alternate ending.
DR6, DR17, DR24, DR39, TH10
Goes well with: *A Cry in the Dark*

DANCER IN THE DARK
Denmark/Sweden/France   2000   C   141 min.   R   Drama
Dir: Lars von Trier
C: Björk, Catherine Deneuve, David Morse, Peter Stormare, Joel Grey,
Jean-Marc Barr, Udo Kier

Selma, a Czech émigré and single mom working in a Washington
State factory, is saving money for an operation to prevent her young

son from going blind—knowing that he may inherit the same disease that is causing her to lose her sight. Selma is also a fan of musicals, because "in a musical nothing dreadful ever happens," so at moments of extreme stress she imagines she's leading everyone in a big production number. It's not like you haven't seen or heard of this before—think writer Dennis Potter's *Pennies from Heaven,* the TV miniseries and movie in which a sheet-song salesman during the Depression escapes his miseries by imagining himself leading his little corner of the world in song. In *Pennies,* however, the tunes were pop standards, while here they're the work of Icelandic singer Björk, who plays Selma. Your taste for her songs and singing style may determine whether you're willing to take the same leap of faith that director Lars von Trier required in his previous film, *Breaking the Waves,* whose story also revolved around an unusual plot twist. It's best to see the film in a widescreen version, where the choreography is shown to its best advantage. The Independent Spirit Awards gave von Trier's audacious film the Best Foreign Film award.

⊙**DVD:** Includes audio commentary by Lars von Trier, producer Vibeke Windelov, and choreographer Vincent Paterson; two behind-the-scenes documentaries; alternate scenes.

DR21, DR39, DR40, XT6

Goes well with: *Breaking the Waves*

DANCING AT LUGHNASA

U.S./U.K./Ireland 1998 C 92 min. PG Drama

Dir: Pat O'Connor

C: Meryl Streep, Michael Gambon, Catherine McCormack, Kathy Burke, Sophie Thompson, Brid Brennan, Rhys Ifans

This adaptation of Brian Friels's acclaimed play may strike some fans of the theater as adding picture-postcard views of the Irish countryside to an essentially interior drama. The setup—five unmarried Irish sisters, ages early twenties to midforties, live a more or less serene life in their 1930s rural homestead until their beloved brother, a priest, returns from a mission in Africa—allowed Friels to explore family dynamics as well as the specter of real poverty lurking just over those emerald green hills. Meryl Streep may be top-billed, but this is truly an ensemble piece, with Catherine McCormack a standout as the youngest sister, who is raising a child born out of wedlock.

⊙**DVD**

DR11, DR32, DR39
Goes well with: *Cries and Whispers*

DARK DAYS

U.S. 2000 B&W 84 min. NR Documentary
Dir: Marc Singer

Delving into what could be literally called a subculture, first-time filmmaker Marc Singer illuminates the world of homeless people who live in the Amtrak train tunnels near New York's Penn Station. What he finds, remarkably, is not despair and hopelessness but a strange kind of vitality and resourcefulness. "You'd be surprised at what the human body can adjust to," one of his subjects observes. It's a largely nonwhite and largely male culture, though the one woman, Dee, is shown to be the only victim of violence when someone burns her "home." (She's soon taken in by a man, and they begin bickering like any couple with a real home.) When some of the men are shown picking through trash for recyclable bottles, for which they'll be paid $60 on a good day, you can't help but admire their initiative. But lest you feel too comfortable, the foraging turns to discarded food outside restaurants and grocers. Amtrak does the group a favor by trying to force them out of their homes; a homeless advocacy group steps in and provides Singer with a happy ending. The film won three awards at Sundance, the Cinematography Award (credited to Singer), Freedom of Expression Award, and the Audience Award.
⊙**DVD**
DO1, DO11
Goes well with: *Streetwise*

DARLING

ESSENTIAL

U.K. 1965 B&W 122 min. NR Drama
Dir: John Schlesinger
C: Julie Christie, Dirk Bogarde, Laurence Harvey, Roland Curran, Jose Luis de Villalonga, Alex Scott

Julie Christie made good on the promise she showed in *Billy Liar,* her first collaboration with director John Schlesinger, in this stunning star vehicle, which won her an Academy Award. Writer Frederic Raphael (also an Oscar winner) concocted a brilliantly witty script that traced the rise to riches and misery of a young woman whose major currency is her beauty. She's a kind of passive-aggressive opportunist, seemingly pushed about by the currents of the Swingin' Sixties, as she becomes a high-fashion model, lover to a series of weak but adoring men, and finally the trophy wife of an Italian count. Christie's dazzling smile is matched by a pout that melted the heart of every male moviegoer in the mid-1960s. The New York Film Critics Circle awarded it three prizes, for Best Film, Best Director, and Best Actress.

DR20, DR39, XT7

Goes well with: *The Marriage of Maria Braun*

DAS BOOT

ESSENTIAL

West Germany   1981   C   210 min.   R   Drama

Dir: Wolfgang Petersen

C: Jürgen Prochnow, Herbert Grönemeyer, Klaus Wennemann, Hubertus Bengsch

It's the best submarine movie ever, but the virtues of *Das Boot* run deeper than simply making you feel giddily claustrophobic about being sealed inside a metal tube thousands of feet beneath the ocean. In its original version, which was shown as a miniseries on German TV, the film revealed complexities about its crew that were not so apparent in the truncated 145-minute theatrical film released to American theaters in 1981. (You may find this version still available on VHS.) The full director's cut was released in 1997 to theaters and then to video. The additional scenes also reinforce *Das Boot*'s greatest virtue: It transcends nationality. (After all, this is a German U-boat crew we're supposed to feel sympathy for.) The long version's remixed soundtrack is another reason to set aside the extra time for it; the pumped-up sound makes those popping rivets and rushing waters sound even scarier.

⊙**DVD:** Director's cut. Includes "making of" and behind-the-scenes featurettes; audio commentary by Wolfgang Petersen.

DR37

Goes well with: *In Which We Serve*

DAVID HOLZMAN'S DIARY

U.S.   1968   B&W   74 min.   NR   Drama

Dir: Jim McBride

C: L. M. Kit Carson, Eileen Dietz, Louise Levine, Lorenzo Mans

In our twenty-first-century world of webcams and personal Internet sites, *David Holzman's Diary* should come as a real surprise to those who think self-reflective media was born with the personal computer. L. M. Kit Carson is the filmmaker of the title, a guy who needs to document his life, or at least the portions of it that pass before the movie camera in his New York apartment, on film. (Not video; he can't view his footage until it is developed.) The conceit works surprisingly well; the film is modest in length, director Jim McBride cleverly works in more at-home situations than you might expect, and Carson's Holzman is a hilariously self-deluding character.

DR22, XT6

Goes well with: *Sherman's March*

DAWN OF THE DEAD

U.S.   1978   C   126 min.   NR   Horror

Dir: George A. Romero

C: David Emge, Ken Foree, Scott Reiniger, Gaylen Ross, Tom Savini

Sequels to horror films are supposed to give the audience more of the same, and on that score, George A. Romero's follow-up to his groundbreaking *Night of the Living Dead* delivers. The flesh-eating zombies are still wandering the land, besieging "normal" humans for something to dine on, and now the gore is offered in (somewhat) living color rather than black-and-white. What gives *Dawn* an extra kick is its setting. The first *Living Dead* film took place largely in an abandoned, isolated rural house; *Dawn*'s human-zombie battlefield is a deserted but well-stocked shopping mall (specifically, the Monroeville Mall east of Pittsburgh, Romero's home turf). The mall gives the quartet of human survivors more places to hide from the zombies, and they are able to employ power tools and other implements in their struggle against overwhelming numbers. But in this chapter, the zombies become more than just monsters; stumbling around the deserted corridors and through the merchandise-laden stores, they are the ultimate consumers, in search of basic sustenance rather than throwaway material goods.

⊙**DVD**

FA9

Goes well with: *Dead Alive*

DAY FOR NIGHT

ESSENTIAL

France/Italy   1973   C   120 min.   PG   Drama

Dir: François Truffaut

C: Jacqueline Bisset, Jean-Pierre Aumont, Valentina Cortese, François Truffaut, Jean-Pierre Léaud, Alexandra Stewart, Dani, Nathalie Baye

François Truffaut saw thousands of films as a film critic before directing his first feature, *The Four Hundred Blows,* in 1959. His fascination with the process of making movies produced this light and likable drama about a production with all the standard problems: a director in love with his leading lady, a diva of an actress who defines the term "high-maintenance," love affairs that are supposed to be clandestine but are really the stuff of daily gossip on the set, and daily script changes. Truffaut plays the film-within-a-film's director (had anyone directed themselves as a filmmaker before *Day for Night*?), Jacqueline Bisset is the object of his affection, Valentina Cortese is the demanding diva, and Jean-Pierre Léaud shows up, too, though not as Antoine Doinel, the role he played in five Truffaut films. *Day for Night* won the Academy Award for Best Foreign Language Film; the New York Film Critics Circle went the Academy one better, tabbing it Best Film, and adding awards for Truffaut (as director) and Cortese.

DR22

Goes well with: *State and Main*

THE DAY OF THE JACKAL

U.K./France   1973   C   141 min.   PG   Thriller

Dir: Fred Zinnemann

C: Edward Fox, Alan Badel, Tony Britton, Cyril Cusack, Michel Lonsdale, Delphine Seyrig, Derek Jacobi

The virtues of solid craftsmanship shouldn't be underestimated, especially when too many filmmakers mistake style for substance. Fred Zinnemann was never regarded as a stylist, but over his long career (whose highlights included Hollywood pictures *From Here to Eternity* and *The Nun's Story,* and the British production *A Man for All Seasons*), he could always be counted on for a solidly produced effort. This adaptation of Frederick Forsyth's novel about a cool assassin hired to take down Charles de Gaulle ranks with Zinnemann's best work. The film runs on two parallel tracks, following both the journey of the assassin through Europe to Paris, the site of his rendezvous with destiny, and the efforts of French police, working with contacts from other countries, to track down the Jackal and stop him. As the police detective in charge of the operation to capture the Jackal, Michel Lonsdale portrays a man as implacable as his foe, coolly played by Edward Fox. Though the outcome is never in doubt, there is a satisfyingly ironic twist ending.

⊙**DVD**

TH9

Goes well with: *Z*

DAY OF WRATH

Denmark   1943   B&W   110 min.   NR   Drama

Dir: Carl Theodor Dreyer

C: Thorkild Roose, Lisbeth Movin, Sigrid Neiiendam, Preben Lerdorff, Anna Svierkier

Danish filmmaker Carl Theodor Dreyer's one-film-a-decade career produced one often-seen masterwork (the 1928 silent *The Passion of Joan of Arc*) and two lesser-known but equally stunning works: *Ordet* and this film. An elderly woman in a seventeenth-century village is accused of witchcraft, and a village elder, the one man whose testimony might save her, refuses to go against the will of the mob. She curses him before she is burned alive, and her curse seems to bear fruit when his second, younger wife falls in love with his visiting son. Filmed during the Nazi occupation of Denmark, *Day of Wrath* offers an implied critique of those who would collaborate with the evildoers rather than follow their consciences, but it also works well outside that context. Dreyer's minimalist technique—no fancy camera or editing tricks distract the viewer from being drawn into this powerful story—perfectly serves his material.

⊙**DVD:** Available in a box set with *Ordet* and *Gertrud,* which also includes a 1995 documentary on Dreyer.

DR19, DR24, DR30

Goes well with: *Ordet*

DAZED AND CONFUSED

U.S.   1993   C   103 min.   R   Comedy

Dir: Richard Linklater

C: Jason London, Wiley Wiggins, Sasha Jenson, Rory Cochrane, Milla Jovovich, Marissa Ribisi, Matthew McConaughey, Ben Affleck, Parker Posey

An invaluable document, *Dazed and Confused* is both a time-capsule look at a specific era and a hilarious view of the contemporary obsession with youthful irresponsibility. It's the last day of high school in a suburban Texas town. The time is the summer of 1976, before disco succeeded head-banging rock (typified by the Led Zeppelin title tune, which unaccountably is not on the film's soundtrack) as the music of the land. As he did in his first film, *Slacker,* writer-director Richard Linklater prefers to offer a montage of characters and stories rather than what might be called a classic three-act dramatic structure. The youthful cast, filled with the familiar faces of future stars, embodies a refreshing take on the familiar teen comedy stereotypes. These kids' idea of higher education involves smoking dope and chugging beer, but Linklater suggests that all of their partying masks a desperate denial of life beyond carefree adolescence. Even without the presence of Zeppelin, the soundtrack rocks on and on with cuts from semiforgotten bands like Black Oak Arkansas and Foghat.

⊙**DVD**

CO5, CO11

Goes well with: *Slacker*

DEAD ALIVE

New Zealand   1992   C   97 min.   NR   Horror

Dir: Peter Jackson

C: Timothy Balme, Diana Peñalver, Elizabeth Moody, Ian Watkin

The last word in zombie movies and on-screen gore, *Dead Alive* is so cartoonish and excessive you can't take it seriously as a horror film, but it's great fun as a spoof of the genre. A nerdy man (Timothy Balme) thinks he has finally found a way to get out from under the thumb of his domineering mother when he falls in love with a lovely local lass. Then Mum is bitten by a rat monkey at the zoo and turns into a foul-mouthed zombie. The nice thing about living in a small village, the film suggests, is that it doesn't take long for zombie bites to get nearly all of the citizenry infected. The film's bravura climax takes place during a house party that gets crashed by a basement full of zombies; our hero is forced to desperate measures (a rotary lawn mower is his weapon of choice) to save himself and his sweetheart. Peter Jackson's second film (his first was a more modest zombie-fest called *Bad Taste*) earned him cult status, and his next effort, the stunning psychological study *Heavenly Creatures,* was his breakthrough. He's now responsible for the *Lord of the Rings* saga.

⊙**DVD**

CO12, FA9

Goes well with: *From Dusk Till Dawn*

DEAD CALM

Australia/U.S. 1989 C 96 min. R Thriller
Dir: Philip Noyce
C: Sam Neill, Nicole Kidman, Billy Zane

Essentially a three-character thriller, *Dead Calm* offers the irresistible, if familiar, premise of the couple out for an excursion who pick up a stranger in distress, only to discover that he's a raging psycho. The twist here is that the action takes place at sea; the couple are on a cruise on their own yacht, and their passenger is "rescued" from a drifting, seemingly abandoned boat. Philip Noyce nicely orchestrates the playing-out of this little setup, and his cast (including the prestardom Nicole Kidman and Billy Zane) play their parts with convincing gusto.

⊙**DVD**

TH2, TH15, TH16

Goes well with: *Knife in the Water*

DEAD MAN WALKING

ESSENTIAL

U.S./U.K. 1995 C 122 min. R Drama
Dir: Tim Robbins
C: Susan Sarandon, Sean Penn, Robert Prosky, Raymond J. Barry,
   R. Lee Ermey, Celia Weston, Lois Smith, Scott Wilson

The debate over capital punishment will never get a better dramatic airing than in this account of the work of Sister Helen Prejean, a Louisiana nun who counsels men on Death Row. Played by Oscar winner Susan Sarandon, Prejean is a woman of enormous religious faith, and one of her biggest challenges comes in the form of a killer who has confessed to the senseless and brutal murder of a young couple. Sean Penn (who won the Independent Spirit award for Best Male Lead) plays the condemned convict, a man seemingly without remorse; his scenes with Sarandon anchor a film rich in emotionally wrenching moments. Even if the film's sympathies are clearly with Sister Helen, the anguish of the victims' parents makes a strong case for those people whose idea of justice involves revenge. The soundtrack, supervised by Tim Robbins and his brother David, is another plus, with music by Pearl Jam's vocalist, Eddie Vedder, the extraordinary Pakistani singer Nusrat Fateh Ali Khan, and Ry Cooder.

⊙**DVD**

DR6, DR8, DR26, DR30

Goes well with: *Let Him Have It*

DEAD OF NIGHT

U.K.   1945   B&W   102 min.   NR   Thriller

Dir: Alberto Cavalcanti, Basil Dearden, Robert Hamer, and Charles Crichton

C: Mervyn Johns, Roland Culver, Antony Baird, Judy Kelly, Miles Malleson, Sally Ann Howes, Googie Withers, Ralph Michael, Michael Redgrave

Anthology horror films are largely of another era, when authors like Saki and Richard Matheson excelled at the literary equivalent, grouping chilling short stories together. This 1945 British warhorse is neatly set up with the dramatic device of a group of travelers, marooned at a house on a dark and stormy night, telling their favorite ghost stories. The first four of the quintet of stories are moderately scary, but the finale, about a ventriloquist (Michael Redgrave) and his very independent-minded dummy, is the equivalent of *The Twilight Zone*'s "Nightmare at 20,000 Feet," a primal scream of an idea brilliantly played and directed. And there's a delightful little kick after the conclusion of that tale as well.

TH3, XT1

Goes well with: *The Innocents*

DEAD RINGERS

Canada/U.S.   1988   C   115 min.   R   Drama

Dir: David Cronenberg

C: Jeremy Irons, Geneviève Bujold, Heidi von Palleske, Barbara Gordon, Shirley Douglas, Stephen Lack

Horror stories about twins are creepy enough, but making the lead characters gynecologists opens up realms of possibilities that movies like *Sisters* and *The Other* never explored. Based on a true story, *Dead Ringers* could only be made (at least this effectively) by David Cronenberg, a filmmaker obsessed with the inner workings, both psychological and physical, of people in extreme situations. Jeremy Irons has never been better, even in his Oscar-winning performance as Claus von Bulow in *Reversal of Fortune,* than he is here in two roles. It's not just that he's required to play both twins; he skillfully imbues them with enough sympathy that we are more fascinated than repulsed by their increasingly odd and perverse behavior toward their patients and each other.

⊙**DVD:** Includes audio commentaries by David Cronenberg, Jeremy Irons, and cinematographer Peter Suschitzky; design gallery; effects footage.

DR11, DR19, DR27

Goes well with: *Twin Falls, Idaho*

DEAR JESSE

U.S.   1997   C/B&W   83 min.   NR   Documentary
Dir: Tim Kirkman

North Carolina native Tim Kirkman opens his film with a witty comparison between himself and longtime senator Jesse Helms, concluding that for much of Helms's career in the U.S. Senate he has been obsessed with gay men, and "for much of my adult life so have I." After graduating from North Carolina State, Kirkman moved to New York City to escape what he considered the crushing homophobic atmosphere in North Carolina, but in 1996, with Helms running for reelection and Kirkman at loose ends personally (he had just broken up with his boyfriend), he returned home to take the pulse of the state. He finds a greater spirit of tolerance, but it's clear that Helms's masterful manipulation of his fearful constituency (he began his career as a race baiter) means he still has the upper hand. The best observation: Kirkman's former minister talking about Helms's "aggressive" brand of ignorance. The most moving scene: Kirkman tries to pin down his father's opinion of Helms and is dismayed when the old man won't condemn the senator. There's a moving epilogue of footage Kirkman shot, on the first day of his project, of a gay couple at a campus; one of the men is Matthew Shepard, two years before he was murdered in the infamous Wyoming hate crime.

DO7, DO9

Goes well with: *Sherman's March*

THE DECLINE OF WESTERN CIVILIZATION

U.S.   1981   C   100 min.   R   Documentary
Dir: Penelope Spheeris

Every pop music scene, however short-lived, deserves a documentary as perceptive and witty as Penelope Spheeris's film about late-1970s Los Angeles punk bands and their devotees. Sporting a cast of musicians mostly forgotten, dead, or both, *Decline* understands the central tenet of punk, that musicianship is secondary to attitude, and throws big gobs of attitude right in our faces. Punk was inevitably a transitional genre, so it's especially important that someone with Spheeris's clear-eyed view of the music world gained access to so many clubs, dressing rooms, back alleys, and bathrooms, where so many musicians and their fans were either shooting up or throwing up. Among the bands featured: X, Black Flag, Fear, Circle Jerks, and Catholic Discipline. (If your eyes are rolling at this point, you're either over fifty or in deep denial that you ever listened to this stuff.)

DO1, DO5, DO11

Goes well with: *The Filth and the Fury*

DEEP END

U.S./West Germany/Poland   1970   C   88 min.   R   Drama

Dir: Jerzy Skolimowski

C: Jane Asher, John Moulder-Brown, Diana Dors, Karl Michael Vogler

Polish filmmaker Jerzy Skolimowski, after running afoul of the Communist authorities in his native country with an anti-Stalinist film called *Hands Up!,* went into exile in the West. This was his second film in English, a disturbing tale of romantic obsession set in a London bathhouse. A fifteen-year-old (John Moulder-Brown) fixes on a coworker, a young woman (Jane Asher) who barely acknowledges him. Her disdain only fuels his fantasies, and the film's strength is that it allows us into the world of someone whose budding sense of love and sex tips into something more twisted, involving total possession of the love object. The Cat Stevens song score offers a running commentary that at first seems appropriate to the blooming of first love, then becomes an ironic counterpoint to its darker impulses.

DR19, DR41

Goes well with: *The Tenant*

THE DEEP END

U.S.   2001   C   99 min.   R   Thriller

Dir: Scott McGehee and David Siegel

C: Tilda Swinton, Goran Visnjic, Jonathan Tucker, Raymond J. Barry, Josh Lucas, Peter Donat, Tamara Hope, Jordan Dorrance

Working from the same book that was the basis for the well-regarded 1949 film noir *The Reckless Moment,* Scott McGehee and David Siegel make several changes from the original story about a middle-class mother who is being blackmailed as a result of an affair between her teenage daughter and an older man. In this version, the teen is a boy, and the setting is not a Los Angeles beach community but the shores of pristine Lake Tahoe. McGehee and Siegel (they produce, direct, and write together) get the most out of both alterations without losing the essence of the story: the resilience of the mother (played by Scottish actress Tilda Swinton) and her unusual relationship with one of the blackmailers (played by Goran Visnjic). It's not love but some sense of respect that develops between them and remains unspoken until the wrap-up, with one remarkable close-up of the two characters.

⊙**DVD:** Includes audio commentary by Scott McGehee and David Siegel; "making of" featurette.

TH1, TH4, TH13, TH16

Goes well with: *The Man Who Knew Too Much*

DELICATESSEN

France 1991 C 102 min. NR Fantasy
Dir: Jean-Pierre Jeunet and Marc Caro
C: Marie-Laure Dougnac, Dominique Pinon, Karin Viard, Jean-Claude Dreyfus

If a funny film could ever be made about cannibalism, *Delicatessen* is it. In an unnamed city of the dismal future, the inhabitants of an apartment building forage for food and put up with meat shortages only because they have their own private source. Their landlord doubles as a butcher, with new tenants soon becoming fresh meat for the rest of the building. Marc Caro and Jean-Pierre Jeunet's dark fantasy (and it's literally dark, too, with the story taking place in some kind of perpetual twilight and the primary color being a burnt umber) is a wonderful companion piece to their second effort, *City of Lost Children*. Both create totally new screen worlds with their own rules and mores, though this film's tone is more delectably lighthearted.

FA3, FA5, XT2, XT6

Goes well with: *City of Lost Children*

THE DEVIL'S PLAYGROUND

Australia 1976 C 107 min. NR Drama
Dir: Fred Schepisi
C: Arthur Dignam, Nick Tate, Simon Burke, Charles McCallum

The suffocating atmosphere of an all-boys private school has produced several superb films (*if . . .* and *Zero for Conduct* among them). *The Devil's Playground* adds religion to the usual mix of adolescents acting out, and the result is a two-sided story, with the kids coming to terms with their biological urges and their priest teachers doing pretty much the same. Ultimately, you get the feeling that the kids will all sort things out as they grow up—unless some of their teachers, unable to cope with the Catholic Church's insistence on abstinence among its clergy, get to them first.

DR19, DR30, DR31, DR41

Goes well with: *if . . .*

DIABOLIQUE
ESSENTIAL

France   1955   B&W   114 min.   NR   Thriller
Dir: Henri-Georges Clouzot
C: Simone Signoret, Véra Clouzot, Paul Meurisse, Charles Vanel

A staple of art-house cinemas from the late 1950s well into the 1960s, *Diabolique* is still powerful stuff. Several inferior remakes, as well as a host of horror and suspense films, have "borrowed" its shocking plot twists. A petty tyrant of a schoolteacher (Paul Meurisse) abuses not only his charges but his wife (Véra Clouzot, the director's spouse) and mistress (Simone Signoret). The women conspire to murder him, and that should be that, except that the body disappears. Director Henri-Georges Clouzot isn't in any rush to tell his story, which may leave some contemporary viewers wondering what all the fuss is about—until that last half hour. The New York Film Critics Circle named it Best Foreign Language Film. *Diabolique* was rereleased theatrically in the U.S. in 1994 with nine minutes of additional footage, reflected in the running time listed here; that version is available on DVD.

⊙**DVD**

TH4, TH5, TH7
Goes well with: *Blood Simple*

DIARY OF A COUNTRY PRIEST
ESSENTIAL

France   1950   B&W   120 min.   NR   Drama
Dir: Robert Bresson
C: Claude Laydu, Nicole Ladmiral, Jean Riveyre, Marie-Monique Arkell, Nicole Maurey, André Guibert, Martine Lemaire

The rigorous filmmaking style of Robert Bresson finds a perfect subject in the day-to-day life of a young cleric assigned to his first parish. The unnamed priest (Claude Laydu) is a study in isolation; he is frequently alone in his study, his daily Mass is usually attended by only one parishioner (we never see his Sunday routine), and his conversations are with one person at a time. He aches for more human contact and approval of his work, but as an older colleague advises him, "A true priest is never loved." Much of the story revolves around his relationship with the parish's wealthiest family: a count (Jean Riveyre), who wants the priest to slow down on any changes to the church's mission, and his wife (Marie-Monique Arkell), grieving over the loss of her young son and indifferent to her teenaged daughter (Nicole Ladmiral), who is clearly attracted to the young priest. The two great accomplishments of Bresson's film are to draw you into discussions of faith, no matter what your beliefs—the final meeting between the priest and the countess is one of the most moving ever filmed—and to dramatize a character's interior turmoil using the simplest film technique: dialogue, voice-over narration, and lingering shots of the priest's agonized face.

⊙**DVD**

DR30

Goes well with: *Priest*

DIARY OF A LOST GIRL

Germany   1929   B&W   104 min.   NR   Drama

Dir: G. W. Pabst

C: Louise Brooks, Fritz Rasp, Josef Ravensky, Sybille Schmitz

Actress Louise Brooks's indelible reputation is based on one film, the magnificent *Pandora's Box*. But her follow-up, also directed by German filmmaker G. W. Pabst in the waning days of silent film, has its perverse charms. As Lulu in *Pandora's Box,* Brooks was a disarmingly innocent sexual predator, but here, as Thymian, a pharmacist's daughter, she is half-victim, half-schemer, wandering through a series of melodramatic episodes (pregnancy by rape, incarceration, marriage into wealth, widowhood) that would sustain a soap opera character for ten seasons. Even at her character's lowest ebb, Brooks maintains an extraordinarily strong sense of self-assurance that few actresses of any era can match.

⊙**DVD:** Includes nine extra minutes not in U.S. prints, and Brooks short "Windy Riley Goes Hollywood."

DR19, DR33, DR39

Goes well with: *Pandora's Box*

THE DINNER GAME

France   1998   C   81 min.   PG-13   Comedy
Dir: Francis Veber
C: Thierry Lhermitte, Jacques Villeret, Francis Huster, Daniel Prévost, Alexandra Vandernoot

Francis Veber's farce is a commentary on the snobbishness of those who find simpleminded folk funny. A group of well-to-do professionals have dinner parties to which each of them brings the stupidest person he can find; the so-called winner is the man whose guest is declared the dumbest of the dumb. Thierry Lhermitte plays a smug publisher who thinks he has a winner in civil servant Jacques Villeret, until a series of mishaps renders Lhermitte beholden to Villeret's sincere generosity. Unlike the characters that Jim Carrey and Adam Sandler play in their more successful comedies, Villeret (and Veber) find some dignity in the fumblings of the less gifted among us. The film clocks in at an economical running time, further proof that the filmmakers don't overplay their hands with this material.

⊙**DVD**

CO7

Goes well with: *The Discreet Charm of the Bourgeoisie*

THE DISCREET CHARM OF THE BOURGEOISIE

ESSENTIAL

France/Italy/Spain   1972   C   101 min.   PG   Comedy
Dir: Luis Buñuel
C: Fernando Rey, Delphine Seyrig, Stéphane Audran, Bulle Ogier, Jean-Pierre Cassel, Michel Piccoli

When *The Discreet Charm* won the Oscar for Best Foreign Language Film of 1972, was the Academy simply honoring the persistence of a seventy-two-year-old filmmaker who began his career collaborating with Salvador Dalí in 1920s Paris, went into exile from his native Spain for 20 years, worked at the Museum of Modern Art's film department and in Hollywood dubbing Spanish-language films, scrambled to make low-budget films in Mexico, returned to Spain for one scandalous film (*Viridiana*) and then caught a second wind in France, beginning with 1967's *Belle de Jour*? Perhaps. But *Discreet Charm* has proved to be one of Buñuel's finest films. It is a comedy with one joke—a group of friends attempt several times to sit down to an elegant dinner party but can never quite complete it—that Buñuel milks in effortlessly imaginative ways. A superior cast of actors (a resource not at his disposal during those long years of exile in Mexico) seems to be having a marvelous time poking fun at social rituals.

⊙**DVD**

CO7, CO8

Goes well with: *The Exterminating Angel*

THE DISH

Australia   2000   C   104 min.   PG-13   Comedy
Dir: Rob Sitch
C: Sam Neill, Kevin Harrington, Tom Long, Patrick Warburton, Genevieve Mooy, Taylor Kane, John McMartin

An endearing comedy about an unlikely subject—the 1969 moon landing—*The Dish* is thoroughly Australian. The Aussies love to make fun of their own sense of isolation and inferiority, but they're just as proud when their country makes a real contribution to history. The untold story of the Apollo 11 mission is that a huge satellite receiver (the film's title character), located in an isolated area in the interior of Australia, provided backup for TV pictures of the moon landing. When technical glitches forced mission control to call on the Aussies, they responded brilliantly—after a few small problems of their own. Sam Neill is the scientist in charge of the operation, and he plays straight man to an engaging gallery of small-town residents (and an American technician, played by Patrick Warburton). *The Dish* never turns its characters into caricatures, and it honestly earns its lump-in-the-throat ending. The funniest bit: At a party to honor the visiting American ambassador (John McMartin), a local rock band plays what they think is the U.S. national anthem.

⊙**DVD**

CO6, CO10, CO11

Goes well with: *Local Hero*

DIVA

ESSENTIAL

France   1981   C   123 min.   R   Thriller
Dir: Jean-Jacques Beineix
C: Wilhelmina Wiggins Fernandez, Frédéric Andréi, Richard Bohringer, Thuy An Luu, Jacques Fabbri

A thriller that's less about story than style, *Diva* was a major hit with those young moviegoers who could tear themselves away from watching music videos on the fledgling MTV. Director Jean-Jacques Beineix was clearly influenced by the flash of music videos in telling the story of a young motorcycle-riding postman (Frédéric Andrei) who secretly tapes performances by his favorite opera singer (real-life opera star Wilhemina Fernandez Wiggins). When one of his bootleg recordings gets mixed up with a tape incriminating some nasty gangsters, the chase is on. Andrei takes his bike right into the Paris Métro (kids, don't try this at home) in the most memorable set piece. The film is clearly in love with the frisson of modern urban life—the neon-lit streets, the effortless mingling of ethnic and racial groups (Andrei's girlfriend is Asian, the diva is African American), the small spaces people hole up in for some sense of privacy.

⊙**DVD**

DR36, TH17, XT6, XT7

Goes well with: *The Usual Suspects*

DIVIDED WE FALL

ESSENTIAL

Czech Republic   2000   C   122 min.   PG-13   Drama
Dir: Jan Hřebejk
C: Bolek Polivka, Anna Šišková, Jaroslav Dušek, Csongor Kassai

World War II dramas that cast a sympathetic light on characters with shifting loyalties are rare, and those that add a comic dimension are rarer still. Jan Hřebejk and his writing collaborator Petr Jarchovský skillfully present this story of a childless Czech couple, Josef and Marie, who take in a former neighbor, a Jew who has escaped from a death camp. Rather than take an obvious route (wife falls in love with the young man, couple learn real lessons in humanism), the film keeps taking wonderfully executed twists and turns. The fourth and key character is Horst, who once worked with Josef for the father of the Jewish fugitive, David Wiener, but now kowtows to the Germans. He's interested in Marie, and guesses the couple's secret early but doesn't tip his hand right away. The story effectively shows how collaborators like Horst were walking a tightrope; afraid that the Nazis will discover they're opportunists, and fretting over confronting their neighbors if Germany loses the war. About halfway through, in a bravura scene involving Marie concealing David in her bed, the tone subtly shifts to absurdist comedy, but it's a mark of the filmmakers' control that they never tip too far in that direction. A nominee for a foreign-language film Oscar, *Divided We Fall* had the misfortune of competing with the sublime (and very popular) *Crouching Tiger, Hidden Dragon.* Any other year, it would have been an easy winner.

⊙**DVD**

DR24, DR38

Goes well with: *Night of the Shooting Stars*

DIVORCE—ITALIAN STYLE

ESSENTIAL

Italy 1961 B&W 104 min. NR Comedy

Dir: Pietro Germi

C: Marcello Mastroianni, Daniela Rocca, Stefania Sandrelli, Leopoldo Trieste

It's easy to overlook this comedy, with its generic title that spawned so many imitators both in Europe and Hollywood. But forty years after its initial release, *Divorce* still sparkles as one of the funniest portraits of the male ego. Marcello Mastroianni is Ferdinando Cefalú, a faded nobleman trying to maintain some sense of dignity while sharing a sprawling, ramshackle house with feuding relatives. His dissatisfaction with his mustachioed wife, Rosalia (Daniella Rocca, in a wonderful good-sport performance) grows keener when cousin Angela (Stefania Sandrelli) returns from school, all grown up and suddenly very desirable. Catholic doctrine (and Italian law) forbid Ferdinando from ending his marriage legally, so he begins to concoct another way to put himself out of his misery. Mastroianni's twitching mustache, his lustful sighs, and his dreamy expressions (he is imagining either ways his wife can die or scenes of bliss with his cousin) create an indelible comic character. The film's original screenplay won an Oscar, and both Mastroianni and director Pietro Germi were nominated as well. A highlight: opening night, in the Sicilian village's lone movie theater, of *La Dolce Vita.*

⊙**DVD**

CO9

Goes well with: *Belle Epoque*

DR. MABUSE THE GAMBLER

Germany 1922 B&W 300 min. NR Action-Adventure

Dir: Fritz Lang

C: Rudolf Klein-Rogge, Alfred Abel, Aud Egede Nissen, Gertrude Welcker, Bernhard Goetzke, Paul Richter

Fritz Lang's first great film also introduced one of cinema's most durable arch-villains, the mad genius Dr. Mabuse, whose great talent is influencing the minds of others (he was an evil forerunner of the Shadow). Originally released as two serials, the first running eight weeks and the second nine, under the title *Dr. Mabuse the Gambler,* it has the pulpy feel of that form, but Lang wasn't just slumming. With his wife, screenwriter Thea von Harbou, he made Mabuse (Rudolf Klein-Rogge) a product of his times—the turbulent post–World War I era in Germany, with its runaway inflation and anything-goes morality among the wealthier classes. Mabuse's first crime is an elaborate stock swindle; his henchmen steal an important international treaty, causing a company's stock price to drop. Mabuse appears in the first of his many disguises on the floor of the stock exchange and begins buying the stock when it hits bottom; when the treaty is conveniently found, he has made the first of his many killings. Mabuse's nemesis is Police Commissioner von Wenk, but the cop is barely able to keep track of the madman, at one point unwittingly sending an ill friend to him for treatment! Accumulating wealth is not Mabuse's aim; as he says, "Nothing is interesting in the long run except playing with human beings and human fates." Lang returned to Mabuse in the early 1930s for *The Testament of Dr. Mabuse,* this time with pointed references to Hitler, whose own henchmen did not take kindly to the film. Try to find the full-length film. Shortened versions are available, but they excise the scenes depicting the breakdown of German society and concentrate on the criminal activities. In one edited set, parts I and II run 120 minutes and 122 minutes, respectively; in another version they run 101 minutes and 87 minutes.

AC1, DR36, TH12

Goes well with: *Les Vampires*

DODES'KA-DEN

Japan   1970   C   140 min.   NR   Drama

Dir: Akira Kurosawa

C: Yoshitaka Zushi, Tomoko Yamazaki, Hiroshi Akutagawa, Noboru Mitani

Japanese filmmaker Akira Kurosawa had been directing films for almost thirty years when he made his first color feature, about the fortunes of a group of people living in a Tokyo slum. Originally running over four hours, it was a big flop in Japan, sending the director into a personal and professional funk, and its distribution in America, at a much shorter running time, was limited. Though it lacks the physical sweep and grand dramatics of his most famous films, *Dodes'ka-den* (the title is from the sound a slow-witted character makes when he pretends to be a train) is still the solid work of a great director. It offers a clear-eyed view of people living day to day on dreams and guile; Kurosawa manages to be sympathetic to the poor without succumbing to sentiment about their plight.

DR36

Goes well with: *Amores Perros*

DOGFIGHT

U.S.   1991   C   92 min.   R   Drama
Dir: Nancy Savoca
C: River Phoenix, Lili Taylor, Richard Panebianco, Anthony Clark, Mitchell Whitfield, Holly Near, Brendan Fraser

A young Marine (River Phoenix) about to ship out from San Francisco to Vietnam in November 1963 picks up an idealistic waitress (Lili Taylor) to bring to a party. His goal isn't a last-minute one-night stand; in fact, he's trying to win a contest for bringing the ugliest girl to the soirée. About the time the waitress discovers his motive, he begins to realize a certain affection for her, and they wind up spending the night wandering the streets of the city. Bob Comfort's script is tough and funny, and even his conceit of setting the story on the eve of JFK's assassination works. Phoenix and Taylor are terrific. He plays a kid who is just beginning to understand that a lifetime of blindly following orders may not be for him, and Taylor embodies a young woman who's a heartbreaking mix of toughness and vulnerability.

DR18, DR24, DR36, XT7

Goes well with: *Who's That Knocking at My Door*

DOLCE VITA, LA.

See *La Dolce Vita*

DON'S PARTY

Australia   1976   C   91 min.   NR   Comedy
Dir: Bruce Beresford
C: John Hargreaves, Pat Bishop, Graham Kennedy, Veronica Lang, Candy Raymond, Harold Hopkins

The gathering in question takes place on the night of an important national election in Australia. Any party at which booze and several shaky marriages are combined has the possibilities for low comedy and high drama; throw in evening-long discussions of politics, and you have the makings of a real wingding. It does help to know some of the political players whose fortunes are at stake, but the setup is generic enough to keep the film's appeal from being too specific. David Williamson adapted his own play, and the film wisely keeps the characters confined to small spaces in order to increase the combustibility of the situations—which are played for laughs, though those laughs sometimes stick in your throat.

⊙**DVD**

CO2, CO8

Goes well with: *High Hopes*

DONT LOOK BACK

ESSENTIAL

U.S.   1967   B&W   96 min.   NR   Documentary

Dir: D. A. Pennebaker

Whatever else Albert Grossman did for Bob Dylan's career as his business manager, hiring D. A. Pennebaker to film Dylan's 1965 tour of England was a stroke of genius. Pennebaker's film didn't turn out to be quite the promotional vehicle Grossman had envisioned, but it's an invaluable record of a performing artist in transition. Dylan bristles so much at being called a folksinger wrapped up in social causes that his subsequent move to a rock sound and more abstract lyrics shouldn't have come as much of a surprise. Joan Baez, whose own promotion of the young Dylan's music gave his career a jump-start, is portrayed here as the odd woman out, as her onetime lover pays more attention to his jokester pal, Bobby Neuwirth. Between snippets of Dylan performing (of which Grossman clearly wished there had been more in the final film), Pennebaker's camera efficiently captures often testy give-and-take sessions between Dylan and an adoring fan, Dylan and two individual reporters, and Dylan and his so-called rival, singer Donovan. If Dylan comes off as casually cruel in all of these encounters, it's also possible to see him a man nearly buckling under the enormous pressure of unrealistic expectations.

⊙**DVD:** Includes five bonus audio tracks.

DO4, DO5

Goes well with: *Thirty Two Short Films About Glenn Gould*

DON'T LOOK NOW

U.K./Italy   1973   C   110 min.   R   Thriller

Dir: Nicolas Roeg

C: Julie Christie, Donald Sutherland, Clelia Mantania, Hilary Mason,
Massimo Serato

Daphne du Maurier's story of a British couple grieving over their
drowned child during a business trip to Venice was brilliantly adapted
by Nicolas Roeg and writers Allan Scott and Chris Bryant. The wife believes that a figure dressed in a familiar red slicker whom she sees only
in fleeting glances may be a reincarnation of her child. When she enlists
the help of two visiting sisters, one a self-proclaimed psychic, the couple's marriage starts to fray. Donald Sutherland, as a rational man involved with the restoration of a church, and Julie Christie, as a mother
who can't let go, are brilliant. No one has suggested the menacing quality of Venice's stately but decaying architecture better than Roeg and his
cinematographer, Anthony Richmond.

DR8, TH3, XT4, XT7

Goes well with: *Carnival of Souls*

THE DREAMLIFE OF ANGELS

France   1998   C   113 min.   R   Drama

Dir: Erick Zonca

C: Elodie Bouchez, Natacha Régnier, Grégoire Colin, Jo Prestia

Working in a factory in a small French town, two disparate women
become unlikely friends and roommates. Isa (Elodie Bouchez) is an
impulsive drifter who adopts a tough exterior to fend off any serious
entanglements. Marie (Natacha Régnier) seems to be more settled,
with a steady boyfriend and an apartment. But the flat actually belongs
to someone else—Marie is only housesitting—and the boyfriend, a
club owner, turns out to be a faithless jerk. Marie's polished façade
starts to crack, and it's Isa who has to hold their lives and friendship together. Director and cowriter Erick Zonca's debut film brilliantly de-
lineates the details of a friendship forged out of isolation. Bouchez and
Régnier shared the Best Actress prize at Cannes for their stunning performances.

⊙**DVD**

DR12, DR39, DR40

Goes well with: *Entre Nous*

DRUGSTORE COWBOY
ESSENTIAL

U.S. 1989 C 100 min. R Comedy

Dir: Gus Van Sant

C: Matt Dillon, Kelly Preston, James Remar, James LeGros, Heather Graham, Beah Richards, Grace Zabriskie, Max Perlich, William S. Burroughs

In this genial adaptation of prison inmate James Fogle's unpublished memoir, Matt Dillon heads up an explosively funny non-nuclear family that includes Kelly Lynch, James LeGros, and Heather Graham, and their main income is derived from holding up drugstores for both cash and the prescription medicines they crave. Gus Van Sant's breakthrough film is that rare comedy about drugs that (a) does not star Cheech and Chong, and (b) does not make people getting high look endearingly goofy. Dillon and his clan are always on the road, going nowhere fast, but it's a helluva ride. Just to add some authenticity, Van Sant tosses in William S. Burroughs as a character who might be described as the Roy Rogers of drugstore cowboys. *Drugstore Cowboy* was a four-time winner at the Independent Spirits, garnering awards for Best Male Lead (Dillon) and Supporting Male (Max Perlich), Screenplay (Van Sant and Daniel Yost), and Cinematography (Robert Yeoman); the screenplay also was honored by the New York Film Critics Circle.

⊙**DVD:** Includes audio commentaries by Gus Van Sant and Matt Dillon.

CO2, DR10

Goes well with: *Trainspotting*

THE DUELLISTS

U.K. 1977 C 101 min. PG Drama

Dir: Ridley Scott

C: Keith Carradine, Harvey Keitel, Edward Fox, Cristina Raines, Robert Stephens, Diana Quick, Tom Conti, Albert Finney

Overcoming some questionable casting and a tendency to be picturesque almost to the point of distraction, Ridley Scott's first film is stronger around the edges than down the middle. This adaptation of Joseph Conrad's story *The Duel* is about a long-running feud between two French army officers of the Napoleonic era. They are played, improbably, by Harvey Keitel and Keith Carradine. Both actors have distinguished themselves in many other films, but Keitel's brooding expressions are the only element between them that works here. In compensation, the supporting cast is tremendously effective, with Albert Finney especially powerful in a small role. Scott and cinematographer Frank Tidy never met a misty morning or painterly sunset they didn't want to include in this film, and the result is a curious tension: an elegant film about two very small-minded people.

DR24, DR37

Goes well with: *The Bridge on the River Kwai*

E

THE EARRINGS OF MADAME DE . . .

ESSENTIAL

France/Italy   1953   B&W   105 min.   NR   Drama
Dir: Max Ophüls
C: Charles Boyer, Danielle Darrieux, Vittorio De Sica, Jean Debucourt,
  Lia Di Leo

Director Max Ophüls's masterwork of social comedy masquerading as straight-faced drama is a delightful excursion into the world of the well-to-do and their silly preoccupations with appearances. Danielle Darrieux is the Madame of the title, perfectly luxe and perfectly inca-pable of real feeling. Mindlessly pawning a pair of earrings given to her by her devoted but clueless husband (Charles Boyer), she sets in motion a series of embarrassing episodes that bring the contours of their love-less marriage into sharp relief. This is the stuff of wonderful farce, but Ophüls is less interested in physical gyrations than in small gesture: the raised eyebrow, the knowing glance, the almost imperceptible shift in tone in a conversation. His camera, which glides in and out of well-appointed chambers and up and down stairs, is like a cat burglar, quietly slipping into a room when no one is looking to steal a few moments from the lives of foolishly pretentious folks.

  DR5, DR19
Goes well with: *La Ronde*

EAST IS EAST

U.K.   1999   C   96 min.   R   Comedy-Drama
Dir: Damien O'Donnell

C: Om Puri, Linda Bassett, Jordan Routledge, Archie Panjabi, Emil
   Marwa, Lesley Nicol, Gary Damer, Emma Rydal

Cultural assimilation get a thorough workout in this comedy-drama
set in early 1970s Britain, when conservative politicians like Enoch
Powell raised the specter of great dark-skinned hordes of immigrants
overwhelming that sceptered isle. Adapted by Ayub Khan-Din from his
own play, *East* follows the fortunes of fish-and-chips shop owner
George (a Pakistani immigrant of twenty-five years' standing), his
British wife, and their seven children, who all look like their father and
sound like their mother. When the oldest son, promised in marriage
under George's customs, bolts from the altar, the battle is on between
the parents over how the remaining offspring, all still living at home,
will be raised. Om Puri, as George, comes on like a brown-skinned
Archie Bunker, with his narrow worldview totally at odds with the reality of children raised to be more independent-minded than he would
like to admit. The film's comedy gets darker as it goes along, until a crucial dramatic scene near the end that feels absolutely right. The funniest
scene: the unveiling of an unusual piece of art by one of the sons during
a very proper social occasion.

⊙**DVD:** Includes audio commentary by Damien O'Donnell.

CO3, DR7, DR11, DR28

Goes well with: *My Son the Fanatic*

EASY RIDER

ESSENTIAL

U.S.   1969   C   94 min.   R   Drama

Dir: Dennis Hopper

C: Dennis Hopper, Peter Fonda, Jack Nicholson, Karen Black, Luke
   Askew, Luana Anders, Robert Walker, Phil Spector, Toni Basil

The success of a cheaply made picture produced outside the studio
system by a couple of renegade actors really messed with people's
minds way back in 1969. Dennis Hopper and Peter Fonda as a pair of
bikers who sell cocaine to finance a cross-country trip from Los Angeles to New Orleans—who knew that film would blow everybody away
at Cannes and make a ton of money at the American box office? (And
how many movies since then have pulled off that feat?) Giving an actor
like Jack Nicholson, who had been kicking around in B movies for a
decade, his big breakthrough; using rock music on the soundtrack as a

narrative device; filming a bad drug experience with a handheld camera; letting the actors improvise their dialogue—man, that's the kind of stuff independent movies do all the time now. Give *Easy Rider* its due; the film broke some kind of solid ground.

⊙**DVD:** Includes "making of" documentary and audio commentary by Dennis Hopper.

DR21, XT5, XT7

Goes well with: *My Own Private Idaho*

EAT DRINK MAN WOMAN

ESSENTIAL

Taiwan   1994   C   124 min.   NR   Drama

Dir: Ang Lee

C: Sihung Lung, Kuei-Mei Yang, Chien-Lien Wu, Yu-Wen Wang, Winston Chao

On the short menu of great films about food, put *Babette's Feast* at the top, followed by this drama about a Taiwanese chef and his three grown daughters. He's a widower whose one way of communicating with his girls is to prepare a weekly family-style dinner for them. He has lost his own ability to taste food, so his generosity is total and complete. Nevertheless, the daughters, each working on her own professional and romantic problems, are reluctant to share with Dad. Like the parents in Ang Lee's previous film, *The Wedding Banquet,* the iron-willed chef is tied to more traditional ways—not only of preparing food but of living to serve and honor your elders. *Eat Drink*'s family dynamics aren't the heavyweight stuff of a Bergman film: This is something closer to the best films of Japanese director Yasujiro Ozu, offering gentle and wise observations about the expectations that adults have for children and how they are rarely met.

⊙**DVD:** Includes interviews with Lee.

DR11, DR39, XT2

Goes well with: *Babette's Feast*

EATING RAOUL

U.S.   1982   C   83 min.   R   Comedy

Dir: Paul Bartel

C: Paul Bartel, Mary Woronov, Robert Beltran, Susan Saiger, Buck Henry, Ed Begley, Jr.

The single men looking for love in this dark comedy don't get their hearts broken; their fate is something worse. Director Paul Bartel stars with Mary Woronov as the Blands, a couple whose idea for supplying meat for their restaurant is to lure wealthy men in search of love to their apartment and turn them into the special of the day. As a forerunner to the darker (and more imaginative) *Delicatessen, Eating Raoul* pushed the envelope on what was funny in screen comedy. Bartel and Woronov worked together in several other films, sometimes with Bartel directing, but they'll best be remembered as a sick version of those lonelyhearts murderers who once peppered the tabloids.

CO2, XT2

Goes well with: *Delicatessen*

THE EDGE OF THE WORLD

U.K. 1937 B&W 74 min. NR Drama
Dir: Michael Powell
C: Niall MacGinnis, Belle Chrystall, John Laurie, Finlay Currie, Eric Berry

Michael Powell called this film a turning point in his life; it was the first project he initiated, and its critical acclaim attracted the attention of famed producer Alexander Korda, who backed several of his films. Powell was inspired to write his screenplay by the abandonment of St. Kilda, an island north of Scotland that had lost too much of its younger population to sustain itself. Forbidden from shooting on St. Kilda (which had been turned into a wildlife refuge), Powell and company journeyed farther north to Foula, an isolated island in the Shetlands with forbidding cliffs. The story is of two families; the Mansons have a twin son and daughter, and the Grays have a son. James Gray loves Ruth Manson, but he disagrees with her brother, Robbie, over the future of the island. When Robbie is killed in a cliff-climbing accident, the families are torn apart, but not for long—there's a pregnancy that brings about a reconciliation, though the island is finally evacuated. The breathtaking scenery competes with the actors for center stage in this moving drama. A bonus feature of the newly restored version on tape is *Return to the Edge of the World,* a lovely documentary Powell made for the BBC in 1978, when he and actor John Laurie (who played the Mansons' father) journeyed back to the island after forty years.

DR34

Goes well with: *I Know Where I'm Going!*

THE EEL

Japan   1997   C   117 min.   NR   Drama
Dir: Shohei Imamura
C: Koji Yakusho, Misa Shimizu, Fujio Tsuneta, Mitsuko Baisho

Dramas about ex-convicts trying to rebuild their lives usually concern habitual offenders who just can't stay out of trouble. In Shohei Imamura's absorbing character study, the ex-con (Koji Yakusho) is a one-time offender who impulsively murdered his wife and her lover when he came home and found them making love. After eight years in prison, he has learned to shut off any emotion toward people, preferring instead to lavish his attention on a pet eel. Inevitably, he is drawn into human contact, first when he opens a barber shop (a trade he learned in prison), next when he saves the life of a suicidal young woman who becomes an unwanted companion. The film's detours into comedy aren't as jarring as you might expect, but most important, Imamura sidesteps the sentimental traps that too often mark this kind of material.
⊙**DVD**
DR21
Goes well with: *The Limey*

8½

ESSENTIAL

Italy   1963   B&W   135 min.   NR   Drama
Dir: Federico Fellini
C: Marcello Mastroianni, Claudia Cardinale, Anouk Aimée, Sandra
   Milo, Barbara Steele, Rossella Falk

A landmark film about the art and soul of moviemaking, Federico Fellini's drama focusing on a director's indecision over the subject for his next project is slyly autobiographical. Fellini had made six features and codirected three others before making this film, thus explaining the title. It opens with a wonderful scene of Guido Anselmi (Marcello Mastroianni) trapped in his car in a tunnel full of vehicles belching exhaust fumes. Before he chokes on the foul air, he is carried up and out of the tunnel, and the story of his imagination lifting him out of dreary everyday life begins. Can he balance the demands of his producers and the women in his life without disturbing his artistic muse? Should he make a film about his past, or maybe his present personal and artistic difficulties? Fellini mixes and matches reality and dreams until you can barely tell the difference—and don't really want to. Few films have captured so accurately the unique consciousness of the artist, for whom every incident and person opens up possibilities for his work. *8½* won an Oscar and the New York Film Critics Circle award for Best Foreign Film; its costumes also picked up an Academy Award.

⊙**DVD:** Two discs. One includes commentary by critic Gideon Bachman; introduction by Terry Gilliam; excerpts from Fellini interviews and letters. Second disc includes "Fellini: A Director's Notebook" and "Nino Rota: Between Cinema and Concert" documentaries.
DR2, DR3, DR22
Goes well with: *Day for Night*

EIGHT MEN OUT

ESSENTIAL

U.S. 1988 C 119 min. PG Drama
Dir: John Sayles
C: John Cusack, Clifton James, Michael Lerner, Christopher Lloyd, John Mahoney, Charlie Sheen, David Strathairn, D. B. Sweeney, Michael Rooker, Perry Lang, Bill Irwin, Studs Terkel, John Sayles, John Anderson, Maggie Renzi

Those who would opt for *Field of Dreams* or *Bull Durham* as the Great American Baseball Movie, like those who thought Duke Snider or Mickey Mantle was the best center fielder playing in New York in the 1950s, are entitled to their opinions. But for me, the Willie Mays of baseball movies is writer-director John Sayles's account of the 1919 World Series, the most infamous scandal in sports history. The Chicago White Sox entered the series heavily favored—and grossly underpaid by their miserly owner, Charles Comiskey. Professional gamblers, alert to the possibilities, offered several Chicago players bribes to ease up on their game so that long-shot bets on their opponents, the Cincinnati Reds, would pay off handsomely. As historian Eliot Asinof did in his source book, Sayles takes us through the setup and payoff step by step; he's sympathetic to the players without minimizing the harm they did to the sport. Among the sensational ensemble cast, the standouts (along with David Strathairn as anguished pitcher Eddie Cicotte) are John Cusack as infielder Buck Weaver, and D. B. Sweeney as outfielder Joe Jackson, two players who fell into the fix without fully understanding its implications until it was too late. Chicago writer Studs Terkel plays a sportswriter whose press box exchanges with Ring Lardner (Sayles) suggest that some observers were aware of the fix as it happened. A bonus: the actors who play the ballplayers really look like athletes in the game scenes.

⊙**DVD**

DR17, DR24, DR35

Goes well with: *This Sporting Life*

EL MARIACHI

U.S./Mexico   1992   C   81 min.   R   Drama

Dir: Robert Rodriguez

C: Carlos Gallardo, Consuelo Gómez, Peter Marquardt, Jaime de Hoyos

Was it really produced for seven thousand dollars, as writer-director Robert Rodriguez claims? However modest the budget was on this agreeably funky comedy thriller, it has energy and style to burn. The title character is a guitar player (Carlos Gallardo) who shows up in a small town where he's mistaken for a nasty criminal. Rodriguez is more interested in action than character, and for a movie shot in two weeks, the film's action sequences are remarkably well choreographed. *El Mariachi* put Rodriguez on the filmmaking map, winning him acclaim from the Independent Spirit Awards (for Best First Feature) and at Sundance (the Audience Award). But none of his subsequent features (including a remake of this film titled *Desperado,* with Antonio Banderas) have quite fulfilled the promise of his debut.

⊙**DVD:** Contains *Desperado;* two featurettes; audio commentary by Robert Rodriguez.

DR6, TH17

Goes well with: *Diva*

EL NORTE

ESSENTIAL

U.S./U.K.   1983   C   139 min.   R   Drama

Dir: Gregory Nava

C: Silvia Gutiérrez, David Villapando, Ernesto Gómez Cruz, Alicia del Lago

A brother and sister fleeing political persecution in Guatemala make it to Los Angeles, the fabled El Norte of many Latin American people's dreams. They are willing to accept minimum-wage jobs for the chance to enjoy better lives, but the American Dream proves elusive. Gregory Nava (who wrote the film with his wife, Anna Thomas) has fashioned one of the best immigrant sagas ever, first demonstrating how difficult the physical journey to America is and then dramatizing how overwhelming the odds are against immigrants with little education and community support. The hope that America holds for so many people is real; Nava and Thomas's great achievement is to dramatize in intimate terms what a strong force that hope is. Their film could be rereleased today with only slight cosmetic changes and still look timely.

DR7, DR28, DR36, DR40

Goes well with: *My Family (Mi Familia)*

ELECTION

U.S. 1999 C 103 min. R Comedy

Dir: Alexander Payne

C: Matthew Broderick, Reese Witherspoon, Chris Klein, Jessica Campbell, Mark Harelik

Reese Witherspoon got the role of her young career in this savage satire of high school politics from the director (Alexander Payne) and writer (Jim Taylor) who gave us *Citizen Ruth*. As Tracey Flick, the student who defines perky, Witherspoon is a ball of Type A energy speaking in complete sentences, surely the only high school student of recent years who uses "like" only as a verb expressing fondness for something and someone. Tracy is running unopposed for student council president until her civics teacher (Matthew Broderick) steps in. Why he urges another student to run against Tracy is a little more complicated than a sense of fair play; you'll have to see this marvelously witty film to find out. The film's greatest inside joke is to cast Broderick, remembered by many filmgoers as the student rebel Ferris Bueller, as a teacher on the other side of the desk. But this is Witherspoon's movie, as she gives a satiric performance that is as skilled as any in recent films. Taylor was honored by both the Independent Spirit Awards and the New York Film Critics Circle for his writing, and the Spirits also awarded the film Best Feature and named Payne Best Director.

⊙**DVD:** Includes audio commentary by Alexander Payne.

CO2, CO5, CO8

Goes well with: *Citizen Ruth*

ELIZABETH

U.K. 1998 C 123 min. R Drama

Dir: Shekhar Kapur

C: Cate Blanchett, Geoffrey Rush, Joseph Fiennes, Richard Attenborough, Christopher Eccleston, Vincent Cassel, Fanny Ardant, Kathy Burke, John Gielgud

Unjustly if understandably neglected in the year that gave us the lighter, more ingratiating *Shakespeare in Love, Elizabeth* is a historical drama of the first rank for one reason: Australian actress Cate Blanchett's central performance. With this film, Blanchett joined Bette Davis and Glenda Jackson in the Hall of Fame of Elizabeth I interpreters (with apologies to *Shakespeare in Love*'s Judi Dench, who was on the screen for all of about ten minutes). This film traces the beginning of Elizabeth's reign as Queen of England; few believed she would be wily enough to ascend to the throne, let alone remain there for an astonishing forty-four years. The almost claustrophobic sense of palace intrigue is matched by the dark tones of Remi Adefarasin's cinematography. The film also offers an impressive array of period costumes and solid supporting performances by Geoffrey Rush and Joseph Fiennes, both of whom also appeared in *Shakespeare in Love.*

⊙**DVD:** Includes "making of" featurette.

DR17, DR24, DR25, DR30, DR39

Goes well with: *Shakespeare in Love*

THE EMIGRANTS
ESSENTIAL

Sweden 1971   C   148 min.   PG   Drama
Dir: Jan Troell
C: Max von Sydow, Liv Ullmann, Eddie Axberg, Allan Edwall

Ideally, you should see this opening chapter of the two-part epic of a Swedish couple emigrating to America in the nineteenth century with its sequel (*The New Land*), but both parts stand on their own. Max von Sydow and Liv Ullmann, long associated with some of the best films of Ingmar Bergman, are the leads, a poor Swedish couple driven from their country by extreme poverty to make a new life in the American midwest. This film concentrates on the difficulties they encounter getting out of Sweden and making their way across the Atlantic and then into the heartland of America. Ullmann, who won the New York Film Critics Circle award for Best Actress, is especially fine as the wife who finds a way to balance deference to her husband with a determination not to be taken advantage of by unscrupulous officials and businessmen.

DR7, DR11, DR24
Goes well with: *The New Land*

THE END OF THE AFFAIR
U.K./U.S.   1999   C   109 min.   R   Drama
Dir: Neil Jordan
C: Ralph Fiennes, Julianne Moore, Stephen Rea, Ian Hart, Jason Isaacs
Graham Greene's semiautobiographical novel tells the story of a World War II–era love affair between a writer and the wife of his best friend, but there's another dimension to this familiar story. Cleverly told in multilayered flashbacks, the film keeps returning to a nearly disastrous episode involving the two lovers that awakens a deeper sense of spirituality in them. Ralph Fiennes, Julianne Moore (nominated for an Oscar) and Stephen Rea are the points of the triangle, and they are all excellent at projecting the requisite measures of guilt, elation, and suspicion that are part of any affair. Writer-director Neil Jordan subtly introduces the extra dimension to the story, and it pays off handsome emotional dividends in the end. Ian Hart, as a private detective, and Jason Isaacs, as a priest-counselor, add excellent support in key roles.
⊙**DVD:** Includes audio commentary by Neil Jordan and "making of" featurette. Also available packaged with 1955 version; no extras on that edition.
DR19, DR24, DR29, DR38, XT4
Goes well with: *Brief Encounter*

THE ENGLISH PATIENT
ESSENTIAL
U.S.   1996   C   162 min.   R   Drama
Dir: Anthony Minghella
C: Ralph Fiennes, Juliette Binoche, Willem Dafoe, Kristin Scott Thomas, Naveen Andrews, Colin Firth, Julian Wadham, Jürgen Prochnow
One of the strongest films to win the big enchilada at the Academy Awards in recent years, this adaptation of Michael Ondaatje's novel of World War II was written and directed by Anthony Minghella. The film deftly switches back and forth between two story lines. A mysterious Hungarian (Ralph Fiennes) suffering burns from a plane crash reveals the events leading up to his accident, involving a love affair with a married woman (Kristin Scott Thomas), to a French nurse (Oscar winner

Juliette Binoche) caring for him in an Italian monastery. The nurse develops yearnings of her own for an Indian soldier (Naveen Andrews) stationed nearby. While Fiennes and Scott Thomas are exquisitely matched as the doomed lovers, Binoche is less effective as the nurse. The subject of wartime romance has produced far too many insipid films, which make the few classics like this film and *Casablanca* all the more satisfying. The film also won Oscars for direction, art direction, cinematography, film editing, sound, costume design, and original dramatic score.

⊙**DVD**

DR19, DR24, DR29, DR38

Goes well with: *The End of the Affair*

THE ENTERTAINER

U.K.   1960   B&W   97 min.   NR   Drama

Dir: Tony Richardson

C: Laurence Olivier, Brenda De Banzie, Roger Livesey, Joan
  Plowright, Daniel Massey, Alan Bates, Shirley Ann Field, Albert
  Finney

Archie Rice is the title character, a broken-down vaudevillian whose career is over for everyone but him. Playwright John Osborne's creation is brilliantly realized by Laurence Olivier in one of his signature roles. Actors and athletes past their prime are among the saddest of cases, as they publicly flaunt their shortcomings before hostile or embarrassed audiences, and Olivier is almost shamelessly brutal in plumbing the depths of Archie's self-deception. Olivier is supported by his future wife, Joan Plowright, and two fresh faces making their screen debuts, Alan Bates and Albert Finney. (Finney and costar Shirley Ann Field would team later that same year to star in *Saturday Night and Sunday Morning,* produced by *Entertainer* director Tony Richardson.)

⊙**DVD**

DR4, DR32

Goes well with: *Mephisto*

ENTRE NOUS

France   1983   C   110 min.   PG   Drama

Dir: Diane Kurys

C: Miou-Miou, Isabelle Huppert, Guy Marchand, Jean-Pierre Bacri,
  Patrick Bauchau

Sidestepping the cliches and sentimentalities that too often plague "women's pictures," Diane Kurys's emotionally resonant and complex drama is a great film about an enduring friendship. The bond between a bourgeois woman (Isabelle Huppert) locked in a comfortable but passionless marriage and an artist (Miou-Miou) married to a well-meaning but ineffectual man remains strong even after their husbands sense that the women are too close for their comfort. It's impossible to think of an American picture about this subject that doesn't reduce the relationship to something sexual (which this is not) or resort to men-are-all-pigs agitprop. Huppert, as good an actress as France has produced in the last twenty years, and Miou-Miou are sensationally effective.

⊙**DVD**

DR11, DR12, DR39

Goes well with: *The Dreamlife of Angels*

ERASERHEAD

ESSENTIAL

U.S.   1977   B&W   90 min.   NR   Fantasy

Dir: David Lynch

C: Jack Nance, Charlotte Stewart, Allen Joseph, Jeanne Bates

In the heyday of midnight movie screenings, when theaters kept their doors open late on weekends with offbeat films designed to attract a knowing audience of buffs and cultists, few films could match the drawing power of *Eraserhead*. David Lynch's debut feature was shot over several years while he was a student at the American Film Institute's Center for Advanced Film Studies, then located on the fabled Greystone estate in the hills overlooking Hollywood. Shooting mostly at night, Lynch employed some of the unused buildings on the grounds for his story of an almost catatonic young man (Jack Nance, here billed as John Nance) with electrified-looking hair, his spastic girlfriend, and their deformed offspring. Nance would become a Lynch regular in both his film and TV projects; he's wonderfully otherworldly in a film that's more a collection of nightmarish images than a straightforward narrative. Like most of Lynch's work, *Eraserhead* uses both arresting visuals and unusual sound effects (the soundtrack often sounds like it was recorded in a machine shop) to place the viewer somewhere south of the consciousness of everyday life.

XT6

Goes well with: *Blue Velvet*

EUROPA EUROPA

France/Germany/Poland   1990   C   115 min.   R   Drama

Dir: Agnieszka Holland

C: Marco Hofschneider, Rene Hofschneider, Julie Delpy, Ashley Wanninger

Among the most harrowing World War II stories of concealed identity is this adaptation of Solomon Perel's memoir, in which he described his attempts as a German Jewish teen to blend in with the Nazis, only to be drafted into Hitler's army. Marco Hofschneider, with his blonde hair, doesn't "look" Jewish, so the deception is perfectly believable, and writer-director Agnieszka Holland sustains an almost unbearable level of suspense by occasionally slipping in moments of dark humor. (Hofschneider's attempts to conceal his circumcised penis are especially funny.) The New York Film Critics Circle awarded *Europa Europa* its Best Foreign Language Film prize.

DR28, DR38

Goes well with: *Au Revoir, les Enfants*

EVE'S BAYOU

ESSENTIAL

U.S.   1997   C   109 min.   R   Drama

Dir: Kasi Lemmons

C: Jurnee Smollett, Meagan Good, Samuel L. Jackson, Lynn Whitfield, Debbi Morgan, Jake Smollett, Diahann Carroll, Vondie Curtis-Hall, Branford Marsalis

Actress Kasi Lemmons made an auspicious directorial debut with this drama of black life, told through the eyes of a ten-year-old girl named Eve Batiste. Her father, Louis (Samuel L. Jackson), a respected back-country doctor, is also a ladies' man, a fact of which her mother (Lynn Whitfield) is all too aware. Although the family is educated and relatively well-to-do, they (and many of their friends) still believe in voodoo and curses, which gives this coming-of-age story an extra dimension. Jurnee Smollett is sensational as Eve, the girl forced to deal with adult realities before she's prepared. The Independent Spirit Awards gave *Eve's Bayou* prizes for Best First Feature and Best Supporting Female performance by Debbi Morgan as Eve's aunt.

⊙**DVD:** Includes "making of" soundtrack featurette; filmmakers' audio commentary; and short film, "Dr. Hugo."

DR11, DR28, DR41, XT4
Goes well with: *King of the Hill*

EVERY MAN FOR HIMSELF AND GOD AGAINST ALL

West Germany 1974 C 110 min. NR Drama
Dir: Werner Herzog
C: Bruno S., Walter Ladengast, Brigitte Mira, Hans Musaus

In 1820s Nuremberg, a mysterious figure appeared one day in the streets, a grown man with no power of speech and the mental capacity of a child. Dubbed Kasper Hauser, he became a lightning rod for both scientists and the superstitious, regarded both as the perfect specimen for testing theories about civilization and as the embodiment of some kind of evil spirit. Werner Herzog's films are often about outcasts and misfits, and this one, based on a true story, may be his best work. It's a meditation that raises provocative questions about society's demands on the individual citizen and the acquisition of knowledge. The film is also known as *The Mystery of Kasper Hauser.*

DR17, DR21
Goes well with: *The Wild Child*

EXCALIBUR

U.K. 1981 C 140 min. R Action-Adventure
Dir: John Boorman
C: Nicol Williamson, Nigel Terry, Helen Mirren, Nicholas Clay, Cherie Lunghi, Corin Redgrave, Paul Geoffrey, Patrick Stewart, Gabriel Byrne, Liam Neeson

It's perplexing how many stiff and lackluster movies have been fashioned from the King Arthur legend, which makes the achievement of John Boorman's boldly imaginative rendering of Malory's *Morte d'Arthur* even more satisfying. Boorman and cowriter Rospo Pallenberg neatly balance the elements of blood, sex, and magic inherent in the story, and Alex Thomson's dazzling camera work makes this a must-see in a wide-screen format. Nicol Williamson offers an interpretation of Merlin that some romantics won't care for (he's a bit daft, see), but Helen Mirren is the definitive Morgana. Watch for Patrick Stewart and the young Liam Neeson in smaller roles. The use of Orff's *Carmina Burana* on the soundtrack is exhilaratingly effective.

⊙**DVD:** Includes audio commentary by John Boorman.
AC8, DR19, DR24

Goes well with: *Crouching Tiger, Hidden Dragon*

EXOTICA

Canada 1994 C 104 min. R Drama
Dir: Atom Egoyan
C: Bruce Greenwood, Mia Kirshner, Arsinée Khanjian, Don McKellar, Elias Koteas, Sarah Polley, Victor Garber

One man's obsession with a dancer at a sex club and a teenaged babysitter—does that sound like the plot of a movie playing at 3 A.M. on the Playboy Channel? In writer-director Atom Egoyan's hands, this is the starting point for an absorbing drama about the fate of seven disparate people. Bruce Greenwood plays a tax collector who spends his nights at the Exotica club, where he's drawn to a dancer (Mia Kirshner) who specializes in dressing up like a school girl in a white blouse and plaid skirt. Keeping a watchful eye on these two are the club's mysterioso disc jockey (Elias Koteas) and Exotica's suspicious owner (Arsinée Khanjian). The tax collector is also friends with a wheelchair-bound man (Victor Garber) and his daughter (the remarkable Sarah Polley), who babysits for his child. And he is auditing the business of a pet-shop owner (Don McKellar) with several secrets. Egoyan unravels his complex story deliberately, drawing out the pleasure of discovery.

⊙**DVD**

DR19, DR27, DR33

Goes well with: *The Sweet Hereafter*

THE EXTERMINATING ANGEL

Mexico 1962 B&W 95 min. NR Comedy
Dir: Luis Buñuel
C: Silvia Pinal, Enrique Rambal, Jacqueline Andere, José Baviera

Suppose you threw a party—and nobody wanted to go home? That's the joke in director Luis Buñuel's masterful skewering of bourgeois mores. The well-to-do guests at a sumptuous party find they cannot cross the threshold when it comes time to say good night, and at first no one seems to mind terribly. When the evening stretches into days of misery, with food and water running low, the guests remain trapped by a strange kind of social inertia. A crowd gathers outside the home, but for some reason no one, even the authorities, can enter the house, and soon the guests begin to starve to death. No one does this surreal material as deftly as Buñuel; this is a wonderful companion piece to his party-can't-get-started comedy, *The Discreet Charm of the Bourgeoisie.*

CO2, CO7

Goes well with: *The Discreet Charm of the Bourgeoisie*

EYE OF GOD

U.S.   1997   C   88 min.   R   Drama

Dir: Tim Blake Nelson

C: Martha Plimpton, Kevin Anderson, Hal Holbrook, Nick Stahl, Richard Jenkins, Margo Martindale, Mary Kay Place

Actor Tim Blake Nelson (*O Brother, Where Art Thou?*) made his debut as a writer-director with a chilling story about an ex-con (Kevin Anderson) and a small-town waitress (Martha Plimpton) who marry as soon as he's out of jail but who both live to regret their impulsiveness. The story is told in flashbacks, framed by the town sheriff (Hal Holbrook) questioning a blood-soaked young boy (Nick Stahl) found wandering a nighttime road. Nelson keeps us off-balance; we know something bad is going to happen but he's very skilled at misdirecting our attention, like a good conjurer. He was nominated for the Someone to Watch prize at the Independent Spirit Awards.

DR30, DR34, XT4

Goes well with: *The Rapture*

THE EYES OF TAMMY FAYE

U.S./U.K.   2000   C   79 min.   PG-13   Documentary

Dir: Fenton Bailey and Randy Barbato

The great accomplishment of this modest and surprisingly affecting documentary is that it wipes all that makeup from the face of Tammy Faye Bakker Messner (not literally) to get some glimpses of the real person. Fenton Bailey and Randy Barbato clearly like Tammy Faye, but they don't worship her. The film lays out her amazing story as a means of showing how one person (two, actually, counting her ex-husband Jim) can be so successful and yet so naïve. The Bakkers built three different religious TV networks, only to see them sold or taken away from them under questionable circumstances. The last instance, of course, followed revelations that Jim had had an affair and that Tammy was suffering from an addiction to pills; Jerry Falwell, according to the film, nobly offered to run the Bakkers' PTL (for Praise the Lord) network for a spell until Jim and Tammy could get back on their feet. Falwell then turned his back on the Bakkers, Jim went to prison, he and Tammy split, she married Jim's chief operations man, he went to prison, she got a talk show with an openly gay man. . . . And there's more, much more. Among the things you will find out about Tammy Faye was that she was exceptionally generous to everyone, including gay people and AIDS sufferers, even when some of her conservative religious brethren were shunning those people. And those hand puppets that Bailey and Barbato have pop up to introduce each segment of the story are a very clever inside joke.

⊙**DVD**
DO4
Goes well with: *The Passion of Joan of Arc*

EYES WITHOUT A FACE

France/Italy   1959   B&W   88 min.   NR   Horror
Dir: Georges Franju
C: Pierre Brasseur, Alida Valli, Edith Scob, Juliette Mayniel

Those nutty scientists and their crazy experiments! Don't they ever go to the movies and learn that it just doesn't pay to play God? Georges Franju's variation of the old story has a provocative twist: the scientist (Pierre Brasseur) is trying to restore the face of his own daughter (Edith Scob), horribly scarred in an auto accident. For his experiments he requires tissue of recently deceased young women, and you can guess what that means. When Daddy finally pushes things a bit too far, daughter releases the laboratory hounds on their tormentor. Franju's camera is so jittery you may require Dramamine before watching, but that adds to the fun; this is a solid little horror film that delivers on its shocks without insulting the viewer with ridiculous plot devices or crude special effects. American distributors retitled this *The Horror Chamber of Dr. Faustus;* why they couldn't leave well enough alone (the title above is a literal translation of the French one) remains a mystery.

FA8
Goes well with: *The City of Lost Children*

FACES
ESSENTIAL

U.S.   1968   B&W   130 min.   R   Drama
Dir: John Cassavetes
C: John Marley, Gena Rowlands, Lynn Carlin, Seymour Cassel, Fred
  Draper, Val Avery

John Cassavetes's breakthrough film, his fourth feature, is about a
pair of one-night stands that don't quite work out. Most of the film alternates between a private party involving a middle-aged married man
(John Marley) and a prostitute (Gena Rowlands), and the man's neglected wife (Lynn Carlin) trying to exact revenge by throwing her own
party at their home with a young man (Seymour Cassel). Cassavetes's
technique is to let his actors improvise from a basic outline, to get closer
to the emotional truth of their characters and scene. You may find this
quite absorbing or awfully self-indulgent. Watching a Cassavetes film is
like being in a bar where the couple in the next booth are having a long
and sometimes violent argument; you want to leave but you also want to
stay to see what will happen. In some of his films it isn't worth the wait;
here and in *A Woman Under the Influence,* it is.

⊙**DVD:** Includes analysis by Cassavetes expert Ray Carney.
DR19, DR27
Goes well with: *A Woman Under the Influence*

FALLEN CHAMP: THE UNTOLD STORY OF MIKE TYSON
U.S.   1993   C   93 min.   NR   Documentary
Dir: Barbara Kopple

At this distance from his heyday, it's hard to recall a time when Mike Tyson wasn't a sick national joke—before the rape, the prison sentence, the chewing on Evander Holyfield's ear, the foray into professional wrestling, and (most disheartening to boxing fans) the eroding of his once-magnificent skills. This portrait by two-time Oscar-winning documentarian Barbara Kopple, made for network television, puts a human face on Tyson, no mean achievement. Kopple was able to gain access to crucial footage of Tyson's early days as a fighter, when he was trained by Cus D'Amato, who became a father figure to the abandoned young man. Seeing how D'Amato and Tyson's managers tried but ultimately failed to put Tyson's best personal and professional interests first is a dispiriting tale of greed overcoming all else; eventually, Tyson ends up in the Don King stable, and the rest is sorry history.

DO10

Goes well with: *When We Were Kings*

THE FALLEN IDOL

U.K.   1948   B&W   94 min.   NR   Drama

Dir: Carol Reed

C: Ralph Richardson, Michèle Morgan, Bobby Henrey, Jack Hawkins, Bernard Lee

Graham Greene has been luckier than most authors whose works have been adapted to the screen, with several solid films (*The End of the Affair, The Third Man*) to steer filmgoers back to his original source material. Count this version of his story "The Basement Room" (which Greene and two other writers adapted for the screen) among the best of his films. Bobby Henrey plays a young boy whose household is served well by an exceptionally ingratiating manservant (Ralph Richardson). The boy, who's a bit of a loner at school, takes the servant as a friend, but when the servant's wife disappears, the boy has to face mounting evidence that his best friend may be a murderer. Carol Reed tells the story mostly from the boy's point of view, but we pick up signals from Richardson early on—his deference seems laced with an occasional taste of tart arrogance.

DR41

Goes well with: *Lawn Dogs*

FANNY AND ALEXANDER

ESSENTIAL

Sweden 1982 C 197 min. R Drama
Dir: Ingmar Bergman
C: Pernilla Allwin, Bertil Guve, Gunn Wollgren, Allan Edwall, Ewa
Fröling, Jan Malmsjö, Erland Josephson, Harriet Andersson

As an autobiographical memoir of youth, Ingmar Bergman's "final"
film (it was announced at the time of its release as his swan song,
though he has made one more film for TV and scripted several others)
is in a class with Fellini's *Amarcord* as fully realized evocations of the
joys and terrors of being a child. Bergman's film, unlike Fellini's, is
about not himself but his father. It's set in turn-of-the-century Sweden,
with the title characters, a young boy (Bergman's father) and his little
sister, watching their parents' marriage weather stormy seas, and
closely observing as various family members come and go and the seasons (especially the year-end holidays) unfold. At the end of his filmmaking career, Bergman seems to have mellowed; the dark, sometimes
morose psychological studies have been replaced by a child's-eye view
of the world. Fanny and Alexander are normal kids, and their day-to-day
concerns are normal, too. A profound film, it's also one of Bergman's
most accessible works. It was named best foreign film by both the
Academy and the New York Film Critics Circle; the former also recognized Sven Nykvist's cinematography, along with the art direction and
costume design, and the NYFCC named Bergman Best Director.
DR3, DR11, DR41
Goes well with: *Amarcord*

FAR FROM THE MADDING CROWD

U.K. 1967 C 169 min. PG Drama
Dir: John Schlesinger
C: Julie Christie, Peter Finch, Alan Bates, Terence Stamp, Prunella
Ransome

John Schlesinger and Julie Christie's third collaboration, following
the delightful comedy *Billy Liar* and the chic drama *Darling,* was this
adaptation of Thomas Hardy's novel about Bathsheba Everdene, a
woman always loved but rarely in love. Bathsheba is a nineteenth-
century version of *Darling's* central character, Diana Scott. Both
women are objects of desire, but they can't seem to find a way to return

the favor. Bathsheba's lovers are, in turn, a dashing but callow soldier (Terence Stamp), a wealthy but older landowner (Peter Finch), and a poor but honest shepherd (Alan Bates). Frederic Raphael (who also wrote *Darling*) did the first-rate adaptation, and to appreciate Nicolas Roeg's stunning cinematography, try to see this film in its original wide-screen glory.

DR18, DR24, DR29

Goes well with: *Darling*

FAREWELL, MY CONCUBINE

ESSENTIAL

China/Hong Kong   1993   C   155 min.   R   Drama

Dir: Chen Kaige

C: Leslie Cheung, Zhang Fengyi, Gong Li, Lu Qi

Arguably the greatest achievement of the new wave of Chinese film-makers, *Farewell, My Concubine* skillfully combines the personal with the political in its fifty-year story of two best friends, male singers at the Peking Opera. Director Chen Kaige wants to show how performing artists, operating in their hermetically sealed world of drama both onstage and backstage, can be oblivious to the political storms raging outside the theater. Leslie Cheung, as the gay singer Douzi, has the most difficult part, and he's sensationally effective; Zhang Fengyi (as Shitou, his friend) and the exquisite Gong Li (as Juxian, Shitou's eventual wife) are also superb. *Farewell* was honored by the New York Film Critics Circle for Best Foreign Language Film (and Best Supporting Actress), but lost the Oscar to the much slighter *Belle Epoque*. It was a rare instance where Academy voters favored comedy over an epic drama of real substance.

⊙**DVD**

DR4, DR19, DR24, DR25

Goes well with: *The Last Metro*

FARGO

U.S.   1996   C   97 min.   R   Comedy

Dir: Joel Coen

C: Frances McDormand, William H. Macy, Steve Buscemi, Harve Presnell, Peter Stormare, Kirstin Rudrüd

The Coen Brothers gained a temporarily wider audience with this acclaimed crime comedy, though some Coenheads complained that it was less stylistically adventurous than their previous efforts. Marge Gunderson, the small-town Minnesota police officer played by Oscar winner Frances McDormand, is a rare Coen commodity: a walking, talking, three-dimensional character. Watching her dogged pursuit of Jerry Lundergard (William H. Macy), the car salesman who has his wife kidnapped so he can share in the ransom her wealthy father will pay, is like watching Columbo operating in drag—her modesty masks an implacable will. Director Joel and producer Ethan Coen's screenplay also won an Oscar, and it's their wittiest work yet, giving everyone from McDormand and Macy to supporting players Steve Buscemi (as one of the hapless kidnappers) and Harve Presnell (as Jerry's obstinate father-in-law) scene after scene of rich, quotable dialogue. The New York Film Critics Circle named *Fargo* Best Film, while the film swept most of the Independent Spirit Awards, picking up Best Feature, Director, Male Lead (Macy), Female Lead, Screenplay, and Cinematography (Roger Deakins).

⊙**DVD**

CO1, CO2

Goes well with: *Bottle Rocket*

FAST, CHEAP & OUT OF CONTROL

U.S. 1997 C/B&W 82 min. PG Documentary

Dir: Errol Morris

The difference between Errol Morris and nearly anyone else working in documentaries (or, as some would prefer, "nonfiction films") is this: Anyone can find four people whose professions are somewhat unusual, as in a topiary gardener, a lion tamer, a scientist who studies hairless moles, and another scientist who builds robots. But no one can inter-weave a quartet of stories with the skill that Morris does. He under-stands that voice-overs in documentaries are often overbearing, so he lets his subjects tell their own stories, or he creates marvelous image montages set to Caleb Sampson's entrancing musical score. Morris's approach is meditative, but you won't find him sucking his thumb over the Big Issues; he's having too much fun telling his stories, and his joy in making films is infectious. The Independent Spirit Awards named *Fast, Cheap* best documentary of 1997.

DO7, DO11

Goes well with: *The Thin Blue Line*

FEED

U.S.   1992   C   76 min.   NR   Documentary
Dir: Kevin Rafferty and James Ridgeway

Owners of the older, larger satellite dish TV systems have one advantage over the new, smaller dish systems: the ability to pick up so-called wild feeds from various networks. These are off-hour transmissions of certain prime-time shows and unguarded moments from news broadcasts during which the reporter and/or subject are waiting to go on the air. Kevin Rafferty and James Ridgeway's documentary is an invaluable look at the early days of the 1992 presidential election through a collection of wild feeds, affording us glimpses of the real men behind the well-crafted façades they present to the public. It's not, as some complain, exploitative; Rafferty and Ridgeway don't set up cameras in these men's homes to film their truly private lives. This is an expedition to a limbo world located between private and public behavior, and one that is available to a shrinking percentage of the American public.

DO9

Goes well with: *The War Room*

THE FILTH AND THE FURY

U.K./U.S.   2000   C/B&W   103 min.   R   Documentary
Dir: Julien Temple

In 1980, British director Julien Temple documented the short but enormously influential life of the British punk band the Sex Pistols in *The Great Rock & Roll Swindle.* Twenty years later, Temple returns to the scene of the crime, with the advantage of historical perspective and access to the band's video archives. Temple interviews the members of the band and its controversial manager, Malcolm McLaren (for some reason, they are shot in darkness obscuring their faces), and it's clear that John Lydon, the band's lead singer, and McLaren are not exchanging Christmas cards. The film's most amusing touch is its use of clips from Laurence Olivier's 1955 film *Richard III,* whose central character was, McLaren admits, an inspiration for his aggressive style of promotion.

⊙**DVD:** Includes audio commentary by Julien Temple and original documentary on the punk rock movement.

DO5

Goes well with: *The Decline of Western Civilization*

FIRES ON THE PLAIN

Japan 1959 B&W 105 min. NR Drama

Dir: Kon Ichikawa

C: Eiji Funakoshi, Mantaro Ushio, Yoshihiro Hamaguchi, Osamu Takizawa

The second of Kon Ichikawa's masterful antiwar films is grittier and less hopeful than its predecessor, *The Burmese Harp*. Like that film, *Fires on the Plain* is set in the closing days of the war, but the mood here is one of desperation, as Japanese soldiers in the Philippines flee the relentless advance of American forces. Surrender is an option only for the few who are willing to risk the purportedly wretched conditions of the POW camps; for most of these men, the choice is between running or fighting against overwhelming odds. *Fires on the Plain* is a raw story of survival: One memorable sequence is shot at foot level, as pairs of worn-out boots are discarded and then picked up by soldiers slogging through the mud. The events are witnessed by a tubercular soldier, Tamura (Eiji Funakoshi), who is separated from his company. His final encounter with two starving soldiers ends in an episode of cannibalism that leaves him dazed and wandering through a barren landscape toward an uncertain fate.

DR37

Goes well with: *The Burmese Harp*

FIREWORKS

Japan 1998 C 103 min. NR Drama

Dir: Takeshi Kitano

C: "Beat" Takeshi, Kayoko Kishimoto, Ren Osugi, Susumu Terajima, Tetsu Watanabe

A Japanese counterpart to some of Joseph Wambaugh's best novels or Clint Eastwood's burned-out cop movies (*Dirty Harry, Tightrope*), director Takeshi Kitano's story follows a veteran police detective through several seemingly uneventful days. What we learn about this man (played by the director under his acting name, "Beat" Takeshi) is that he's carrying a heavy load of guilt and sorrow: His wife is dying of cancer, his former partner is paralyzed and suicidal, and he's still mulling over a botched arrest that led to another detective's death. He has to shift gears between talking tough with the gangsters who are tempting him with bribes, and offering sympathy and support for the two people in his life who are near or contemplating death. Takeshi is a remarkable actor, reminiscent of John Garfield at his brooding best.

⊙**DVD**
DR8, DR36
Goes well with: *Chungking Express*

A FISTFUL OF DOLLARS

Italy/West Germany/Spain 1964 C 96 min. R Action-Adventure
Dir: Sergio Leone
C: Clint Eastwood, Gian Maria Volonté, Marianne Koch, Wolfgang Lukschy

A truly international production: The story is a remake of a Japanese film, the director is Italian, the locations Spanish, the star American. It's the first of director Sergio Leone's "Dollars" trilogy of Westerns, followed by *For a Few Dollars More* and *The Good, the Bad and the Ugly.* The source material is *Yojimbo,* Akira Kurosawa's violently comic tale of a freelance samurai who allows warring clans in a small town to bid for his services while he dispatches dozens of men on whichever side isn't paying him that day. Clint Eastwood, coming off eight seasons on the TV program *Rawhide,* plays an Old West version of the samurai, the serape-wearing, cigar-chewing Man with No Name. This was a new kind of Western hero, less interested in dispatching justice than in getting his fair share of whatever money is floating around. Mark this as the beginning of the end for the genre, or the next logical step in its progression; either way, like *Yojimbo,* it's a darkly funny film.

⊙**DVD**
AC5, AC6
Goes well with: *Yojimbo*

FITZCARRALDO

West Germany/Peru 1982 C 157 min. PG Drama
Dir: Werner Herzog
C: Klaus Kinski, Claudia Cardinale, José Lewgoy, Miguel Angel Fuentes

Among the most fascinating obsessives ever portrayed in films is the title character in Werner Herzog and Klaus Kinski's most lavish collaboration. Brian Sweeney Fitzgerald was a visionary, a nineteenth-century Irishman who dreamed of building an opera house in the Peruvian rain forests and bringing the great Enrico Caruso there. Herzog began his film with Jason Robards as Fitzcarraldo (the local Indians' name for Fitzgerald), but Robards took ill with a form of jungle fever, and fortunately Herzog's longtime collaborator (and frequent adversary) Klaus Kinski was available to fill in. As good an actor as Robards is, this is a part the wild-eyed Kinski seems born to play. Fitzcarraldo's plan involved dragging an immense steamship over a small mountain to avoid traveling upstream through rapids, and that feat—which Herzog insisted on duplicating during the production (no digital effects for Werner!)—is the film's highlight. (All of this and more is well documented in Les Blank's film *Burden of Dreams*.) *Fitzcarraldo* is a bit in love with the audacity of itself, so the film feels like it stops every once in a while to look in the mirror, but it's an undeniably fascinating tale that could only be told by this matchless team.

⊙**DVD:** Includes audio commentary by Werner Herzog.

AC2, DR1, DR17, DR21

Goes well with: *Burden of Dreams*

THE FIVE SENSES

Canada   1999   C   105 min.   R   Drama

Dir: Jeremy Podeswa

C: Mary-Louise Parker, Philippe Volter, Gabrielle Rose, Molly Parker, Daniel MacIvor, Marco Leonardi, Brendan Fletcher, Nadia Litz

Jeremy Podeswa's drama, set in and around an urban apartment/office building, is a model of restraint. From the title you would guess correctly that his stories are connected to sight, hearing, taste, smell, and touch, but the beauty of Podeswa's work lies in its ability to create characters and situations that seem to incidentally embroider ideas about the senses. Rona (Mary-Louise Parker) bakes cakes for special occasions, though she has a lousy sense of taste for both food and men; Richard (Philippe Volter) is an eye doctor who's first seen eavesdropping on his neighbors through the air shafts, even though he is losing his hearing; Robert (Daniel MacIvor) is Rona's best pal, a bisexual with a highly developed sense of smell but bad intuition for romance; Ruth (Gabrielle Rose) is a massage therapist losing touch with her teenage daughter, Rachel (Nadia Litz), who in turn loses touch with a child she's supposed to be watching in a park when Rachel sneaks away to spy on a couple making love. Podeswa glides smoothly among these tales of urban heartbreak, allowing us to do our own eavesdropping and spying, all the while carefully pulling us in to these characters' lives.

⊙**DVD**
DR12, DR19, DR20, DR36
Goes well with: *Short Cuts*

FLIRTING

Australia   1990   C   100 min.   R   Drama
Dir: John Duigan
C: Noah Taylor, Thandie Newton, Nicole Kidman, Bartholomew Rose

John Duigan's sequel to *The Year My Voice Broke* follows Andy
(Noah Taylor) to an all-boys' boarding school. He's still the sensitive kid
from the first film, but whereas he spent all his time in that one yearning for an untouchable love, here he meets a girl (Thandie Newton)
from a neighboring school, and they fall in love. Like Freya, his love
object in *Year,* she's a bit of a loner, in part because she's a Ugandan exchange student and is scorned by some of her snootier classmates (including Nicole Kidman, in an early role). Duigan has an easy way with
his actors, and though there are few surprises here, it's a solid story, and
both Taylor and Newton are very appealing.

DR19, DR31, DR41
Goes well with: *The Year My Voice Broke*

FLIRTING WITH DISASTER

ESSENTIAL

U.S.   1996   C   92 min.   R   Comedy
Dir: David O. Russell
C: Ben Stiller, Patricia Arquette, Téa Leoni, Alan Alda, Mary Tyler
    Moore, George Segal, Lily Tomlin, Josh Brolin, Richard Jenkins,
    Celia Weston

If most American comedies of the last twenty years are fast food—
predictable, safe, and ultimately unsatisfying—*Flirting with Disaster* is
that little hole-in-the-wall ethnic joint with a menu full of surprises.
Ben Stiller plays a man with a wife and new baby and no idea who his
real parents are. He's adopted, and that hasn't bothered him until the
birth of his son. So he's off with his wife (Patricia Arquette), their baby,
and a graduate student (Téa Leoni) interested in documenting his
case—and maybe in him as well. Their cross-country adventures wind
up in New Mexico, where both sets of parents meet amid farcical circumstances that would do the Marx Brothers proud. George Segal and

Mary Tyler Moore are Stiller's adoptive parents, and Alan Alda and Lily Tomlin are the real deals, a pair of 1960s dropouts with a thriving business. In David O. Russell's film, the adventure lies in its delightful surprises. People are not what they seem, either by design or by circumstance, and Russell is a virtuoso at playing a series of variations on that theme.

⊙**DVD**

CO3, XT5

Goes well with: *Slums of Beverly Hills*

FOR A FEW DOLLARS MORE

Italy/Spain/West Germany/Monaco   1965   C   130 min.   NR
Action-Adventure

Dir: Sergio Leone

C: Clint Eastwood, Lee Van Cleef, Gian Maria Volonté, Jose Egger, Klaus Kinski

The title could be a cynic's summation of why Sergio Leone and Clint Eastwood reteamed for a follow-up to the surprising success of their first film together, *A Fistful of Dollars.* But the second of the "Dollars" trilogy (followed by *The Good, the Bad and the Ugly*) is quite entertaining, with Leone elaborating on the stylistics of the first film (long, drawn-out staredowns before guns start blazing, dialogue pared to the bone, every character an archetype of Western movie mythology) and Eastwood's Man with No Name no longer the loner. His partner of sorts is Col. Douglas Mortimer, played with great aplomb by veteran character actor Lee Van Cleef. Their mutual goal is to capture a nasty bandit named Indio (Gian Maria Volonté); their motivations are very different. Watch for Klaus Kinski, in an early role, as a hunchback. Ennio Morricone's score, as in all of Leone's major films, is a key element.

⊙**DVD**

AC6

Goes well with: *A Fistful of Dollars*

FORBIDDEN GAMES

ESSENTIAL

France   1951   B&W   102 min.   NR   Drama

Dir: René Clément

C: Brigitte Fossey, Georges Poujouly, Louis Herbert

War through the eyes of children: It's a surefire way to get the film audience's emotions stirred up, but it also allows the filmmaker to push well-worn buttons that can cheapen the effect of the drama. The beauty of Réne Clément's film is that while little Paulette (the remarkable Brigitte Fossey, five years old when the film was shot) is a completely innocent victim, losing her refugee parents to strafing German planes, her rescuers, the rural Dolle family, are something else. M. Dolle refuses to take Paulette in until he realizes that the neighbors they're feuding with are likely to win some kind of service medal if they take her in first. Bickering among themselves and cynical of the French army's effort against the invading Germans, the Dolles are not your lovable peasant types. Paulette forms a bond with ten-year-old Michel (Georges Poujouly), and they lay out an animal cemetery in an abandoned mill; it's their way of dealing with ever-present death, but also Michel's means of escaping the casual brutality and ignorance of his family. Winner of the Best Foreign Language Film prize from the New York Film Critics Circle, and an honorary Oscar.

DR8, DR12, DR38, DR41

Goes well with: *Au Revoir, les Enfants*

FORGOTTEN SILVER

New Zealand   1996   C/B&W   53 min.   NR   Comedy
Dir: Costa Botes and Peter Jackson
C: Sam Neill, Leonard Maltin, Harvey Weinstein, John O'Shea

If you've never heard of New Zealand silent filmmaker Colin McKenzie and his lost biblical epic *Salome,* don't go scrambling for your copy of *The Film Encyclopedia* or clicking on the Internet Movie Database. McKenzie is a fictional character, created by writers Peter Jackson and Costa Botes for this spot-on mockumentary, originally shown on New Zealand television. Botes and Jackson tell McKenzie's story through faux archival footage interlaced with straight-faced interviews with the likes of actor Sam Neill, film historian Leonard Maltin, and Hollywood mogul Harvey Weinstein. The film's modest length is just right to sustain this joke, which is to film history what *This Is Spinal Tap* is to rock and roll.

⊙**DVD:** Includes interviews with Jackson, Botes, cast, and crew; special effects shots.

CO10, CO12

Goes well with: *Waiting for Guffman*

42 UP

ESSENTIAL

U.K.   1999   C/B&W   134 min.   NR   Documentary
Dir: Michael Apted

Michael Apted's provocative and affecting documentary series began in 1964 with the release of *7 Up,* when he assisted director Paul Almond in gathering a group of thirteen British schoolchildren to ask them about their lives and their futures. Apted took over the task of checking on the subjects every seven years to see how they were progressing in life. Only *28 Up* (which I haven't seen), *35 Up,* and *42 Up* are available on video, and only *42 Up* is on DVD. The later chapters offer plenty of clips from the earlier ones to allow you to familiarize yourself with the cast. At 42, most are settled in fairly conventional lives, some are on second marriages, but given the opportunity to reflect on what they've achieved (and haven't), each rises to the occasion with thoughtful observations. Two subjects declined to appear in *35 Up:* Symon (the only black person) and Charles (who produces documentaries for TV—does he know something from his job?). For *42 Up* Charles is still missing, but Symon is back, with a new wife and son. The most memorable Up-er continues to be Neil, who was homeless in Scotland at 28 and living in public housing on one of the Shetland Islands at 35. However, at 42, he is back in London, a two-time elected councilman in his Hackney neighborhood. He still lives on public assistance, but his struggles to reenter society are symbolized by his friendship with one of the other subjects, Bruce, an idealistic math teacher recently married for the first time. Apted wraps up this entry with questions about class and how being in the films has affected the participants' lives.

⊙**DVD:** Includes audio commentary by Michael Apted.
DO7
Goes well with: *35 Up*

THE FOUR HUNDRED BLOWS

ESSENTIAL

France   1959   B&W   99 min.   NR   Drama
Dir: François Truffaut
C: Jean-Pierre Léaud, Patrick Auffray, Claire Maurier, Albert Rémy, Jeanne Moreau, Jean-Claude Brialy

The two great autobiographical films are Federico Fellini's *8½* and this, François Truffaut's amazing debut. The former is about a man wracked by indecision over his professional and personal life; *The Four Hundred Blows* is a fiercely honest film about a boy on the cusp of adolescence. At twelve, Antoine Doinel is, as my father used to say, a good boy but a poor boy—poor in emotional resources at a time in his life when he most needs them. His parents are so busy arguing that his problems are less than an afterthought to them; they're an annoyance. "Why do you do these things to me?" each keeps saying, as though Antoine's acting up in school or running afoul of shopkeepers and police is designed to hurt them. Antoine has few friends, so he retreats onto the streets of Paris and into its movie theaters, just as the young Truffaut did. Even if the film's details don't always match those of Truffaut's youth, the pain and humiliation Antoine experiences is by all accounts a perfect match to that of his creator's youth. Jean-Pierre Léaud played Doinel here and in four subsequent features directed or codirected by Truffaut, but their first collaboration is still their best.

⊙**DVD:** Two editions: Criterion (out of print) contains audio commentary by Professor Brian Stonehill, Robert Lachenay, and cowriter Marcel Moussey. Winstar edition contains audio commentary by Glenn Kinney.

DR3, DR11, DR41, XT7
Goes well with: *La Promesse*

4 LITTLE GIRLS
U.S.   1997   C/B&W   102 min.   NR   Documentary
Dir: Spike Lee

Spike Lee's documentary, made for HBO and given a limited theatrical release, has its roots in his student filmmaking days at New York University, when he determined to make a documentary about the September 1963 bombing of a black church in Birmingham, Alabama, that took the lives of four adolescent girls. Not until he had established himself as this country's premier African American filmmaker—and enough time had passed for the families of the girls to feel they were ready to cooperate—could Lee realize his dream. This is a straightforward document; Lee understands that to embellish the story would not be showing it the proper respect. All of the interviews, with family, friends, and a lawyer whose efforts to bring one of the perpetrators to justice finally bore fruit over thirty years after the crime, are exceptionally moving, but it's the footage from that time, when it took such a heinous crime to rally a nation to the cause of civil rights, that most effectively conveys the ability of this story to move us forty years after the fact.

⊙**DVD**

DO2, DO3

Goes well with: *Get on the Bus*

THE FOUR MUSKETEERS

U.S.   1974   C   108 min.   R   Action-Adventure

Dir: Richard Lester

C: Oliver Reed, Raquel Welch, Richard Chamberlain, Frank Finlay, Michael York, Christopher Lee, Jean-Pierre Cassel, Geraldine Chaplin, Faye Dunaway, Charlton Heston, Roy Kinnear

It's the first and reportedly only instance of a filmmaking team (producers Alexander and Ilya Salkind and director Richard Lester) making two films for the price of one. The Salkinds and Lester filmed a very lengthy adaptation (by George MacDonald Fraser) of the Dumas classic and then—much to the surprise of the cast—released the story in two parts. Needless to say, lawsuits ensued—but they weren't over the quality of the films, which are as good a pair of swashbucklers as you'll ever see, full of marvelously staged physical action, throwaway gags, and knowing commentary on the politics of the era. Lester understood that the Dumas material could be treated with a certain lightness (which predominates in the first film, *The Three Musketeers*), but that it was also a serious story about honor, betrayal, and loyalty (and those themes are explored here). Here's one example where everyone in the cast (and it's a sensational one, from Oliver Reed as a brooding Athos down to the great comic actor Roy Kinnear as the bumbling manservant Planchet) is back for the sequel.

⊙**DVD**

AC8, CO6, DR24, DR25

Goes well with: *The Three Musketeers*

FOUR WEDDINGS AND A FUNERAL

ESSENTIAL

U.K.   1994   C   117 min.   R   Comedy

Dir: Mike Newell

C: Hugh Grant, Andie MacDowell, Kristin Scott Thomas, Simon Callow, Rowan Atkinson, James Fleet, John Hannah, Charlotte Coleman, Corin Redgrave

The pursuit is everything in any good romantic comedy; after all, it's not much fun watching a couple meet and instantly fall in love to live happily ever after. Richard Curtis's screenplay for this 1994 hit is textbook stuff, starting with the title, which sets up the five occasions on which our couple encounter each other. Hugh Grant plays a well-meaning young man, smart but slightly ill at ease in any social occasion that involves anyone other than his close cadre of friends. The other half of this dynamic duo is American actress Andie MacDowell, an actress who can be sensational with the right script (as here and in *sex, lies and videotape*). The film also benefits enormously from a good supporting cast, led by the sad-eyed Kristin Scott Thomas, who's sure that she and Hugh are meant for each other. She and his other pals form a witty Greek chorus for the romance unfolding before them.

⊙**DVD**

CO9

Goes well with: *Notting Hill*

THE FOURTH MAN

Netherlands   1983   C   104 min.   NR   Drama

Dir: Paul Verhoeven

C: Jeroen Krabbé, Renée Soutendijk, Thom Hoffman

Dutch director Paul Verhoeven got the attention of American filmgoers with this outrageously sexy thriller that presaged his most notorious Hollywood project, *Basic Instinct.* In both films, a man in sexual thrall to a woman has to wonder if she's really a killer. Jeroen Krabbé plays a poet who is ambivalent about his new lover (Renée Soutendijk) in more ways than one: he's bisexual and attracted to her current lover as well. Unlike the basically tawdry *Instinct,* this film has a sense of humor about its main character's confusions and suspicions.

⊙**DVD:** Includes audio commentary by Paul Verhoeven and storyboards.

DR19, DR33, TH7

Goes well with: *Pandora's Box*

FROM DUSK TILL DAWN

U.S.   1996   C   108 min.   R   Horror

Dir: Robert Rodriguez

C: Harvey Keitel, George Clooney, Quentin Tarantino, Juliette Lewis, Salma Hayek, Cheech Marin, Tom Savini, Fred Williamson, John Saxon, Kelly Preston, Ernest Liu

Not on any critic's top ten, and unlikely to be discussed in polite circles, *From Dusk till Dawn* is a guilty pleasure par excellence. For the first hour or so, it comes off as just another road picture about two escaped convict brothers (George Clooney and Quentin Tarantino) using a family (Harvey Keitel, Juliette Lewis, and Ernest Liu) and their RV to escape a botched holdup. Tarantino's script is functionally gritty, with the brothers exchanging unpleasantries with the religious Keitel on their way to a rendezvous at a notorious Mexican bar called the Titty Twister. Unbeknownst to all concerned, the bar is a front for a gang of vampire strippers, and the action that ensues in the film's final half hour is mind-boggling in its relentless fury. If you'd like to take a break from watching Jane Austen adaptations or Antonioni studies of modern alienation, you've come to the right place. The special-effects makeup is by Tom Savini, who did the honors for George Romero's *Night of the Living Dead* series.

⊙**DVD**
FA9
Goes well with: *Dawn of the Dead*

THE FULL MONTY
U.K./U.S.   1997   C   95 min.   R   Comedy
Dir: Peter Cattaneo
C: Robert Carlyle, Tom Wilkinson, Mark Addy, Lesley Sharp, Emily
   Woof, Steve Huison
The angry young men who inhabited the British cinema of the early 1960s, railing against the injustices against the working classes, have been replaced by a generation of, um, male strippers dancing to Donna Summer. Not a very pretty sight, especially when said strippers sport the kind of bodies built in pubs rather than health clubs. Simon Beaufoy's screenplay cleverly backs his desperate characters (led by Robert Carlyle, the Steve Buscemi of British film) into their show-biz careers. It's hard to imagine American working-class joes with this kind of let-it-all-hang-out attitude; British blue-collar pride may be bowed but it's not broken, and its sense of humor is also intact. The film's original musical score won an Oscar.

⊙**DVD**
CO8, CO10
Goes well with: *The Commitments*

FUN

U.S. 1993 C 105 min. NR Drama
Dir: Rafal Zielinski
C: Alicia Witt, Renée Humphrey, William R. Moses, Leslie Hope

Bored Teens on a Crime Spree. Ho-hum, what else is new? But look here, these kids are a pair of girls with no criminal records, and they weren't just shoplifting at the 7-11—they murdered an old woman who let them into her home out of nothing more than kindness. James Bosley's script, adapted from his play, breaks up the events of this disquieting tale into jagged chunks; as the film begins, Bonnie (Alicia Witt) and Hillary (Renée Humphrey) are already in detention and being interviewed by a sympathetic counselor (Leslie Hope) and a skeptical journalist (William R. Moses). The story is told in flashbacks, presumably showing what a stagebound play could not. Those who would like to use this story to decry the decline of contemporary America should note the similarities between the events and characters of *Fun* and those of Peter Jackson's equally disturbing *Heavenly Creatures,* based on a true story that took place half a world away (in New Zealand) and nearly fifty years ago. The Sundance festival gave *Fun* a Special Jury Recognition Prize for Witt's and Humphrey's performances.

DR6, DR12, DR20, DR27, DR41
Goes well with: *Heavenly Creatures*

THE FUNERAL

Japan 1984 C 124 min. NR Comedy
Dir: Juzo Itami
C: Nobuko Miyamoto, Tsutomu Yamazaki, Kin Sugai, Ichiro Zaitsu

Juzo Itami's debut film is an odd mixture of black humor and stonefaced drama, reportedly inspired by his experiences with his father-in-law's funeral. Tsutomu Yamazaki and Nobuko Miyamoto play a married couple who work in TV commercials; they're called away from a shoot by the death of her father. In the three days that follow, the bills steadily mount, uninvited guests create scenes (an old flame of Yamazaki's character won't leave him alone until they have clandestine sex in the woods), relatives arrive and spend half the night drinking, and the kids won't sit still. Itami pokes fun at the Japanese observance of ritual by showing his couple watch a home video, *The ABCs of a Funeral,* to learn the correct way to accept condolences, even when you're overcome with grief. The film's comic tone is set almost immediately by the actor who plays the funeral director; he's a dead ringer for Jonathan Winters.

⊙**DVD**

CO3, CO8

Goes well with: *Shall We Dance?*

FUNNY BONES

U.K./U.S. 1995 C 126 min. R Comedy

Dir: Peter Chelsom

C: Oliver Platt, Lee Evans, Richard Griffiths, Leslie Caron, Jerry Lewis, Oliver Reed

Living in the shadow of a show-biz parent was never more painful than in Peter Chelsom's remarkable comedy. Oliver Platt plays a stand-up comedian whose Vegas debut is greeted with stunned silence, even from his old man (Jerry Lewis), a famous comic. Platt retreats to his father's native England to lick his wounds and try to learn, at a seaside resort where his dad got his own start, just what it takes to make people laugh. There, he discovers an amazing three-man comedy team, two geezers and an elastic-limbed young man (Lee Evans) whose odd act has a connection to his father. It's a wonderfully eccentric companion to Chelsom's first film, *Hear My Song*, which was about a show-biz quest, though of a more conventional nature. Platt is one of those dependable character actors who can shine in the spotlight with the right material, and he's got it here. Lewis gets a chance, as in Martin Scorsese's *King of Comedy*, to play an entertainer with a grand sense of his own legend.

CO3, CO10

Goes well with: *Hear My Song*

G

GALLIPOLI

Australia 1981 C 110 min. PG Drama
Dir: Peter Weir
C: Mark Lee, Mel Gibson, Bill Kerr, Robert Grubb

World War I still occupies a special place in the hearts of many Australians, long after its veterans have died, because it was the country's debut on the world stage. (Australia did not become a federation until the turn of the century.) Plus, Australians' longtime resentment of their British colonial masters found a perfect flash point in the 1915 battle on the Gallipoli peninsula in Turkey, where thousands of Australian soldiers needlessly died due to questionable tactics by British officers. Peter Weir's film is that rare document that can be taken as both a call to the glory of battle and an antiwar statement; its young men (personified by criminally handsome leads Mel Gibson and Mark Lee) are seen as only so much cannon fodder by commanders too proud to admit their incompetence. The use of Albinoni's "Adagio" brilliantly underscores the emotional devastation of the battle.

⊙**DVD:** Includes interview with Peter Weir.

DR37

Goes well with: *"Breaker" Morant*

THE GARDEN OF THE FINZI-CONTINIS

ESSENTIAL

Italy/West Germany 1971 C 95 min. R Drama
Dir: Vittorio De Sica
C: Dominique Sanda, Lino Capolicchio, Helmut Berger, Fabio Testi, Romolo Valli

The power of money to act as insulation from harsh realities is the theme of Vittorio De Sica's brilliant portrait of a wealthy Italian family of Jews who don't believe that the persecution of their people will affect them. Adapted from an autobiographical novel by Giorgio Bassani, *Garden* takes place between 1938 and 1943, when even the most privileged of families felt the sting of anti-Semitism. The story is told through the eyes of Giorgio (Lino Capolicchio), a middle-class Jew who loves the aristocratic Micol (Dominique Sanda), daughter of the Finzi-Continis. The dreamy aura of the film, most of it taking place during the lush summer months, almost lulls us into thinking, like the Finzi-Continis, that the approaching storm of deportation will somehow veer around their lovely walled garden. *Garden* won the Academy Award for Best Foreign Language Film.

⊙**DVD**

DR5, DR11, DR28, DR38

Goes well with: *Rules of the Game*

GAS FOOD LODGING

U.S.   1992   C   101 min.   R   Drama

Dir: Allison Anders

C: Brooke Adams, Ione Skye, Fairuza Balk, James Brolin, Robert Knepper, Donovan Leitch

A trio of women—a truck-stop waitress and her two adolescent daughters—are the focus of Allison Anders's breakthrough film, which offers fresh insights into the familiar story of the single mom trying to make ends meet and keep her kids out of trouble. Brooke Adams, persuasively worn down but resilient, is the mom who's stuck in a New Mexico trailer park with a dead-end job, her hopes riding on her two girls, played by Ione Skye and Fairuza Balk. Skye is the cynical older daughter whose determination not to be like her mom gets undercut by her experimentation with sex. Balk is the younger, dreamier kid who is sure there must some way out of here, even if it's only through her imagination. As the wayward husband/father to this family on the verge of nuclear meltdown, James Brolin is convincing as a onetime cowboy stud whose better days are behind him. Anders won Best New Director from the New York Film Critics Circle, while Balk picked up the Best Female Lead award from the Independent Spirit Awards.

DR11, DR34, DR39, DR41

Goes well with: *Out of the Blue*

GATES OF HEAVEN

U.S. 1978 C 85 min. NR Documentary

Dir: Errol Morris

A documentary about pet cemeteries could be the occasion for ninety minutes of cheap jokes at the expense of people who fret over headstones for their toy poodles. What makes Errol Morris's film so unexpectedly moving is the filmmaker's uncanny ability to give these people their due without patronizing them. In documenting the closing of one San Francisco–area cemetery and the transfer of its occupants to another, it successfully dramatizes the emotional bonds people have with their pets. But it never loses perspective on the enormous amount of time and money being spent on interring dead animals. Morris lets his subjects tell the story; he's averse to knowing voice-overs that explain too much. It's possible to see the film as a commentary on our misplaced priorities for humans as well. Morris's camera never blinks, and, more important, it never winks.

DO7, DO11

Goes well with: *Fast, Cheap & Out of Control*

THE GENERAL

Ireland/U.K. 1998 B&W 124 min. R Drama

Dir: John Boorman

C: Brendan Gleeson, Jon Voight, Adrian Dunbar, Sean McGinley, Maria Doyle Kennedy, Angeline Ball, Eamonn Owens

Not to be confused with the magnificent Buster Keaton silent film, *The General* is a stunning portrait of a man undone by his own sense of invulnerability. Martin Cahill, a Dublin criminal, was a larger-than-life character whose gang pulled off both art heists and petty thefts, mostly at his own whim. Cahill continued to live in a working-class neighborhood, because, as the film suggests, he saw himself as a kind of Robin Hood, tweaking society's swells just for the sheer pleasure of getting away with it. His twisted sense of morality extended to his home life; he was married but publicly kept a second home with his wife's sister. Brendan Gleeson, slouching and shambling but with a violent gleam in his eyes, is an Irish Tony Soprano, and Jon Voight is marvelous as the cop who unsuccessfully tries to bring Cahill down. That job eventually falls to the IRA, an organization that tried to throw in with Cahill but did not take kindly to his suggestions to bugger off. See this film in a wide-screen version if you can. John Boorman was himself a victim of one of Cahill's burglaries.

⊙**DVD**

DR1, DR6, DR17, TH12

Goes well with: *The Long Good Friday*

GEORGY GIRL

U.K. 1966 B&W 100 min. NR Comedy

Dir: Silvio Narizzano

C: James Mason, Alan Bates, Lynn Redgrave, Charlotte Rampling, Bill Owen, Claire Kelly

1966 was a coming-out year for the Redgrave sisters. Vanessa was nominated for an Oscar for *Morgan!* and appeared in Michelangelo Antonioni's hip hit *Blowup*. Little sis Lynn also got an Oscar nomination, for playing the lead in this delightful Cinderella comedy. She's Georgy, the overweight roommate of the oh-so-slender Meredith (the stunning Charlotte Rampling). Meredith is the woman Georgy wants to be, and Meredith's wacky boyfriend, Jos (Alan Bates), is the man she wants. But there is a man in Georgy's life, too: James Leamington (James Mason), a wealthy middle-aged chap who also happens to employ Georgy's parents as his servants. The script (by Peter Nichols and Margaret Foster, from Foster's novel) sorts out these complications by offering up a series of unusual domestic arrangements until we reach a predictable and satisfying conclusion.

CO9, XT7

Goes well with: *Bridget Jones's Diary*

GERTRUD

Denmark 1964 B&W 116 min. NR Drama

Dir: Carl Theodor Dreyer

C: Nina Pens Rode, Bendt Rothe, Ebbe Rode, Baard Owe

Carl Theodor Dreyer's last film lacks the religious dimensions of his best-known work (*The Passion of Joan of Arc, Day of Wrath, Ordet*), but it is about a spiritual quest. Gertrud, a woman in her forties, is desired by three men: Gustav, her lawyer husband; Erland, her younger lover, a pianist; and Gabriel, a poet and her former lover. The problem with all of them is summed up by Gabriel in a scrap-paper note Gertrud once found: "A woman's love and a man's work are mortal enemies." There's no surprise in how Gertrud resolves her dilemma, but there's plenty of pleasure for viewers as we watch her work things through. Dreyer's spare sets and minimal editing (he lets the camera follow people through a scene, or pans back and forth between two characters) force you to concentrate on the faces, the words, the slightest movements as signals of emotional distress.

⊙**DVD:** Available in a box set with *Day of Wrath* and *Ordet,* including a 1995 documentary on Carl Dreyer.

DR24, DR39

Goes well with: *The House of Mirth*

GET ON THE BUS

U.S. 1996 C 120 min. R Drama

Dir: Spike Lee

C: Ossie Davis, Charles S. Dutton, Andre Braugher, De'aundre Bonds, Albert Hall, Roger Guenveur Smith, Isaiah Washington, Thomas Jefferson Byrd, Richard Belzer, Gabriel Casseus

Financed by fifteen African American celebrities (among them Danny Glover, Will Smith, and Wesley Snipes), Spike Lee's story of the Million Man March is a low-budget labor of love that deserved a much better fate at the box office. Viewers fearful that Lee would use the occasion to climb on a soapbox and even offer a sympathetic treatment of the march's organizer Louis Farrakhan were mistaken on both counts. The film is about a journey to the march, with a busload of men traveling from Los Angeles to Washington, D.C. Even though Reggie Rock Bythewood's script insists that the passenger list has to resemble a Whitman's Sampler of the community (the actor, the ex-con and his son, the gay couple, the conservative Republican, the old man, etc.), that conceit works out fine. Over the course of the trip, every character's story is sketched in economically, and there is plenty of interaction among them—these guys don't agree on much beyond the fact that black men need to stand together and literally be counted. The magnetic Andre Braugher, Ossie Davis (a Spike Lee regular), and Roger Guenveur Smith are the standouts in a first-rate ensemble cast; Richard Belzer is very funny as the white man at the front of the bus, the driver who gets his walking papers midtrip.

⊙**DVD:** Includes audio commentary by Spike Lee.

DR28, XT5

Goes well with: *School Daze*

GHOST DOG: THE WAY OF THE SAMURAI
U.S./France/Germany/Japan   1999   C   116 min.   R   Drama
Dir: Jim Jarmusch
C: Forest Whitaker, John Tormey, Cliff Gorman, Henry Silva

You've been given a job as a favor by someone to whom you owe a debt, and it's a job you do well, but it's also nasty work, so how do you justify your existence? If you're a black hit man named Dog, whose life was saved by a Mafia boss and who now works for the mob as a hitman, you adhere to a code of ethics based on the ancient Japanese warriors that Toshiro Mifune played in so many great action movies. Forest Whitaker is the sad-eyed Dog in writer-director Jim Jarmusch's contemplative, wry, and sometimes violent story set in a New Jersey city that closely resembles Jarmusch's hometown of Akron, Ohio, with its crumbling old buildings and neighborhood taverns. As in his best films, Jarmusch's mix of deadpan humor and ruminations on weighty matters invites repeat viewings.

⊙**DVD:** Includes deleted footage; "making of" featurette; music video; isolated music score.

DR6, DR21, DR36, TH9
Goes well with: *The American Friend*

GHOST WORLD
ESSENTIAL

U.S./U.K.   2001   C   111 min.   R   Comedy-Drama
Dir: Terry Zwigoff
C: Thora Birch, Scarlett Johansson, Steve Buscemi, Brad Renfro, Illeana Douglas, Bob Balaban, Teri Garr

Is it possible for a satire to be melancholy? That's the strange and wonderful achievement of this adaptation of Daniel Clowes's comic book series. The film follows the adventures of Enid, a girl caught in what Clowes calls the "magic time" between the end of high school and the beginnings of college or a job. Enid (Thora Birch) and her best friend Becky (Scarlett Johansson) aren't going to college, but there is this thing about getting a job, at least for Enid, who wears Buddy Holly–style horn-rims and a so-what expression. While Becky works at a coffee shop, Enid takes on the unpaid job of finding a woman for Seymour (Steve Buscemi), a collector of rare 78s who admits that he "doesn't relate to 99 percent of society." Director Terry Zwigoff (who cowrote the script with Clowes) accurately captures the sad desperation of these characters. This is a very funny film, to be sure, but it's also a very sobering look at people out of step with the world at large. Buscemi won Best Supporting Actor from the New York Film Critics Circle.

⊙**DVD:** Includes "making of" featurette; deleted/alternate footage; music video.

CO2, CO5, DR21, DR41

Goes well with: *Crumb*

GIMME SHELTER

ESSENTIAL

U.S.   1970   C   91 min.   R   Documentary
Dir: Albert Maysles, David Maysles, and Charlotte Zwerin
C: The Rolling Stones, Melvin Belli

In 1969, pioneering documentary filmmakers Albert and David Maysles wanted to make a documentary about Woodstock; they lost the rights, however, and consoled themselves with permission to film the Rolling Stones' U.S. tour later that same year. Inspired by the success of Woodstock and by their own free concert the month before Woodstock in London's Hyde Park, the Stones planned another free show to wrap up their tour, in December at the Altamont Speedway, near San Francisco. The peaceful vibes that attended Woodstock were nowhere near Altamont, and the Maysles' cameras captured scenes right out of Bosch. It might have made for great material for the bad boy Stones, except it was all too true and gruesomely violent. The planning for the concert had been helter-skelter at best, and the topper was that security was provided by the Hell's Angels. A man named Meredith Hunter who approached the stage flashing a gun during the Stones' set was stabbed by several zealous Angels, and it's all here in living color. The film's most chilling moments take place in the Maysles' editing room, with Mick Jagger watching the murder over and over, entranced (as are we) by the sheer stupidity of the tragedy.

⊙**DVD:** Includes footage censored from original release; audio commentary by Albert Maysles and Charlotte Zwerin; outtakes; restoration demonstration.

DO2, DO5

Goes well with: *One Day in September*

GIRL ON THE BRIDGE

France 1999 C 92 min. R Drama

Dir: Patrice Leconte

C: Daniel Auteuil, Vanessa Paradis, Demetre Georgalas, Bertie Cortez

Knife thrower in need of target meets suicidal young woman about to leap from bridge; love ensues. Ah, if it were only that easy. Patrice Leconte's film is a delirious story of the redemptive power of love and the difficulties inherent in any show-biz relationship. Gabor (Daniel Auteuil) is attracted to Adele (Vanessa Paradis), but he's so respectful of her fragility that he underplays his hand; she's in need of someone who will take charge of more than just her résumé. Jean-Marie Dreujou's camera swoops and glides around these two erstwhile soul mates, as the act goes on the road and then on to the high seas as a cruise ship attraction.

DR4, DR18, XT5

Goes well with: *The Hairdresser's Husband*

GIRLFIGHT

U.S. 2000 C 110 min. R Drama

Dir: Karyn Kusama

C: Michelle Rodriguez, Jaime Tirelli, Paul Calderon, Santiago Douglas, Ray Santiago, John Sayles

You don't have to like boxing to like this story of a Latina high school student who channels her anger by training to be a fighter at a run-down Brooklyn gym. Played by Michelle Rodriguez, Diana Guzman has a glower that would do Sonny Liston proud and just enough self-awareness to understand that the discipline of a physical regimen would give her a better chance at the success her embittered widowed father, Sandro (Paul Calderon), never enjoyed. Their strained relationship fuels her determination, and she's lucky to have a trainer, Hector (Jaime Tirelli), who drops his resistance to her working out in his gym as soon as he senses her determination. The story almost takes a fatal turn when Diana falls for another fighter, Adrian (Santiago Douglas), and then has to face him in the ring, but writer-director Karyn Kusama has built up so much goodwill by that point that she can be forgiven for irony overkill. Yes, that is coexecutive producer John Sayles as Mr. Coolidge, one of Diana's teachers. Rodriguez won the Debut Performance prize from the Independent Spirit Awards; the film won the Grand Jury Award (Dramatic) and Director's Award (Dramatic) at Sundance.

⊙**DVD**
DR11, DR35, DR39
Goes well with: *The Governess*

GO

ESSENTIAL

U.S.   1999   C   103 min.   R   Drama
Dir: Doug Liman
C: Sarah Polley, Katie Holmes, Desmond Askew, Taye Diggs, William
Fichtner, J. E. Freeman, Jane Krakowski, Jay Mohr, Scott Wolf

Working with the same kind of time-fractured intertwined-narrative style as *Pulp Fiction,* director-cameraman Doug Liman's propulsive twenty-four hours in the lives of several Southern California young people is bracing stuff. The focus is on Ronna (Sarah Polley), who agrees to work Christmas Eve so a fellow grocery store checkout clerk (Desmond Askew) can go to Vegas with his buddies. Ronna also gets involved with two actors (Jay Mohr and Scott Wolf) and a drug deal. The film's funniest scene involves a holiday dinner hosted by a very strange cop (William Fichtner) and his wife. Just to tantalize us, Liman and screenwriter John August suggest alternative possibilities to their narratives as well. *Go* doesn't give you time to think about what screwups most of its characters are, and Liman keeps the tone consistently light, so that even in its scariest moment (a hit-and-run in a parking lot at a rave concert), you have the feeling that things are going to work out. And they do. Mostly.

⊙**DVD:** Includes "making of" featurette; audio commentary by Doug Liman; deleted scenes.

DR10, DR36, DR41, XT4
Goes well with: *Trainspotting*

THE GO-BETWEEN

U.K.   1971   C   116 min.   PG   Drama
Dir: Joseph Losey
C: Julie Christie, Alan Bates, Dominic Guard, Margaret Leighton,
Michael Gough, Michael Redgrave, Edward Fox

The third collaboration between director Joseph Losey and writer Harold Pinter (following *The Servant* and *Accident*) is a marvelously evocative adaptation of a story by L. P. Hartley. A middle-aged man recalls a summer in his youth when he served as a messenger between an aristocratic woman (Julie Christie) and her secret lover (Alan Bates), a farmer whom her family would scorn if they knew of her affection for him. We know it's only a matter of time before the lovers are discovered, but before they are, we're totally in sync with the boy and his vicarious thrill at being party to a secret. The story is told in flashback, with Michael Redgrave playing the grown-up messenger, and the story ends on a bittersweet coda. Christie and Bates were a terrific romantic team in *Far from the Madding Crowd,* and they're just as good here.

DR5, DR19, DR29, DR41, XT4

Goes well with: *Far from the Madding Crowd*

GODS AND MONSTERS

ESSENTIAL

U.S./U.K.   1998   C   105 min.   R   Drama
Dir: Bill Condon
C: Ian McKellen, Brendan Fraser, Lynn Redgrave, Lolita Davidovich, David Dukes, Kevin J. O'Connor, Jack Betts, Rosalind Ayres

Director James Whale's output during the 1930s was slim but memorable, with *Frankenstein, Bride of Frankenstein, The Old Dark House,* and *The Invisible Man* still capable of chilling and amusing audiences today. However, Whale's abrupt retirement in the early 1940s (allegedly to take up painting) and his mysterious death in a swimming pool in 1957 have inspired plenty of speculation, most of it focusing on his homosexuality. Christopher Bram's excellent novel about Whale's final days, *Father of Frankenstein,* was faithfully adapted by writer-director Bill Condon, whose script won an Academy Award. The always brilliant Ian McKellen plays Whale, and Brendan Fraser (taking a respite from doofus comedies) is the gardener in whom Whale takes an interest. Whale isn't portrayed as a randy old predator, but he's clearly a man with regrets for missed opportunities. The film's highlight is a party at the home of George Cukor, a director who managed to sustain his own career despite common knowledge of his homosexuality; the actors portraying Boris Karloff (Jack Betts) and Elsa Lanchester (Rosalind Ayres), who were the stars of *Bride of Frankenstein,* are uncanny lookalikes.

⊙**DVD:** Includes audio commentary by Bill Condon and featurette: "The World of Gods and Monsters: A Journey with James Whale."

DR12, DR17, DR19

Goes well with: *Apartment Zero*

THE GOOD, THE BAD AND THE UGLY

ESSENTIAL

Italy/Spain   1966   C   161 min.   R   Action-Adventure
Dir: Sergio Leone
C: Clint Eastwood, Lee Van Cleef, Eli Wallach, Rada Rassimov

The final film in the "Dollars" trilogy from Sergio Leone and Clint Eastwood is also the best, and on the short list of the best Westerns ever made. Eastwood's Man with No Name again encounters bounty hunter Col. Douglas Mortimer (Lee Van Cleef, reprising his role from *For a Few Dollars More*). Along with a lowlife (Eli Wallach, reprising his *Magnificent Seven* bandido shtick), each man possesses partial information on the location of a treasure chest. The story takes place during the American Civil War, so the title characters spend a lot of their time working their way through and around battle zones. Leone's tongue-in-cheek approach doesn't undercut the thrills, and the final showdown (which *must* be seen in wide-screen) is the last word in Mexican stand-offs. Flamboyant, operatic, and a whole lot of fun.

⊙**DVD:** Includes fourteen minutes of footage unreleased in the U.S. AC6, XT8
Goes well with: *The Killer*

GOSFORD PARK

ESSENTIAL

U.K./U.S./Italy/Germany   2001   C   137 min.   R   Comedy-Drama
Dir: Robert Altman
C: Michael Gambon, Kristin Scott Thomas, Maggie Smith, Charles Dance, Jeremy Northam, Bob Balaban, Alan Bates, Helen Mirren, Eileen Atkins, Derek Jacobi, Emily Watson, Richard E. Grant, Kelly Macdonald, Clive Owen, Ryan Phillippe, Stephen Fry

Proving again that he is the undisputed master of multistoried filmmaking, Robert Altman deftly navigates the rooms and, most important, the stairways of an English country estate for a unique comedy-drama of class rituals disguised as a whodunit. Based on an idea by Altman and actor Bob Balaban and fleshed out by actor-writer Julian Fellowes, *Gosford Park* is set in 1932 during a shooting party weekend reminiscent of Jean Renoir's *Rules of the Game.* The guests assemble, the servants bustle, and intrigue abounds, both upstairs and downstairs and sometimes in between. It may take you more than one viewing to get all of the characters sorted out, but it's not hard work at all, thanks to Fellowes's witty script and performances by the cream of the British acting ranks. Among the standouts are Emily Watson as an impetuous maid, Helen Mirren and Eileen Atkins as a feuding pair of servants (yes, there is a definite pecking order downstairs as well), Clive Owen as a tight-lipped valet, Kelly Macdonald as a newly hired maid, Maggie Smith as her tart-tongued boss, and Jeremy Northam as the actor-singer Ivor Novello (in fact, in his evening clothes Northam looks more like Cary Grant). Altman's direction and Mirren's supporting performance (it's hard to figure out who the leads are here) were honored by the New York Film Critics Circle; Fellowes's screenplay won an Academy Award.

CO7, DR5, DR24

Goes well with: *Rules of the Game*

THE GOVERNESS

U.K.   1998   C   112 min.   R   Drama

Dir: Sandra Goldbacher

C: Minnie Driver, Tom Wilkinson, Florence Hoath, Jonathan Rhys-Meyers, Harriet Walter

A film with a lot on its plate, *The Governess* is a satisfying meal composed of generous helpings of illicit romance, the bitter fruits of anti-Semitism, professional exploitation, and a crash course in the early days of photography. Minnie Driver plays a young Jewish woman who escapes persecution in mid-nineteenth-century London for a job as a governess to an inventor and his family living on a remote Scottish island. Her employer (Tom Wilkinson) is dabbling in photography, and soon enough the governess is involved with him both professionally and romantically. Director Sandra Goldbacher's script makes Driver's predicaments (concealing her ethnic identity, concealing her affair, concealing her displeasure when she doesn't get credit for her ideas) believable and provocative.

⊙DVD

DR19, DR24, DR39

Goes well with: *Hester Street*

GRAND ILLUSION

ESSENTIAL

France   1937   B&W   117 min.   NR   Drama

Dir: Jean Renoir

C: Jean Gabin, Pierre Fresnay, Erich von Stroheim, [Marcel] Dalio, Dita Parlo

It's a working blueprint for an entire genre of films, and one of the great antiwar films as well. Jean Renoir's World War I drama, based on the exploits of a flyer comrade of Renoir's who escaped seven times from German captivity, has all the elements of the POW drama: the jaunty prisoners, the cultured commandant, the prisoners' theatrical presentation designed to boost the moral of the men, the cat-and-mouse games over package deliveries, and the inevitable escape attempts. Jean Gabin is common-man Marechal, Pierre Fresnay is the aristocratic Boeldieu, Dalio is the Jewish landowner Rosenthal, and Erich von Stroheim is the neck-braced von Rauffenstein, the German with a melancholy view of the world. ("I used to be a combatant," he complains, "now I'm a bureaucrat, a policeman.") The understanding between him and Boeldieu: This is, as Renoir himself described it, "a gentleman's war." Released on the eve of World War II, the film is almost nostalgic in its reverence for the grace of the officers, while conveniently ignoring the horror of the trenches and the poison gas attacks. Winner of the Best Foreign Language Film prize from the New York Film Critics Circle. Be sure to see the full-length version, best viewed on the excellent Criterion DVD release.

⊙**DVD:** Includes audio commentary by historian Peter Cowie; restoration demonstration; theatrical trailer, with Jean Renoir discussing his war experiences.

DR26, DR37

Goes well with: *The Bridge on the River Kwai*

GREAT EXPECTATIONS
U.K. 1946 B&W 118 min. NR Drama
Dir: David Lean
C: John Mills, Valerie Hobson, Bernard Miles, Francis L. Sullivan, Finlay Currie, Martita Hunt, Jean Simmons, Alec Guinness

David Lean's pair of Dickens films (this one and *Oliver Twist*) are, more than fifty years after their release, still models of filmmaking excellence. Opening with the justly celebrated graveyard scene with Pip and the convict Magwitch, *Great Expectations* fulfills all of our expectations for memorable characters and absorbing narrative. John Mills is the perfect adult Pip, and Jean Simmons is enchanting as Estella. Making his film debut as Herbert Pocket, Alec Guinness also began a long-running association with Lean. Photographed by Oscar winner Guy Green.

⊙**DVD**
DR5, DR18, DR29, DR41
Goes well with: *Oliver Twist*

THE GREY FOX

Canada   1982   C   92 min.   PG   Action-Adventure
Dir: Phillip Borsos
C: Richard Farnsworth, Jackie Burroughs, Wayne Robson, Ken Pogue

An amiable Western about Bill Miner, a true-life Canadian outlaw, *The Grey Fox* provided a rare starring role for former stuntman Richard Farnsworth, who had begun showing his face to the camera in the late 1970s in supporting roles. And what a wonderful face it is: At sixty-three years of age, Farnsworth's weathered mug, anchored by an almost dapper white mustache, makes him look like he stepped right out of a history textbook on the old west. *Fox* is a story of changing times for an outlaw, who goes into jail as a stagecoach robber and emerges thirty-three years later to find that trains are a bit harder to hold up. The best scene: Miner goes to an early motion-picture show and discovers that outlaws can live forever on the big screen.

AC6, DR14, DR21
Goes well with: *Things Change*

GREY GARDENS

U.S.   1976   C   95 min.   PG   Documentary
Dir: Ellen Hovde, Albert Maysles, David Maysles, Muffie Meyer, and
   Susan Froemke

The lifestyles of the rich and nearly famous. Filmmakers Albert and David Maysles pay their respects in an odd way to Edith Bouvier Beale (aged seventy-nine) and her daughter Edie (fifty-seven), who live in a condemned mansion in East Hampton, New York. Would we be interested in the Beales if they weren't, respectively, the aunt and cousin of Jacqueline Bouvier Onassis? Not likely; they would just come off as a couple of rich old eccentrics who have slid into embarrassing behavior. The Maysles may be commenting on America's insatiable appetite for anything connected to the Kennedy family and its branches—or they may just be wallowing in it. Given the serious nature of their other work, I prefer to think the former.

This is one of the Maysles brothers' strongest works because it goes well beyond the specificity of the celebrity connection to become a rich portrait of two women locked in the past: Edith in an idealized version of her marriage (which broke up over twenty years ago), Edie in a series of thwarted youthful romances. Edie, who moved in with her mother in 1952, wants to leave her but knows she can't, and the dance of love and regret and affection and recrimination that the two women perform over and over for the Maysles' camera is breathtakingly sad.

⊙**DVD**

DO4

Goes well with: *Salesman*

THE GRIFTERS

U.S.   1990   C   114 min.   R   Thriller

Dir: Stephen Frears

C: Anjelica Huston, John Cusack, Annette Bening, Pat Hingle, Henry Jones, J. T. Walsh, Charles Napier

The best movie versions of pulp writer Jim Thompson's novels (the first version of *The Getaway, Coup de Torchon*) reflect both his dim view of humanity and his dark sense of humor. *The Grifters,* adapted by Donald Westlake, a crime novelist with his own fine sense of dark humor, is a small step below the best of Thompson. It's about a trio of con artists, played by Anjelica Huston, John Cusack, and Annette Bening. Huston is Cusack's mother, Bening his would-be girlfriend, and the triangulation is as deliciously complicated as you might expect. The film's one weakness is Cusack, who talks a good con game but never seems as comfortable as a truly dishonest character as his female costars. Free bonus: Coproducer Martin Scorsese narrates. Huston and the film won Independent Spirit Awards.

⊙**DVD**

TH2, TH5, TH13

Goes well with: *House of Games*

H

THE HAIRDRESSER'S HUSBAND

France   1992   C   84 min.   R   Drama
Dir: Patrice Leconte
C: Jean Rochefort, Anna Galiena, Roland Bertin, Maurice Chevit

Like *Shampoo, The Hairdresser's Husband* answers the question "Can giving (or getting) a haircut be sexy?" with a resounding yes. Jean Rochefort plays Antoine, a man who recalls his first sexual awakening, when he was twelve years old, at the skilled hands of a buxom hairdresser. His ambition in life—to be the man who goes to bed every night with the hairdresser—is finally fulfilled forty years later when he meets Mathilde (Anna Galiena), who conveniently (1) is the only barber in her shop, (2) does only men's hair, and (3) is both lovely and available. After a brief, two-haircut courtship, they settle into a dreamlike marriage. Anyone surprised by the film's slow, subtle turn to darkness hasn't been observing the signals. Writer-director Patrice Leconte understands that this is novella-size material, and he wisely does not overextend the story, making its wrap-up, with a bittersweet final line, all the more satisfying.
DR18

Goes well with: *Girl on the Bridge*

HAIRSPRAY

ESSENTIAL

U.S.   1988   C   96 min.   PG   Comedy
Dir: John Waters
C: Sonny Bono, Ruth Brown, Divine, Colleen Fitzpatrick, Michael St. Gerard, Debbie Harry, Ricki Lake, Leslie Ann Powers, Jerry Stiller, Pia Zadora, Ric Ocasek

Baltimore filmmaker John Waters's breakthrough film is an affectionate piece of nostalgia about Charm City's teen dance TV shows of the 1950s. Waters wisely retains one very large collaborator from his early days: Divine, the three-hundred-pound transvestite, who here plays Edna Turnblad, the live-and-let-live mom of Tracy (played by Ricki Lake, before she slimmed down and got a talk show deal). Fans of Waters's earlier, cruder films, such as *Pink Flamingos,* complained that he sold out with a bigger budget and less edgy material; but like Dylan going electric, it's the same singer, but with a slightly different sound. Waters got to stock this film with some of his favorite pop culture icons, like Sonny Bono (between his gig as Cher's straight man and his gig as a congressman) and Pia Zadora. Lake and Divine are a marvelous team, and they're ably supported by Jerry Stiller as Mr. Turnblad, Bono and Debbie Harry as the obnoxious parents of Tracy's bitchy rival, and Miss Rhythm herself, singer Ruth Brown, as a record-store owner who loves to let her black and white customers dance to the latest tunes right in the store. Another plus: a soundtrack packed with semiobscure period tunes, including the short-lived dance craze "The Madison."

⊙**DVD:** Available in *John Waters Collection #1: Hairspray/Pecker.* Includes audio commentaries on this film by Waters and Ricki Lake.

CO5

Goes well with: *Cry-Baby*

HALLOWEEN

ESSENTIAL

U.S. 1978 C 91 min. R Horror

Dir: John Carpenter

C: Donald Pleasence, Jamie Lee Curtis, Nancy Loomis, P. J. Soles, Charles Cyphers

Spawning far too many sequels and way too many imitators, John Carpenter's spooky film about a seemingly indestructible masked killer is still a primer for getting the biggest bang for your buck. Carpenter tapped into a basic fear—your home turning into a house of horrors—with his tale of Michael Myers, an escaped mental patient whose murderous career began on Halloween night fifteen years before, when he was a little boy. The familiar critical interpretation that the killer punishes teens who have sex makes no sense, since his main target seems to be the virginal Laurie, played by newcomer Jamie Lee Curtis. Myers and his pursuer, Dr. Loomis, played by Donald Pleasence, are modern variations of the killing machine Cesare and his creator from *The Cabinet of Dr. Caligari*. Loomis didn't create Myers, but he had fifteen years to cure him, so he feels responsible for his still-murderous ways.

⊙**DVD**

FA7, TH16

Goes well with: *White of the Eye*

HAMLET (1948)

ESSENTIAL

U.K.   1948   B&W   153 min.   NR   Drama

Dir: Laurence Olivier

C: Laurence Olivier, Eileen Herlie, Basil Sydney, Felix Aylmer, Jean Simmons, Stanley Holloway, Peter Cushing

The virtues of Laurence Olivier's masterful version of Hamlet begin with the director and star himself. At the age of forty, he might have seemed too old to play the lead, but his Hamlet is less the petulant young man than the genuinely anguished adult. Even if Olivier and his colleagues didn't film the entire play (as Branagh did in the next entry), they bit off a two-and-a-half-hour chunk that is quite a satisfying portion. Jean Simmons is especially fine as Ophelia; though she was twenty-two years Olivier's junior in real life, they seem a perfect match here. As with his magnificent *Henry V*, Olivier opens up the play, shooting on location in Elsinore, Denmark, without losing sight of the fact that Shakespeare's matchless language is the true star of all his plays. Olivier's performance and the film both won Academy Awards.

⊙**DVD**

DR11, DR24, DR25, DR32

Goes well with: *Henry V* (1945)

HAMLET (1996)

U.S./U.K.   1996   C   242 min.   PG-13   Drama

Dir: Kenneth Branagh

C: Kenneth Branagh, Julie Christie, Derek Jacobi, Kate Winslet, Rufus Sewell, Richard Briers, Brian Blessed, Gérard Depardieu, Charlton Heston, Rosemary Harris, Jack Lemmon, Billy Crystal, Robin Williams, Richard Attenborough, John Gielgud, John Mills

Kenneth Branagh hasn't done a film of *Richard III* yet, but give him time. He has already given us versions of two of Laurence Olivier's three great Shakespeare screen adaptations, this one and *Henry V*. Branagh's decision to film the entire text of *Hamlet,* a first on the big screen, was a risky one, which he may have tried to offset by updating the story to the nineteenth century and by hiring an amazingly eclectic cast. His calculations don't always pay off, but the film looks so smashing (see it in widescreen for Alex Thomson's sharp 70mm images), you can forgive its lapses. And thanks to the miracle of home video, you can choose to watch the film in more digestible chunks over two or three sittings. Julie Christie as Gertrude, Derek Jacobi as Claudius, and Kate Winslet as Ophelia are standouts, and even Charlton Heston as the Player King fits right in. But Jack Lemmon is not up to his small role as Marcellus, and Billy Crystal and Robin Williams are distractions rather than additions. Branagh is a much more frantic Hamlet than we're used to; if the Danes had had Ritalin in the nineteenth century, Gertrude might have slipped him some. If Branagh interprets the nefarious Richard III with this kind of gusto, he won't just be over the top but out of the theater.

DR11, DR24, DR25, DR32

Goes well with: *Henry V* (1989)

A HANDFUL OF DUST

U.K.   1988   C   118 min.   PG   Drama

Dir: Charles Sturridge

C: James Wilby, Kristin Scott Thomas, Rupert Graves, Judi Dench, Anjelica Huston, Alec Guinness

Aside from spending a week with the magnificent TV miniseries *Brideshead Revisited,* your best shot at getting a heady dose of Evelyn Waugh on your TV screen (and in under two hours) is to rent this film. Director Charles Sturridge, who did the honors on *Brideshead,* collaborated with Tim Sullivan and Derek Granger on an adaptation of Waugh's 1934 satire of British society. Tony Last (James Wilby) is a well-meaning but naïve chap whose marriage to lovely but utterly ruthless Brenda (Kristin Scott Thomas) is a joke told behind his back everywhere they go. When Brenda sues him for divorce, Tony's response is not to start life over again among his so-called friends but to lose himself in the jungles of South America, where he finds someone who really does need him, though in a most unexpected way. Watch for Judi Dench and Anjelica Huston in small roles. On the basis of *Brideshead* and this film, which get both the letter and the wicked spirit of Waugh just right, Sturridge should be given the key to Waugh's library by a generous film producer.

DR5, DR29
Goes well with: *Angels and Insects*

HAPPINESS

ESSENTIAL

U.S. 1998 C 139 min. NR Comedy-Drama
Dir: Todd Solondz
C: Jane Adams, Jon Lovitz, Philip Seymour Hoffman, Dylan Baker, Lara Flynn Boyle, Cynthia Stevenson, Molly Shannon, Louise Lasser, Ben Gazzara, Camryn Manheim, Jared Harris, Elizabeth Ashley

It's a difficult film to recommend. After all, it's about three sisters, one (Jane Adams) who dumps a boyfriend who then commits suicide, another (Lara Flynn Boyle) who is the obsession of a neighbor (Philip Seymour Hoffman) who derives sexual pleasure from obscene phone calls, and a third (Cynthia Stevenson) who is unknowingly married to a pedophile. If you're still reading this entry, be assured that writer-director Todd Solondz steers us through some pretty rocky waters with a modicum of tact, and he manages to make nearly everyone (including the child molester, bravely played by Dylan Baker) objects of compassion rather than scorn or disgust. In fact, there are a lot of laughs, as there surely should be in a film called *Happiness;* but again, they are not at the expense of poor, deluded creatures we can look down upon just because they live in New Jersey.

⊙**DVD**
CO2, DR11, DR20, DR21
Goes well with: *Short Cuts*

A HARD DAY'S NIGHT

ESSENTIAL

U.K. 1964 B&W 85 min. G Musical
Dir: Richard Lester
C: John Lennon, Paul McCartney, George Harrison, Ringo Starr, Wilfrid Brambell, Norman Rossington, Victor Spinetti

It's a shame that not every great pop group gets the chance to make a movie as witty, inventive, and exhilarating as the Beatles did with writer Alun Owen and director Richard Lester. John, Paul, George, and Ringo acquit themselves quite well as actors—but then, they're essentially playing themselves in this day-in-the-life docudrama. There's a wisp of a plot, involving getting the Fab Four to a TV studio for a live show, but Owen and Lester are more interested in commenting on the vagaries of fame and pop trends (a fashion designer, not recognizing George, asks him questions about what's hot with today's kids and then dismisses his answer when they don't fit his agenda) and packing in musical numbers that, because there is hardly a story, have little to do with what's going on. The "Can't Buy Me Love" number, shot with the lads frolicking in an open field, recalls Lester's debut film, a short called "The Running Jumping & Standing Still Film" that is included on the DVD.

⊙**DVD:** Includes additional footage; interview with Richard Lester; early Lester short, "The Running Jumping & Standing Still Film."

CO10, MU2, XT7

Goes well with: *Help!*

HARD EIGHT

U.S.   1996   C   101 min.   R   Drama

Dir: Paul Thomas Anderson

C: Philip Baker Hall, John C. Reilly, Gwyneth Paltrow, Samuel L. Jackson, Philip Seymour Hoffman

In his debut feature, writer-director Paul Thomas Anderson was already displaying the triple-threat talents that marked his next two films, the independently produced *Boogie Nights* and the studio production *Magnolia*. Anderson writes wonderfully taut and tantalizingly enigmatic dialogue, he elicits top-notch work from his actors, and he has an unerring sense of where to put the camera (and when to move it) to get the most out of every scene. John C. Reilly and Philip Baker Hall (who have appeared in all three Anderson films) are, respectively, a young gambler down on his luck and a veteran of the tables who takes the kid under his wing. Gwyneth Paltrow, as a clueless waitress/hooker, and Samuel L. Jackson, as a small-time hood with big ambitions, complete the essentially four-character story. Best scene: Reilly describing how his pants caught on fire while he was waiting in line to see a movie.

⊙**DVD:** Special Edition contains audio commentary by Paul Thomas Anderson, cast, and crew; deleted footage; three Sundance Institute Filmmaker Lab scenes.

DR12, DR13, DR16

Goes well with: *Croupier*

HARD-BOILED

Hong Kong 1992 C 126 min. NR (R) Action-Adventure
Dir: John Woo
C: Chow Yun-Fat, Tony Leung, Teresa Mo, Philip Chan

Director John Woo's last Hong Kong–based film is a doozy. It's the familiar Woo story about twin sons of different mothers, with rogue cop (Chow Yun-Fat) facing off against an undercover man who moonlights as a hit man (Tony Leung). These guys understand each other all too well, but all the which-side-of-the-law-am-I-really-on dramatics are secondary to the action scenes. There are three set pieces that are staged as well as any you've ever seen: the opening shoot-out in a restaurant filled with live birds in cages, a gun battle in a warehouse involving nearly every wheeled vehicle except a tricycle, and the protracted finale, a siege in a hospital, much of which takes place in a maternity ward. No babies or birds were harmed during the making of this film, but lots of nameless extras do bite the dust in fairly spectacular fashion.

⊙**DVD:** Includes audio commentaries by John Woo, producer Terence Chang, writer Roger Avary, and critic Dave Kehr. DVD is unrated version.

AC1, AC5, XT6
Goes well with: *The Killer*

THE HARDER THEY COME

Jamaica 1973 C 103 min. R Drama
Dir: Perry Henzell
C: Jimmy Cliff, Janet Barkley, Carl Bradshaw, Ras Daniel Hartman

The movie that put reggae on the map and in the ears of American music lovers, *The Harder They Come* is a likably crude film about an erstwhile Jamaican pop star. He's frustrated with the practices of the music business, which only recognizes artists willing to slip extra money to promoters and disc jockeys, so he turns to a life of crime. Suddenly, he's a wanted man—both by the police and by record buyers, who are exposed to his music because disc jockeys are willing to play his songs now that he's notorious. Real-life reggae star Jimmy Cliff acquits himself well as an actor, and sings the title tune and "You Can Get It If You Really Want."

⊙**DVD:** Includes audio commentaries by Perry Henzell and Jimmy Cliff, and interview with Chris Blackwell, founder of Island Records.

DR6, DR23
Goes well with: *Payday*

HARLAN COUNTY, U.S.A.

ESSENTIAL

U.S.   1976   C   103 min.   PG   Documentary
Dir: Barbara Kopple

Fighting the good labor fight seems to be a story for history books, as strikers in almost any line of work, from professional athletes to air traffic controllers, are looked on as inconveniencing our lives rather than as fighting for a fair piece of the pie and decent working conditions. Barbara Kopple's Oscar-winning documentary focuses on Kentucky coal miners and their struggle against the Eastover Mining Company, a subsidiary of Duke Power, and it all seems like much longer ago than twenty-five years or so. The issues are simpler and the sides more clearly drawn here than in her next Oscar winner, *American Dream,* but that doesn't diminish the drama of a large company trying to take advantage of workers it suspects won't fight for their rights.

DO1

Goes well with: *American Dream*

THE HARMONISTS

Germany/Austria   1997   C   126 min.   R   Drama
Dir: Joseph Vilsmaier
C: Ben Becker, Heino Ferch, Ulrich Noethen, Heinrich Schafmeister,
   Max Tidof

They were a real singing group, formed in Germany in the 1920s by five singers and their pianist, who loved American popular music and transformed both American and German standards with their richly complex harmonizing. This dramatic recreation of their careers begins on a note of such optimism that you know there has to be trouble ahead, especially because three of the singers are Jewish. On a trip to New York in the mid-1930s, as this film shows, the group was divided about staying, some of its members convinced that the Nazis meant business and others not wanting to believe that the most popular singing group in Germany could be harassed. Like *Mephisto,* this is a superb dramatization of how performing artists can wrap themselves in a cocoon and ignore the political realities of their time. The musical numbers, and they are numerous, are sensational.

DR23, DR24, DR28
Goes well with: *Mephisto*

HEAR MY SONG

U.S./U.K.   1991   C   104 min.   R   Drama

Dir: Peter Chelsom

C: Ned Beatty, Adrian Dunbar, Shirley Anne Field, Tara Fitzgerald, David McCallum

A show-biz fable with some slight resemblance to actual events, *Hear My Song* is a genial British comedy about a nightclub owner and promoter who is too sharp for his own good. Adrian Dunbar (who cowrote the script with director Peter Chelsom) is Mickey, the man who promises the moon and then has to deliver to an outraged community and, more important, his put-upon girlfriend (Tara Fitzgerald) and her mum (Shirley Anne Field). Since the last "mystery artist" he hired turned out not to be famed tenor Josef Locke but an impostor, Mickey goes to Ireland in search of the reclusive Mr. Locke (Ned Beatty). Dunbar plays the kind of hustler you can love, and the finale, while totally predictable, is sure to bring a lump to the throat of any lover of great singing.

DR23

Goes well with: *Funny Bones*

HEARTLAND

U.S.   1979   C   96 min.   PG   Drama

Dir: Richard Pearce

C: Rip Torn, Conchata Ferrell, Barry Primus, Lilia Skala, Megan Folsom

In 1910, Wyoming was still a relatively unsettled area of the West; it had been a state for only twenty years, and the population was 145,000 souls, most of them scraping out a living on small ranches or farms or in newly opened coal mines. Elinore Randall Stewart was one of those souls, a single mother determined to try life on the frontier who hired herself out as a housekeeper to a bachelor rancher. Cinematographer-turned-director Richard Pearce and writer Beth Ferris do a lovely job in translating Stewart's diaries to film. Rather than hire some lovely starlet and dashing leading man, they chose two character actors, Conchata Ferrell and Rip Torn, for the leads, and what the film loses in glamour it more than makes up for in authenticity and true grit.

⊙**DVD:** Includes interviews with Beth Ferris and producer Annick Smith.

DR24, DR39

Goes well with: *The New Land*

HEATHERS

ESSENTIAL

U.S.   1989   C   102 min.   R   Comedy

Dir: Michael Lehmann

C: Winona Ryder, Christian Slater, Shannen Doherty, Lisanne Falk, Kim Walker

High school comedies come in two flavors: light and dark. The light ones largely pander to arrested or actual adolescents who see male horniness as the ultimate tragedy of the human condition. It's possible to make a *smart,* light high school comedy (see *Dazed and Confused*), but the truly smart ones illuminate the darker side of dating and the struggle for social acceptance. As dark as they come is *Heathers,* which benefits from a very mean script by Daniel Waters about a small clique of girls and their latest initiate, Veronica, played with ferocious intelligence by Winona Ryder. Should she follow the dictates of the Heathers, or throw in with J.D., the dangerous new guy (Christian Slater) in school? (Jack Nicholson should have demanded some kind of credit for Slater's smugly leering line deliveries.) Caught between the devil and the deep blue blazers of the Heathers, Veronica does what any respectable girl should do, in an ending that was reportedly forced on the filmmakers but works anyway. The Independent Spirit Awards tabbed it as Best First Feature.

⊙**DVD:** Includes audio commentaries by Winona Ryder and Christian Slater.

CO2, CO5

Goes well with: *Pump Up the Volume*

HEAVENLY CREATURES

ESSENTIAL

New Zealand   1994   C   99 min.   R   Drama

Dir: Peter Jackson

C: Melanie Lynskey, Kate Winslet, Sarah Peirse, Diana Kent, Clive Merrison

After making two acclaimed but little-seen horror comedies (*Bad Taste* and *Dead Alive*), New Zealand director Peter Jackson set out to film a different kind of horror tale, the true story of teenagers Pauline Parker and Juliet Hulme. In 1954 the pair, who had formed a friendship that their parents found disturbingly close, committed a desperate act when Pauline's mother refused her daughter's request to join the Hulmes in their move to South Africa. Jackson and cowriter Frances Walsh were nominated for an Oscar for their original screenplay, which constructed the "Fourth World," a universe imagined by the two girls, filled with the music of Mario Lanza, images of the brooding Orson Welles, and large stone statues that come to life in menacingly erotic ways. Melanie Lynskey and the young Kate Winslet throw themselves wholly into their performances, and the result is a persuasive depiction of adolescent friendship run amok. (Some years later, it was revealed that the grown-up Hulme had been writing popular mystery novels under the name Anne Perry.)

DR12, DR17, DR27, DR41

Goes well with: *Fun*

HEDWIG AND THE ANGRY INCH

U.S.   2001   C   95 min.   R   Comedy-Musical
Dir: John Cameron Mitchell
C: John Cameron Mitchell, Michael Pitt, Miriam Shor, Stephen Trask, Andrea Martin, Alberta Watson

In the competition for Most Outstanding Movie About Rockin' Drag Queens, it's difficult to decide between *Hedwig* and *Priscilla, Queen of the Desert*. *Priscilla* definitely has the best scenery, but *Hedwig* has the clear edge in music. John Cameron Mitchell, who originated the role off-Broadway, gives a dynamite performance as the East Berlin boy originally named Hansel by his German mom (Alberta Watson) and American G.I. dad, now touring America in sequins and form-fitting gowns, playing a series of gigs at outlets of the Bilgewater restaurant chain. He sings and struts around the salad bar with such unapologetic verve that you can't help but love him. And Hedwig is not an easy man/woman to love; he spurns the affections of his lead guitarist (Stephen Trask, who cowrote the script and authored many of the snappy songs) and vengefully pursues a former protégé, Tommy Gnosis (Michael Pitt). Hell hath no fury like a transsexual rock singer scorned.

⊙**DVD:** Includes audio commentary by John Cameron Mitchell; documentary, "Long Story Short: The Forging of a Cult Legend From Stage to Screen"; deleted scenes with optional commentary; sing-along feature.

CO10, MU2

Goes well with: *The Adventures of Priscilla, Queen of the Desert*

HELLRAISER

U.K. 1987 C 94 min. R Horror

Dir: Clive Barker

C: Andrew Robinson, Clare Higgins, Ashley Laurence, Sean Chapman

As is usually the case with horror film series, it's all downhill after the first film, but the opener in the Clive Barker set is a doozy. The bare bones of the story—a man's brother (who is also his wife's ex-lover) lives in their attic as a skeletal creature who requires fresh blood to restore his flesh—should be enough to either entice you or have you quickly skipping to other entries in this book. Andrew Robinson (*Dirty Harry* fans will recall him as the psychotic villain of that film) is the bewildered Larry, Clare Higgins is his wife, who is all too willing to help an old boyfriend, and Ashley Laurence is their teenage daughter, the one character who gets to scream a lot at all the weirdness going on in her house. Barker wrote and directed this stylishly fun exercise in gruesomeness; subsequent chapters in the series are for hardcore fans of the genre only.

⊙**DVD:** Special Edition contains audio commentary by Clive Barker and "making of" featurette.

FA9

Goes well with: *The Addiction*

HELP!

U.K. 1965 C 90 min. NR Musical

Dir: Richard Lester

C: John Lennon, Paul McCartney, George Harrison, Ringo Starr, Leo McKern, Eleanor Bron, Victor Spinetti, Roy Kinnear, Patrick Cargill

The Beatles' second film, under the astute direction of Richard Lester, surpasses *A Hard Day's Night* in many ways. Lester and ace cinematographer David Watkin have fun with the use of color, both in the modish interiors and in outdoor locations from London to the Austrian Alps to the Salisbury Plain to the Bahamas. The song set is just as inspired, with "Ticket to Ride" and "You've Got to Hide Your Love Away" as highlights. The story is a macguffin: A vaguely Indian cult needs a sacred ring for a religious ceremony, Ringo is wearing it, so they dispatch a team of agents to steal it. But it does give Lester the opportunity to work in funny business for his supporting cast, including Leo

McKern as High Priest Clang, Eleanor Bron as Priestess Ahme, Victor Spinetti as Foot, a megalomaniac scientist, and the inimitable Roy Kinnear (a Lester regular) as Algernon, Foot's fat, bumbling assistant. Best scene: John leading a pub full of drinkers in a sing-along to the last movement of Beethoven's Ninth Symphony.

⊙**DVD:** Includes deleted footage; silent footage from the set and premiere; two newsreels; radio interview.

CO10, CO12, MU2

Goes well with: *A Hard Day's Night*

HENRY V (1945)

ESSENTIAL

U.K.   1945   C   137 min.   NR   Drama

Dir: Laurence Olivier

C: Laurence Olivier, Robert Newton, Leslie Banks, Renee Asherson, Esmond Knight

It's on everyone's shortlist of favorite Shakespeare films, and why not? Laurence Olivier made his directing debut with this stirring call to arms, shot during the dark days of World War II (hint hint). Along with *Children of Paradise,* it's the best film ever made on a European home front. The opening is a pip: It begins on the stage of the Globe Theatre, and just as we think that Olivier is going to film a stagebound production, the camera swoops onto the plains of Agincourt and we get a full-fledged movie, packed with battle scenes and castle settings. Olivier picked up a special Oscar for his work here, and his performance was lauded by the New York Film Critics Circle.

⊙**DVD:** Includes liner notes and commentary by Bruce Eder; *Book of Hours* visual reference.

DR24, DR25, DR32

Goes well with: *Hamlet* (1948)

HENRY V (1989)

ESSENTIAL

U.K.   1989   C   137 min.   PG-13   Drama

Dir: Kenneth Branagh

C: Kenneth Branagh, Derek Jacobi, Brian Blessed, Alec McCowen, Ian Holm, Richard Briers, Robert Stephens, Robbie Coltrane, Christian Bale, Judi Dench, Paul Scofield, Emma Thompson

If Olivier could do it, then Kenneth Branagh was going to give it a try. Both men made their film directing debuts with adaptations of one of Shakespeare's most muscular plays. Inevitably, the comparisons would favor Olivier's version, in part because of its wartime context: Larry rallying England at a time of need and so forth. Branagh offers a less glorious view of war and its attendant politics, geared to an era more skeptical of the machinations that put so many lives at risk. (At least in Henry's day the leader put himself on the front line with the troops he was ordering into battle.) Branagh's Henry is a splendid performance (nominated for an Oscar, as was his direction), and he has surrounded himself with the cream of the British acting corps, including Derek Jacobi as the Narrator, Judi Dench as Mistress Quickly, Ian Holm as Fluellen, Paul Scofield as the French King, and Branagh's then-wife Emma Thompson as Katherine. An Oscar winner for costume design.

⊙**DVD**

DR24, DR25, DR32

Goes well with: *Hamlet* (1996)

HENRY FOOL

U.S.   1998   C   137 min.   R   Drama

Dir: Hal Hartley

C: Thomas Jay Ryan, James Urbaniak, Parker Posey, Maria Porter, James Saito, Kevin Corrigan

Writer-director Hal Hartley's early films (*The Unbelievable Truth, Trust*) were modest stories about oddball characters adrift in a world bereft of physical and emotional anchors. *Henry Fool* is a more ambitious version of those stories, with an expansive running time that threatens to expose the holes in its narrative. The title character is a drifter who's both charismatic and irritating, a kind of lowlife Sheridan Whiteside who comes to influence the life of aspiring writer Simon Grim. Thomas Jay Ryan's performance as Henry always threatens to spin out of control, but you can't take your eyes off the guy, if only because Hartley deftly dangles the possibility that Henry is a total fake, and part of you wants to see him get his comeuppance. A bold, flawed, but fascinating film.

DR12, DR21

Goes well with: *The Unbelievable Truth*

HENRY: PORTRAIT OF A SERIAL KILLER

ESSENTIAL

U.S. 1990 C 90 min. NR Drama
Dir: John McNaughton
C: Michael Rooker, Tracy Arnold, Tom Towles

There are no Freudian explanations à la *Psycho*. There is no social or geographical context à la *American Psycho*. There are no philosophical considerations à la *The Minus Man*. There is just Henry (Michael Rooker), a Chicago guy who likes to kill people because, well, it's something to do. The screenplay, by director John McNaughton and Richard Fire, does not portray Henry as a maladjusted nut, nor is he a smooth talker on the order of Ted Bundy. He's a quiet loner who occasionally lashes out, with little warning, in a homicidal rage. Henry's pal from their days in prison, Otis (Tom Towles), is all too easily drawn into the world of murder until it's too late to back out. The story's most vulnerable victim is Otis's sister, Becky (Tracy Arnold), who offers the one faint ray of hope in this dark tale until she, too, is pulled under. This is a disturbing film for its clear-eyed view of horror and its victims and abettors.

⊙**DVD:** DVD edition runs 130 minutes and is the uncut, unrated director's version. Includes interview with John McNaughton.

DR6, TH15, XT7
Goes well with: *The Minus Man*

HESTER STREET

U.S. 1975 B&W 92 min. PG Drama
Dir: Joan Micklin Silver
C: Steven Keats, Carol Kane, Mel Howard, Dorrie Kavanaugh, Doris Roberts

Joan Micklin Silver's directorial debut is a lovely historical drama about the adjustments a Jewish couple make when they emigrate from Russia to New York's Lower East Side at the turn of the century. Unlike the story of young Vito Corleone, portrayed in the second *Godfather* film a year before *Hester Street* was released, this drama focuses mainly on the woman's problems. Upon joining her husband in New York she is dismayed to see how quickly he has dropped the customs of their life in the Old World, but the times and her cultural upbringing don't give her much latitude to disagree or criticize. Carol Kane's luminous performance was nominated for an Oscar.

DR7, DR36, DR39
Goes well with: *The Governess*

HIGH AND LOW

ESSENTIAL

Japan   1963   C/B&W   142 min.   NR   Drama
Dir: Akira Kurosawa
C: Toshiro Mifune, Tatsuya Mihashi, Yutaka Sada, Tatsuya Nakadai

Not many filmmakers work from material as diverse as Shakespeare and Ed McBain, but then Akira Kurosawa was, film for film, the greatest director of all time, for both his versatility and consistency. *High and Low* is a police procedural about a businessman victimized by a kidnapper, but Kurosawa brings an extra moral dimension to the material. Toshiro Mifune plays the central figure, a man whose well-publicized windfall in his business dealings attracts the wrong kind of attention: A desperate young man snatches his boy for ransom. Mifune's agony becomes more complicated when it's learned that the kidnapper took the chauffeur's son by mistake. The morality play comes first, taking place almost entirely in one room; once the decision to pay has been made, we follow the scrupulous police work that leads to the perpetrator, whose motive is more than mercenary. Don't be put off by the long running time; this film hasn't one slow moment. (There is only one shot in color, at the film's end, for dramatic emphasis.)

⊙**DVD**
DR5, DR6, TH1, XT8
Goes well with: *The Day of the Jackal*

HIGH ART

Canada/U.S.   1998   C   101 min.   R   Drama
Dir: Lisa Cholodenko
C: Ally Sheedy, Radha Mitchell, Patricia Clarkson, Tammy Grimes

The journalist who gets too involved in his or her subject is the setup for too many half-baked movies that are in a big hurry to get the principals romantically hooked up, ignoring the more interesting issues of the relationship. Writer-director Lisa Cholodenko adds something different to the romantic angle—both characters are women—but she also gives more than equal time to the office politics and career crises that beset the protagonist, played by Radha Mitchell.

She's an inexperienced writer for a trendy art magazine who takes on the challenge of tracking down a once-acclaimed photographer (Ally Sheedy) who is now a recluse. As Sheedy's drug-addled companion, Patricia Clarkson adds touches of humor around the edges of a fairly downbeat tale. Director Lisa Cholodenko's script won an award at the Sundance festival.

DR2, DR10, DR19, DR39

Goes well with: *Basquiat*

HIGH HOPES

U.K. 1988 C 112 min. PG Comedy-Drama
Dir: Mike Leigh
C: Philip Davis, Ruth Sheen, Edna Doré, Philip Jackson, Heather Tobias, Lesley Manville, David Bamber

Writer-director Mike Leigh's "comeback" film (he had debuted in 1971 with *Bleak Moments,* then worked for seventeen years in TV and on the stage) is a time-capsule comedy-drama about the England that Margaret Thatcher helped create, with greed the norm and the working classes left to fend for themselves. Cyril and Shirley (Philip Davis and Ruth Sheen) are a working-class couple, Martin and Valerie (Philip Jackson and Heather Tobias) are grotesque strivers, Laetitia and Rupert (Lesley Manville and David Bamber) are smug got-it-mades. The film is painful, funny, and painfully funny, but it is most successful when it concentrates on Cyril and Shirley, whose loving relationship contains a dark undercurrent, and on Cyril and Valerie's mum (Edna Doré), who's living alone and teetering on the edge of senility. As characters, Valerie is too shrill and Martin too crass, while Laetitia and Rupert are creations that would work better in the pages of a Martin Amis or Tom Wolfe novel. The film's centerpiece is a comic sequence detailing each couple's bedtime routine, ending on a somber note in a beautifully observed exchange between Cyril and Shirley.

CO8, DR5

Goes well with: *Life Is Sweet*

HIGH TIDE

Australia 1987 C 101 min. PG-13 Drama
Dir: Gillian Armstrong
C: Judy Davis, Jan Adele, Claudia Karvan, Colin Friels

It's almost impossible to overrate the performances of Judy Davis, who in films both great and small always delivers. Here she plays Lilli, a woman whose pathetic career as a backup singer for an Elvis impersonator comes to an abrupt end when she's sacked and left stranded in a small seaside town in Australia. She meets a young woman named Bet (Jan Adele), who is something of a singer herself as well as working in a fish factory and driving an ice cream van. The two women have something else in common: Bet is the daughter Lilli abandoned years ago to pursue her show-biz ambitions. Director Gillian Armstrong runs with the premise of Laura Jones's screenplay in an agreeably zigzag pattern. Armstrong and Davis seem made for each other; they both master the subtleties of any situation or character and nicely avoid making the obvious point in any scene.

DR11, DR39

Goes well with: *Limbo*

HILARY AND JACKIE

U.K.   1998   C   120 min.   R   Drama

Dir: Anand Tucker

C: Emily Watson, Rachel Griffiths, James Frain, David Morrissey, Charles Dance, Celia Imrie

The title promises a portrait of two women, and the film is structured to offer two points of view on some of the events. But this is clearly Hilary du Pré's view of her story and that of her famous sister, cellist Jacqueline du Pré, who died at the age of forty-two from multiple sclerosis. Hilary was herself an accomplished flautist, and as Frank Cottrell Boyce's adaptation of Hilary and her brother Piers du Pré's book *A Genius in the Family* shows, Jackie's determination to outstrip her sister also proved her undoing. What Jackie was left with was an unfulfilled life, despite a marriage to handsome pianist Daniel Barenboim and worldwide acclaim. "I never asked to be a cellist," she moans at one point. Emily Watson (as Jackie) and Rachel Griffiths (as Hilary) overcome some (though not all) of the film's limitations with affecting performances. The best scene is played twice, from both sisters' points of view; when "Hils" announces to her sister that she's going to marry, she is oblivious to Jackie's despair that the two of them will never be so close again.

⊙**DVD:** Includes "making of" featurette.

DR2, DR11, DR17, DR23
Goes well with: *Isadora*

HIROSHIMA, MON AMOUR

ESSENTIAL

France/Japan 1959 B&W 91 min. NR Drama
Dir: Alain Resnais
C: Emmanuelle Riva, Eiji Okada, Stella Dassas, Pierre Barbaud

Director Alain Resnais takes on the most cataclysmic moment of World War II in his story of an affair between a Japanese architect and a French actress. She is working on location on an antiwar film in Hiroshima, and as the film begins their affair is at its height. He tells her she has seen nothing in Hiroshima, since he was in the city on August 6, 1945, and witnessed the horror first-hand. But she has her own wartime horror story to tell, a romance with a German soldier that ended with his death and her imprisonment and ostracization by her community. Marguerite Duras's screenplay works for about the first seventy minutes of the film, but then it begins to repeat itself to no great effect, and a long nighttime sequence seems to go on forever. Still, the black-and-white images (by Sacha Vierney and Mikio Takhashi), especially the opening montage of bodies intertwined, are always striking, and the power of the film's subject matter is undeniable. The New York Film Critics Circle awarded it Best Foreign Language Film.

DR19, DR38, XT4, XT7
Goes well with: *The English Patient*

HOLLYWOOD SHUFFLE

U.S. 1987 C 81 min. R Comedy
Dir: Robert Townsend
C: Robert Townsend, Anne-Marie Johnson, Starletta Dupois, Helen Martin

It would be heartening to report that Robert Townsend's comedy about a black actor's struggles to get meaningful work in Hollywood is full of outdated jokes. But the truth is that dignified leading roles for African Americans are still rare in mainstream films. Townsend, who cowrote with Keenen Ivory Wayans, plays Bobby, a thespian with modest aspirations that are still far too ambitious for most producers he reads for. His fantasies, especially one of a black acting school that teaches its pupils how to come on like Stepin Fetchit's babbling butlers, are among the funniest scenes in an uneven but worthwhile film.

⊙**DVD**

CO10, DR28

Goes well with: *The Big Picture*

HOOP DREAMS

ESSENTIAL

U.S.   1994   C   170 min.   PG-13   Documentary

Dir: Steve James

The virtually untouched subject of nonwhite high school athletes and the sacrifices and pressures they endure finally has the great film it deserves. Filmmakers Steve James (who directed), Fred Marx, and Peter Gilbert found two products of the Chicago housing projects, Arthur Agee and William Gates, and followed them for several years. Agee and Gates get scholarships to a suburban high school whose alumni include former NBA star Isaiah Thomas. The details of how these two modest young men deal with a two-hour commute to and from school, plus the rising expectations of coaches, fellow students, and, most significant, their families, make the nearly three-hour running time fly by. College is in their futures, but is real stardom and the elusive goal of a professional career? We know the answer, but confirming it is an immensely satisfying experience.

DO7, DO10

Goes well with: *The Loneliness of the Long Distance Runner*

HOPE AND GLORY

ESSENTIAL

U.K.   1987   C   113 min.   PG-13   Drama

Dir: John Boorman

C: Sarah Miles, David Hayman, Derrick O'Connor, Susan Wooldridge, Sammi Davis, Ian Bannen, Sebastian Rice-Edwards, Jean-Marc Barr

The two best films of 1987, *The Last Emperor* and *Hope and Glory,* were both historical dramas, but there the similarities end. Bernardo Bertolucci's epic cut a huge swath through twentieth-century Chinese history, while John Boorman's more modest film focused on a brief period in England. That period was the dark days during the Second World

War, when London was under attack from German bombers. Boorman's film offers a unique perspective: that of Bill Rohan, a nine-year-old boy. (Any resemblance to the director's own experiences is reportedly not coincidental.) For Bill (Sebastian Rice-Edwards), the bombings provide more excitement than horror; while adults walk around the ruins of buildings muttering about the awful waste, Bill and his pals turn them into playgrounds in which they act out their own war games. This is not to say that *Hope and Glory* cheapens the drama of living in wartime. It is, in fact, the film that Steven Spielberg might have made of *Empire of the Sun* but didn't: a delightful, moving, and wholly authentic kid's-eye view of a world gone slightly mad, and how he and his family cope. Of special note among the performances is the splendid Ian Holm as Bill's grandfather.

⊙**DVD**

DR3, DR38, DR41

Goes well with: *Forbidden Games*

THE HOURS AND TIMES

U.S. 1991 B&W 60 min. NR Drama

Dir: Christopher Münch

C: David Angus, Ian Hart, Stephanie Pack, Robin McDonald

The four days that John Lennon and the Beatles' manager, Brian Epstein, spent in Barcelona during the spring of 1963 are the subject of this modest, effectively mounted film. Epstein was a homosexual, so speculation about the two men's friendship has always revolved around a "Did they or did they not?" line of questioning. The film suggests they almost did, but if that were all it was about, you wouldn't be reading about it here. David Angus (as Epstein) and Ian Hart (as Lennon—he also played him in *Backbeat*) portray two men heading in different directions. Epstein's sense that he can't keep up with the whirlwind of fame that is beginning to engulf (and isolate) John and his mates is made painfully clear, while John comes across as more secure and confident, in spite of the working-class upbringing that has made him a social inferior of the more urbane Epstein. It's a fascinating character study, and both actors (especially Hart, a dead ringer for the young Lennon) are up to writer-director Christopher Münch's material. The film won a Special Jury Recognition prize at the Sundance festival.

DR12, DR17

Goes well with: *Backbeat*

HOUSE OF GAMES

U.S.   1987   C   102 min.   R   Thriller
Dir: David Mamet
C: Lindsay Crouse, Joe Mantegna, Mike Nussbaum, Lilia Skala, J. T.
   Walsh, Willo Hausman, Ricky Jay, William H. Macy

Playwright David Mamet's debut as a film director cleverly allows
the audience to identify with the character who's sure she knows a con
game when she sees it. Psychiatrist Margaret Ford (Lindsay Crouse) is
treating a patient driven to the brink of suicide by Mike, a slick con man
(Joe Mantegna, a frequent player in Mamet's stage work who has also
appeared in many Mamet films). Margaret confronts Mike, then gets
sucked into exploring his world, all the while thinking she's above being
fooled—partly because Mike is giving her the grand tour, partly because she has a college degree and he doesn't. Mamet clearly loves the
Chinese-box world of cons, and he revels in the language of that world.
For those who willingly suspend disbelief at the movies, there's a kind
of masochistic pleasure in getting fooled, too.

⊙**DVD**
TH2, TH5
Goes well with: *The Spanish Prisoner*

THE HOUSE OF MIRTH

ESSENTIAL

U.K./U.S./France/Germany   2000   C   140 min.   PG   Drama
Dir: Terence Davies
C: Gillian Anderson, Eric Stoltz, Dan Aykroyd, Eleanor Bron, Terry
   Kinney, Anthony LaPaglia, Laura Linney, Elizabeth McGovern,
   Jodhi May

Shamefully ignored on its original release, the best movie adaptation
of Edith Wharton's work deserves a better fate on video. Lily Bart
(Gillian Anderson) is a woman of very modest means who, at the age of
twenty-nine, is trying not to notice that time is growing short for her to
find a suitable husband. Her choice between Sim Rosedale (Anthony La-
Paglia), a successful businessman, and Lawrence Selden (Eric Stoltz), a
writer with not many more assets than she, is complicated by two other
relationships, with a wealthy aunt (Eleanor Bron) and the even more
wealthy Gus Trenor (Dan Aykroyd), who agrees to lend her money for
investments. Anderson is a marvel, offering a complex portrait of a
woman whose confidence is also her undoing, as she makes one bad de-

cision after another until she is left with almost no options in life. Writer-director Terence Davies manages to do the nearly impossible, surpassing Martin Scorsese's first-rate version of Wharton's *The Age of Innocence* with a film that packs an even stronger emotional punch.

⊙**DVD:** Special Edition contains audio commentary by Terence Davies and deleted scenes with commentary.

DR5, DR24, DR29, DR39

Goes well with: *My Brilliant Career*

HOUSEHOLD SAINTS

U.S. 1993 C 124 min. R Drama
Dir: Nancy Savoca
C: Tracey Ullman, Vincent D'Onofrio, Lili Taylor, Judith Malina, Michael Rispoli, Victor Argo, Michael Imperioli, Illeana Douglas

It ain't *The Godfather* trilogy, but it's a good start. How many films about Italian-Americans have focused on the women? From Vito Corleone to Jake LaMotta, it's men men men men. So give this three-generation saga of an Italian-American family some credit for starting to even the score by offering a trio of amazingly rich female characters. Carmela Santangelo (Judith Malina) is the superstitious first-generation immigrant who is embarrassed when her daughter, Catherine (Tracey Ullman), is wed to a man (Vincent D'Onofrio) who wins her in a pinochle game. Catherine's daughter, Teresa (Lili Taylor), grows up to be a religious girl who sees visions and believes that she has a great future as a saint. Director Nancy Savoca and her husband, Richard Guay, adapted Francine Prose's novel about religion, food, and sex (and its denial) while retaining its humor and without cheapening the characters. Each woman is given her due, and all three actresses are superb, especially Taylor as a woman who chooses to serve God rather than men. Taylor was named Best Supporting Female by the Independent Spirit Awards.

DR11, DR21, DR30

Goes well with: *Antonia's Line*

HOW I WON THE WAR

U.K. 1967 C 109 min. NR Comedy
Dir: Richard Lester
C: Michael Crawford, John Lennon, Roy Kinnear, Jack MacGowran, Michael Hordern, Lee Montague, Alexander Knox

A rare antiwar film set in World War II, *How I Won the War* is a satire of wartime reminiscence: The events the film shows are quite at odds with the memories of its narrator. Ernest Goodbody (Michael Crawford) somehow rises to the rank of officer, even though he's clearly a few bullets shy of a full clip. He is placed in charge of a ragtag outfit with the unlikely mission of setting up a cricket pitch in the Egyptian desert. Director Richard Lester and writer Charles Wood illustrate the absurdity of war in several imaginative ways, such as using color to symbolize the deaths of individual soldiers in the company, even backing out at one point to show two middle-aged women in a newsreel theater commenting on the film's action. Lester cast Beatle John Lennon (whom he directed in *A Hard Day's Night* and *Help!*) as Gripweed, one of Goodbody's ineffectual soldiers. If some of the experimental techniques fall a bit flat, the message that Wood and Lester offer, about the absurdity of all armed conflict, hasn't dated at all.

⊙**DVD**

CO2, DR37

Goes well with: *The Life and Death of Colonel Blimp*

HOWARDS END

ESSENTIAL

Japan/U.K.   1992   C   140 min.   PG   Drama
Dir: James Ivory
C: Anthony Hopkins, Vanessa Redgrave, Helena Bonham Carter, Emma Thompson, James Wilby, Sam West, Jemma Redgrave

It's a film of superlatives: the best adaptation of an E. M. Forster novel; the supreme achievement of the long-running team of producer Ismail Merchant, director James Ivory, and writer Ruth Prawer Jhabvala; and the home of Emma Thompson's most affecting and accomplished performance. Thompson is Margaret Schlegel, whose friendship with Ruth Wilcox (Vanessa Redgrave) pulls their contrasting families into social situations together. The rest of the wealthier, more conservative Wilcox clan, led by Henry (Anthony Hopkins), find the open-minded Schlegels too common, and there's even more conflict after Ruth's death, when it's learned that she left her country house (called Howards End) to Margaret. The filmmakers are in sync with every nuance of Forster's acutely observed novel of class, compromise, and reconciliation. The final scene between Thompson and Hopkins is a stunner. Thompson won Best Actress accolades from both the Academy and the New York Film

Critics Circle; Oscars also went to Jhabvala's screenplay and the film's art direction.

⊙**DVD**

DR5, DR11, DR29

Goes well with: *The Remains of the Day*

HURLYBURLY

U.S. 1998 C 122 min. R Drama

Dir: Anthony Drazan

C: Sean Penn, Kevin Spacey, Robin Wright Penn, Chazz Palminteri, Garry Shandling, Anna Paquin, Meg Ryan

David Rabe's play about Hollywood wannabes deals with the timeless questions that attend many stories set in Southern California. Do people trying to make it in the movie business deceive one another? Are men in Southern California even more eager than their brethren elsewhere to use women as sexual playthings? Are drugs or alcohol the last refuge of creatively bankrupt people? Rabe makes these and other topics a lot funnier than they have any right to be, and Sean Penn, Kevin Spacey, and Chazz Palminteri, as the three stooges of the Hollywood Hills, illustrate Rabe's themes with brio and conviction. Kudos, too, to Meg Ryan in a rare gritty role and Anna Paquin in her first adult part.

⊙**DVD:** Special Edition contains audio commentaries by Sean Penn, Anthony Drazan, David Rabe, composer David Baerwald, and social commentator Janet Brown.

DR10, DR27, DR32

Goes well with: *The Player*

I

I AM CUBA

Cuba/Soviet Union   1964   B&W   140 min.   NR   Drama
Dir: Mikhail Kalatozov
C: Sergio Corrieri, Salvador Vud, José Gallardo, Raúl García, Luz
  María Collazo, Jean Bouise

I Am Cuba is to Communist propaganda what *Triumph of the Will* is
to Nazi propaganda. Whatever you think of the effects of Fidel Castro's
revolution on Cuba, you cannot deny the sheer filmmaking brilliance of
I Am Cuba. Set in the days leading up to Castro's victory over Batista,
this is not, for the most part, a hectoring lesson in the power of the pro-
letariat. Soviet filmmaker Mikhail Kalatozov, working with cinematographer Sergei Urusevsky, has filmed a Cuba that is so sensual, so
physically alive, you wonder why anyone would live anywhere else.
There are four stories: the encounter between a young prostitute and a
sleazy American (all Americans in this film are sleazy), the desperate
actions of a sugarcane farmer who learns that his boss has sold out to
United Fruit, the martyrdom of a student activist, and the politicization
of a peasant in the Sierra Maestra. The script, by poets Yevgeny Yev-
tushenko and Enrique Piñeda Barnet, is not especially sophisticated, but
it's the camerawork that's the show: In no other film, surely, does the
camera swoop and pan so much. *I Am Cuba* was not released in America until 1995, when directors Francis Ford Coppola and Martin Scorsese "presented" it to a filmgoing public that would look beyond its
politics to its greatness as a piece of filmmaking.
  ⊙**DVD**

DR25, XT1
Goes well with: *Before Night Falls*

I KNOW WHERE I'M GOING!
U.K. 1945 B&W 91 min. NR Drama
Dir: Michael Powell and Emeric Pressburger
C: Wendy Hiller, Roger Livesey, Finlay Currie, Pamela Brown, Petula
 Clark

Among the most beguiling romantic films ever made, *I Know Where I'm Going!* is also very much a cult item. Here and in several other films (notably *Black Narcissus*), the filmmaking team of Michael Powell and Emeric Pressburger (who share producing, directing, and writing credits) show an interest in the intoxicating effect of the landscape on the human psyche. Joan Webster (Wendy Hiller) is a headstrong Londoner who announces to her father in the film's opening scene that she is about to marry a wealthy man (her boss, in fact) and that the wedding is to take place on an isolated island off the coast of Scotland. When bad weather stalls her journey at the ferry port, she meets a handsome young naval officer (Roger Livesey), and the effects of the wild weather and the beguiling terrain begin to work on her resolve. It's a charming and predictable movie about the unpredictability of romance. (Footnote: Livesey could not get out of a play commitment in London, so Powell and Pressburger shot all of his interior scenes on studio sets there and used doubles for the exterior shots.)

 ⊙**DVD:** Includes audio essay by historian Ian Christie; behind-the-scenes stills and home movies narrated by Powell's widow, Thelma Schoonmaker Powell; 1994 documentary *I Know Where I'm Going! Revisited;* excerpts from Powell's films *The Edge of the World* and *Edge of the World Revisited.*

DR18
Goes well with: *The Edge of the World*

I SHOT ANDY WARHOL
U.S./U.K. 1996 C 106 min. R Drama
Dir: Mary Harron
C: Lili Taylor, Jared Harris, Stephen Dorff, Martha Plimpton, Danny
 Morgenstern, Lothaire Bluteau, Michael Imperioli, Donovan
 Leitch, Tahnee Welch, Jill Hennessey
 Like Mark David Chapman and Lee Harvey Oswald, Valerie Solanas

gained her fifteen minutes of fame by attempting to assassinate a cultural icon. In 1968, she shot artist Andy Warhol several times. Miraculously, he survived. Solanas was an aspiring artist who felt that Warhol had encouraged her career and then ignored her; given Warhol's indiscriminate if low-key enthusiasm for almost everything connected to pop culture, Solanas was probably right. But as the founder and sole member of SCUM (the Society for Cutting Up Men), she saw Andy as an oppressor rather than as a onetime patron. Lili Taylor's astonishing performance, in which we see the pathos of the truly delusional personality, anchors the film; she won a Special Jury Prize at the Sundance festival. The film also captures the ambience of Warhol's world and the downtown New York art scene of the late 1960s perfectly. Jared Harris is an even better Warhol than David Bowie was in *Basquiat,* a dreamy exterior covering a steely frame—no wonder he survived the attempt on his life.

⊙**DVD**

DR17, DR21, DR39

Goes well with: *Basquiat*

IF . . .

U.K. 1968 C/B&W 111 min. R Drama
Dir: Lindsay Anderson
C: Malcolm McDowell, David Wood, Richard Warwick, Robert Swann, Christine Noonan

This stylish study of a student rebellion at an English boys' boarding school was a timely release, coming at the height of youthful rebellion in Europe and the States over Vietnam. But its real inspiration, at least stylistically, was French filmmaker Jean Vigo's *Zero for Conduct,* a thirty-five-year-old film about the same subject. Like Vigo, writer David Sherwin and director Lindsay Anderson pepper their narrative with surrealistic episodes, alternating between color and black-and-white cinematography. (Anderson has claimed the switch was driven by budget rather than style.) Malcolm McDowell is the dashing leader of the rebel students who call themselves the Crusaders; his naked wrestling with a young waitress earned *if . . .* an X rating, sealing its status as an outlaw film. (The movie was later rerated R.) Thirty years later, it seems fairly tame, but it's not as if privilege and caste have disappeared from the English public school, either.

DR31, DR41

Goes well with: *Zero for Conduct*

IKIRU

ESSENTIAL

Japan 1952 B&W 143 min. NR Drama
Dir: Akira Kurosawa
C: Takashi Shimura, Nobuo Kaneko, Kyōko Seki, Miki Odagiri

Two years before he played the robust lead in *The Seven Samurai,* actor Takashi Shimura gave his finest performance in a very different role for director Akira Kurosawa. Kanji Watanabe is a city-government bureaucrat who seems to be playing out the string, both at his job and at home. Then he learns that he has terminal cancer, and after an initial wallow in self-pity, he resolves to do something more with his life than reviewing and passing on forms. Using his lifetime of experience with the government, he rams through a project to convert a junkyard into a playground for children. Kurosawa's deliberate pace serves to intensify the mood of this somber yet hopeful tale. Rather than make a feel-good movie in which Watanabe's coworkers and family rally around him, Kurosawa portrays Watanabe as a lonely crusader—no one can understand why this playground is so important to him. Shimura, with his mournful eyes, seems to shrink into his suit as the story progresses, shuffling through office corridors with a mixture of resignation and determination.

DR8, DR14, DR16
Goes well with: *A Woman's Tale*

THE IMPOSTORS

U.S. 1998 C 108 min. R Comedy
Dir: Stanley Tucci
C: Stanley Tucci, Oliver Platt, Alfred Molina, Lili Taylor, Tony Shalhoub, Steve Buscemi, Allison Janney, Richard Jenkins, Isabella Rossellini, Campbell Scott, Billy Connolly, Dana Ivey, Hope Davis

It has the feel of "Hey kids, let's put on a show," and the ringmaster of this lovely little farce (that's a genre description, not a backhanded compliment) is writer-director-star Stanley Tucci. He has gathered several cast members from his first effort, *Big Night,* and added several other great talents, including one uncredited ringer. It's *Some Like It Hot* meets *A Night at the Opera,* as two bumbling actors flee for their lives and end up as stowaways on an ocean liner filled with eccentrics. Tucci and Oliver Platt prove to be a first-rate Laurel and Hardy team, and everyone in the supporting cast seems to be having a great time. So will you.

⊙**DVD**

CO10

Goes well with: *Big Night*

IMPROMPTU

U.K./France   1991   C   109 min.   PG-13   Comedy-Drama

Dir: James Lapine

C: Judy Davis, Hugh Grant, Mandy Patinkin, Bernadette Peters, Julian Sands, Ralph Brown, Georges Corraface, Emma Thompson

Movies in which famous personages sit around a country home and yak at each other, just like you and me and our friends on holiday, usually have an aura of fake intimacy about them, as though the filmmakers are trying hard to pretend that none of these people wound up with major entries in encyclopedias. Count *Impromptu* as the rare exception to that stunningly crafted generalization; it gathers George Sand (Judy Davis), Franz Liszt (Julian Sands), Frédéric Chopin (Hugh Grant), Alfred de Musset (Mandy Patinkin), and Eugène Delacroix (Ralph Brown) together for a weekend of playing around and conversations on matters both high and low. Sand's romantic pursuit of the distracted Chopin is the linchpin of the story, and director James Lapine orchestrates the nearly farcical action quite neatly. As always, Davis is intense and totally believable; Grant is surprisingly effective as the soulful Pole; Emma Thompson as a starstruck duchess and Patinkin as Musset both overact but to amusing effect.

⊙**DVD**

CO6, DR2, DR17

Goes well with: *Mrs. Parker and the Vicious Circle*

IN THE BEDROOM

U.S.   2001   C   130 min.   R   Drama

Dir: Todd Field

C: Tom Wilkinson, Sissy Spacek, Nick Stahl, Marisa Tomei, William Mapother, William Wise, Celia Weston, Karen Allen

The setting for this drama of a family's sorrow and regret is one of the loveliest towns in New England: Camden, Maine. Nestled at the foot of a hill in a picturesque harbor, Camden must seem to its many visitors an enchanted place where nothing could ever go wrong. But for the Fowler family—Matt (Tom Wilkinson), his wife, Ruth (Sissy

Spacek), and their college-age son, Frank (Nick Stahl), something does go very very wrong. Frank's summer fling with an older woman (Marisa Tomei) trying to shed a violent husband (William Mapother) ends in a moment of violence. The film skillfully charts how Matt, an easygoing doctor, and Ruth, a music teacher who's wound tighter than her husband, respond to their tragedy: first by growing apart, then by coming together in a scheme to purge their sorrow. Actor-turned-director Todd Field, adapting Andre Dubus's story "Killers," is in tune with the dynamics of a small town, where your private sorrow is public knowledge and you keep running into people you don't want to.

DR11, DR34

Goes well with: *The Sweet Hereafter*

IN THE COMPANY OF MEN
ESSENTIAL

U.S.   1997   C   97 min.   R   Drama
Dir: Neil LaBute
C: Aaron Eckhart, Stacy Edwards, Matt Malloy

Playwright Neil LaBute's debut film has the feel of someone trying to have the last word on misogyny, and it nearly succeeds. Aaron Eckhart and Matt Malloy play a couple of frustrated office workers on assignment in another city. Because they presume they are superior to all women, they decide to play a little game with a temporary worker, a deaf woman (Stacy Edwards). They both pursue her (without letting on that they know each other) and then dump her hard. There, now didn't that feel better, boys? LaBute plugs in to the disgruntled male zeitgeist also illustrated in *American Beauty, American Psycho,* and *Fight Club,* but in some ways his vision is even bleaker than the ones offered in those films. The writing is what carries the film; LaBute understands how socially impotent men communicate through swaggering generalizations about the world in general and women in particular. The New York Film Critics Circle gave the film its Best First Film award, while the Independent Spirit Awards recognized Eckhart's performance and Labute's screenplay, and Sundance awarded its Filmmaker's Trophy to the entire production.

⊙**DVD:** Includes audio commentaries by Neil LaBute and the cast.

DR20, DR27

Goes well with: *Who's That Knocking at My Door*

IN THE NAME OF THE FATHER

Ireland/U.K./U.S. 1993 C 133 min. R Drama
Dir: Jim Sheridan
C: Daniel Day-Lewis, Pete Postlethwaite, Emma Thompson, John Lynch, Corin Redgrave, Daniel Massey

The excesses of the British authorities in dealing with the real threat of terrorism in Northern Ireland get a thorough airing in this drama based on a true case. Gerry Conlon (Daniel Day-Lewis) is arrested on flimsy evidence for a series of pub bombings in 1974. His father (Pete Postlethwaite) is also hauled in, along with several of Conlon's friends. The script by director Jim Sheridan and Terry George meticulously re-creates the horror of false imprisonment and the growing sense of outrage among activists that the British police were trying to get quick convictions to satisfy public thirst for some kind of retribution. Emma Thompson plays the attorney who endures public charges of being an IRA supporter to get Conlon and his father free. It's a rousing drama fueled by Oscar-nominated performances by Day-Lewis and Postlethwaite.
⊙**DVD**
DR17, DR25, DR26
Goes well with: *Cal*

IN THE REALM OF THE SENSES

Japan/France 1976 C 105 min. NC-17 Drama
Dir: Nagisa Oshima
C: Tatsuya Fuji, Eiko Matsuda, Aio Nakajima, Meika Seri

More than twenty-five years after its release, *In the Realm of the Senses* is still the most sexually explicit film ever released to non-"adult" movie theaters. But this film is not about the joys of sex; writer-director Nagisa Oshima sees the consuming relationship between a prostitute (Eiko Matsuda) and her married lover (Tatsuya Fuji) as a dead end for both participants. Oshima based his screenplay on a real incident in 1936 in which a dazed woman was found wandering the streets of a Japanese city with a man's severed genitals. Oshima suggests that the couple were reacting to Japan's increasing military mobilization by escaping into their private world of pleasure, and he also makes it clear from the very beginning that the prostitute is the real engine that drives this *amour fou* to its inevitable destination. It's a provocative reversal of expectations; we don't expect to see a woman be the aggressor in a sexual relationship. *Senses* is a sobering commentary on voyeurism as well, daring us to watch two actors actually having sex while we wait in the knowledge that the characters they portray will come to a bad end.

⊙**DVD:** Available in subtitled or dubbed editions.

DR19, DR27, DR33

Goes well with: *Last Tango in Paris*

IN WHICH WE SERVE

U.K.   1942   B&W   115 min.   NR   Drama

Dir: Noel Coward and David Lean

C: Noel Coward, John Mills, Bernard Miles, Celia Johnson, Kay Walsh, Joyce Carey, Michael Wilding, James Donald, Richard Attenborough, Daniel Massey, Juliet Mills

Is it "impossibly patronizing," or can it be said that "unlike most WWII films, this masterpiece doesn't date one bit"? This drama of men from a sunken destroyer sitting in their life raft and recalling how they got there (in extended flashbacks) is indisputably the ultimate in stiff upper lips, from none other than Noel Coward, who wrote, codirected with newcomer David Lean, and starred as the commander. The author of the negative assessment is respected British critic Tom Milne, while the second quote is from American critic and historian Leonard Maltin, who gives the film four stars in his invaluable annual guide. Milne's perspective that the film is a "reminder of strictures of snobbery and privilege in the services" is correct, but that doesn't diminish the emotional impact of its story. And after all, that's Coward there on the rubber raft with his men; it's not like he sent them off to battle while observing through heavy lenses.

DR37

Goes well with: *The Bridge on the River Kwai*

THE INNOCENTS

U.K.   1961   B&W   100 min.   NR   Drama

Dir: Jack Clayton

C: Deborah Kerr, Michael Redgrave, Peter Wyngarde, Megs Jenkins, Pamela Franklin, Martin Stephens

Henry James is well served by this stylish interpretation of *The Turn of the Screw.* Screenwriters William Archibald and Truman Capote are sensitive to James's nuances and add a few of their own in the story of a governess (Deborah Kerr) whose visions of dead servants place her young charges in more danger than they should be. Kerr, an actress who was respected and yet strangely underrated over the course of her long career, gives her best performance here; she slowly reveals the pathology behind Miss Giddens's good intentions without ever turning her into a raving psycho. Director Jack Clayton and cinematographer Freddie Francis deserve credit, too, for creating a wonderfully suggestive atmosphere in which Miss Giddens's fantasies can flourish.

DR27, DR29, TH3

Goes well with: *Don't Look Now*

INTO THE ARMS OF STRANGERS: STORIES OF THE KINDERTRANSPORT

U.S./U.K.   2000   C/B&W   122 min.   PG   Documentary

Dir: Mark Jonathan Harris

The tales of the more than ten thousand children who found refuge away from the threats of the Nazis finally get their own film. In the wake of Kristallnacht (November 9, 1938), when the Nazis' murderous intentions became clear to many Jews, an agreement was reached with Great Britain to take in boatloads of youngsters. (England was the only country willing to relax its immigration laws; the United States considered the matter but decided that separating children from their parents was wrong.) The memories of several Kindertransport children are interwoven with vintage footage of them being herded into holiday camps, where they waited for sponsoring families to take them in. Among the interviewees in this Oscar-winning documentary is actor-director Richard Attenborough, whose family sponsored a pair of Jewish girls.

⊙**DVD:** Includes audio commentaries by the filmmakers.

DO3, DO7

Goes well with: *The Last Days*

ISADORA

U.K.   1968   C   168 min.   PG   Drama

Dir: Karel Reisz

C: Vanessa Redgrave, James Fox, Jason Robards, Ivan Tchenko, John Fraser, Bessie Love

Like T. E. Lawrence, Isadora Duncan, the high priestess of modern dance, seems too big a personality to be contained in one film. This

sprawling mess of a movie commemorates her with a fearlessly energetic performance by Vanessa Redgrave, but it's not much more successful than Ken Russell's famed hour-long documentary at leaving us
with an understanding of what made Isadora tick. Not only was Isadora
an innovative dancer, but she led the kind of tempestuous personal life
that today would earn her a nightly slot on *Entertainment Tonight.* The
film was originally released in December 1968, only in Los Angeles, in
order to qualify for the Academy Awards; that print ran 177 minutes.
The distributor thought better of that version and began hacking away at
it, adding a new title, *The Loves of Isadora.* (Said loves were stage designer Gordon Craig, played by James Fox; sewing machine magnate
Paris Singer, played by Jason Robards; and Russian poet Sergei Ess-
enin, played by Ivan Tchenko.) At a little over two hours, the film still
managed to make sense, but barely. Happily, much of the cut footage
has since been restored in a special video edition of 168 minutes.

DR4, DR17

Goes well with: *Lola Montès*

IVAN THE TERRIBLE, PART ONE
ESSENTIAL

Soviet Union   1943   B&W   99 min.   NR   Drama
Dir: Sergei Eisenstein
C: Nikolai Cherkasov, Ludmila Tselikovskaya, Serafima Birman

Sergei Eisenstein's last film was half triumph, half disaster for the
filmmaker. Originally conceived as a three-part film on Czar Ivan IV,
who tried to consolidate the Russian empire in the sixteenth century and
was considered by the Soviet powers to be a national hero, it was never
completed. Part One, detailing Ivan's rise to power and his conquering
of Siberia, earned Eisenstein great acclaim from Stalin and his cohorts.
But Eisenstein suffered a heart attack after finishing Part Two. While he
was recuperating, the film was shown to Stalin, who detested its portrayal of Ivan's increasing paranoia and his use of the *oprichniki,* an
early version of the KGB, to crush his internal enemies. Although the
film was withdrawn, Stalin approved the filming of the third chapter,
but Eisenstein's poor health prevented the project from ever going into
production. He died in 1948, and Part Two didn't debut in the Soviet
Union for another ten years. Both films are marvelously constructed
and beautifully photographed, the most accessible of all of Eisenstein's

films, with a stunning central performance by Nikolai Cherkasov and a musical score by Sergei Prokofiev (who had also done the honors on Eisenstein's *Alexander Nevsky*).

⊙**DVD:** Includes liner notes by critic Rob Edelman.

DR17, DR25

Goes well with: *Alexander Nevsky*

IVAN THE TERRIBLE, PART TWO

ESSENTIAL

Soviet Union 1946 C/B&W 85 min. NR Drama

Dir: Sergei Eisenstein

C: Nikolai Cherkasov, Serafima Birman, Mikhail Nazvanov, Pavel Kadochnikov

For a description, see entry for *Ivan the Terrible, Part One*.

⊙**DVD:** Includes liner notes by critic Rob Edelman.

DR17, DR25

Goes well with: *Alexander Nevsky*

J

JEAN DE FLORETTE
ESSENTIAL

France/Switzerland/Italy   1986   C   122 min.   PG   Drama
Dir: Claude Berri
C: Yves Montand, Gérard Depardieu, Daniel Auteuil, Elisabeth Depardieu

The first of a two-part adaptation of a Marcel Pagnol novel, *Jean de Florette* tells a story of evil triumphant over good. (Part two, *Manon of the Spring,* reverses that outcome.) An arrogant farmer (Yves Montand) and his dimwitted son (Daniel Auteuil) conspire to cheat a former tax collector who has inherited a neighboring piece of land, concealing the existence of a natural spring that would help the novice farmer to get his crops started. Gérard Depardieu is terrific as the hunchback who is heartbreakingly trusting of his neighbors. The film offers exquisite views of the Provence countryside that was the setting for so many Pagnol stories, but director Claude Berri and writer Gerard Brach never let us forget the vagaries of the farming life, so dependent on the whims of the weather as well as the goodwill of your fellow man.
⊙**DVD**
DR29
Goes well with: *Manon of the Spring*

JOUR SE LÈVE, LE.
See *Le Jour Se Lève*

JU DOU

China/Japan 1989 C 95 min. PG-13 Drama
Dir: Zhang Yimou and Yang Fengliang
C: Gong Li, Li Wei, Li Bao-Tian, Zhang Yi

As one of the first films from mainland China to be released in the United States, *Ju Dou* carried a special badge of distinction. It was banned by Chinese authorities; they found its story, set in the 1920s, of a woman defying her older husband by having an affair with his nephew, to be an implied critique of contemporary (and mostly elderly) political leaders. Things got even stickier when it was submitted to the Academy as China's official entry for the foreign-language film Oscar, and nominated. The second of Zhang Yimou's six films with actress Gong Li is among the best, both for her radiant performance and for the director's use of color—the action takes place mainly in a textile factory—to match or offset the changing moods of the story.

⊙**DVD**
DR19, DR24, DR39
Goes well with: *Raise the Red Lantern*

JUGGERNAUT

U.K. 1974 C 110 min. PG Thriller
Dir: Richard Lester
C: Richard Harris, Omar Sharif, David Hemmings, Anthony Hopkins,
    Shirley Knight, Ian Holm, Roy Kinnear, Freddie Jones

The plague of disaster movies in the mid-1970s did produce one authentically great film. Richard Alan Simmons's script concerns a mad bomber who calls himself Juggernaut. He places seven steel drums containing high explosives aboard an ocean liner, then calls the company that owns the ship just after it departs from England with 1,200 passengers. His demand is an immense ransom. The film neatly cuts back and forth between the attempts of the authorities to track down the bomber and the action aboard the ship, where a bomb squad is helicoptered in to try to defuse the situation. One strength of this film is its cast; the standouts are Richard Harris and David Hemmings as the leaders of the bomb squad, Shirley Knight as a woman having an on-again off-again affair with the ship's captain (Omar Sharif), Roy Kinnear as a steward desperately trying to cheer up an increasingly nervous passenger list, and Anthony Hopkins as an executive of the shipping company whose wife and children are on the ship. *Juggernaut* is more interested in exploring character than in staging big action scenes, and, as in all his best films, Lester captures the rueful humor behind the tension in any situation.

TH1

Goes well with: *High and Low*

JULES AND JIM

ESSENTIAL

France   1961   B&W   104 min.   NR   Drama
Dir: François Truffaut
C: Jeanne Moreau, Oskar Werner, Henri Serre, Marie Dubois

Any filmmaker who tries to work in the risky area of the romantic triangle has to contend with the very long shadow of François Truffaut's masterful rendition of the Henri Roché novel. (Roché's only other novel, *Two English Girls,* also about a romantic triangle, was made into a stunning but underseen film by Truffaut.) Set in the World War I era, the story focuses on Catherine (Jeanne Moreau), the free-spirited woman loved by best buddies Jules (Oskar Werner) and Jim (Henri Serre). Can their friendship survive this romantic rivalry? How will the outbreak of war affect this German and Frenchman? For a time, the trio seem to be having so much fun (without a hint that sex could come between them) that we're lulled into a state of bliss. Surely they'll work it out, *oui? Mais non.* Catherine has to choose, but of course she can't, and the bittersweet ending is both inevitable and perfectly appropriate. It is a tribute to the blinding power of young love and friendship. A real plus: Georges Delerue's deliriously romantic score.

⊙**DVD**

DR12, DR18, DR29

Goes well with: *Two English Girls*

K

KAGEMUSHA
Japan 1980 C 159 min. PG Drama
Dir: Akira Kurosawa
C: Tatsuya Nakadai, Tsutomu Yamazaki, Kenichi Hagiwara, Jinpachi Nezu

Akira Kurosawa made two magnificent costume epics near the end of his career, this film and *Ran*. As a sign of respect for their colleague (and as a dramatic illustration of how difficult it was for Japan's greatest director to get financing), American filmmakers Francis Ford Coppola and George Lucas produced this film. In the sixteenth century, a warlord's clan devises a plan to disguise his death: They persuade a common thief to pose as their fallen leader and keep the peace, in a very broad manner of speaking. The thief has to fool not only the enemy but the warlord's family. Kurosawa effortlessly combines the intimate story of a man living a lie (but enjoying his newfound privileges nonetheless) with several battle scenes that confirm the director's reputation as the best large-scale action filmmaker of them all. Tatsuya Nakadai is perfection as both the warlord and his impostor.

DR24, DR25, DR37
Goes well with: *Ran*

KAMA SUTRA: A TALE OF LOVE
India 1996 C 114 min. NR Drama
Dir: Mira Nair
C: Indira Varma, Sarita Choudhury, Naveen Andrews, Ramon Tikaram

It's a bit of a come-on, that title, like something you'd find in the listings for your cable or satellite dish adult channels. (Not that you ever watch any of those films, of course.) But Mira Nair's film is that rarity, an intelligent story of how women can use their sexuality to gain a measure of power. The story is set in sixteenth-century India, when women were essentially slaves, bound by custom reinforced by religion. Maya (Indira Varma) is a servant who attracts the eye of a randy prince, and she determines that the way out of a future of drudgery is to make him her slave by means of the title text. What she doesn't count on is losing him to her "friend," a pouty princess (Sarita Choudhury) who has, after all, been reading the same book. The film was criticized by some as conservative, as if these women had much of a choice when it came to wielding some sense of power in their lives. The cinematography by Declan Quinn won an Independent Spirit Award. The film is available in both R-rated (113 min.) and unrated versions on video; the difference is not in the dialogue.

⊙**DVD:** Includes audio commentary by Mira Nair.

DR24, DR33, DR39

Goes well with: *Raise the Red Lantern*

KANAL

ESSENTIAL

Poland   1956   B&W   97 min.   NR   Drama

Dir: Andrzej Wajda

C: Teresa Izewska, Tadeusz Janczar, Wienczlaw Glinski, Wladyslaw Sheybal

It's astonishing to realize how few films have dealt with the subject of resistance movements during World War II. *Kanal,* the second film in Andrzej Wajda's trilogy of wartime Poland (bracketed by *A Generation* and *Ashes and Diamonds*), is set literally underground, in the sewers beneath Warsaw in 1944, when the remnants of the partisan movement is trying to escape the Nazis. It's not a movie for claustrophobics, but it is exciting and intelligent filmmaking, as Wajda and screenwriter Jerzy Stefan Sawinski sketch in a half-dozen characters' stories amid the chaos.

DR36, DR38

Goes well with: *Ashes and Diamonds*

KANDAHAR

Iran/France   2001   C   85 min.   NR   Drama

Dir: Mohsen Makhmalbaf

C: Niloufar Pazira, Hassan Tantai, Sadou Teymouri

No film released in 2001 enjoyed better timing than this drama set in Afghanistan. The story concerns Nafas, a journalist returning to her homeland after years abroad to find her sister, who is still living in the title city. In a letter to Nafas, the sister has threatened to kill herself in the wake of a land-mine accident that destroyed her legs. For a woman to enter Taliban-ruled Afghanistan alone and travel overland to anywhere in the interior was a daunting task, and the film follows Nafas's struggles to seek protection from a series of guides and groups. Aside from a helicopter, which carries her to the border in the opening scene, and a tape recorder she uses to record her thoughts, there is almost nothing in this film that suggests that it takes place in the twentieth century. Mohsen Makhmalbaf based his script on his lead actress's own life; she had tried to reenter Afghanistan in the early 1990s to visit a desperate friend. The narrative sometimes bogs down in scenes that don't quite pay off, but the director's eye for the stark beauty of desert landscapes more than compensates. This is an invaluable record of an era that we can only hope has ended in the wake of September 11.

DR7, DR39, XT5
Goes well with: *The Circle*

KICKING AND SCREAMING

U.S.   1995   C   96 min.   R   Comedy
Dir: Noah Baumbach
C: Josh Hamilton, Eric Stoltz, Olivia d'Abo, Chris Eigeman, Parker Posey, Jason Wiles, Elliott Gould

We're in the Twilight Zone here, where college students hang on for years after they've allegedly graduated, afraid to confront the so-called real world. Director Noah Baumbach (who cowrote with Oliver Berkman) rounds up the usual suspects and then manages to breathe new life into a flagging genre. It's an updated version of *Diner* in which the men play Peter Pan while their girlfriends move on into adulthood—and then the guys sit around and complain about their inability to sustain a relationship. If you loved Chris Eigeman in the Whit Stillman movies *Metropolitan* and *Barcelona,* you'll love him here, doing his too-clever-by-half shtick. It works, and so does the rest of the cast, including the always exquisite Parker Posey.

CO5
Goes well with: *Dazed and Confused*

THE KILLER
ESSENTIAL

Hong Kong 1989 C 110 min. NR Action-Adventure
Dir: John Woo
C: Chow Yun-Fat, Sally Yeh, Danny Lee, Kenneth Tsang

The movie that lifted Hong Kong action director John Woo from semiobscurity to worldwide fame, *The Killer* also gave a big career boost to frequent Woo star Chow Yun-Fat. He plays Jeffrey Chow, a hired assassin who bungles a job in a crowded nightclub. When Jenny (Sally Yeh), a beautiful singer, is accidentally blinded in the crossfire, Chow feels responsible for raising money for a sight-restoring operation. A detective (Danny Lee) in pursuit of Chow learns of his plan, and the two develop a kind of grudging respect for each other—a motif of Woo's best work. Oh yes, the two adversaries' nicknames on the street are Mickey Mouse and Dumbo. It is as corny as it sounds, but the real attraction in any Woo film are the action scenes, and the shoot-out finale in a church (which Woo restaged in his Hollywood film *Face/Off*) is a mind-blower, filled with shafts of light and fluttering doves.

⊙**DVD:** Includes audio commentaries by John Woo and producer Terence Chang; deleted scenes.

TH9, XT6
Goes well with: *Hard-Boiled*

THE KILLING FIELDS
U.K. 1984 C 141 min. R Drama
Dir: Roland Joffe
C: Sam Waterston, Haing S. Ngor, John Malkovich, Julian Sands, Craig
  T. Nelson, Bill Paterson, Athol Fugard, Spalding Gray

Leave it to the Brits to beat us Yanks to the punch and make one of the best films about Southeast Asia's tumult during the 1970s. Sam Waterston plays *New York Times* reporter Sidney Schanberg, who remained in Cambodia even after American personnel were evacuated in anticipation of the fall of Phnom Penh to the Khmer Rouge in 1975. As brave as Schanberg was, his actions did place Dith Pran, his translator, in peril, and much of the film dramatizes Pran's capture, torture, and eventual escape to be reunited with Schanberg. Haing S. Ngor as Pran won a supporting actor Oscar in his debut performance; equally impressive was the work of director Roland Joffe, also making his debut after a career in theater and documentaries. Chris Menges won an Oscar and a

New York Film Critics Circle award for his brilliant cinematography, which captures the beauty of a land ravaged by a senseless war. Jim Clark's film editing was also an Oscar winner.

⊙**DVD:** Includes audio commentary by Roland Joffe.

DR17, DR26, DR38

Goes well with: *The Year of Living Dangerously*

KIND HEARTS AND CORONETS

U.K.   1949   B&W   104 min.   NR   Comedy

Dir: Robert Hamer

C: Dennis Price, Alec Guinness, Valerie Hobson, Joan Greenwood, Hugh Griffith

Before the term "black comedy" was coined, *Kind Hearts and Coronets* was tickling audiences with its audacious story of a man who lays waste to an entire family in order to come into a title he believes rightfully belongs to him. This killing spree is set in Edwardian England, when a title attached to your name was in some ways more important than being a millionaire. Dennis Price plays Louis, the man who would be duke, but the main reason this film remains a perennial favorite is Alec Guinness, who plays all eight victims of Louis's dastardly plan. *Kind Hearts* is the most beloved product of Britain's Ealing Studios, which churned out a raft of sophisticated and satirical comedies in the 1940s and 1950s, including *The Ladykillers* and *The Lavender Hill Mob.*

CO1, CO3

Goes well with: *The Ladykillers*

KING OF THE HILL

U.S.   1993   C   103 min.   PG-13   Drama

Dir: Steven Soderbergh

C: Jesse Bradford, Jeroen Krabbé, Lisa Eichhorn, Karen Allen, Spalding Gray, Elizabeth McGovern

Writer A. E. Hotchner is best known for his biography of Ernest Hemingway, but on the basis of this film, his memoir of growing up during the Depression should be rediscovered. As a twelve-year-old, Hotchner found himself living alone in a ramshackle St. Louis hotel when his mentally unstable mother was hospitalized and his salesman father took to the road to support his fractured family. Soderbergh neither sentimentalizes the material nor turns it into something grotesque; this is a tale of survival, and Aaron (Jesse Bradford) proves a resourceful kid at fooling inquisitive adults into thinking he's not on his own. Jeroen Krabbé and Lisa Eichhorn are good in the limited roles of Aaron's parents, but this is Bradford's film, and he's a natural, with a lot of help from Soderbergh's sensitive direction and script.

DR11, DR24, DR41

Goes well with: *The Four Hundred Blows*

THE KINGDOM

Denmark 1994 C 279 min. NR Comedy
Dir: Lars von Trier and Morten Arnfred
C: Ernst-Hugo Järegård, Kirsten Rolffes, Ghita Nørby, Søren Pilmark, Holger Juul Hansen

Fans of the TV series *St. Elsewhere,* about a run-down Boston hospital and its valiant staff and weird assortment of patients, may be drawn to Lars von Trier's miniseries for its similar setting. But Danish TV is clearly a more wide-open medium than its American network counterpart, allowing von Trier to populate his darkly comic stories with ghosts, oversexed doctors, corrupt administrators, and a pair of dishwashers with Down's syndrome who offer running commentaries on the latest action. Shot in desaturated color with frequent use of handheld cameras, the narrative is fractured enough that if one thread doesn't hold you, he'll soon pick up another one. This is, to borrow from critic Michael Weldon, psychotronic TV, whose only rival stateside would be HBO's determinedly grim prison series *Oz.*

CO2

Goes well with: *Blue Velvet*

KISS OF THE SPIDER WOMAN

U.S./Brazil 1985 C/B&W 119 min. R Drama
Dir: Hector Babenco
C: William Hurt, Raul Julia, Sonia Braga, José Lewgoy

Manuel Puig's novel of mismatched cellmates—a rabid revolutionary and a dreamy gay man—in a Latin American jail is both schematic and wonderfully allusive, and the movie has the same shortcomings and virtues. Foremost among the latter are the lead performances by Raul Julia and William Hurt. Naturally, Hurt, in the flashier role of Molina, the man who dreams about movie stars rather than facing reality, got all the acclaim as well as the Oscar. But the underrated Julia is superb as well; Valentin is the character transformed by the shared experience, and Julia is totally convincing at portraying the subtle shifts in this ideologue's thinking. Hector Babenco and screenwriter Leonard Schrader skillfully mix gritty jailhouse confrontations with Molina's gauzily imagined scenes from his favorite film, starring the luscious Sonia Braga in the title role. The Independent Spirit Awards honored the film with the Special Distinction Award.

DR25, DR26, DR29
Goes well with: *Strawberry and Chocolate*

KNIFE IN THE WATER
ESSENTIAL

Poland 1962 B&W 94 min. NR Drama
Dir: Roman Polanski
C: Leon Niemczyk, Jolanta Umecka, Zygmunt Malanowicz

A modestly mounted but stunning feature debut, Roman Polanski's three-character psychodrama set the tone for much of his best work to come. A couple on their way to a weekend on their sailboat pick up a handsome young hitchhiker, and pretty soon he's crewing for them as well. No good can come of this, but Polanski and cowriters Jerzy Skolimowski and Jakub Goldberg reveal the fissures in the relationship between Andrzej (Leon Niemczyk) and Christine (Jolanta Umecka) a few cracks at a time. By the time someone goes overboard, you're almost relieved that there isn't blood on the decks instead. Polanski is brilliant at portraying the mind games people play with one another and on themselves. This was a preview of great things to come, and from *Repulsion* through *The Tenant,* Polanski proved himself the master of the psychological thriller.

⊙**DVD**
DR27
Goes well with: *Dead Calm*

THE KRAYS
U.K. 1990 C 119 min. R Drama
Dir: Peter Medak
C: Billie Whitelaw, Gary Kemp, Martin Kemp, Susan Fleetwood, Charlotte Cornwell, Kate Hardie, Victor Spinetti

British crime dramas come in two flavors, nasty and truly nasty, and *The Krays* falls nicely into the latter camp, in part because it's all true. (Well, with a few changes for dramatic purposes.) Ronald and Reggie Kray were twin sons of the same monstrous mum, and they ruled their little East End corner of the London underworld with panache and persuasiveness in the late 1950s and 1960s. Philip Ridley's script follows R&R from their teen years as boxers through their blighted military service (much of it spent in prison) and on to their thriving "business" operations, headquartered in a modest pool hall. Singers Martin and Gary Kemp (of Spandau Ballet) are eerily effective as the twins, one of them ever the ladies' man (when he weds in 1965, you feel like his wife has been handed a death sentence), the other a tormented homosexual. You can look no further than the Krays' mother, played by Billie Whitelaw in a performance to rival that of Faye Dunaway as Joan Crawford, to understand the boys' twisted view of morality.

DR1, DR6, DR17, XT7

Goes well with: *The General*

KURT & COURTNEY

U.K. 1998 C 95 min. R Documentary

Dir: Nick Broomfield

C: Courtney Love

If filmmaker Nick Broomfield comes knocking on your door with his cameraman, you know you're in big trouble. Broomfield spends a lot of time tracking down people who knew famous people (or people who knew people who knew famous people), and said famous people are usually infamous. Case in point: Kurt Cobain, gifted, troubled, and dead musician, and his widow, Courtney Love. Did Kurt kill himself, or did he have help, and what does Courtney know about this? Broomfield's film is about much more than solving a mystery. This is the culture of celebrity laid bare in all its wretched splendor. Broomfield includes too much about his own difficulties in getting people to talk, but that does seem to be part of the point after a while. He is the stand-in for all of us who would love to get to the bottom of whatever mystery trouble us about a famous person.

⊙**DVD**

DO4, DO5

Goes well with: *The Filth and the Fury*

KWAIDAN

Japan   1964   C   164 min.   NR   Horror

Dir: Masaki Kobayashi

C: Rentaro Mikuni, Michiyo Aratama, Tatsuya Nakadai, Keiko Kishi,
Katsuo Nakamura, Takashi Shimura, Ganemon Nakamura, Noboru
Nakaya

A four-story horror film, *Kwaidan* may disappoint audiences who
are used to fast-moving and bloody tales of mad killers. It's based on the
writings of Lafcadio Hearn, a European who moved to Japan and in
1895 became a naturalized citizen. Hearn absorbed the folk culture of
his adopted land, as evidenced in these spooky stories of a faithless
samurai, a blind musician who plays for the ghost of a dead child emperor, two woodcutters menaced by an evil snow witch, and a swordsman possessed by the soul of a rival warrior. The magnificent sets (by
art director Shigemasa Toda), lush wide-screen cinematography (by
Yoshio Miyajima), and striking use of sound effects and traditional
Japanese music (by Toru Takemitsu) make *Kwaidan* one of the most
technically impressive films you'll ever see. In other words, it's best experienced on DVD.

⊙**DVD**

FA9, XT1, XT8

Goes well with: *Nosferatu the Vampyre*

L

L'ATALANTE

ESSENTIAL

France 1934 B&W 89 min. NR Drama
Dir: Jean Vigo
C: Michel Simon, Dita Parlo, Jean Dasté, Gilles Margaritis

Director Jean Vigo is the Buddy Holly of French filmmaking: He died young (at twenty-nine, of leukemia) and left a small but disproportionately influential body of work. His third and last film is one of the screen's great romances, about a couple (Dita Parlo and Jean Dasté) who live on a barge that floats through France. They're in love, they fight, she disappears, he goes searching for her, and . . . Ah, no fair peeking. Vigo imbues his characters with a wonderfully prickly kind of humanity—they are both very specific and generic lovers, who have to come to an understanding about each other for their affection to take root. Vigo, the son of an anarchist who mysteriously died in prison when young Jean was twelve, is aware of life's absurdities, but he's also a romantic, and the tension between these strains of thought informs both *L'Atalante* and his wonderful schoolboy fantasy *Zero for Conduct*. A Jean Vigo Prize is still awarded annually, nearly seventy years after his death; filmmakers as diverse as François Truffaut and Lindsay Anderson have acknowledged Vigo's influence on their work.

DR18, DR36
Goes well with: *Dogfight*

L'AVVENTURA

ESSENTIAL

France/Italy 1960 B&W 145 min. NR Drama

Dir: Michelangelo Antonioni

C: Monica Vitti, Gabriele Ferzetti, Lea Massari, Dominique Blanchar, James Addams

In retrospect, it seems that everything Michelangelo Antonioni did in nearly twenty years of filmmaking before *L'Avventura* was in preparation for it, and everything afterward was a variation of it. *L'Avventura* isn't just Antonioni's acknowledged masterpiece; it is one of the greatest films ever made. Two years after its release, a critics' survey by the respected film magazine *Sight and Sound* already had placed it second on its all-time Ten Best list (after *Citizen Kane*). The story breaks into two parts: Anna (Lea Massari) disappears during an outing on a nearly deserted island off the coast of Sicily; then her fiancé, Sandro (Gabriele Ferzetti), and best friend, Claudia (Monica Vitti), travel through the country, ostensibly tracking down reports of her appearance, while they begin an affair. *L'Avventura* is an astonishingly modern film; its characters use sex to relieve their boredom and are in turn bored by their own pleasures; its visual style is cool, detached, and deliberate. Antonioni and his cinematographer, Aldo Scavarda, frame the characters largely in isolation; even when they're making love, they don't seem to be connecting at all (both Anna and Claudia are caught by the camera looking over Sandro's shoulder, their eyes betraying ennui). No filmmaker ever saw the world quite the way Antonioni did, and while he made several excellent films after *L'Avventura,* he had set the bar impossibly high. The Criterion DVD is highly recommended, both for its pristine images and for the excellent commentary by Gene Youngblood.

⊙**DVD:** Two-disc set: includes audio commentary by film historian Gene Youngblood; documentary, "Antonioni, Documents and Testimonials"; Antonioni writings read by Jack Nicholson; Nicholson's reminiscences of Antonioni; reprint of Antonioni's statement about the film after its premiere at the 1960 Cannes Film Festival.

DR19, DR20, XT5

Goes well with: *Pierrot le Fou*

LA BELLE NOISEUSE

ESSENTIAL

France/Switzerland 1991 C 240 min. NR Drama

Dir: Jacques Rivette

C: Michel Piccoli, Jane Birkin, Emmanuelle Béart, Marianne Benicourt, David Burszstein, Gilles Arbona

In most films about artists, we watch a painter slapping oil on a canvas, a musician sitting thoughtfully at the piano, a writer pounding the keys of the typewriter, but we still have no idea how that painting, that symphony, or that novel really came into being. Jacques Rivette (along with cowriters Pascal Bonitzer and Christine Laurent) explicates the process with the story of Edouard, a middle-aged painter (Michel Piccoli) inspired to resume work after a ten-year hiatus when he meets Marianne (Emmanuelle Béart), an aspiring writer. Marianne reminds him of a subject he had long wanted to paint but never had the right model for. She agrees to pose for him, much of the time in the nude. Rivette daringly lets many scenes run in real time; the moments when Edouard gets out his brushes and paints and other equipment tick on and on, as we feel Marianne's tension over the uncertainty of her decision. But we also see Edouard in the process of getting his artistic chops back, creating sketch after sketch in preparation for a full-blown painting. *La Belle Noiseuse* is also about the casual selfishness of the artist; Edouard is nearly oblivious to Marianne's physical discomfort, and once he begins working, he's only vaguely aware of his much younger wife, Liz (Jane Birkin). Edouard's final decision about the disposition of his painting reveals that he understands the process was more important than the actual result. Bernard Dufour did the drawings and paintings; the musical score is drawn from the works of Igor Stravinsky. This is an immensely rewarding film, well worth its lavish running time.

DR2

Goes well with: *The Blood of a Poet*

LA CÉRÉMONIE

France/Germany 1995 C 111 min. NR Drama
Dir: Claude Chabrol
C: Isabelle Huppert, Sandrine Bonnaire, Jacqueline Bisset, Jean-Pierre Cassel, Virginie Ledoyen, Valentin Merlet

A bourgeois family enjoys opera telecasts on a lavish home-theater system while the maid watches music videos on the modest TV in her room; everyone is happy, right? Not when director Claude Chabrol is on hand to stir up a little class warfare. Working from a novel by Ruth Rendell, Chabrol and cowriter Caroline Eliacheff carefully set up the possibilities for trouble: Dad (Jean-Pierre Cassel) is sure that the local postmistress (Isabelle Huppert) is opening the family mail, while the maid (Sandrine Bonnaire) strikes up a friendship with the same woman.

Mom (Jacqueline Bisset, speaking French!) is on her second marriage, and teen daughter (Virginie Ledoyen) has serious boyfriend problems. Bonnaire and Huppert are the best young French actresses of the last twenty years, and their teaming here as a pair of outcasts who share a resentment toward their social betters is sublime.

DR5, DR12, TH14

Goes well with: *The Discreet Charm of the Bourgeoisie*

LA DOLCE VITA

ESSENTIAL

Italy 1960 B&W 175 min. NR Drama
Dir: Federico Fellini
C: Marcello Mastroianni, Anita Ekberg, Anouk Aimée, Yvonne Furneaux, Magali Noël, Alain Cuny, Lex Barker

When a movie's title enters the popular lexicon, should we merely genuflect at its feet and move on to the next title? Federico Fellini's best-known film, which won the foreign film prize from the New York Film Critics Circle, helped kick off a subgenre dismissively titled by one critic the Come Dressed as the Sick Soul of Europe Parties movies. Here in the States, we always suspected that the folks across the pond were decadent, and Fellini gives us ample evidence in his tale of a jaded society reporter (Marcello Mastroianni) stumbling through Rome, observing the absurdities of contemporary urban life. He covers a series of parties, he follows a buxom actress (Anita Ekberg) around until her boyfriend assaults him, he covers the story of two children who claim to have had visions of the Virgin Mary, and there are more parties. There is a character named Paparazzo, who is a persistent photographer of everyone and everything that might be termed famous; now you know the origin of the term "paparazzi." It should be clear by now if someone made a movie like this today, everyone would be screaming about how relevant it is to our star-struck, scandal-obsessed, sensation-soaked print and electronic media. *Grazie,* Signor Fellini, for being so prescient.

DR20, DR36, XT7

Goes well with: *Divorce—Italian Style*

LA FEMME NIKITA

France/Italy 1990 C 117 min. R Action-Adventure
Dir: Luc Besson

C: Anne Parillaud, Jean-Hughes Anglade, Tcheky Karyo, Jeanne Moreau, Jean Reno

It's trashy fun, and it clearly has struck a nerve, spawning an American remake (*Point of No Return*) and a TV series (using the original title). Welcome to the brave new world where movie women can handle a gun just as well as their male counterparts, while showing minimal emotion at the carnage they can create. The antiheroine is a punk terrorist (Anne Parillaud) who is given a reprieve from a death sentence by government agents interested in reprogramming her to become an undercover assassin, channeling her skill at mayhem (and her indifference to morality) into "positive" ends. It's the Dirty Dozen Minus Eleven, with a Sex Change. The movie is about as cynical as possible without being totally misanthropic. The opening scene, a violent drugstore shootout, is staged with such verve that you think director Luc Besson can't possibly keep up the energy, but he somehow does.

⊙**DVD**

AC5, TH6

Goes well with: *The Killer*

LA PROMESSE

Belgium/France/Luxembourg/Tunisia   1996   C   93 min.   NR Drama

Dir: Jean-Pierre Dardenne and Luc Dardenne

C: Jérémie Rénier, Olivier Gourmet, Assita Ouedraogo, Rasmané Ouedraogo

A fifteen-year-old boy's world should revolve around riding go-carts, not a promise he makes to a dying man, but such is the fate of Igor in this closely observed coming-of-age drama. Igor works for his father, Roger, who smuggles illegal immigrants into France and helps them get menial labor, profiting from the fees they pay him and the substandard housing he provides. When an African man (Rasmané Ouedraogo) whose wife (Assita Ouedraogo) and infant Igor has befriended is killed in a construction accident, Roger covers up the death for fear of attracting attention from the authorities. But it is Igor who is left to deal with the promise he made to the man to take care of his family. Jérémie Rénier and Olivier Gourmet star as the son and father, bound by love but eventually torn apart by Igor's guilt and sense of obligation. Directors Jean-Pierre and Luc Dardenne (they are brothers) filmed much of the story with handheld cameras, to reinforce the unsettled emotions of its main character.

⊙**DVD**
DR11, DR28, DR40, DR41
Goes well with: *Pelle the Conqueror*

LA RONDE

ESSENTIAL

France 1950 B&W 97 min. NR Drama
Dir: Max Ophüls
C: Anton Walbrook, Serge Reggiani, Simone Simon, Simone Signoret, Daniel Gélin, Danielle Darrieux, Fernand Gravet, Odette Joyeux, Isa Miranda, Jean-Louis Barrault, Gérard Philipe

Perhaps it's the setting—late-nineteenth-century Vienna, where the easy circular gliding of the waltz symbolized a kind of casual attitude toward romance among the upper classes. Or it's the author—Arthur Schnitzler, who probed said classes with wit and perception in his plays and novels (one of the latter was updated for Stanley Kubrick's *Eyes Wide Shut*). But it must be the director—Max Ophüls, master at portraying sophisticated but faded elegance with an ever-moving camera. Anton Walbrook is our narrator for this adaptation (by Ophüls and Jacques Natanson) of a Schnitzler play, and his witty observations provide the overlay on a chain of love affairs that eventually work their way into a circle. When American directors try this material, it inevitably looks silly and contrived; some concepts are best left to a specific time, place, and, most important, director.

DR5, DR19
Goes well with: *The Earrings of Madame de . . .*

LA STRADA

ESSENTIAL

Italy 1954 B&W 108 min. NR Drama
Dir: Federico Fellini
C: Anthony Quinn, Giulietta Masina, Richard Basehart, Aldo Silvani

A transitional film for Federico Fellini, *La Strada* proved his first big success with American audiences, winning the Academy Award and New York Film Critics Circle prize for best foreign-language film. Its story of Zampano, a traveling strongman (Anthony Quinn), and Gelsomina, his waifish traveling companion (Giulietta Masina, the director's wife), has elements of the postwar neorealist approach in its depiction of the desolate towns along their journey. But in focusing on only three characters (including Richard Basehart, a tightrope walker known as the Fool), Fellini distills *La Strada* into something resembling a fable: Zampano is heartless physical strength, Gelsomina is spiritual innocence, the Fool is intelligence and wit. Zampano and Gelsomina briefly join a circus, where they meet the Fool; this is an early appearance in a Fellini movie of the circus as a metaphor for life. Nino Rota's haunting theme is a key element. The film holds its age well, thanks in large part to Masina, an exceptionally expressive actress who would have been right at home in the silent days of moviemaking.

DR12, DR16, DR21, XT5

Goes well with: *The Bicycle Thief*

LA TRAVIATA

Italy   1982   C   105 min.   G   Musical

Dir: Franco Zeffirelli

C: Teresa Stratas, Placido Domingo, Cornell MacNeil, Alan Monk

La Traviata proves that a great opera can be translated into a great film, but the risks are so great (big expense for a limited audience) that it's not surprising that few filmmakers have tried. Franco Zeffirelli has the great advantage of working on both stages and movie sets, so he understands the sense of reality that film can impart to very theatrical material. Verdi's opera, based on the Dumas novel *Lady of the Camelias* (known to all Garbo lovers as *Camille*), is grand melodrama—the dying woman of easy virtue concealing her illness from her young nobleman lover. Zeffirelli respects the genre but understands that for all the lavish costumes and dazzling sets, it still comes down to the vocal performers making Verdi's music. And in Teresa Stratas and Placido Domingo, he has the goods. Yes, Domingo was too old to play Alfredo, but when he opens his mouth, you can forgive and forget that. And Stratas is, well, to die for. As Violetta's health declines, Stratas looks more beautiful, her singing more ethereal.

⊙**DVD**

DR5, DR18, MU1

Goes well with: *Carmen*

THE LADY VANISHES

ESSENTIAL

U.K.   1938   B&W   97 min.   NR   Thriller

Dir: Alfred Hitchcock

C: Margaret Lockwood, Michael Redgrave, Paul Lukas, Dame Mae Whitty, Googie Withers, Cecil Parker, Linden Travers, Catherine Lacey, Naunton Wayne, Basil Radford

Said lady being a lovely old governess on a train bound from a fascist-held Balkan country to England. Said lady being played by Dame Mae Whitty, an actress possessing the most appropriate of surnames. Her eyes sparkle, and she almost sings her dialogue, but her chatty governess does disappear about twenty minutes into this delightful thriller, one of Alfred Hitchcock's all-time best. Her newfound friend (played by Margaret Lockwood) can't find her, and no one else on the car is aware of the old lady's existence, let alone her whereabouts. The passenger list includes a self-absorbed musicologist (Michael Redgrave), a friendly brain surgeon (Paul Lukas), and two chaps (Naunton Wayne and Basil Radford) who talk about nothing but cricket. All is not what it seems, including the identity of the governess, but there's no point in spoiling the fun (and this is one of Hitchcock's most purely enjoyable films). *The Lady Vanishes* was a huge hit and a critical success, and it attracted the attention of Hollywood producer David O. Selznick, who brought Hitchcock to America to make *Rebecca.* The timing couldn't have been better for Hitchcock, with wartime restrictions in England severely curtailing film production.

⊙**DVD:** Includes introduction by Tony Curtis.

TH6, TH11, TH16

Goes well with: *The 39 Steps*

THE LADYKILLERS
ESSENTIAL

U.K. 1955 C 90 min. NR Comedy

Dir: Alexander Mackendrick

C: Alec Guinness, Katie Johnson, Cecil Parker, Herbert Lom, Peter Sellers, Danny Green, Frankie Howard

Britain's Ealing Studios produced at least a half-dozen great comedies in the early 1950s, but none darker or funnier than this one, written by William Rose. A gang of crooks hole up in a rooming house run by a sweet little old lady. While they decide what to do with their swag from a robbery, they realize that their landlady, Mrs. Wilberforce, may be on to them, so they turn their attentions to devising a surefire way to dispose of her. Katie Johnson, a veteran character actress, got to shine late in her career as the indestructible Mrs. W; she won the British version of the Oscar for her performance. Her would-be assassins are brilliantly played by Alec Guinness (with an overbite a vampire would die for), Cecil Parker, Herbert Lom, and a young and rather chubby Peter Sellers. Having committed a successful crime, these men are feeling invulnerable, and our delight lies in watching each one outsmart himself.

CO1, CO2

Goes well with: *The Lavender Hill Mob*

LAND AND FREEDOM

Italy/Spain/U.K./Germany 1995 C 109 min. NR Drama
Dir: Ken Loach
C: Ian Hart, Rosana Pastor, Icíar Bollaín, Tom Gilroy

For an event that had such an immediate and long-running impact on world history, the Spanish Civil War has been woefully underrepresented on film, *For Whom the Bell Tolls* being one notable exception. It's especially exciting, then, to report that director Ken Loach and writer Jim Allen's drama about a young Liverpudlian fighting on the side of the Loyalists isn't just a terrific re-creation of that era, it's also a well-drawn portrait of the political divisions within the ranks of the anti-Franco forces. Ian Hart is the Communist worker who signs up to fight the fascists, only to discover that not everyone in Spain is happy to have him and his comrades in arms and ideology walking around their countryside. *Land and Freedom* is clearly on the side of the Loyalists, but Loach and Allen understand that no political movement is free of division and dissent.

DR24, DR25, DR37

Goes well with: *Burnt by the Sun*

LANTANA

ESSENTIAL

Australia/Germany 2001 C 121 min. R Drama
Dir: Ray Lawrence
C: Anthony LaPaglia, Geoffrey Rush, Barbara Hershey, Kerry Armstrong, Rachael Blake, Vince Colosimo, Daniella Farinacci, Glenn Robbins

Watching *Lantana* unfold is like being in on a wonderful voyage of discovery, so I can't tell too much about it without spoiling that experience. The film opens with a shot of the title plant, which grows in dense bushes, and as the camera moves inside the thick growth of one stand of lantana, we see what looks like a corpse. For an hour or more of the story, we aren't even sure who that body might belong to, but the stories that intertwine like the branches of lantana are so intriguing it doesn't matter. They involve four couples living in and around Sydney, Australia. A police detective (Anthony LaPaglia) is cheating on his wife (Kerry Armstrong), and a psychoanalyst (Barbara Hershey) treating the wife is also having her own marital problems with her doctor husband (Geoffrey Rush) in dealing with the senseless murder of their young daughter. Meanwhile, two working-class couples are friends and neighbors but going in opposite directions: one (Vince Colosimo, Daniella Farinacci) get along even though the husband is out of work, and the other (Rachael Blake, Glenn Robbins) are separated and unsure of their future. The secrets that people keep from each other form a recurring and beautifully understated theme. Andrew Bovell adapted his own play, *Speaking in Tongues,* but he clearly reworked the material, because starting with that allusive title, the film displays a marvelous feel for landscape and location. *Lantana* virtually swept the Australian Film Institute Awards in 2001, winning seven equivalents of our Oscars.

DR18, DR19, DR32, DR36

Goes well with: *The Five Senses*

THE LAST DAYS

ESSENTIAL

U.S.   1998   C/B&W   90 min.   PG-13   Documentary
Dir: James Moll

In 1944, with the Allies on the offensive in Europe and the Nazi empire beginning to crumble, Hitler and his minions were not about to surrender on one front. In the face of certain defeat, they kept intact their plans for the Final Solution, deporting thousands of Jews to concentration camps to be experimented upon and murdered. This documentary, a well-deserving Oscar winner, tells the story of five Hungarians— Irene Zisblatt, Renée Firestone, Alice Lok Cahana, Bill Basch, and Tom Lantos (who went on to become a long-serving congressman from California)—who all survived the Nazi invasion of their homeland in 1944. All are shown in both interview sessions and on trips of remembrance with their children or grandchildren back to Hungary (some of which is now Ukraine) and to the sites of the death camps where all but Lantos spent time. In some ways, the most distressing portion of their stories involve how their neighbors and so-called friends turned on them once the German army arrived in Hungary. "You were a hunted animal twenty-four hours a day," Lantos recalls, shaking his head in wonder. The film was produced by Steven Spielberg's Shoah Foundation, formed in the wake of his experiences making *Schindler's List.*

⊙**DVD:** Includes featurette on the Shoah Foundation and deleted footage.

DO3, DO7

Goes well with: *Shoah*

THE LAST DAYS OF CHEZ NOUS

Australia   1993   C   96 min.   R   Drama

Dir: Gillian Armstrong

C: Lisa Harrow, Bruno Ganz, Kerry Fox, Miranda Otto

Director Gillian Armstrong makes thoughtful, well-observed films that have flown below the radar of most filmgoers. Exhibit A: this absorbing drama set in a working-class neighborhood of Sydney, Australia, about the domestic arrangements of an aspiring novelist named Beth (Lisa Harrow), her French husband, J.P. (Bruno Ganz), her teenage daughter, Annie (Miranda Otto), and the new ingredient in the mix, Beth's wayward sister, Vicki (Kerry Fox). Vicki shakes up the comfort level of the household in ways that are both beneficial (a new sense of energy and some variation on the daily rituals and routines) and damaging (a fling with J.P.). Helen Garner's screenplay gives each of the four principals their full due, and Armstrong masterfully allows our sympathies to shift by the moment without confusing our ultimate loyalty to Beth. Harrow is superb at portraying Beth's stability and her vulnerability.

DR11, DR39

Goes well with: *High Tide*

THE LAST DAYS OF DISCO

U.S.   1998   C   113 min.   R   Comedy

Dir: Whit Stillman

C: Chloë Sevigny, Kate Beckinsale, Chris Eigeman, Mackenzie Astin, Matt Kesslar, Robert Sean Leonard, Jennifer Beals

It's no exercise in nostalgia—not coming from Whit Stillman, master of the comedy of manners. Kate Beckinsale and Chloë Sevigny play roommates in New York of the early 1980s; they both work at entry-level jobs, and they are sure that hanging out at a disco is the coolest thing they can do. Beckinsale's Charlotte is the girl who thinks she's got it all down, and she's a champion bluffer when confronted with her ignorance or inexperience. Sevigny's Alice is more trusting and in some ways less needy than Charlotte. They're a wonderful pair of guides to Manhattan social mores, and they get lots of help from Des, the assistant manager of their favorite disco, played by the inimitable Chris Eigeman, who appeared in Stillman's *Metropolitan* and *Barcelona*. As in both of those earlier films, nothing much "happens" here, just a lot of hanging out and subtle shifting of social alliances. As the title states, this is an end-of-an-era film, though in this case the participants are wholly unaware that the times they are a-changin'.

⊙**DVD:** Includes interactive menus.

CO5, CO7, CO8, CO9

Goes well with: *Metropolitan*

THE LAST EMPEROR
ESSENTIAL

Italy/U.K./China   1987   C   218 min.   PG-13   Drama
Dir: Bernardo Bertolucci
C: John Lone, Joan Chen, Peter O'Toole, Ying Ruocheng, Victor Wong, Dennis Dun, Ryuichi Sakamoto

Making a commitment to see this epic story of Pu Yi, either for the first time or to ensure that it's as good as you remembered, would involve watching the director's cut, which added almost an hour to the film. (The running time above reflects this version.) If there was one general criticism of Bernardo Bertolucci's Oscar winner when it was originally released, it was of the film's sometimes choppy narrative, which skipped over periods in the life of China's last monarch. Clearly Bertolucci had been pressured to produce a final cut whose running time would not intimidate audiences, especially since the subject matter was relatively obscure. Bertolucci and cowriter Mark Peploe are interested in how Pu Yi's story spans nearly all of the history of China in the twentieth century, from his pampered youth in the Forbidden City to his exile during World War II, when he became a stooge for the Japanese, and on to his imprisonment during Mao's Cultural Revolution. John Lone plays the grown-up emperor, a man with money to burn and little but his sense of dignity to cling to. Give the producers of this film big points for persuading secretive Chinese officials to allow filming inside the Forbidden City. The film's early images of splendor are breathtaking, but it's the later stages of the emperor's life that are the most dramatically and historically interesting. Vittorio Storaro's Oscar-winning images are best seen in a letterboxed version. The film won all nine Oscars for which it was nominated (for picture, director, adapted screenplay, art direction, cinematography, costume design, editing, score, and sound), as well as the New York Film Critics Circle award for Cinematography.

⊙**DVD:** Director's cut.

DR17, DR24, DR25

Goes well with: *Farewell, My Concubine*

THE LAST LAUGH

ESSENTIAL

Germany 1924 B&W 87 min. NR Drama
Dir: F. W. Murnau
C: Emil Jannings, Maly Delschaft, Max Hiller, Hans Unterkircher

A silent film with minimal dialogue, *The Last Laugh* is a tribute to the genius of two people: actor Emil Jannings and director F. W. Murnau. Jannings plays a proud doorman at a swanky hotel. The symbol of his self-regard is his fancy uniform, with braids, buttons, epaulets—everything short of service ribbons and decorations. Jannings is best at the moments when he thinks no one is watching; his chest puffs out a few more inches and you can see him imagining that he is indeed a very important man. A demotion to washroom attendant—his age precludes heavy lifting—is a devastating event for him, and he desperately conceals his change in status from his wife and neighbors. Murnau and cameraman Karl Freund experiment with subjective point of view; the doorman's agitated state is expressed with wobbly shots that go in and out of focus. The technique binds us even closer to his plight. Jannings proves himself the equal of Chaplin in wringing pathos out of screen pantomime.

⊙**DVD**

DR14

Goes well with: *Ikiru*

THE LAST METRO

France 1980 C 133 min. PG Drama
Dir: François Truffaut
C: Catherine Deneuve, Gérard Depardieu, Jean Poiret, Heinz Bennent,
    Andréa Ferréol

François Truffaut's drama, set during the Nazi occupation of Paris, is a well-crafted story of people who have to mute their emotions. It's as though the Nazis turn every conversation into a whisper. Catherine Deneuve plays the director of a struggling theater company; her Jewish husband is hiding out in the basement of their theater, and she sneaks off to see him whenever she can. Gérard Depardieu is the new man in her life, a forceful actor who successfully auditions for a role in the company's new play. Truffaut and writer Suzanne Schiffman play with our expectations that these people will fall in love; after all, isn't that what actors do when they are working together night after night? Before he became a filmmaker, Truffaut was a critic who attacked the tradition of "quality" French cinema, and his first films, seemingly shot off the cuff and about ordinary characters and their problems, followed through on his critique. *The Last Metro* looks and plays more like the films Truffaut the critic detested, but it's moving and involving nonetheless, one of the best screen portraits of life in the theater.

⊙**DVD**
DR4, DR38
Goes well with: *Children of Paradise*

LAST TANGO IN PARIS
ESSENTIAL

France/Italy   1972   C   129 min.   X   Drama
Dir: Bernardo Bertolucci
C: Marlon Brando, Maria Schneider, Jean-Pierre Léaud

It hardly needs an introduction, unless you've been on a desert island with Tom Hanks and a volleyball since 1972. Marlon Brando gives his greatest performance here, even better than *On the Waterfront,* because his character is harder to love or even like but fascinating nonetheless. He's Paul, an American in Paris grieving over the suicide of his wife, who meets Jeanne, a young woman seeking to rent an apartment. Jeanne (Maria Schneider) is about to embark on a life with her fiancé (Jean-Pierre Léaud), a self-obsessed filmmaker who's making a documentary about her. The affair between these two souls is sexually explicit (though certainly less shocking thirty years later) for a good reason; Bernardo Bertolucci and cowriter Franco Arcalli set it up as a no-questions-asked liaison. Paul needs some connection to life again, but he's also bitter about his inability to understand women; Jeanne is looking for a way to escape the Big Brother camera of her husband and establish a connection to someone focused solely on her. No other actor could bring a combination of gravitas and playfulness to this role like Brando. Also of note: the work of Bertolucci's frequent cinematographer Vittorio Storaro, capturing the autumnal light of Paris in both interior and exterior scenes. (Also available in an R-rated version.)

⊙**DVD**

DR8, DR19, DR27, DR33, XT7

Goes well with: *In the Realm of the Senses*

LAST YEAR AT MARIENBAD

ESSENTIAL

France/Italy   1961   B&W   93 min.   NR   Drama

Dir: Alain Resnais

C: Delphine Seyrig, Giorgio Albertazzi, Sacha Pitoeff

A fascinating picture puzzle or pretentious piffle? Director Alain Resnais and writer Alain Robbe-Grillet's generic (no character has a name) drama has three people moving mysteriously in and around an immense chateau, speaking ominously to one another. Is X (Giorgio Albertazzi) really the former lover of A (Delphine Seyrig), and is M (Sacha Pitoeff) really her husband? *Marienbad* is a wavelength movie; you're either tuned in from the start or you're just picking up a lot of static for ninety-three minutes. It's consistent with other Resnais films about memory and time dislocation (for example, *Hiroshima, Mon Amour* and *Muriel*), but its abstraction invites scorn from people who don't believe movies can indulge in this kind of literary conceit. Bottom line: You can't have an informed opinion without seeing for yourself.

⊙**DVD**

XT6

Goes well with: *Hiroshima, Mon Amour*

LATE SPRING

Japan   1949   B&W   108 min.   NR   Drama

Dir: Yasujiro Ozu

C: Chishu Ryu, Setsuko Hara, Yumeji Tsukioka, Haruko Sugimura

The specifics are rooted in Japanese tradition, but the overall sentiment is universal in Yasujiro Ozu's moving drama of a father-daughter relationship. Somiya, a widowed professor, lives with his grown daughter Noriko in a quiet suburb of Tokyo. She's happy to care for him, but he comes to understand that she needs a life of her own. He gently tries to persuade her to marry, but she's dead set against it, especially with her best friend from their school days offering a cynical view of marriage after a bitter divorce. Finally, Somiya plays a trump card to force the situation, and Noriko reluctantly submits to his wishes. Ozu regular Chishu Ryu is quietly authoritative as Somiya, but this is actress Setsuko Hara's film. In the drama's first half hour, Noriko is a gay, almost giggly young woman; as the realization that she is going to lose her well-ordered existence dawns on her, she turns somber and almost bitter. And Hara's immensely appealing face seems to age ten years in a story span of only a few months. Ozu's unusual technique—most scenes are shot from just above floor level—intensifies our involvement with the characters.

DR11

Goes well with: *An Autumn Afternoon*

THE LAVENDER HILL MOB
U.K.   1951   B&W   78 min.   NR   Comedy
Dir: Charles Crichton
C: Alec Guinness, Stanley Holloway, Sidney James, Alfie Bass

All by itself, Britain's Ealing Studios put the bite back in British comedy in the 1950s with films such as *Kind Hearts and Coronets, The Ladykillers,* and this droll caper story. Alec Guinness (who starred in all three) plays a mousy bank clerk with a foolproof plan to pull off a brazen heist of gold bullion and convert it into Eiffel Tower paperweights. His accomplices, played by Stanley Holloway, Sidney James, and Alfie Bass, are sure they're not only smarter than the police but smarter than the man who devised the plan to make them rich, so the fun lies in watching them get away with the crime while also trying to one-up each other. And yes, that is a young Audrey Hepburn in the film's opening scene. T.E.B. Clarke's clever story and screenplay won an Oscar.

CO1

Goes well with: *The Ladykillers*

LAWN DOGS
U.K.   1998   C   100 min.   R   Drama
Dir: John Duigan
C: Kathleen Quinlan, Sam Rockwell, Christopher McDonald, Bruce McGill, Tom Aldredge, Mischa Barton

A lawnmower man who lives in a broken-down trailer in the woods befriends a lonely girl new to a sterile suburban enclave. Is this going to be a cutesy little drama about a mismatched pair of needy outcasts, or maybe something kinkier? It's neither. Devon (the remarkable Mischa Barton) is a girl who knows secrets about her two-faced parents (Kathleen Quinlan and Christopher McDonald). Their new neighborhood (the latest, we would guess, in a long series of them) yields only one possible friend, Trent (Sam Rockwell), a psychologically damaged veteran who senses a soulmate in Devon. (Trent, who mows lawns for a living and resides in a trailer, is a darker version of Rockwell's "The Kid" in *Box of Moonlight*.) Her attitude toward him is complicated by her first rumblings of sexuality, but the film suggests that this is only part of the attraction. Naomi Wallace's script neatly sets up an us-against-the-world dichotomy; not only are Devon's parents hypocrites, but there's a pack of neighborhood bullies who don't miss an opportunity to harass Trent. John Duigan handles this unusual coming-of-age story with care, and the film stays on course to a satisfying wrap-up.

⊙**DVD**

DR12, DR21, DR41

Goes well with: *Box of Moonlight*

LAWRENCE OF ARABIA

ESSENTIAL

U.K. 1962 C 221 min. PG Drama
Dir: David Lean
C: Peter O'Toole, Alec Guinness, Anthony Quinn, Jack Hawkins, Claude Rains, Anthony Quayle, Arthur Kennedy, Omar Sharif, Jose Ferrer

It won't be playing at the multiplex any time soon, so your only chance to see one of the greatest movie spectacles is at home. Our advice: watch a letterboxed print on as a big a screen as you can find. Yes, there are plenty of virtues besides Freddie Young's magnificent cinematography of the desert, starting with Peter O'Toole's riveting portrayal of one of this century's great enigmas. T. E. Lawrence was a little mad, or maybe completely cuckoo, to go off in search of his destiny as the leader of Arab forces fighting the Turks in the 1910s and 1920s. It's fashionable among critics to deride this film for not resolving Lawrence's contradictions—and filming did go on hiatus while screenwriter Robert Bolt and director David Lean tried to work out some of those problems. But ultimately, no screen biography, even one that's over three-and-a-half hours long, can resolve the complexities of a man like Lawrence. It's a stunning visual record of his accomplishments and offers a subject for further study. Winner of seven Academy Awards, including Best Picture and awards for direction, art direction, color cinematography, editing, score, and sound.

⊙**DVD:** Two discs: One includes a DVD-ROM with historical photographs and an interactive map of the Middle East. Second includes a "making of" documentary; a conversation with Steven Spielberg; four featurettes.

DR7, DR17, DR25, DR37, XT8

Goes well with: *The Bridge on the River Kwai*

LE JOUR SE LÈVE

France 1939 B&W 93 min. NR Drama
Dir: Marcel Carné
C: Jean Gabin, Jacqueline Laurent, Jules Berry, Arletty, Mady Berry

Before Bogart, there was Jean Gabin, who played dozens of fatalistic heroes in French films of the 1930s. These were the heavy-lidded guys who looked great in trench coats and always had a cigarette dangling from their lips and a mademoiselle on one arm whimpering, "Cheri, we can't go on like this." Along with the classic POW drama *Grand Illusion,* this is Gabin 101, a story of a murderer holed up in an apartment, waiting during a long night for the police to storm the building. That's the setup—the story is how he got painted into this corner. It involves one other guy (Jules Berry) and two dames (Arletty and Jacqueline Laurent), and it's still the same old story, that fight for love and glory, a case of do or die. But what really matters is Gabin working his way toward his doom with a shrug and a sigh. Director Marcel Carné and writer Jacques Prévert are working with archetypes, but they imbue every gesture, every prop, with immense meaning. Were it not for the sublime *Children of Paradise,* this would be the film they'd be remembered for.

DR18, DR27, XT4

Goes well with: *Rififi*

LEAVING LAS VEGAS

ESSENTIAL

U.S. 1995 C 111 min. R Drama

Dir: Mike Figgis

C: Nicolas Cage, Elisabeth Shue, Julian Sands, Richard Lewis, Steven Weber, Valeria Golino, R. Lee Ermey, Mariska Hargitay, Laurie Metcalf

This story of a man who drinks himself to death would be almost unbearable to watch were it not for the fact that it's really about the woman who tries to stop him. Mike Figgis adapted John O'Brien's novel about Ben, a man with no future. We glimpse him losing his job at a movie studio, and there's a suggestion that there have been other indignities. So Ben decides to run the table in, where else, Sin City, where the sight of a man with a drink in his hand and a suicidal look in his eye is no big deal. What Ben doesn't count on is meeting a prostitute named Sarah and falling in love with her. But he's past redemption, and Figgis boldly shifts the focus of the story to Sarah as she recounts Ben's last days to an unseen listener. For Sarah, Ben's death proves to be her ticket out of a life of degradation. Nicolas Cage lets his sad eyes and naturally slurry voice do a lot of the work, and his reward was a well-deserved Oscar and the New York Film Critics Circle award. Elisabeth Shue, recognized by the Independent Spirit Awards, matches him as the outwardly brave but inwardly desperate Sarah. The NYFCC and Independent Spirits gave the film their Best Picture awards, and the Independent Spirits also recognized Declan Quinn's cinematography. There is an unrated version available.

⊙**DVD:** Uncut, unrated version.

DR9, DR18, DR27, DR29

Goes well with: *Last Tango in Paris*

LES VAMPIRES

ESSENTIAL

France 1915 B&W 399 min. NR Action-Adventure

Dir: Louis Feuillade

C: Musidora, Edouard Mathé, Marcel Lévesque, Jean Aymé, Louis Leubas

Les Vampires is a remarkable artifact of the days when movies were inventing themselves. Watching this clever though not especially sophisticated silent serial is like reading a collection of classic Dick Tracy cases. First off, it is not about blood-sucking ghouls: The villains are members of a criminal gang that preys on the good citizens of Paris. Their foil is intrepid reporter Philippe Guerande (Edouard Mathé) and his comic sidekick, Oscar Mazamette (Marcel Lévesque), but the bad guys are the real attractions here. Sporting names like Doctor Nox, Satanas, and Irma Vep (it's an anagram) and an arsenal of unusual weapons and disguises, the Vampires seem to be everywhere, and they operate like modern terrorists, often creating havoc for its own sake. Director Louis Feuillade, one of the pioneers of silent film, worked with his cast and crew under strained conditions; they were shooting while men were dying in the trenches not far from their Paris locations. Perhaps wartime restrictions account for the empty streets in the film's exteriors, which contribute to the spooky atmosphere.

⊙**DVD:** Includes essay by Fabrice Zagury; "For the Children," three-minute comedy sketch by cast and crew to raise money for French war orphans; "Bout de Zan and the Shirker," eight-minute comedy featuring child actor Bout de Zan from Episode 8 of *Les Vampires*.

AC1, TH12

Goes well with: *Dr. Mabuse the Gambler*

LET HIM HAVE IT

U.K./France/Netherlands   1991   C   115 min.   R   Drama
Dir: Peter Medak
C: Christopher Eccleston, Paul Reynolds, Tom Courtenay, Tom Bell, Eileen Atkins

In 1952 London, two petty criminals, Christopher Craig and Derek Bentley, were confronted on the roof of a warehouse they had broken into. Craig had a gun, and when a detective approached the pair, Bentley said, "Let him have it, Chris." In the shooting that followed, a policeman was mortally wounded. Both men were convicted of murder, but Craig was sixteen, too young to be sentenced to death, so Bentley, a slow-witted, epileptic nineteen-year-old, was the one who was executed. The outrage that greeted his sentence helped lead to the abolition of the death penalty in Great Britain, and this film documents the whole case, leaning with great sympathy toward the bewildered Bentley (Christopher Eccleston). Director Peter Medak (*The Krays*) and writers Neal Purvis and Robert Wade resist turning poor Bentley into an out-and-out martyr, but their outrage toward a system hell-bent on vengeance and unwilling to consider the ambiguity of Bentley's famous line is stirring.

DR6, DR17

Goes well with: *Dance with a Stranger*

LIAM

Germany/U.K./France   2000   C   91 min.   R   Drama
Dir: Stephen Frears
C: Ian Hart, Claire Hackett, Anthony Borrows, David Hart, Megan Burns

Jimmy McGovern's script for this drama, based in 1930s Liverpool, makes for an amazingly economical film, managing to juggle enough dramatic balls for a movie twice its length. Liam (Anthony Borrows) is an eight-year-old boy about to receive his First Holy Communion, and anyone raised in the Catholic Church will get a jolt of recognition from the scenes of his teacher drumming the fear of God into him. (McGovern also wrote the incisive script for *Priest,* a more complex portrait of the Church.) Liam's dad (Ian Hart) is a working man who blames his newfound unemployment on the twin forces of Irish immigrants (providing cheap labor) and Jewish businessmen; he's also angered at the Church's seeming indifference to his plight. Inconveniently (and unbeknownst to him), his teenage daughter, Teresa (Megan Burns), has taken a job as a maid in the home of a Jewish family, where she becomes privy to a secret that causes her great distress. Director Stephen Frears skillfully orchestrates these stories toward a shattering climax.

DR11, DR24, DR28, DR30, DR41
Goes well with: *The Butcher Boy*

THE LIFE AND DEATH OF COLONEL BLIMP

U.K.   1943   C   163 min.   NR   Drama
Dir: Michael Powell and Emeric Pressburger
C: Roger Livesey, Deborah Kerr, Anton Walbrook, John Laurie

The debut film of the Archers, a partnership formed by Michael Powell and Emeric Pressburger (the two shared credits on producing, directing, and writing, though their previous credits suggest that Powell directed and Pressburger scripted), is one of their best films. It's loosely based on a comic strip character, here referred to General Clive Candy, not a very auspicious name for a military man. The story is told mainly in flashback, as Candy reflects back on his life of service to His Majesty, beginning with World War I, when he strikes up a friendship with a German counterpart. Candy's reflections are prompted by his disgust over what he sees as dishonorable tactics on both sides during the Second World War, a position that hardly endeared the film to

British authorities when it was released in the middle of the war. The film was severely edited, and for years it was difficult to see a complete print. In America, to add insult to injury, the film was released in black-and-white, negating one of its strongest virtues, the Technicolor cinematography by Georges Périnal. Roger Livesey is magnificent as the increasingly disillusioned Candy, Anton Walbrook is his *Deutsche freund,* and in her breakthrough film, Deborah Kerr plays the three women in Candy's life. A laserdisc edition featured Powell and his American acolyte Martin Scorsese discussing the production on an alternate soundtrack; one can only hope that a DVD release with the same feature is imminent.

DR16, DR37, XT4

Goes well with: *How I Won the War*

THE LIFE AND TIMES OF HANK GREENBERG

U.S. 2000 C/B&W 98 min. PG Documentary
Dir: Aviva Kempner

Greenberg (1911–1986) was the first great Jewish baseball player, a slugger who hit as many as 58 home runs and drove in as many as 183 runs in his best seasons with the Detroit Tigers. His career paralleled the rise of fascism and the onset of World War II—which cost him three seasons in the prime of his career. Aviva Kempner spent years gathering clips of Greenberg in action and interviewing surviving relatives and contemporaries (including actor Walter Matthau and Congressman Carl Levin) for this wonderful portrait of an athlete who became an inevitable symbol, as well as a target for prejudice. Greenberg's last season was spent in the National League in 1947, where he crossed paths with another athlete/symbol, Jackie Robinson. There are also generous excerpts from interviews with Greenberg, who proved to be as articulate off the field as he was talented between the lines.

⊙**DVD:** Includes audio commentary by Aviva Kempner; deleted interview material; Yiddish subtitles with English translation.

DO10

Goes well with: *One Day in September*

LIFE IS BEAUTIFUL

ESSENTIAL

Italy 1997 C 116 min. PG-13 Drama
Dir: Roberto Benigni

C: Roberto Benigni, Nicoletta Braschi, Giorgio Cantarini, Giustino Durano

After more than fifty years of somber documentaries and dramas commemorating the suffering of the victims of the Holocaust, was it time to offer a lighter point of view? Writer-director-star Roberto Benigni thought so, as did ticket buyers (this was the most popular foreign-language film released in the U.S. until *Crouching Tiger, Hidden Dragon* flew by it) and members of the Academy of Motion Picture Arts and Sciences (who gave the film two Oscars, for Best Foreign Language Film and for Benigni's lead performance). If you buy the film's premise—a lovable guy who is sent to the death camps with his young son can make a game out of the experience to shield his boy from the horrors of their new life—it's on the basis of Benigni's energetic performance. Though his depiction of the camp is a little sterile, Benigni does not cheapen the suffering. He sincerely wants us to believe that some people will do anything to protect their loved ones from harm, and the film's bittersweet ending does remind us of the sacrifices brave people make to accomplish that goal.

⊙**DVD:** Includes "making of" featurette.

DR11, DR16, DR26, DR38

Goes well with: *Au Revoir, les Enfants*

LIFE IS SWEET

U.K. 1990 C 102 min. R Comedy

Dir: Mike Leigh

C: Alison Steadman, Jim Broadbent, Claire Skinner, Jane Horrocks, Stephen Rea, Timothy Spall, David Thewlis

Writer-director Mike Leigh's second "comeback" film (see *High Hopes* for the first) is a rollicking comedy about a family of four compass points. Andy (Jim Broadbent) is a dreamer à la Ralph Kramden, hoping to make it big with a rolling food cart. Wendy (Alison Steadman) is the Alice Kramden type, but a little wackier; she's working as a waitress in a new upscale restaurant run by their friend Aubrey (Timothy Spall). Their twin teenage daughters (Jane Horrocks and Claire Skinner) are like British versions of the *Parent Trap* duo, one serious and anal, the other rebellious and spiky—and both want Andy and Wendy off their backs *this very minute.* In the hands of fifteen Hollywood writers, this would be a moderately successful sitcom, but Leigh isn't interested in one-liners and two-dimensional characters. Life is

sweet, all right; it's also messy, frustrating, demanding, confounding, irritating—but never boring, at least when Leigh is at the controls.
CO3
Goes well with: *High Hopes*

LIFE OF BRIAN.
See *Monty Python's Life of Brian*

LIGHT SLEEPER
U.S. 1992 C 103 min. R Drama
Dir: Paul Schrader
C: Willem Dafoe, Susan Sarandon, Dana Delaney, David Clennon, Mary Beth Hurt, Victor Garber, Jane Adams

If John Letour, the alienated New Yorker played by Willem Dafoe in this chilling little drama, reminds you of a movie about a New York cab driver named Travis Bickle who went a little nuts and tried to kill a politician, there's a good reason. Paul Schrader penned *Taxi Driver,* and he wrote and directed this film, too. Letour is a forty-year-old drug courier and compulsive journal keeper, but he's not remotely homicidal, just depressed. His boss (Susan Sarandon) may be getting out of the business, and he knows that's the kick he needs to get a new career going. But, but, but . . . Dafoe's deliberateness and hollow-eyed look work perfectly in sync with Schrader's vision of lonely men locked in prisons of indecision and bad decisions. The film is not as glum as that may sound; there are moments of wry humor along the way. Dana Delaney is especially good as the woman who tries to save LeTour but can't do the same for herself.
⊙DVD
DR10, DR20, DR21, DR36, XT7
Goes well with: *Affliction*

LIKE WATER FOR CHOCOLATE
ESSENTIAL
Mexico 1992 C 113 min. NR Drama
Dir: Alfonso Arau
C: Lumi Cavazos, Marco Leonardi, Regina Torné, Mario Iván Martínez, Ada Carrasco

Food and sex: the irresistible combination fueled Laura Esquivel's novel and this hit adaptation, written by the author and directed by her then-husband, actor Alfonso Arau. Lumi Cavazos plays Tita, the youngest of three daughters caught under the thumb of a domineering mother, who teaches her the ways of the kitchen. Tita loves Pedro (Marco Leonardi), but he has been promised in marriage to her older sister. Wedding vows are put aside once Pedro gets second helpings of Tita's specialty dishes. All this intrigue is played out against the Mexican Revolution, so there are soldiers riding in and out of town and bullets flying between and during meals. It's a marvelously sensual movie, lingering in the mind the way a good meal stays on the tongue.

⊙**DVD**

DR18, DR29, XT2

Goes well with: *Babette's Feast*

LIMBO

U.S.   1999   C   126 min.   R   Drama

Dir: John Sayles

C: Mary Elizabeth Mastrantonio, David Strathairn, Vanessa Martinez, Kris Kristofferson, Casey Siemaszko

John Sayles is a successful novelist and short-story writer turned filmmaker, and his films have a writer's feel for place and character. This drama is set in a coastal Alaskan town whose economy is shifting from harvesting and processing fish to serving tourists on excursions to what most people think of as the last wilderness in America. David Strathairn plays Joe, an ex-fisherman who now takes freelance jobs as a guide; Mary Elizabeth Mastrantonio is Donna, an itinerant singer he meets and begins an affair with; and Vanessa Martinez is her daughter, Noelle. For at least half of its running time, the film seems to be treading water, as Joe and Donna court and Noelle fumes over what she thinks is her mother making another bad choice in men. Then Joe's brother, Bobby (Casey Siemaszko), shows up in town asking for a very special favor that involves using Joe's boat. The four set out to a remote location, and what develops, while not totally unexpected, has dire consequences for the original trio. By slowly working his way to the final act, Sayles gains our sympathy for these flawed people, creating almost unbearable tension over their fates.

⊙**DVD:** Includes audio commentary by John Sayles.

DR11, DR34

Goes well with: *Lone Star*

THE LIMEY

U.S.   1999   C   90 min.   R   Thriller

Dir: Steven Soderbergh

C: Terence Stamp, Peter Fonda, Lesley Ann Warren, Luis Guzman, Barry Newman, Joe Dallesandro

A film of modest ambitions, *The Limey* succeeds on every level and even rewards repeated viewings. Writer Lem Dobbs creates a hard case, Wilson, a cockney ex-con played by the magnetic Terence Stamp, with steely eyes and clipped voice to match. He's on a mission, just out of British jail and seriously upset that his estranged daughter wound up dead in Los Angeles. Police rule her death in a car crash an accident, but Wilson senses that her relationship with a middle-aged record producer named Terry Valentine (Peter Fonda) led to her death. As in *Out of Sight,* Steven Soderbergh fractures the narrative with illuminating flashbacks that include footage of Stamp from a 1967 film, *Poor Cow,* in which he played a similar character. *The Limey* makes good use of Los Angeles locations, particularly Valentine's Hollywood Hills home, with its swimming pool suspended over a cliff. Fonda is very persuasive as an amoral Angeleno, and character actor Barry Newman is devilishly menacing as his chief of security. A first-class addition to the film noir hall of fame.

⊙**DVD:** Includes audio commentaries by Steven Soderbergh and Lem Dobbs; 1960s "documentary" with footage of Terence Stamp, Peter Fonda, Lesley Ann Warren, and Joe Dallesandro.

TH13, TH14, XT4

Goes well with: *The Underneath*

LIVE FLESH

Spain/France   1997   C   100 min.   R   Drama

Dir: Pedro Almodóvar

C: Liberto Rabal, Francesca Neri, Javier Bardem, Angela Molina, Penélope Cruz

Pedro Almodóvar fans expecting his usual campy hijinks, with cross-dressers and sultry ladies prancing through brightly decorated homes, may feel a little let down by this film, but it's one of his strongest. Working from Ruth Rendell's thriller, Almodóvar and cowriters Ray Loriga and Jorge Guerricaechevarría have fashioned an unexpectedly touching story out of frankly melodramatic material. Víctor (Liberto Rabal), a punk involved romantically with Elena (Francesca Neri), a drug user, accidentally shoots and wounds a cop (Javier Bardem) during a confrontation at Elena's apartment. When Víctor gets out of jail, he finds that Elena has married the policeman, and they are pillars of the community. Almodóvar underplays the simmering passions between David and Elena (complicated by the fact that the cop is a paraplegic as a result of the shooting), and the result is a movie that's just as entertaining as his comedies but more rewarding.

⊙**DVD**

DR18

Goes well with: *All About My Mother*

LIVING IN OBLIVION

U.S.   1995   C/B&W   91 min.   R   Comedy

Dir: Tom DiCillo

C: Steve Buscemi, Catherine Keener, Dermot Mulroney, Danielle von Zerneck, James LeGros

It might be called *Revenge of the Filmmaker.* In 1991, writer-director Tom DiCillo made a film called *Johnny Suede,* starring a then-unknown Brad Pitt. *Johnny* tanked with critics and ticket buyers. So DiCillo turned around and made a film based (at least in part) on his experiences making *Johnny Suede.* The critics were happy this time around, and you will be, too, especially knowing who the model was for preening actor Chad Palomino (played by James LeGros). Steve Buscemi, in full Irritated as Hell mode, plays the director of the low-budget film *that will not get made until everybody shuts up and pays attention to me right now!* Catherine Keener, a DiCillo regular, is the film-within-a-film's female lead; Dermot Mulroney is the ditsy cameraman; and the whole enterprise has the loose feel of a home movie done by real professionals.

CO10

Goes well with: *Day for Night*

LOCAL HERO

ESSENTIAL

U.K.   1983   C   111 min.   PG   Comedy

Dir: Bill Forsyth

C: Peter Riegert, Burt Lancaster, Fulton Mackay, Denis Lawson, Norman Chancer, Peter Capaldi, Jenny Seagrove

It's *Brigadoon* without music or dancing, but with lots more laughs. Peter Riegert plays Mac MacIntyre, troubleshooter for a Houston oil company, assigned to scope out a Scottish seaside village the firm wants to buy and replace with an oil refinery. The first curve ball: The inhabitants are nearly unanimous in favor of the sale, but they don't want to tip their hands to Mac, hoping to drive up the price. Mac is also under strict orders from Felix Happer (Burt Lancaster), his astronomy-mad boss, to report on doings in the northern skies over the village. Writer-director Bill Forsyth hits all the right notes in this utterly charming comedy, in which first Mac and then Happer are beguiled by the charms of the village. The musical score by Mark Knopfler is a big plus, adding just the right touch of wistfulness. The film is a total original that would charm the crankiest of misanthropes into a smile. Forsyth's screenplay won an award from the New York Film Critics Circle.

⊙**DVD**

CO4, CO8, CO11

Goes well with: *The Coca-Cola Kid*

LOCK, STOCK AND TWO SMOKING BARRELS

U.S./U.K.   1998   C   106 min.   R   Thriller

Dir: Guy Ritchie

C: Jason Flemyng, Dexter Fletcher, Nick Moran, Jason Statham, Steven Mackintosh, Vinnie Jones, Sting

Could anyone be surprised, after seeing this triumph of style over substance, that its director would marry Madonna, popular culture's foremost exponent of same? That doesn't mean you have to love Madonna's music to appreciate how much fun Guy Ritchie has with the British tough-boys crime genre. Four mates with cotton between their ears get into big-time debt to a big-time mobster at a big-time poker game, so it's off to Let's Make a Drug Deal Land for some quick cash. That puts them into more hot water with some nasty Jamaicans and some lowlife homeboys, and pretty soon guns are blazing and crosses are being doubled and tripled. It's about as loud and shallow as you might expect, but Ritchie and his filmmaking mates aren't taking themselves too seriously. Unlike a certain pop diva.

⊙**DVD**

CO1, TH5, TH11

Goes well with: *Pulp Fiction*

LOLA MONTÈS
ESSENTIAL

France/West Germany 1955 C 110 min. NR Drama
Dir: Max Ophüls
C: Martine Carol, Peter Ustinov, Anton Walbrook, Oskar Werner, Ivan Desny

It shouldn't be the first Max Ophüls you see, especially because it's his last film. At one time regarded as his masterpiece (and by at least one respectable critic as the greatest film ever made), *Lola* has one too many flaws to be called either. It's the true story of a show-biz legend of sorts, a courtesan turned circus sideshow performer whose only duty is to sit still and allow people to gaze upon her. The film starts with her final humiliation and backtracks, in a series of flashbacks, to her career as the lover of, among many others, Franz Liszt and Ludwig I, King of Bavaria. Ophüls is less interested in the facts of Lola's life than in the celebrity she achieved based on them and the rumors and apocryphal stories they spawned. The film was released at 140 minutes, to disapproval from audiences and support from Ophüls's fellow filmmakers. Its distributor cut and cut it, rearranging its story in chronological order, but in 1969, a 100-minute version was released to general acclaim. The star of any Ophüls film is his relentlessly prowling camera (the cinematographer here was Christian Matras), so you should see this film in a letterboxed edition. Its biggest drawback is its putative star, Martine Carol, who is a stiff in the lead role. (Critics who claim her performance is somehow intentional are only rationalizing.)
⊙**DVD**
DR4, DR17, XT4, XT8
Goes well with: *Isadora*

LONE STAR
ESSENTIAL

U.S. 1996 C 134 min. R Drama
Dir: John Sayles
C: Kris Kristofferson, Chris Cooper, Elizabeth Peña, Joe Morton, Ron Canada, Miriam Colon, Clifton James, Matthew McConaughey, Frances McDormand

John Sayles's most ambitious work pays equally big dividends with a tangled story of small-town Texas lives intersecting. Sheriff Sam Deeds (Chris Cooper) has more than the usual criminal element to deal with. He keeps getting dragged into the past, both by his former high school sweetheart (Elizabeth Peña), who married another guy after their parents nixed their romance, and by the resurrection of a long-ago murder involving his own father (Matthew McConaughey), also a sheriff, and the man he replaced (Kris Kristofferson), a notorious racist. Another story thread involves the discovery of some human remains on the firing range of a nearby Army base, run by a black colonel (Joe Morton) with father-son issues of his own. Wherever his films take place, Sayles seems to have immersed himself in the local culture; this feels like a film a native Texan would have made. And the ending is a stunner, wrapping up the biggest mystery of the story in heartbreaking fashion. Peña's performance won her an Independent Spirit Award.

⊙**DVD**

DR7, DR28, DR34, XT4

Goes well with: *Limbo*

THE LONELINESS OF THE LONG DISTANCE RUNNER

U.K. 1962 B&W 103 min. NR Drama
Dir: Tony Richardson
C: Michael Redgrave, Tom Courtenay, Avis Bunnage, Peter Madden, Alec McCowen, James Fox, Julia Foster

It hasn't aged quite as well as some of its fellow Angry Young Man films from the era (among them *Look Back in Anger* and *This Sporting Life*), but there's still an integrity to this story that demands respect. Tom Courtenay plays Colin, a reform school lad who is chosen to compete in the school's big cross-country race, during which he recalls the events that landed him in trouble: the death of his father, his mother's profligate spending of the insurance money, his few moments of happiness with a young girl, and the robbery of a bakery. Tony Richardson, working from Alan Sillitoe's adaptation of his own short story, wants us to sympathize with Colin, but he stacks the deck a bit too much, with Michael Redgrave's craven headmaster—who uses Colin's athletic gifts to bring glory to the school even as he abuses him personally—a figure of caricature. A stinging conclusion is the film's best moment.

DR21, DR31, DR35, DR41, XT4

Goes well with: *This Sporting Life*

THE LONG GOOD FRIDAY

U.K. 1980 C 114 min. R Drama
Dir: John MacKenzie

C: Bob Hoskins, Helen Mirren, Eddie Constantine, Dave King

Bob Hoskins had small roles in three films before being chosen to play the lead in this stunning crime drama, and he makes the most of his first break. Coming on like a combination of Edward G. Robinson (in his stubby, glowering appearance) and James Cagney (in his manic intensity), Hoskins plays a London crime boss whose empire is under siege from unknown forces. He spends much of the story raging about town, threatening rivals and colleagues alike, as bombs mangle his businesses and assassinations reduce his work force. Helen Mirren brings a welcome measure of dignity to the clichéd role of the long-suffering mistress. Barrie Keefe's tart screenplay and John MacKenzie's muscular direction work in perfect sync. It ain't *The Sopranos,* but it'll do, it'll do.

⊙**DVD:** Includes liner notes by critic Michael Sragow.

DR6, DR36, XT7

Goes well with: *The General*

LONGTIME COMPANION

U.S.   1990   C   96 min.   R   Drama

Dir: Norman René

C: Stephen Caffrey, Patrick Cassidy, Brian Cousins, Bruce Davison, Dermot Mulroney, Mary-Louise Parker, Campbell Scott

Being the first film to deal with any serious subject is no guarantee of quality. *Longtime Companion* has the distinction of being a first-rate drama as well as the first big-screen take on the AIDS epidemic. It's set among a group of well-to-do New York gay men, beginning in the summer of 1981 with the first reports of the virus and working its way through the ensuing decade. Writer Craig Lucas focuses on the characters, avoiding any political statements. By 1990, everyone knew the score on AIDS, which is what makes these men's initial reactions of disbelief and denial so heartbreaking. Among the ensemble cast, the standout performance comes from Bruce Davison, who won supporting actor awards from the Independent Spirit Awards and the New York Film Critics Circle. The Sundance festival bestowed its Audience Award on the film.

⊙**DVD**

DR8, DR12, DR19

Goes well with: *Before Night Falls*

LOOK BACK IN ANGER

ESSENTIAL

U.K.   1959   B&W   99 min.   NR   Drama

Dir: Tony Richardson

C: Richard Burton, Claire Bloom, Edith Evans, Mary Ure, Donald Pleasence

Richard Burton had been working in films for ten years before he confirmed his sterling reputation as a stage actor. As playwright John Osborne's viciously articulate creation Jimmy Porter, Burton is the epitome of the angry young man who seemed to inhabit every other British drama of the late 1950s and early 1960s. He's sure that the System is stacked against him and every other honest working man. Jimmy is too busy ranting to do much work himself, but why should he, since the government would take most of his pay in taxes to subsidize the System? Porter's so magnetic (as Burton plays him) that it's no surprise that both his wife (Mary Ure) and her best friend (Claire Bloom) can't stay away from him. In truth, Jimmy's most honest relationship with a woman is with dear old Mrs. Tanner (Edith Evans), a political lefty who has a soothing effect on Jimmy's seething psyche.

⊙**DVD**

DR21, DR32, XT7

Goes well with: *Saturday Night and Sunday Morning*

LOS OLVIDADOS

ESSENTIAL

Mexico   1950   B&W   88 min.   NR   Drama

Dir: Luis Buñuel

C: Alfonso Mejía, Roberto Cobo, Stella Inda, Miguel Inclán

Working a continent away from his Italian colleagues, director Luis Buñuel offered his own version of the street life that Vittorio de Sica and Roberto Rossellini were documenting. But Buñuel's Mexico City was not a city ravaged by war with its residents trying to reconstruct their lives. The urban poor whom Buñuel chose to portray weren't lovable urchins, either; that would hardly fit into his jaded worldview. This is an unblinking look at a hell on earth that neither sensationalizes nor patronizes its subject. It's also a masterful combination of gritty realism and Buñuel's trademark surrealism, as in the ongoing dream one of the younger thieves has about the Virgin Mary. Leave it to Buñuel, beginning the second phase of his career after years of exile from Franco-ruled Spain, to work his favorite target, the Catholic Church, into a movie about street punks.

DR36, DR41

Goes well with: *Pixote*

THE LOUISIANA STORY

ESSENTIAL

U.S.   1948   B&W   77 min.   NR   Documentary

Dir: Robert Flaherty

The last film by documentary film pioneer Robert Flaherty is a curiosity. It's a dramatized story, but it often has the feel of a nonfiction film; it's a lyrical poem to the natural world, but its subject is how an oil company can set up a temporary drilling operation in a virgin swamp and leave no evidence behind when it departs. Standard Oil sponsored the film, so a sanguine view of industrial pollution is guaranteed. But Flaherty is no hack for hire; he and cinematographer Richard Leacock (who went on to become a pioneer of the cinema verité movement) may be under the thumb of Big Oil, but they spend much of the film's running time exploring the swamp through the eyes of a young boy (Joseph Boudreaux) whose father (Lionel Le Blanc) leases the land to the oil men. Virgil Thomson's lovely musical score is another plus.

DO8

Goes well with: *Man of Aran*

M

ESSENTIAL

Germany   1931   B&W   99 min.   NR   Thriller

Dir: Fritz Lang

C: Peter Lorre, Ellen Widmann, Inge Landgut, Gustav Gründgens

M is that unusual film that seems to be inventing a subgenre while simultaneously offering twisted variations on it. Fritz Lang, his reputation already secured by the silent classics *Dr. Mabuse the Gambler* and *Metropolis,* made an effortless transition to sound with this haunting story, based on a real-life case of a madman who preyed on Dusseldorf's children. (The location was changed to Berlin in the film.) On the evidence of *M,* Lang was still a silent director at heart, for much of the film's power comes from its imagery: dark shadows, furtive figures, abandoned children's toys. As the sweating, bug-eyed, oddly childlike killer, Peter Lorre was so effective that he was forever typecast as villains and weak links. Lang and cowriter Thea von Harbou (his wife) turn the world of criminal detection upside down; Berlin's ineffective police can't catch the killer, but when they crack down on all criminal activities, the city's underworld organizes to catch the killer themselves. It's a mark of Lorre's greatness that his plea-bargaining speech at his "trial" by a very large jury of his peers almost turns our sympathies toward him.

⊙**DVD:** Includes liner notes by critic Stanley Kauffmann.

TH15

Goes well with: *Dr. Mabuse the Gambler*

MA SAISON PRÉFÉRÉE

France 1993 C 124 min. NR Drama
Dir: André Téchiné
C: Catherine Deneuve, Daniel Auteuil, Marthe Villalonga, Jean-Pierre
Bouvier, Chiara Mastroianni, Carmen Chaplin

In this absorbing drama, Catherine Deneuve and Daniel Auteuil play estranged siblings, Emilie and Antoine, whose prickly relationship is exacerbated by a family crisis: Their elderly mother is no longer self-reliant. The film is neither protracted psychodrama nor predictable sentiment. Emilie and Antoine are no prizes—her marriage is falling apart and his disdain for bourgeois conventions has left him a bitter man—and writer-director André Téchiné offers neither one the moral high ground in dealing with their mutual problem. It's a subtly powerful examination of how adult siblings try to come to grips with the reasons their lives have diverged so much. Chiara Mastroianni, the young actress playing Deneuve's daughter, is her real-life daughter by actor Marcello Mastroianni.

⊙**DVD:** DVD title: *My Favorite Season.*

DR11

Goes well with: *A Sunday in the Country*

MAD MAX

Australia 1979 C 93 min. R Action-Adventure
Dir: George Miller
C: Mel Gibson, Joanne Samuel, Hugh Keays-Byrne, Steve Bisley

Mel Gibson is Max, a cop with a lovely wife and child and a swaggering attitude reflected in his very high-powered automobile. Sometime in the near future, he is trying to make the backroads of Australia safe for motorists. But this being down under, where machismo is a state religion, there are an inordinate number of badasses roaming the highways, many interested only in creating mayhem. Director George Miller revs up the sound, swivels his camera like Elvis's hips, and creates a world in which there are, like the steak house chain's ads say, "No rules." That allows Max (especially after his wife and child are brutally murdered by bikers) to rev up his engine and dispatch a little Dirty Harry–style justice. The sequel, *The Road Warrior,* is even better. (*Max* caught on with American audiences only after its distributor dubbed the dialogue; the Aussie accents proved too thick to understand.)

⊙**DVD:** Special edition includes original Australian dialogue; audio commentary; two documentaries, "Mel Gibson: The Birth of a Star" and "Mad Max: The Film Phenomenon."

AC1, AC5, AC7

Goes well with: *The Road Warrior*

THE MADNESS OF KING GEORGE

U.K.   1994   C   107 min.   PG-13   Drama

Dir: Nicholas Hytner

C: Nigel Hawthorne, Helen Mirren, Ian Holm, Rupert Everett, Rupert Graves, John Wood, Amanda Donohoe

History tells us that England's King George III started behaving a bit loopy not long after the American colonies were lost. This adaptation of Alan Bennett's play is one of those doctor-detective movies, in which Bennett and director Nicholas Hytner offer their own diagnosis of a famed nut job. Funny and surprisingly touching, often at the same moment, *Madness* succeeds in being entertaining and provocative without feeling definitive. Nigel Hawthorne is splendidly ambiguous as the mad monarch. Ultimately, every good film about any royal family is only as good as its intrigue, and this one has plenty of it, with the Prince of Wales (Rupert Everett) going mad himself at the prospect of ascending to the throne to take over for dear old dotty Dad, while the queen (the ever-reliable Helen Mirren) tries to hold the fort with the help of a strange parson turned doctor (Ian Holm). A jolly good show that won an Oscar for its art direction.

⊙**DVD**

DR17, DR25

Goes well with: *Mrs. Brown*

A MAN ESCAPED

France   1956   B&W   102 min.   NR   Drama

Dir: Robert Bresson

C: François Leterrier, Charles Le Clainche, Maurice Beerblock, Roland Monod

Jean Renoir may have written the book on POW movies with *Grand Illusion,* but director Robert Bresson deserves credit for adding his own touches to the genre. Bresson's drama, based on a true World War II story, isn't about a band of brothers digging their way out under the noses of the Nazis. As is usually the case in a Bresson film, the story is pared down to basics: one man and a plan. (He relents toward the end and allows another prisoner in on the deal.) The real-life prison depicted here was in Lyons; ten thousand resistance fighters and partisans were housed there during its short history, and seven thousand of them died of natural causes or were executed. We do know from the voice-over that our hero is racing against time—his captors will eventually get around to shooting him for his activities on the outside. Even though the ending is announced by the title, the tension, as in any well-crafted suspense film, is nearly unbearable. Moreover, by dispensing with any details other than the escape preparations, Bresson offers an implicit commentary on the frivolousness of other films, with their joking asides and colorful collection of bunkhouse characters.

DR26, DR38

Goes well with: *Grand Illusion*

A MAN FOR ALL SEASONS

U.K.   1966   C   120 min.   G   Drama
Dir: Fred Zinnemann
C: Paul Scofield, Wendy Hiller, Leo McKern, Robert Shaw, Orson Welles, Susannah York, John Hurt, Vanessa Redgrave

Robert Bolt's adaptation of his play about the power struggle between Henry VIII and Thomas More is a film whose reputation has suffered, it seems, solely because it had the temerity to win six Academy Awards. Unlike, say, *Gladiator,* this film has real substance, and a true-life hero instead of a fictional one. Paul Scofield is More, the man who defied his king when said monarch came looking for justification for his own defiance of the Catholic Church. Robert Shaw is Henry, a blustering fool who has painted himself into a corner and would rather have More's head chopped off than admit he's wrong. The cast also includes the splendid Wendy Hiller as Alice More, Orson Welles as Cardinal Woolsey (he has only one scene, but it's a pip), and, in the appropriately brief role of Anne Boleyn, newcomer Vanessa Redgrave. Director Fred Zinnemann's solid craftsmanship in service of this material shouldn't be underestimated or dismissed. Oscars went to the film, Zinnemann, Scofield, Bolt, cinematographer Ted Moore, and costume designers Joan Bridges and Elizabeth Haffenden. The New York Film Critics Circle also honored the film, Zinnemann, Scofield, and Bolt.

⊙**DVD**
DR17, DR25, DR30
Goes well with: *The Passion of Joan of Arc*

MAN OF ARAN

ESSENTIAL

U.K. 1934 B&W 73 min. NR Documentary
Dir: Robert Flaherty

Pioneering documentary filmmaker Robert Flaherty journeyed to one of the Aran Islands, west of Ireland's Galway Bay, for a film that is long on poetry and short on hard information. Much of what we see was created for the camera—the "family" is a composite of three photogenic islanders, a dangerous venture into stormy seas would not normally be attempted, a hunt for gigantic basking sharks was something the islanders hadn't attempted in years—but the essence of the film is true. The Aran Islands are almost all rock, and those who choose to live there face punishing weather and primitive living conditions, much like the family in Flaherty's debut feature, *Nanook of the North*. Ultimately, this is a film of startling images: waves pounding on jagged rocks, a young boy casting his fishing line off a cliff that appears to be one hundred feet high and then casually sitting on the edge of the precipice, awaiting a tug on the line.

DO8
Goes well with: *Nanook of the North*

MAN OF IRON

ESSENTIAL

Poland 1981 C 152 min. PG Drama
Dir: Andrzej Wajda
C: Jerzy Radziwilowicz, Krystyna Janda, Marian Opaina, Irena Byrska, Wieslawa Kosmalska, Lech Walesa

Andrzej Wajda's follow-up to *Man of Marble* (see below) was an amazingly timely film; one of its "stars" is Lech Walesa, the leader of Poland's Solidarity movement, which began in the shipyards at Gdansk. That is where *Man of Marble* left off, with filmmaker Agnieszka (Krystyna Janda) finally tracking down the son of a discredited labor leader of the 1950s. Maciek Tomczyk (played by Jerzy Radziwilowicz, who also played the character's father in *Man of Marble*) is now one of the Solidarity leaders. He's haunted by his father's death during a 1970 workers' demonstration and determined to continue the struggle for labor rights. As in *Man of Marble,* the story is framed by a journalist, in this case a harried radio reporter assigned to discredit the current uprising. The more he learns about Tomczyk and his past, the more reluctant he is to play ball with his Communist masters. The film combines old newsreel footage, re-created dramatic scenes set in the past, and, most astonishing, actual scenes of the shipworkers' successful action. Walesa is seen in many news clips, and he even appears in the fictional narrative, as a guest at Tomczyk's wedding.

DR25, DR40, XT4

Goes well with: *Medium Cool*

MAN OF MARBLE

ESSENTIAL

Poland   1977   C   160 min.   NR   Drama

Dir: Andrzej Wajda

C: Krystyna Janda, Jerzy Radziwilowicz, Tadeusz Lomnicki, Jacek Lomnicki

It has been called the *Citizen Kane* of Polish filmmaking, and that's a double-edged compliment. Director Andrzej Wajda's drama about a discredited worker hero of the 1950s garnered the kind of acclaim that has greeted few films on their initial release. And in their narrative method, Wajda and screenwriter Aleksander Scibor-Rylski have borrowed heavily from Orson Welles's masterpiece. The film begins in the present, with a student filmmaker, Agnieszka (Krystyna Janda), setting out to make her "diploma film" about Tadeusz Birkut (Jerzy Radziwilowicz), a onetime hero of the working class who mysteriously ran afoul of Communist officials and eventually fell off everyone's radar screen. She collects newsreel and state-sponsored films featuring Birkut and interviews those who knew him; the narrative includes lengthy flashbacks to the 1950s. The story of Birkut's fall from grace allows Wajda to expose the corruption of the state government, which was more interested in promoting productivity than in maintaining any quality controls over construction (Birkut was a bricklayer). Janda gives an intense performance—at one point, she looks like she's going to eat a lit cigarette, she's smoking it so furiously—but the film really belongs to Radziwilowicz, who possesses some of the charisma of Zbigniew Cybulski, the young star of Wajda's *A Generation* and *Ashes and Diamonds*. The story continues in *Man of Iron*.

DR22, DR25, DR40, XT4
Goes well with: *Man of Iron*

THE MAN WHO FELL TO EARTH
U.K. 1976 C 140 min. R Science Fiction
Dir: Nicolas Roeg
C: David Bowie, Rip Torn, Candy Clark, Buck Henry, Bernie Casey

Nicolas Roeg and writer Paul Mayersburg turned Walter Tevis's excellent science-fiction novel inside out for this amazing film, arguably the best of Roeg's career. Singer David Bowie, only a few years removed from his Ziggy Stardust character, plays an alien who tries to save his drought-stricken planet by journeying to our own. He's already aware, from intercepting TV transmissions, that Earth's surface is 70 percent water. Once "Newton" has landed, he finds himself seduced—by his new wife (Candy Clark, in a very touching performance), by the luxurious lifestyle he enjoys thanks to his amazing business acumen, and, most significant, by television. Newton, like Chance the otherworldly gardener in *Being There,* likes to watch. Meanwhile, shadowy government agents are investigating Newton's past, which doesn't exist. Roeg expands on the basic premise of Tevis's book with dazzling imagery; much of what we see is from Newton's point of view, and because he takes in much more information than any human, we're always racing to keep up with his thoughts. Make sure you're watching the restored 140-minute version of the film; tapes of the original 118-minute U.S. release may still be in circulation.
⊙**DVD**
DR20, DR21, FA1
Goes well with: *Every Man for Himself and God Against All*

THE MAN WHO KNEW TOO MUCH
U.K. 1934 B&W 75 min. NR Thriller
Dir: Alfred Hitchcock
C: Leslie Banks, Edna Best, Peter Lorre, Nova Pilbeam, Frank Vosper, Pierre Fresnay

Hitchcock remade this film (in 1956, with James Stewart and Doris Day), but he didn't really need to, as the original, featuring Peter Lorre's English-language debut as (what else?) the villain, is a real corker. A gang of spies kidnaps the daughter (Nova Pilbeam) of a seemingly innocent couple (Leslie Banks and Edna Best), though we know that in fact they've accidentally learned an important detail about the villains' dastardly plans. Banks and Best are shown as resilient and resourceful parents, and her talent as a sharpshooter comes in very handy. In fact, they come off as a smarter and in some ways more attractive couple than Stewart and Day. As in his two other great British films of the 1930s, *The 39 Steps* and *The Lady Vanishes,* Hitchcock sprinkles liberal doses of humor throughout the proceedings.

☉**DVD:** Includes introduction by Tony Curtis.

TH1, TH6

Goes well with: *The 39 Steps*

THE MAN WITH A MOVIE CAMERA
ESSENTIAL

Soviet Union   1929   B&W   69 min.   NR   Documentary
Dir: Dziga Vertov

Russian director Dziga Vertov and his chief collaborators, his wife (editor Elizaveta Svilova) and his brother (cinematographer Mikhail Kaufman), believed that fictional films were corrupting influences on audiences, that the true goal of cinema should be to present life as it is lived. Before you turn the page, know that *The Man with a Movie Camera* is a marvelous thrill ride, a brilliantly photographed, propulsively edited day-in-the-life portrait of a city from dawn till dusk, or as the opening title describes it, "An excerpt from the diary of a cameraman." (The filmmakers actually shot their footage in several cities, including Moscow, Kiev, and Odessa.) There is no voice-over and no titles (other than an opening statement), just images. The film's only "star" is the title character; we sometimes see Kaufman scrambling around to line up his shots. The DVD features a musical score, composed from suggestions made by the director, by a group called the Alloy Orchestra (though you'd swear it was Philip Glass).

☉**DVD:** Includes audio commentary and first-rate liner notes by historian Yuri Tsivian.

DO8, XT6

Goes well with: *I Am Cuba*

MANON OF THE SPRING
ESSENTIAL

France   1986   C   113 min.   PG   Drama
Dir: Claude Berri

C: Yves Montand, Emmanuelle Béart, Daniel Auteuil, Hippolyte Girardot, Elisabeth Depardieu

The second part of the story begun with *Jean de Florette* provides a
most satisfactory wrap-up. It takes place ten years after that film's conclusion; the young daughter, Manon (Emmanuelle Béart), of the farmer
unwittingly swindled by his neighbors, has grown up into a lovely
young woman. She discovers belatedly how her late father was ruined
by Soubeyran and his nephew, Ugolin (Yves Montand and Daniel Auteuil, reprising their roles), and seeks revenge. This being a Marcel Pagnol story, set in the lovely countryside of Provence, said revenge is not
accomplished with firearms. Ugolin's infatuation with Manon allows
her the pleasure of really sticking it to him and his uncle. Béart's breakthrough performance as Manon is exquisite, and Auteuil, as the nephew
who is too weak to resist his uncle's dominance, is tremendously affecting in the pivotal role.
⊙**DVD**
DR29
Goes well with: *Jean de Florette*

THE MARRIAGE OF MARIA BRAUN

ESSENTIAL

West Germany   1978   C   120 min.   R   Drama
Dir: Rainer Werner Fassbinder
C: Hanna Schygulla, Ivan Desny, Gottfried John, Klaus Löwitsch

Rainer Werner Fassbinder's relatively short but amazingly prolific
career began several years before this film was released, but for many
American filmgoers this was their first exposure to his work, and it remains one of his strongest films. Hanna Schygulla is Maria, the woman
who is wed in the middle of a World War II air raid and barely gets to
know her husband before he's swallowed up in the chaos of the war. She
carries on with her life as though she had never married, although in
fact her marriage seems to open up some kind of strange force in her.
Maria becomes a successful businesswoman after the war, taking full
advantage of the opportunities available to anyone (but especially a
woman willing to use sex whenever necessary) with ambition. *Maria
Braun* is one of Fassbinder's more conventional films, playing much
like the melodramas of one of his favorite Hollywood directors, Douglas Sirk. It's a chance to glimpse one man's depiction of the tumultuous
years that followed Germany's defeat.

DR1, DR24, DR39
Goes well with: *Antonia's Line*

MARTIN

U.S.   1978   B&W   95 min.   R   Horror
Dir: George A. Romero
C: John Amplas, Lincoln Maazel, Christine Forrest, Elayne Nadeau,
Tom Savini, George A. Romero

Michael Weldon, the author of *The Psychotronic Encyclopedia of Film* and its follow-up, *The Psychotronic Video Guide,* two indispensable reference works on weird and wacky films, declared in his first book that this vampire film was director George A. Romero's best work to date. And nothing Romero—the director best known for *Night of the Living Dead*—has done since the book was published in 1983 has changed that evaluation. As frightening as *Living Dead* was, *Martin* gets to you in more subtle and profound ways. Martin (John Amplas) is an eighteen-year-old who thinks he may be a vampire, just because he loves the taste of blood. He has no fangs—he uses syringes and razor blades on his victims—and he's not disturbed by crucifixes or garlic, but he persists in thinking of himself as the undead. Romero's screenplay offers the ambiguous proposition that Martin may be mentally disturbed, and the film plays with our perceptions of outcast teens and how "dangerous" they really are to both themselves and society. Martin's elderly cousin (played by Lincoln Maazel, father of classical conductor Lorin Maazel) feeds Martin's obsession by claiming that the boy is Nosferatu, but it's clear that the old man has been watching too many late-night movies. When Martin becomes a regular caller on an all-night radio talk show, the film kicks into a darkly comic mode.

⊙**DVD:** Includes audio commentary by George A. Romero.
FA9
Goes well with: *The Addiction*

MATEWAN

U.S.   1987   C   130 min.   PG-13   Drama
Dir: John Sayles
C: Chris Cooper, Will Oldham, Mary McDonnell, Bob Gunton, James
Earl Jones, Gordon Clapp, Maggie Renzi, David Strathairn, John
Sayles

Released at a time of declining union membership, during the administration of Ronald Reagan, a president who earned the enmity of organized labor for breaking the air traffic controllers' union, *Matewan* is typical of filmmaker John Sayles's career. In telling a story sympathetic to a labor organization, based on an obscure incident in the 1920s, Sayles proves himself impervious to fashion, preferring to work with subjects that interest him. He also understands there's more to labor-management disputes than black hats for management and white hats for labor. In the coal mines near Matewan, West Virginia, Stone Mountain Coal decides to increase profits by reducing wages. A union organizer (Chris Cooper) shows up in town to bring the workers together, but his job is complicated by the fact that the company has hired blacks and immigrant Italians who will work for reduced wages, thus exploiting the white miners' racist attitudes. *Matewan* reflects Sayles's impeccable feel for time and place and the issues that touch the lives of ordinary people. The filmmaker has an uncredited role as a preacher.

⊙**DVD:** Available in an Indie Collector's Pack, which also includes *Breaking the Waves* and *Traveller.*

DR24, DR40

Goes well with: *Harlan County, U.S.A.*

MAYA LIN: A STRONG CLEAR VISION

U.S. 1994 C 96 min. NR Documentary
Dir: Freida Lee Mock

The most graceful, eloquent, and understated of all memorials in Washington, D.C., is the one dedicated to the veterans of the Vietnam War. It's the best-known work of Maya Lin, who won the design competition while still a student at Yale University. The idea of recognizing that chapter of American history was itself controversial, but Lin's spare design provoked outrage even among supporters of the project. This Oscar-winning documentary is of the point-and-shoot school, but with a subject as fascinating as Lin (whose other work is showcased here), less is more.

DO4

Goes well with: *The Governess*

MEDIUM COOL

ESSENTIAL

U.S. 1969 C 110 min. R Drama
Dir: Haskell Wexler
C: Robert Forster, Verna Bloom, Peter Bonerz, Marianna Hill, Harold Blankenship, Peter Boyle

Produced independent of the studio system, *Medium Cool* miraculously managed to get distributed by Paramount Pictures. It is nearly a one-man production—written, directed, and photographed by Haskell Wexler, who also coproduced with his brother, Jerrold. Haskell Wexler is an esteemed cinematographer and political activist who wanted to look at the role of a news cameraman during especially tumultuous times. He couldn't have picked a better time and place to make this film, the summer of 1968 in Chicago. John Cassellis (Robert Forster) is a "shooter" for a Chicago TV station, oblivious to the building tension over the forthcoming National Democratic Convention. His apolitical attitude starts to crumble as he becomes involved with Eileen (Verna Bloom) and her son Harold (Harold Blankenship), West Virginia natives who are living in a slum awaiting word from Verna's husband, who is in Vietnam. As a dramatist, Wexler isn't subtle about portraying John's growing politicization; what gives the film its real power is its documentary flavor. Shooting a confrontation between police and antiwar demonstrators, for instance, Wexler and his crew found themselves caught in no-man's-land. When a tear gas canister landed at his feet, an assistant cried out, "Watch out, Haskell; it's real!" The moment stayed in the film. *Medium Cool* questioned how detached any journalist could be in covering a story, a rarity in films to that moment. Paramount opened the film in August 1969; in those days, studios actually released movies of substance during the summer.

⊙**DVD:** Includes audio commentaries by Haskell Wexler, editorial consultant Paul Golding, and actress Marianna Hill.

DR25, DR36, XT7

Goes well with: *Man of Iron*

MEETING VENUS

U.K./Japan/U.S.   1991   C   117 min.   PG-13   Drama
Dir: István Szabó
C: Glenn Close, Niels Arestrup, Erland Josephson, Johanna ter Steege, Jay O. Sanders, Maria de Medeiros

A wonderfully wry backstage drama about the world of modern opera, *Meeting Venus* offers a timely look at the new Europe, unified in principle but divided in fact. Glenn Close is a Swedish opera diva, Niels Arestrup is her Hungarian conductor, and they do their best to bring the great nations of Europe together by having an affair during rehearsals for a Paris production of Wagner's *Tannhäuser.* If only the rest of the company picked up on their good vibrations; the film is strongest when it details (in largely comic terms) union nitpicking and feuds exacerbated by barely simmering nationalistic prejudices. Close is a good singer, but the producers wisely chose to dub in Kiri Te Kanawa's singing voice.

DR23

Goes well with: *Topsy-Turvy*

MEMORIES OF UNDERDEVELOPMENT

Cuba   1968   B&W   104 min.   NR   Drama
Dir: Tomás Guttiérez Alea
C: Sergio Corrieri, Daisy Granados, Eslinda Núñez, Beatriz Ponchora

The first film from Castro's Cuba to enjoy wide distribution in the United States is a surprisingly ambivalent and melancholy drama of a man who both welcomes and dreads the changes taking place in his country. Set in the months between the 1961 Bay of Pigs invasion and the 1962 Missile Crisis, the story centers on the musings of Sergio (Sergio Corrieri), who in the opening scenes is sending his parents and his unhappy wife off to America. He's happy to be rid of them and other bourgeois friends fleeing to the north, but not because he's a committed Communist. "Cubans waste their talents adapting to every moment," Sergio observes. "They always need someone to think for them." Living in a high-rise apartment on a modest income as a landlord (his father's furniture business, which he used to manage, has been taken over by the state), Sergio spends his days wandering the city in search of women or recalling past loves, including a German girl he almost married. When he seduces and abandons a young woman named Elena (Daisy Granados), he's confronted by her angry brother and parents and forced to defend himself against rape charges. Sergio's the ultimate outsider and observer (he often retreats to a telescope on his balcony to spy on the city) whose musings suggest that his own development is arrested. This is a bold look at the mixed blessings of the revolution from a unique perspective.

DR25

Goes well with: *Strawberry and Chocolate*

MENACE II SOCIETY

U.S.   1993   C   97 min.   R   Drama
Dir: Allen Hughes and Albert Hughes

C: Tyrin Turner, Larenz Tate, Jada Pinkett, Vonte Sweet, Samuel L. Jackson, Charles S. Dutton, Glenn Plummer, Bill Duke

Twin brothers Allen and Albert Hughes made an especially dynamic debut with this chilling account of teen sociopaths growing up way too fast on the streets of Los Angeles. If *Boyz N the Hood* seemed too polite a picture of troubled black youth, this should meet your minimum daily requirements for mayhem. Tyrin Turner plays Caine, the kid who's too far gone to be saved by his loving girlfriend (Jada Pinkett), but it's Larenz Tate's charismatic performance as his buddy O-Dog that is at the cold, cold heart of this film. As Luis Buñuel did in *Los Olvidados,* the Hughes brothers refuse to excuse or mitigate these punks' actions, but the film doesn't wallow in violence for its own sake. Of the many urgent dispatches from the streets of America's inner cities in the 1990s, this film holds up best. Lisa Rinzler's cinematography won an Independent Spirit Award.

⊙**DVD:** Includes interview with the Hughes Brothers.

DR6, DR28, DR36, DR41

Goes well with: *Slam*

MEPHISTO

Hungary 1981 C 144 min. NR Drama
Dir: István Szabó
C: Klaus Maria Brandauer, Krystyna Janda, Ildikó Bánsági, Karin Boyd, Rolf Hoppe

The apolitical individual who willfully ignores the tide of history until he nearly drowns is the subject of Hungarian director István Szabó's brilliant study of blind ambition. Hendrik Hoefgen (Klaus Maria Brandauer) is a German stage actor in the 1930s who's understandably excited about jumping from provincial theater work to parts on the Berlin stage. As the Nazis rise to power, Hendrik dismisses them as thugs, only to find himself abandoned by his patron, Dora, who flees to America to escape the coming Holocaust, and by his wife, Barbara, who moves to Paris to work against the rise of fascism in Europe. Even in the face of government censorship, Hendrik declares that he is "married to the theater," assuming that being an artist exempts him from any other considerations. His black mistress is threatened, and Hendrik manages to pull some political strings to get her out of the country, but by then his pact with the devil has been sealed. Klaus Maria Brandauer offers an indelible portrait of a man whose need for approval from anyone who can grant it is his undoing. Academy Award winner for Best Foreign Language Film.

⊙**DVD:** Includes interviews with István Szabó and Klaus Maria Brandauer.

DR1, DR4, DR38

Goes well with: *Farewell, My Concubine*

MERRY CHRISTMAS, MR. LAWRENCE

Japan/New Zealand/U.K.   1983   C   122 min.   R   Drama
Dir: Nagisa Oshima
C: Tom Conti, David Bowie, Ryuichi Sakamoto, Takeshi, Jack Thompson

One of the more unusual entries in a genre crowded with excellent films, *Merry Christmas* offers what appears at first to be the standard POW setup. The Japanese commandant is a martinet, the British prisoners all offer veddy stiff upper lips, there are scenes of torture, and discussions of honor and duty. But Nagisa Oshima, making his first film in English (well, half in English) offers some twists: the commandant, Captain Yonoi, is played by Japanese music star Ryuichi Sakamoto, and he's carrying a torch for blond, handsome Jack Celliers, played by British music star David Bowie. Sakamoto composed the film's score, and although there are no duets for him and Bowie—the film is not *that* strange—Oshima does impart a more elliptical and poetic style to the proceedings than most fans of the genre are used to. Tom Conti is the title character, the only bilingual man in the camp. It's a bit like *Billy Budd* meets *The Bridge on the River Kwai,* with a decidedly Japanese flavor.

DR7, DR26, DR37

Goes well with: *The Bridge on the River Kwai*

METROPOLIS

ESSENTIAL

Germany   1926   B&W   120 min.   NR   Science Fiction
Dir: Fritz Lang
C: Brigitte Helm, Gustav Frölich, Rudolf Klein-Rogge, Fritz Rasp

The first great science-fiction epic is also one of silent film's great technical achievements. Fritz Lang employed the cream of German film technicians (including cameraman Karl Freund and special effects artist Eugen Shufftan) to create a city of the future; the film is full of effects that are still dazzling today. Written by Thea von Harbou (then Lang's wife), *Metropolis* was reportedly inspired by a trip Lang made to New York. His city of the early twenty-first century is divided between an above-ground civilization of sleek skyscrapers, flying cars, and the indolent wealthy, and an underground maze of machinery and cave dwellings for the workers who operate the city's complex infrastructure. An evil scientist (Rudolf Klein-Rogge) creates a robot version of the worker's champion, a young woman named Maria (Brigitte Helm), to lead the workers in a doomed revolt that will allow him to create a whole army of robot workers. The story is confusing, in part because the film was originally three hours long; the full-length version was never released in the United States. But it's the look of the film that has influenced so many science fiction films. In 1984 composer Giorgio Moroder created a new *Metropolis,* editing it to try to smooth out the kinks in the story, color-tinting some sequences, and adding rock-and-roll songs to the soundtrack. It's not as awful as it sounds, partly because Lang's visual razzle-dazzle still shines through.

⊙**DVD:** Includes interactive menu.

FA3, FA5, FA8

Goes well with: *Android*

METROPOLITAN
ESSENTIAL

U.S. 1990 C 98 min. PG-13 Comedy
Dir: Whit Stillman
C: Carolyn Farina, Edward Clements, Christopher Eigeman, Taylor Nichols, Allison Rutledge-Parisi

It might have been called *Jane Austen in Manhattan,* but that title was already taken (by an obscure 1980 film.) Writer-director Whit Stillman's debut is a unique look at the very rich from a semioutsider's perspective. Its protagonist, Tom (Edward Clements), does not have the family money and connections to be part of a clique of young debs and their escorts calling themselves the Sally Fowler Rat Pack, but they permit him to hang out with them anyway, possibly because enough of them find him amusing in a middle-class sort of way. Stillman's great achievement here is to humanize the wealthy snobs without ever letting us forget that they are very different from you and me. (Maybe this should have been called *Fitzgerald in Manhattan,* with Tom as the Nick Carraway stand-in.) The cast of good-looking young actors fill out their

roles nicely, most memorably Chris (here billed as Christopher) Eigeman, creating the character of the great social bluffer that he reprised in
several Stillman films. *Metropolitan* won Best New Director from the
New York Film Critics Circle, and Best First Feature from the Independent Spirit Awards.

CO5, CO7

Goes well with: *The Last Days of Disco*

MI VIDA LOCA

U.S.   1994   C   92 min.   R   Drama
Dir: Allison Anders
C: Angel Aviles, Seidy Lopez, Jacob Vargas, Marlo Marron, Salma
  Hayek

An invaluable look at a subject rarely explored in films, the lives of
the inner-city women left behind when their husbands are all dead or in
jail. The setting is Echo Park, an area of East Los Angeles that's not on
any tourist maps. Five stories intermingle, told both by actual crime
widows and by Latina actresses with short résumés. (Salma Hayek
proved to be the one breakout performer.) If the ride is a bit bumpy—
writer-director Allison Anders indulges some characters a bit too
much—it's a ride well worth taking for a glimpse at a social problem as
timely now as when this film was made, almost ten years ago.

DR6, DR28, DR36, DR39

Goes well with: *My Family (Mi Famila)*

A MIDNIGHT CLEAR

U.S.   1992   C   107 min.   R   Drama
Dir: Keith Gordon
C: Peter Berg, Kevin Dillon, Arye Gross, Ethan Hawke, Gary Sinise,
  Frank Whaley

Working from William Wharton's novel, actor-turned-writer-and-
director Keith Gordon fashioned a deeply felt antiwar film set in the
final days of World War II. In the dead of winter, a small reconnaissance
squad of American soldiers is in a standoff with an equal number of
German soldiers. There is nothing much to fight for, and every soldier
is aware that peace may soon be at hand. The young Americans are
caught between duty and self-preservation, and Gordon gives every
possible side of the debate its due without turning the film into a talk-

ing-heads show. The story moves inexorably toward a confrontation that underscores the daily dilemma in any combat soldier's life.

DR37

Goes well with: *The Burmese Harp*

MIFUNE

Denmark/Sweden 1999 C 99 min. R Drama

Dir: Søren Kragh-Jacobsen

C: Anders W. Berthelsen, Iben Hjejle, Jesper Asholt, Emil Tarding

Kresten, a newlywed businessman, is called to his family farm with the news that his father has died, leaving Kresten's mentally impaired brother, Rud, to fend for himself. That neither relative was at the wedding is an indication of Kresten's estrangement from them. Unable to secure housing for his brother, Kresten stays on at the dilapidated farm with Rud, hiring a live-in maid to care for the place. The woman who answers his ad, Liva, has her own problems; she's a prostitute on the lam from a man who has been harassing her with obscene phone calls. Liva is soon joined by her teenage brother, Bjarke, who is adrift after being kicked out of a boarding school she was paying for. It's not surprising that the quartet forms an ad-hoc family—the outcasts Rud and Bjarke bond, and Kresten and Liva fall in love—but the film exhibits an emotional honesty about its troubled characters that's refreshing. All four lead performers (including Iben Hjejle, familiar to fans of the John Cusack comedy *High Fidelity*) make strong impressions. The title reference is to Japanese actor Toshiro Mifune, star of many samurai films, which are a source of ritual games between Kresten and Rud. This was shot under the restrictions of Dogma 95, a set of filmmaking rules agreed to by a collective of Danish filmmakers—like *The Celebration,* another film about family strife set in a country house.

⊙**DVD:** Includes audio commentary by Søren Kragh-Jacobsen.

DR11

Goes well with: *The Celebration*

THE MINUS MAN

U.S. 1999 C 112 min. R Drama

Dir: Hampton Fancher

C: Owen Wilson, Janeane Garofalo, Brian Cox, Sheryl Crow, Mercedes Ruehl, Dennis Haysbert, Dwight Yoakam

Hampton Fancher's film is a scrupulous adaptation that both respects its source and adds some flourishes of its own. *The Minus Man* is based on Lew McCreary's tale of a serial killer who packs a flask of poisoned liquor along with his own twisted philosophy of life and death. Vann Siegert wants to relieve the suffering of others, even though his victims haven't reached the stage where they've considered calling Dr. Kevorkian. Vann is usually half-right: These people *are* unhappy with life, and since in his twisted judgment they can't see any way out of their misery, he's there to help. Vann takes a room with a troubled couple (Brian Cox and Mercedes Ruehl) and a job at the post office, courting a colleague (Janeane Garofalo), but he's undeterred from his mission in life. Owen Wilson, brilliantly funny as the half-smart crook Dignan in *Bottle Rocket,* is perfectly charming and cold-blooded as Vann. McCreary has a cameo as a victim in a restaurant.

⊙**DVD**

DR8, DR29, TH15

Goes well with: *White of the Eye*

MISHIMA

U.S.   1985   C/B&W   120 min.   R   Drama

Dir: Paul Schrader

C: Ken Ogata, Masayuki Shionoya, Junkichi Orimoto, Naoko Otani, Roy Scheider (narrator)

A rare stylized biography that works, *Mishima* is an impressionistic account of the life and works of author, actor, director, and militarist Yukio Mishima. The film alternates between black-and-white accounts of his life and color sequences that expound on selected writings. Woven throughout are the events of November 25, 1970, the last day of Mishima's life. A strong believer in restoring Japan to its traditional, pre–World War II values, he and several members of his own paramilitary force tried to take over an army barracks in Tokyo; Mishima ended the siege by committing ritual suicide. Paul Schrader (who cowrote the screenplay with his brother, Leonard, and Leonard's wife, Chieko) is well aware that a man of Mishima's prodigious talent and contradictions (he lived a life of well-publicized luxury while condemning materialism) can, within the limitations of a two-hour film, only be glimpsed. This is easily the most mesmerizing film Schrader has directed, thanks in large part to the contributions of cinematographer John Bailey, production and costume designer Eiko Ishioka, and composer Philip Glass.

⊙**DVD:** Special Edition contains "Inside Mishima" documentary; audio commentary by Paul Schrader; deleted scene.

DR2, DR17, XT6

Goes well with: *Providence*

THE MISSION

U.K.   1986   C   125 min.   PG   Drama

Dir: Roland Joffe

C: Robert De Niro, Jeremy Irons, Ray McAnally, Aidan Quinn, Cherie Lunghi, Liam Neeson, Daniel Berrigan

Following his successful debut with *The Killing Fields,* Roland Joffe turned his attention to another conflict, the eighteenth-century struggle between Spain and Portugal for the riches of South America. Robert Bolt's script is more interested in the war for men's souls than in armies clashing over gold and other treasures. Jeremy Irons plays Gabriel, a Jesuit missionary whose work among the natives involves protecting them from slavers more than providing actual spiritual nourishment. The convert he does make is Mendoza (Robert De Niro), a slave trader who sees the error of his ways and joins Gabriel's cause. But the politics of the Church (personified in Ray McAnally's wicked prelate, Altamirano) and the economic imperatives of both European countries overwhelm all else, turning the natives against the men who have their best interests at heart. As he did for *The Killing Fields,* Chris Menges won an Oscar for cinematography, and there is a tremendously moving musical score by Ennio Morricone.

DR7, DR24, DR30

Goes well with: *Black Robe*

MISSISSIPPI MASALA

U.S.   1991   C   118 min.   R   Drama

Dir: Mira Nair

C: Denzel Washington, Sarita Choudhury, Roshan Seth, Sharmila Tagore, Charles S. Dutton, Joe Seneca

All on its own, the struggles of an Indian family living in Greenwood, Mississippi, would be the stuff of arresting drama. They are refugees not from the subcontinent but from political unrest in Uganda, where turmoil in 1972 created a mass exodus of foreign-born workers and diplomats. Even after eighteen years, the father longs to return to Uganda; like anyone uprooted from a comfortable life, he's irrationally fixated on re-creating it. But his daughter Mina (Sarita Choudhury) is a young woman of twenty-two, eager to make her way in America, where she has lived for most of her life. When Mina meets a handsome African American businessman (Denzel Washington), the film's conventional romance takes over, and as attractive a couple as they are, it's the fringe benefits of this film, exploring the pockets of ethnic culture in the most unlikely places, that recommend it.

DR7, DR18, DR19, DR28

Goes well with: *Broken English*

MRS. BROWN

U.K./U.S./Ireland   1997   C   103 min.   PG   Drama
Dir: John Madden
C: Judi Dench, Billy Connolly, Geoffrey Palmer, Antony Sher

She was Victoria, Queen of England, but the gossips began calling her Mrs. Brown. Still grieving four years after the death of her husband, Victoria (Judi Dench) is shaken out of her lethargy by an unlikely source: Mr. Brown, a Scots horseman (Billy Connolly) who also happens to be one of her servants. His intentions seem to be most honorable, but tongues will wag over almost anything the royals do. Yes, it's a not-so-sly commentary on the egregious coverage given to Diana Spenser and Sarah Ferguson. Dench is magnificent as a woman slowly coming out of her shell but retaining her dignity (after all, this is Victoria), but Connolly almost steals the show. The robust comedian tamps down the urge to play Brown broadly, and he finds the heart of a man who knows his place but is not afraid to offer a hand to someone in need, whoever they might be. Dench could have won an Oscar here; instead she won for her next collaboration with John Madden, *Shakespeare in Love*.

⊙**DVD**

DR8, DR17, DR24, DR25

Goes well with: *The Madness of King George*

MRS. DALLOWAY

U.K./Netherlands/U.S.   1997   C   97 min.   PG-13   Drama
Dir: Marleen Gorris
C: Vanessa Redgrave, Natascha McElhone, Rupert Graves, Michael Kitchen, Alan Cox, Lena Headey

The best Virginia Woolf adaptation (from a very slim field), *Mrs. Dalloway* expands Woolf's story of a middle-aged woman's day of crisis (a party to give and a flood of memories to deal with) by fleshing out its backstory. Writer Eileen Atkins addresses the common complaint that movie characters' motivations aren't clear by offering a more detailed look at the choices Clarissa made in her youth, which informed the rest of her life. Vanessa Redgrave is appropriately fluttery as Mrs. D, and as the young Clarissa, Natasha McElhone gives us a sense of the woman she could have become. It may not be a movie for Woolf purists, who want the letter of the novel better respected, but it does the more important job of capturing the author's style and her creation's sense of regret.

⊙**DVD**

DR18, DR29, DR39, XT4

Goes well with: *Gertrud*

MRS. PARKER AND THE VICIOUS CIRCLE

U.S. 1994 C/B&W 125 min. R Drama

Dir: Alan Rudolph

C: Jennifer Jason Leigh, Campbell Scott, Matthew Broderick, Andrew McCarthy, Peter Gallagher, Jennifer Beals, Gwyneth Paltrow, Sam Robards, Martha Plimpton, Wallace Shawn, Lili Taylor, David Thornton, James LeGros, Keith Carradine, Nick Cassavetes, Jane Adams, Heather Graham

Initial reactions to this portrait of writer Dorothy Parker and her literary associates centered on Jennifer Jason Leigh's performance as Parker. Speaking as though her jaws were wired shut, Leigh may strike you as irritatingly mannered or appropriately conflicted. This juror votes for the latter; Leigh can be an actress whose tics overcome her talent (as in the Coen brothers' *Hudsucker Proxy*), but here she is the one character among many famous personages who comes off in fully three dimensions. Even if Parker wasn't the biggest talent at the famed Algonquin Round Table, she was often treated as if she were by the likes of Robert Benchley (Campbell Scott), Charles MacArthur (Matthew Broderick), Edna Ferber (Lili Taylor), Harold Ross (Sam Robards), and George S. Kaufman (David Thornton). Writer-director Alan Rudolph knows he hasn't got a chance of fully fleshing out all of these complex characters, so he keeps our eye on Dorothy. This version of the Round Table is a lot of smart people playing at being clever without being profound, reinforcing Dorothy Parker's sense that that was the limit of her own talent.

DR2, DR12, DR17

Goes well with: *Impromptu*

MR. DEATH: THE RISE AND FALL OF FRED A. LEUCHTER, JR.

U.S.   1999   C   92 min.   PG-13   Documentary

Dir: Errol Morris

Errol Morris has illuminated a number of rich subjects in his documentaries, but none so poignant as Fred A. Leuchter, Jr., a self-described expert in devices of capital punishment. In the first third of this film Leuchter shows off his bona fides, explaining how a good electric chair or gas chamber or gallows should work—his definition of "good" being a quick and relatively painless death for the prisoner. But Morris was attracted to Leuchter for more than his profession; Leuchter had become a consultant to a Holocaust denier, who employed him to collect samples from the walls of Auschwitz in order to prove that Jews were never gassed there. That Leuchter would include a side trip to the former camp during his honeymoon is just one of many jaw-dropping moments in this surprisingly moving (and bitterly funny) tale of man's limitless capacity for self-deception.

⊙**DVD**

DO4

Goes well with: *Fast, Cheap & Out of Control*

MR. HULOT'S HOLIDAY

ESSENTIAL

France   1953   B&W   86 min.   NR   Comedy

Dir: Jacques Tati

C: Jacques Tati, Nathalie Pascaud, Michèle Rolla, Valentine Camax

Comedy filmmaker Jacques Tati is a bridge from the silent clowns (Charlie Chaplin, Buster Keaton, Harold Lloyd) to our contemporary buffoons (Peter Sellers, Jerry Lewis, Jim Carrey). His second feature debuted his indelible creation, Monsieur Hulot, who was to Tati what the Little Tramp was to Chaplin: a sounding board for all the absurdities of modern life, a figure of sanity in a world gone a little mad. Striding about with an odd stiff-legged gait, wearing a rumpled raincoat, and carrying an umbrella (no matter what the weather), Hulot always manages to walk away from any situation unruffled, even when he has left a pile of rubble in his wake. For Tati, dialogue was superfluous; this film's only sounds are music and effects. The sight gag was his comic means of expression, and M. Hulot's trip to a seaside resort offers beaucoup possibilities.

⊙**DVD:** DVD title: *Monsieur Hulot's Holiday.*

CO4

Goes well with: *Mon Oncle*

MON ONCLE

France 1958 B&W 116 min. NR Comedy

Dir: Jacques Tati

C: Jacques Tati, Jean-Pierre Zola, Adrienne Servantie, Alain Bécourt

The second of Jacques Tati's Hulot films (preceded by *Mr. Hulot's Holiday* and followed by *Playtime* and *Traffic*) is a transitional film. The polite but slightly nutty world of *Holiday* is still in evidence here in Hulot's ramshackle apartment building and slightly seedy neighborhood, but most of the action takes place in the hideously "modern" house occupied by Hulot's sister and brother-in-law and their young son, Gerard. It's a nightmare version of those houses whose "conveniences" are annoyingly mechanical contraptions and whose furniture has everything to do with sleek design and nothing to do with comfort. Gerard and Hulot are pals because they are both uninterested in this chamber of horrors, preferring instead to wander the backstreets and fields of their village in search of adventures. There are wonderful running gags—a fish fountain, a procrastinating street sweeper—and lovely collisions between old and new, typified when a defective length of hose (from a factory named PLASTAC) is hauled away in a horse-drawn trash cart. In *Playtime,* Tati's next film, *everything* is "modern"—except, of course, for the inimitable Hulot with his rumpled raincoat and umbrella, walking with his storklike gait through one disaster after another. Voted Best Foreign Language Film by the Academy and by the New York Film Critics Circle.

⊙**DVD:** Includes introduction by director/performer Terry Jones, and 1947 Tati short, "L'ecole des facteurs."

CO3, CO8

Goes well with: *Playtime*

MONA LISA

U.K. 1986 C 104 min. R Drama

Dir: Neil Jordan

C: Bob Hoskins, Cathy Tyson, Michael Caine, Robbie Coltrane, Clarke Peters, Kate Hardie, Sammi Davis

Bob Hoskins, such a raging bull in his breakthrough role as the crime boss in *The Long Good Friday,* is a tame pussycat in this drama, but he's no less magnetic. George is a low-level hood just out of prison, and his old boss, Mortwell (Michael Caine), offers him a job chauffeuring Simone (Cathy Tyson), one of Mortwell's most popular call girls, to and from her jobs. You can guess the rest, but it's great fun watching Hoskins play the little man struggling to maintain his dignity. Caine gets to tap into his nasty side; his clipped vocal cadence turns every word he says into a little knife. Newcomer Tyson makes Simone into more than a one-trick pony; she is a woman aching for someone to show her a way out, but afraid to take that first step. The film's only misstep is the overuse of Nat King Cole's title tune. Hoskins won the Best Actor prize from the New York Film Critics Circle.

⊙**DVD:** Includes audio commentaries by Neil Jordan and Bob Hoskins.

DR6, DR19, XT7

Goes well with: *My Son the Fanatic*

MONSIEUR HULOT'S HOLIDAY.

See *Mr. Hulot's Holiday*

MONTEREY POP

ESSENTIAL

U.S.   1969   C   98 min.   NR   Documentary

Dir: James Desmond, Barry Feinstein, D. A. Pennebaker, Albert Maysles, Roger Murphy, Richard Leacock, Nick Proferes

The first great music-festival documentary offers a time-capsule look at the opening kiss of the fabled summer of love. In June 1967, producer Lou Adler and musician John Phillips of the Mamas and the Papas invited a cross-section of pop acts to perform for three days near the California town of Monterey. Not every act made it into the final cut (some by choice—the Grateful Dead were unhappy with their performance), but the ones that did were almost uniformly sensational. The performers include the Who, Simon and Garfunkel, the Mamas and the Papas, Hugh Masekela, Eric Burdon and the Animals, Canned Heat, Ravi Shankar, the Jefferson Airplane, and Country Joe and the Fish. This was a coming-out party of sorts for three major performers: Otis Redding (who was just beginning to cross over to a white audience),

Jimi Hendrix (who astonished the crowd by setting his guitar on fire), and Janis Joplin (who stunned everyone, including Cass Elliott of the Mamas and the Papas, seen saying "Wow!" after Joplin's performance of "Ball and Chain"). A four-CD set of performances from the festival is available, but when you hear how ragged the musicians sound on disc, you understand the power of the visuals. This was rock-and-roll image-making in its infancy; MTV was still more than a decade away. (A deluxe DVD edition is reportedly in the works.)

DO6, DO11

Goes well with: *Easy Rider*

MONTY PYTHON AND THE HOLY GRAIL

U.K.   1975   C   90 min.   PG   Comedy

Dir: Terry Gilliam and Terry Jones

C: Graham Chapman, John Cleese, Terry Gilliam, Eric Idle, Terry Jones, Michael Palin

The Pythons' take on the Arthurian legends is their first attempt at telling a story on film. It's better than nearly all the *Saturday Night Live* spin-off films, but you can still sense that the boys are keener on individual bits than on creating a coherent narrative. Python fans have already devoured this and regurgitated it to their friends, but if you have never been exposed to any of the work of Messrs. Chapman, Cleese, Gilliam, Idle, Jones, and Palin, this is a fine place to start. There are lots of references to filmmaking itself; knights are seen galloping on nothing but their own legs, while their servants use coconuts to create the sound of horses' hooves striking the ground. It isn't all silly fun, either; the Pythons want everyone to know that while Arthur was fruitlessly searching for the Holy Grail, his countrymen were starving in miserable conditions. Warning to the faint-hearted: dismemberment scene played for laughs, dead ahead.

☉**DVD:** Special Edition two-DVD set contains twenty-four seconds of previously unseen footage; two audio commentary tracks by Terry Gilliam, Terry Jones, John Cleese, Eric Idle, and Michael Palin; "Follow the Killer Rabbit" feature; sing-alongs; "making of" documentary; "How to Use Your Coconuts" educational film; 1974 BBC documentary *On Location with the Pythons;* Shakespeare's *Henry IV* subtitle option.

CO6, CO12

Goes well with: *The Three Musketeers*

MONTY PYTHON'S LIFE OF BRIAN

U.K.   1979   C   93 min.   R   Comedy

Dir: Terry Jones

C: Graham Chapman, John Cleese, Terry Gilliam, Eric Idle, Terry Jones, Michael Palin

Considering that the Pythons made only four feature films as a group (and one of them was a collection of sketches from their TV show), we should be especially grateful that one of their subjects was organized religion. Born at the same time as Jesus, Brian (Graham Chapman) comes to be mistaken for the Messiah. Miracles don't come off, nonsensical sermons are delivered, clueless groups of disciples gather and bump into one another, and crucifixions abound. Spoofing the finale of *Spartacus,* dozens of crucified men sing the Eric Idle tune "Always Look on the Bright Side of Life." Further explication is unnecessary; if you're not chuckling in anticipation of catching up on your Monty Python, you should be looking for another brand of comedy that respects family values and all that. Also known as *Life of Brian.*

⊙**DVD:** Two versions. Criterion contains "making of" documentary; audio commentaries by John Cleese, Terry Gilliam, Eric Idle, Terry Jones, and Michael Palin; and deleted scenes. The Anchor Bay version contains no extras.

CO6, CO12

Goes well with: *The Ruling Class*

MONTY PYTHON'S THE MEANING OF LIFE

U.K.   1983   C   103 min.   R   Comedy

Dir: Terry Jones

C: Graham Chapman, John Cleese, Terry Gilliam, Eric Idle, Terry Jones, Michael Palin

The last, and unfortunately the weakest, of their four feature films still finds the boys in commendable form. They get in one more jab at the Catholic Church (the "Every Sperm Is Sacred" sing-along), there is a grisly sketch involving attempts to harvest body organs from live donors, and the rip-snorting finale involves the exploding Mr. Creosote (Terry Jones in a fat suit that makes him look slightly smaller than the Goodyear blimp). Overall, it's like the last album by a band whose members can't wait to get out and do solo recordings.

⊙**DVD**

CO12

Goes well with: *And Now for Something Completely Different*

MOONLIGHTING

U.K. 1982 C 97 min. PG Drama

Dir: Jerzy Skolimowski

C: Jeremy Irons, Eugene Lipinski, Jirí Stanislav, Eugeniusz Haczkiewicz

Aside from the box-office-driven casting of Jeremy Irons, this drama of a Polish work crew trapped outside their homeland when martial law is declared in December 1981 is a tightly wrapped story of dislocation. Irons is Nowak, the foreman of a three-man crew hired by a wealthy Brit who figures it's cheaper to import laborers than use the homegrown variety to renovate his flat. The men are working without permits, and when Nowak discovers that the Polish military has imposed restrictions on everyday life, he must improvise to extend the job and keep his men from knowing the truth. Polish writer-director Jerzy Skolimowski obviously made this one from the heart, and his anguish over things going from bad (Communist dictatorship) to worse (military dictatorship) is evident in every scene. And the sad-eyed Irons is perfectly cast, except for his rudimentary Polish.

DR7, DR40

Goes well with: *La Promesse*

MOTHER NIGHT

U.S. 1996 C 114 min. R Drama

Dir: Keith Gordon

C: Nick Nolte, Sheryl Lee, Alan Arkin, John Goodman, Kirsten Dunst, Arye Gross, Frankie Faison, David Strathairn

Filming the events in any novel is easy; it's getting the tone of the work right that confounds many filmmakers. Keith Gordon and producer Robert B. Wiede (who collaborated on the screenplay) know what makes the best works of Kurt Vonnegut unique, if this adaptation of his 1966 novel is any indication. The story involves Howard Campbell (Nick Nolte, in excellent form), an American playwright hired by U.S. intelligence to broadcast stingingly anti-Semitic speeches from Germany during World War II; they're encoded with valuable information to help the Allied cause. Campbell recedes into obscurity after the war, only to be tracked down by Israeli intelligence agents, white suprema-cists, and a German wife he thought had died. Vonnegut presented all of this in a matter-of-fact style laced with bitterly black humor, and Gor-don matches his prose style perfectly on the screen, thanks in part to a first-rate cast (Sheryl Lee is a standout as Campbell's wife). You can glimpse Vonnegut in a street scene near the end of the film; whether he appeared to place his imprimatur on Gordon and Wiede's efforts is not known, but he must have been pleased with the final results.

⊙**DVD**

DR21, DR29, DR38, XT4

Goes well with: *The Tin Drum*

MOUNTAINS OF THE MOON

U.S.   1990   C   135 min.   R   Action-Adventure
Dir: Bob Rafelson
C: Patrick Bergin, Iain Glen, Richard E. Grant, Fiona Shaw, Delroy Lindo, Roshan Seth, Anna Massey

A great historical subject, the 1858 journey of Richard Burton and John Hanning Speke to discover the source of the Nile, is the subject of this marvelous film. William Harrison and Bob Rafelson adapted Har-rison's novel about the two men and borrowed from their journals as well to re-create the arduous expedition. Like the two explorers in *Burke and Wills,* Burton (Patrick Bergin) and Speke (Iain Glen) were an odd couple of the bush: Burton the lusty adventurer and anthropologist, Speke the dilettante who's along for the ride just so he can write a best-seller about it. (It further mucks things up that Speke more than admires the manly Burton.) Special mention should be made of Fiona Shaw's witty performance as Isabel Adams Burton, the one woman who could keep a hold on Burton, and of Roger Deakins's breathtaking cine-matography.

⊙**DVD**

AC2, DR12, DR17

Goes well with: *Burke and Wills*

MS. 45

U.S.   1981   C   84 min.   R   Drama
Dir: Abel Ferrara
C: Zoë Tamerlis, Steve Singer, Jack Thibeau, Peter Yellen, Jimmy Laine
"Equal time for the ladies" is the motto of Abel Ferrara's cheesy but ef-

fective vigilante melodrama. Drawing liberally from the execrable *Death Wish* series (as well as classier films like *Repulsion* and *Carrie*), writer Nicholas St. John sees New York as hell on earth for women. Thana (Zoë Tamerlis), a mute garment worker, is raped twice in the same day (the first rapist is played by Ferrara, who's billed as Jimmy Laine). Literally unable to communicate her pain and rage to the few friends she has, she acquires a gun (easily, of course) and begins a campaign of terror against any man who dares approach her. And that turns out to be most of the men in her neighborhood. Ferrara and St. John are after more than visceral thrills here; this is a stylish portrait of urban isolation. And they refuse to endorse Thana's behavior, as evidenced in the finale, a costume party in which she comes totally unhinged while dressed up as a nun.

⊙**DVD**

DR36, DR39, TH14

Goes well with: *The Addiction*

MUCH ADO ABOUT NOTHING

U.K.   1993   C   111 min.   PG-13   Comedy

Dir: Kenneth Branagh

C: Kenneth Branagh, Michael Keaton, Robert Sean Leonard, Keanu Reeves, Emma Thompson, Denzel Washington, Richard Briers, Kate Beckinsale, Brian Blessed, Phyllida Law

Kenneth Branagh brushes us all up on our Shakespeare with his second go at the Bard, following the rousing *Henry V* with an equally charming version of this romantic comedy. Unlike some recent Shakespeare films that pride themselves on original casting at the expense of sense and harmony (and that would include Branagh's own *Hamlet*), this film integrates its diverse cast with a minimum of distraction and a maximum of pleasure. Branagh and Emma Thompson make the most of their last film together with splendid performances as Benedick and Beatrice, but the real surprises are more-than-effective turns by Michael Keaton as Constable Dogberry and Keanu Reeves as Don John. Denzel Washington is a splendid Don Pedro; we never feel acknowledgement of his race is necessary. Also of note: Kate Beckinsale's lovely Hero, and Phyllida Law (Thompson's real-life mom) as Ursula. The Tuscan countryside never looked sunnier. A delight from start to finish.

⊙**DVD**

CO9, DR32

Goes well with: *Shakespeare in Love*

MULHOLLAND DRIVE

ESSENTIAL

France/U.S.   2001   C   146 min.   R   Drama
Dir: David Lynch
C: Naomi Watts, Laura Elena Harring, Justin Theroux, Ann Miller, Dan Hedaya, Angelo Badalamenti, Mark Pellegrino, Robert Forster, Diane Baker, Chad Everett, James Karen

Mulholland Drive began life as a pilot for a series on ABC, the same network that gave David Lynch the opportunity to do the sometimes brilliant *Twin Peaks*. When ABC gave Lynch the thumbs-down on the *Mulholland Drive* series, a French producer stepped in and offered to finance some additional shooting and postproduction work that would turn the opening episode of a TV series into a self-contained movie. The result is Lynch's spookiest and most intriguing film since *Blue Velvet*. (*The Straight Story* was intriguing but hardly spooky, though it had Lynch's fingerprints all over it.) Naomi Watts and Laura Elena Harring play Los Angeles roommates thrown together by circumstance: Watts is an aspiring actress, Betty is staying at her aunt's apartment, where she finds Harring (who takes the name Rita from a film poster for Rita Hayworth's *Gilda*) recovering from a car accident that gave her amnesia. We're one step ahead of Betty, knowing that "Rita" was about to be murdered before the accident, but it doesn't take long before we're many steps behind Lynch and his convoluted script, which takes a severe left turn at the two-hour mark. It is possible to read this break in the narrative as one part "reality" and one part dream, but to say which is which would be giving away too much to a first-time viewer. Watts is sensational in the role of the innocent Betty (reincarnated as something less attractive in the last thirty minutes), and there are amusing side performances from a gallery of faces so familiar and yet so strange that they threaten to turn this film into an homage to Fellini. Finally, *Mulholland Drive* is a poison-pen valentine to Hollywood, with its pretentious young directors, its lascivious aging actors, and its scummy money men "suggesting" that a film could be improved by hiring a certain young actress. Winner of Best Picture from the New York Film Critics Circle.

⊙**DVD**

DR12, DR19, DR22, DR27, DR36, XT4
Goes well with: *Apartment Zero*

MURIEL

France/Italy   1963   C   115 min.   NR   Drama
Dir: Alain Resnais
C: Delphine Seyrig, Jean-Pierre Kérien, Nita Klein, Claude Sainval,
  Jean-Baptiste Thierrée

Director Alain Resnais continues his investigations into time and memory that began with *Hiroshima, Mon Amour* and would continue with *Providence.* The character of Muriel is already dead when the story begins, the victim of callous French soldiers stationed in war-ravaged Algeria. One of those soldiers, Bernard (Jean-Baptiste Thierrée), is back in France, living with his stepmother, Hélène (Delphine Seyrig), and haunted by his memories of the war. Hélène has her own past to deal with in the form of an ex-lover who drops by to visit with his new girlfriend, prompting her to recall their happier days together. Resnais splinters this basic story with flashes of memories. Bernard tries to come to grips with his complicity in murder, while Hélène is trapped by longing that can never be satisfied. It's a rewarding film, but don't rent it if you're not prepared to sit up and pay close attention.

DR11, DR27, DR38, XT4
Goes well with: *Hiroshima, Mon Amour*

THE MUSIC OF CHANCE

U.S.   1993   C   98 min.   NR   Drama
Dir: Philip Haas
C: James Spader, Mandy Patinkin, M. Emmet Walsh, Charles Durning,
  Joel Grey

The chance encounter that goes wrong. Jim (Mandy Patinkin) picks up a hitchhiker, Jack (James Spader), a scruffy card sharp with a proposition: If Jim finances him in a high-stakes game of poker with a couple of eccentric millionaires, they can divide the proceeds. What J&J don't reckon on is losing so big that they're forced into a kind of indentured servitude to the millionaires (Charles Durning and Joel Grey) who have taken their money. It may take a while to figure out that Paul Auster's novel, adapted by Philip Haas and his wife, Belinda, isn't meant to be taken literally; note that the eccentrics' last names are Flower and Stone. But the movie doesn't descend into pretentious symbolism, either, grounded by Spader's quirky turn and Haas's adept direction.

DR13, DR26
Goes well with: *Hard Eight*

MY BEAUTIFUL LAUNDRETTE

ESSENTIAL

U.K. 1985 C 98 min. R Drama
Dir: Stephen Frears
C: Saeed Jaffrey, Roshan Seth, Daniel Day-Lewis, Gordon Warnecke,
Derrick Branche, Shirley Anne Field

London's thriving Asian community has a prolific literary (and filmic) chronicler in Pakistani writer Hanif Kureishi. His screenplay for this drama (which was originally shown on British TV) also features a new take on the gay scene, with its central characters, Johnny (Daniel Day-Lewis) and Omar (Gordon Warnecke), passionate (and interracial) lovers. Kureishi and director Steven Frears are not interested in simply creating a collection of noble Asian emigrés beset by resentful Brits howling for tougher immigration laws. Saaed Jeffrey plays an immigrant businessman who is both charming and aggressive; you can admire how successful that combination has made him, but it doesn't make you like him. Omar's dilemma is that he wants to open his own business (see title), but he has a bigger heart than most of his countrymen. That may endear him to certain members of the community, but will it be enough to shake off the thick blanket of prejudice he's under every day? For his breakthrough film, Day-Lewis picked up a Best Supporting Actor award from the New York Film Critics Circle, and Kureishi got the Best Screenplay Award.

DR7, DR19, DR28, DR36, DR40, XT7
Goes well with: *My Son the Fanatic*

MY BEST FIEND

U.K./Germany/Finland/U.S. 1999 C 95 min. NR Documentary
Dir: Werner Herzog
C: Klaus Kinski, Werner Herzog

Three films that director Werner Herzog and actor Klaus Kinski made together—*Aguirre, the Wrath of God; Nosferatu the Vampyre;* and *Fitzcarraldo*—are among Herzog's best, and certainly feature Kinski's three greatest performances. But, as the title of this documentary suggests, it was not the smoothest of working relationships. Herzog put his cast and crew through hellish location shoots on two of the films, and Kinski was, as clips from the sets of *Aguirre* and *Fitzcarraldo* show, not reticent about letting the filmmaker know when he was out of line. In their younger days, the men had actually been roommates for a time, and Herzog is shown walking through their old apartment, pointing to walls that Kinski had destroyed in fits of rage. *Fiend* is a portrait of a very talented and exceptionally difficult man (he died in 1991)—or make that "men," since it's as much (implicitly) about Herzog as it is about Kinski.

⊙**DVD**

DO4, DO5

Goes well with: *Fitzcarraldo*

MY BODYGUARD

U.S. 1980 C 96 min. PG Drama

Dir: Tony Bill

C: Chris Makepeace, Adam Baldwin, Martin Mull, Ruth Gordon, Matt Dillon, John Houseman, Joan Cusack, George Wendt

My Bodyguard is a modest coming-of-age story about an undersized high school student taking a stand. Chris Makepeace is Clifford, a new kid in a Chicago school who can't hang on to his lunch money, so he literally hires Ricky (Adam Baldwin), a hulking but reticent classmate, for protection. The film is more interesting around the edges than down the middle, where its message of might-makes-right is hardly inspirational. The cast is packed with familiar faces: Ruth Gordon and Martin Mull as Clifford's grandmother and father, Matt Dillon as one of the bullies, and Joan Cusack and George Wendt in small roles. It's an important film in the American independent movement, if only because it was a surprise box-office hit, proving that the little guy has a chance in the marketplace, too.

⊙**DVD**

DR31, DR41

Goes well with: *The Chocolate War*

MY BRILLIANT CAREER

Australia 1979 C 101 min. G Drama

Dir: Gillian Armstrong

C: Judy Davis, Sam Neill, Wendy Hughes, Robert Grubb

The breakthrough film for both director Gillian Armstrong and actress Judy Davis is the wonderfully realized story of Sybylla, a woman living on a remote ranch in turn-of-the-century Australia. Eleanor Whitcombe's script, based on an autobiographical 1901 novel by Miles Franklin (a pseudonym for Stella Franklin), focuses on a familiar dilemma: Should Sybylla give in and marry a wealthy landowner (Sam Neill) or pursue her dream of becoming a writer? Her mobility is limited by geography and economics (she is working to pay off her poor parents' debts) as well as custom. Davis comes on like Glenda Jackson crossed with the young Katherine Hepburn, playing a fiercely intelligent woman whose intensity both attracts and scares off men. In real life, Franklin was a lesbian, but the film sidesteps that issue to concentrate on Sybylla's struggle for respect, no matter what her sexual orientation.

DR17, DR39

Goes well with: *The Governess*

MY FAMILY (MI FAMILIA)

U.S.   1995   C   128 min.   R   Drama

Dir: Gregory Nava

C: Jimmy Smits, Esai Morales, Edward James Olmos, Eduardo López Rojas, Jenny Gago, Elpidia Carillo, Jennifer Lopez, Mary Steenburgen, Scott Bakula

The ambitious saga of a Hispanic clan in Los Angeles, covering several generations, Gregory Nava's story might have worked better as a TV miniseries, allowing time to flesh out some of the characters and story lines. Still, it has power and conviction on its side, as well as the charismatic Jimmy Smits at the center of the story. He's Jimmy Sánchez, a writer who looks back on his family's history, starting in the 1920s, when his grandfather, according to Sánchez lore, walked from Mexico to L.A. Nava, who wrote the script with his wife, Anna Thomas, also made *El Norte,* a more sharply focused film about Hispanic immigrants to Southern California.

DR7, DR11, DR28, DR36

Goes well with: *El Norte*

MY FAVORITE SEASON.

See *Ma Saison Préférée*

MY LEFT FOOT

Ireland   1989   C   103 min.   R   Drama

Dir: Jim Sheridan

C: Daniel Day-Lewis, Brenda Fricker, Ray McAnally, Hugh O'Conor, Fiona Shaw, Cyril Cusack, Adrian Dunbar

Writer/painter Christy Brown was a movie waiting to happen. Virtually paralyzed by cerebral palsy (his one usable appendage supplies the film's title), he managed to carve out an artistic career that was the envy of most able-bodied people. Jim Sheridan's film (cowritten by the director and Shane Connaughton) avoids the obvious pitfalls in telling this triumph-over-adversity tale, thanks in large part to Daniel Day-Lewis's performance. Day-Lewis doesn't just nail all the technical tics of Brown's struggle to lead a relatively normal life, he makes him a less-than-noble figure—Brown was no twinkle-eyed saint—without diminishing his accomplishments. Brenda Fricker's performance as Brown's patient mother also avoids the cliches inherent in that familiar role. Oscars went to both performers; the New York Film Critics Circle named it Best Film and Day-Lewis Best Actor, while the Independent Spirit Awards tabbed *My Left Foot* Best Foreign Film.

⊙**DVD**

DR2, DR15, DR17

Goes well with: *The Waterdance*

MY LIFE AS A DOG

Sweden   1985   C   101 min.   PG-13   Drama

Dir: Lasse Hallström

C: Anton Glanzelius, Tomas von Brömssen, Anki Lidén, Melinda Kinnaman

Don't hold it against this film that it was a surprise hit with filmgoers and inspired a TV series. After all, so did *M*A*S*H,* which is still a great film in spite of its bowdlerization for television. *My Life* is a genuinely winning comedy, based on an autobiographical novel, about a twelve-year-old boy sent to live with relatives in a small town in the 1950s. His overactive imagination allows him to adjust to being the new kid everywhere he turns. It's not *The Four Hundred Blows*—director Lasse Hallström isn't drawing from the kind of raw material that Truffaut did—but it's no gauzy remembrance of youth, either. The characters are mostly small-town eccentrics, giving a nice edge to the story. The Independent Spirit Awards and the New York Film Critics Circle awarded *My Life as a Dog* their Best Foreign Film prizes.

⊙**DVD**

DR34, DR41

Goes well with: *The Secret of Roan Inish*

MY NIGHT AT MAUD'S

ESSENTIAL

France   1969   B&W   105 min.   PG   Comedy

Dir: Eric Rohmer

C: Jean-Louis Trintignant, Françoise Fabian, Marie-Christine Barrault,
Antoine Vitez

Though this was the third installment in Rohmer's "Six Moral Tales,"
it was the first Rohmer film most Americans had seen, and it immediately
split the filmgoing public into two camps. There were those who could
not get enough of Rohmer's witty dissections of bourgeois life, and those
who felt, like Gene Hackman's character in the 1975 film *Night Moves,*
that watching a Rohmer film was like watching paint dry. The story here
revolves around a Catholic engineer (Jean-Louis Trintignant) who is as
much in love with the idea of love as he is with the strict dogma of his
Church. Although he is determined to marry a woman (Marie-Christine
Barrault) he has only seen at Mass, he is intelligent enough to know that
an offer to spend the night with a divorcée (Françoise Fabian) is not something he should refuse. The offer has some strings attached, and the night
is all talk and no action, which isn't giving anything away. The joy of
watching a Rohmer film lies in observing people who think they have the
world figured out come up short on their predictions. Rohmer's screenplay was honored by the New York Film Critics Circle.

⊙**DVD**

CO9, DR30

Goes well with: *The Tao of Steve*

MY OWN PRIVATE IDAHO

ESSENTIAL

U.S.   1991   C   102 min.   R   Drama

Dir: Gus Van Sant

C: River Phoenix, Keanu Reeves, James Russo, William Richert, Rod-
ney Harvey, Flea, Grace Zabriskie, Udo Kier

It's a road movie, it's a male love story, it's Shakespeare. Gus Van
Sant's third feature, following up on the brilliant *Drugstore Cowboy,* is
a continuation of that film's exploration of unusual family configura-

tions. Male hustler Mike (River Phoenix) and more-or-less straight Scott (Keanu Reeves) travel the highways and byways of the Pacific Northwest, partly in search of action and partly in search of Mike's mom. In Portland, Oregon, Mike is anointed the future "king" by a jolly thief (William Richert), and if some of their dialogue sounds familiar, it's because they're using the words of good Prince Hal and Falstaff. Amazingly, all of this somehow hangs together, in part because the film has a consistently dreamlike quality that downplays narrative in favor of rich imagery. The Independent Spirit Awards honored Phoenix's performance, Van Sant's screenplay, and the musical score by Bill Stafford.

DR19, DR21, XT5, XT6

Goes well with: *Drugstore Cowboy*

MY SON THE FANATIC

U.K.   1997   C   89 min.   R   Drama

Dir: Udayan Prasad

C: Om Puri, Rachel Griffiths, Stellan Skarsgård, Akbar Kurtha, Gopi Desai

Writer Hanif Kureishi (*My Beautiful Laundrette*) continues to monitor the cultural clashes between Asian immigrants and their British countrymen in this drama about a Pakistani taxi driver and his domestic problems. Parvee (Om Puri) is a man of small ambitions; he has been driving a cab for twenty-five years, and his modest pleasures include a glass or two of scotch and listening to American jazz and rhythm-and-blues records (LPs, not CDs). When his son Farid (Akbar Kurtha) begins to get "funny ideas," they're not about assimilation; he's going the other way, back to a more ascetic and less Western lifestyle. Farid soon invites a religious leader to board with the family, and Parvee watches with dismay as his wife, Minoo (Gopi Desai), chooses to eat in the kitchen, separate from the men in the house. The film is less interesting when it concentrates on Parvee's involvement with Bettina (Rachel Griffiths), a prostitute he regularly ferries to and from her jobs; *Mona Lisa* already has that route well-mapped. Puri's performance as a man scrambling to justify his existence is the best reason to see this film; it's a neat reversal of his character in *East Is East*.

⊙**DVD**

DR7, DR11, DR19, DR28

Goes well with: *East Is East*

THE MYSTERY OF KASPER HAUSER.
See *Every Man for Himself and God Against All*

MYSTERY TRAIN
U.S./Japan 1989 C 113 min. R Comedy
Dir: Jim Jarmusch
C: Masatoshi Nagase, Youki Kudoh, Screamin' Jay Hawkins, Cinqué
Lee, Nicoletta Braschi, Elizabeth Bracco, Joe Strummer, Steve
Buscemi, Rufus Thomas, Tom Waits (voice only)

Arguably Jim Jarmusch's best film, *Mystery Train* is certainly the best evocation of the spirit of Elvis Presley. It's a trio of comic stories set in and around a rundown Memphis hotel that has heartbreak oozing out of every crack in its linoleum. A Japanese couple (Masatoshi Nagase, Youki Kudoh) are staying there while they make the requisite pilgrimages to all the holy shrines—Graceland, the Sun studios, the King's grave. An Italian woman (Nicoletta Braschi) taking her husband's coffin back to Rome has to share her room with a very talkative American gal (Elizabeth Bracco) and later has her own religious experience with the King. An English punk (Joe Strummer) who fancies himself Elvis drives around town with a gun looking for trouble. Jarmusch demonstrates that Elvis is an international phenomenon that has helped define foreigners' view of America, for better or worse. Elvis is like God—he's everywhere and can mean whatever you want for any occasion. In addition to Strummer, formerly of the Clash, three musicians play supporting roles: Screamin' Jay Hawkins and Rufus Thomas, plus Tom Waits as the omnipresent voice of a radio disc jockey.
⊙**DVD**
CO10, XT1
Goes well with: *Night on Earth*

NAKED

ESSENTIAL

U.K. 1993 C 131 min. NR Comedy-Drama
Dir: Mike Leigh
C: David Thewlis, Lesley Sharp, Katrin Cartlidge, Greg Cruttwell, Claire Skinner

You may want to punch out Johnny, the character David Thewlis plays in Mike Leigh's scabrous satire, within the first ten minutes of this film. He's a woman hater, a leech, a man who's articulate enough to get your attention but too dyspeptic to keep it for long. And yet, there's something about him. . . . Maybe it's the characters he's given to bounce off of: his pliant girlfriend (Lesley Sharp), her flatmate (Katrin Cartlidge), who is all too willing to have sex with Johnny, and their landlord (Greg Cruttwell), whose behavior toward women makes Johnny look positively sensitive. Mike Leigh takes big risks in this satire of self-loathing modern men (and the women who put up with them), and most of them pay off, in part thanks to David Thewlis's masterful central performance, a winner with the New York Film Critics Circle. Not an easy film to like, but a film easily admired.

CO2, CO8, DR21
Goes well with: *Henry Fool*

THE NAKED KISS

U.S. 1964 B&W 93 min. NR Drama
Dir: Samuel Fuller
C: Constance Towers, Anthony Eisley, Michael Dante, Virginia Grey, Patsy Kelly, Betty Bronson

Before he became a filmmaker in the late 1940s, Sam Fuller was a reporter for several New York papers and a decorated soldier in World War II. He brought elements of both of those experiences to his filmmaking technique; Fuller approached every script with the attitude that life is war, and he was going to record that combat as truthfully as possible. In his greatest film, Fuller, who wrote all of his scripts, exposes the hypocrisy of a small town toward its newest citizen, Kelly (Constance Towers). Her secret is that she has fled the city and her life as a prostitute to make a new start. She takes up with Grant (Michael Dante), whose prominent family has given Grantville its name. He knows of her past and is willing to marry her, but he has a secret of his own. A violent confrontation between them forces the town to take sides, and even after she's proven right, Kelly understands that she can't stay in Grantville. It's melodramatic material, but Fuller presents it with such verve (from the opening confrontation between Kelly and her pimp) and conviction that it's easy to forgive its contrivances.

⊙**DVD**

DR34, DR39

Goes well with: *Ruby in Paradise*

NANOOK OF THE NORTH

ESSENTIAL

U.S.   1922   B&W   79 min.   NR   Documentary
Dir: Robert Flaherty

Director Robert Flaherty was a pioneer in nonfiction film, creating documentaries before the term was coined. For his first completed film, he traveled to the eastern shore of Canada's Hudson Bay to film the daily activities of an Eskimo family during the winter of 1920–21. Rather than hoping to catch significant moments in the lives of his subjects by just hanging around, he encouraged them to stage scenes for him. (He even set up printing equipment and a minitheater on location to show his subjects what he was up to, as a means of maintaining their trust in him.) Whether this process made the film less authentic has been debated for many years, but few question the basic truthfulness of Flaherty's intentions in recording the struggles of a family living among the harshest conditions on the planet.

⊙**DVD:** Includes interview with Frances Flaherty, widow of Robert

Flaherty and coeditor; excerpts from documentary *Flaherty on Film;* gallery of Flaherty's photographs of life in the Arctic.

DO8

Goes well with: *Man of Aran*

NAPOLÉON

ESSENTIAL

France 1927 B&W 235 min. NR Drama

Dir: Abel Gance

C: Albert Dieudonné, Antonin Artaud, Pierre Batcheff, Alexandre Bernard, Abel Gance

Among the greatest spectacles in the history of silent film, Abel Gance's masterful take on the life and times of M. Bonaparte has also provided one of the most stirring stories of film restoration: historian Kevin Brownlow's twenty-year labor of love to recover long-lost footage and present it in a form as close to the original print as possible. The version available on video is one that director Francis Ford Coppola "presented," with a score by his father, Carmine. Film scholars may quibble over how much it matches Brownlow's intentions, but it is still an impressive film. Gance was less a great storyteller than a technical innovator, employing mobile cameras and optical effects that were new to the language of filmmaking. The film's climax, presented in a wide-screen triptych, was a sensation at its original release and wowed even seen-it-all audiences in the 1980s when the film enjoyed limited theatrical release. Like *Lawrence of Arabia, Napoléon* will lose some of its impact on the TV screen, but if you're serious about completing your film history education, this is required viewing.

DR17, DR25

Goes well with: *The Last Emperor*

NELLY AND MONSIEUR ARNAUD

France/Italy/Germany 1995 C 103 min. NR Drama

Dir: Claude Sautet

C: Emmanuelle Béart, Michel Serrault, Jean-Hugues Anglade, Claire Nadeau, Michel Lonsdale

An unusually satisfying character study of two people in transition, *Nelly and Monsieur Arnaud* tells the story of a young woman who, as the famous advice columnist would say, wakes up and smells the coffee one day. Her husband has been out of work and moping around their apartment, and her own professional life is floundering. Then Nelly (Emmanuelle Béart) meets the mysterious businessman Monsieur Arnaud (Michel Serrault), who offers to pay off her debts, no questions asked. She soon extricates herself from the marriage and finds herself working as an editor on Arnaud's memoirs. If this were another kind of film, M. Arnaud would soon be spying on Nelly as she conveniently takes showers at his apartment and forgets to close the door all the way. But, thankfully, this is not that kind of film, though Arnaud's feelings for Nelly are not without passion. There are other characters as well: Arnaud's editor (Jean-Hugues Anglade), who benefits from Nelly's need for affection as she rebounds from her marriage, and another mysterious figure (Michel Lonsdale) who frequently visits Arnaud's apartment. Claude Sautet and his writing partners, Jacques Fieschi and Yves Ulmann, tell us just enough about Nelly, M. Arnaud, and these other characters to beguile us, and the lead actors honestly earn our sympathies, even when they're being almost impossibly stubborn about their life choices.

⊙**DVD**

DR12

Goes well with: *Un Coeur en Hiver*

THE NEW LAND

ESSENTIAL

Sweden   1972   C   161 min.   PG   Drama

Dir: Jan Troell

C: Max von Sydow, Liv Ullmann, Eddie Axberg, Hans Alfredson, Monica Zetterlund, Per Oscarsson

In the concluding chapter of the nineteenth-century saga begun with *The Emigrants,* Karl-Oskar (Max von Sydow) and Kristina (Liv Ullmann) have arrived in America after their arduous journey from Sweden. They settle in the midwest and try to make a go of it as farmers, but the inevitable catastrophes of weather and hostile Indians almost overcome them. *The Emigrants,* for all the difficulties presented, was at least a hopeful story; Karl-Oskar and Kristina were leaving a Sweden gripped by economic depression for something they knew would be better. In *The New Land,* the reality of what they're up against hits them—and us—hard. When Karl-Oskar pushes on to prospect for gold in the southwest, you have to admire his optimism in the face of so much adversity. As in *The Emigrants,* Ullmann's luminous performance is the anchor.

DR7, DR11, DR24

Goes well with: *The Emigrants*

NEWSFRONT

Australia   1978   C   110 min.   PG   Drama

Dir: Philip Noyce

C: Bill Hunter, Gerard Kennedy, Angela Punch, Wendy Hughes, Chris Haywood, Bryan Brown

Several generations of filmgoers have grown up without any first-hand knowledge of newsreels and their importance in conveying images of world events in the days before television took over that job. Philip Noyce's debut film is a tribute to the brave cameramen who put themselves on the front lines of many battles and smack in the middle of developing disasters to bring back the pictures that millions of moviegoers were eager to see. The episodic story is set in the 1940s and 1950s, which allows us to witness both great events and the dying days of the form, as that box in the living room began to replace a trip to the theater for the latest pictures of world leaders and earthquake victims. Noyce and his editors skillfully combine real newsreel footage with re-created shots, and the cast is uniformly adept at conveying the devil-may-care attitude of the newsreel men and women.

DR22, DR24

Goes well with: *Boogie Nights*

NIGHT OF THE LIVING DEAD

ESSENTIAL

U.S.   1968   B&W   96 min.   R   Horror

Dir: George A. Romero

C: Duane Jones, Judith O'Dea, Russell Streiner, Karl Hardman, Keith Wayne

It is crudely shot, the writing is rudimentary, and there is only one skilled performance. Nevertheless, *Night of the Living Dead* is on the short list of great horror films, for one simple reason: *It is so damned scary.* The rules of this game are simple: Corpses are rising from their slabs and stalking the living for food; once you have been bitten by a zombie, you can become one; you can kill a zombie with a shot to the head. Now, lock seven people in an isolated rural cabin surrounded by zombies and watch what happens. Duane Jones plays the one occupant who keeps his cool, and the fact that he is black does not go without comment by several of the other characters. George Romero and writer John Russo tap into some primal fears: claustrophobia, pursuit by a mindless mob, and a world turned upside down. The gore seems pretty restrained, given the last thirty years of nonstop bloodletting in horror films with much bigger budgets and much punier imaginations.

⊙**DVD:** Available in two editions. Special Edition contains audio commentaries by George A. Romero, John Russo, cast, and crew; "Night of the Living Bread" parody. The 30th Anniversary Edition contains audio commentaries by John Russo, cast, and crew; all-new musical score; original 90-minute "edit" of the film; behind-the-scenes featurette; music video; collector's booklet.

FA9

Goes well with: *Dawn of the Dead*

THE NIGHT OF THE SHOOTING STARS

Italy   1982   C   106 min.   R   Drama
Dir: Paolo Taviani and Vittorio Taviani
C: Omero Antonutti, Margarita Lozano, Claudio Bigagli, Massimo Bonetti

The Taviani brothers' breakthrough film is an evocation of the final days of World War II, as American troops advance through Tuscany. The film has the aura of a series of fables, and indeed, the framing device for the story is a bedtime story told by a mother to her young son—she's recalling what she saw as a six-year-old. The citizens of San Martino await the arrival of the Americans, but, fearful of the vengeful Germans, some of them strike out through the countryside to meet their liberators. Along the way, they have to evade not only the Germans but also the Italian fascists. The Tavianis blend rueful humor and stark violence—a gun battle in a field between the citizens and the fascists is the film's highlight—in a movie that combines the best of the neorealist tradition and the more fanciful elements of Federico Fellini's best work.

DR34, DR38, XT5
Goes well with: *Paisan*

NIGHT ON EARTH

France/Germany/Japan/U.S. 1991 C 129 min. R Comedy-Drama
Dir: Jim Jarmusch
C: Winona Ryder, Gena Rowlands, Giancarlo Esposito, Armin Mueller-Stahl, Rosie Perez, Isaach De Bankolé, Béatrice Dalle, Roberto Benigni, Paolo Bonacelli, Matti Pelonpää

Nearly every episodic film works in fits and starts, and Jim Jarmusch's portrait of five cab drivers in five cities is no exception. The weakest is the opening, a pas de deux in L.A. between Winona Ryder and casting agent Gena Rowlands. The funniest is set in Helsinki, with a melancholy driver (Matti Pelonpää) calming three rowdy drunks with a story that sounds like Garrison Keillor translated into Finnish. The other three tales are set in New York (with redoubtable Armin Meuller-Stahl as the driver), Paris (a standoff between an African immigrant and a blind young woman), and Rome (Roberto Benigni mugging as only he can). Jarmusch clearly has a lot of affection for his drivers, and a few of the passengers as well; this may be his most tender comedy yet. Frederick Elmes's cinematography won an Independent Spirit Award.

DR36, XT1, XT7
Goes well with: *Mystery Train*

NIGHTS OF CABIRIA

Italy/France 1957 B&W 117 min. NR Drama
Dir: Federico Fellini
C: Giulietta Masina, François Périer, Franca Marzi, Dorian Gray, Amedeo Nazzari

Federico Fellini's second collaboration with his actress wife, Giulietta Masina, is not quite up to the sublime heights of *La Strada,* though both won Oscars for Best Foreign Language Film. Here, Masina plays a woeful Roman prostitute who is successful enough to have her own home but not savvy enough to avoid hooking up with men who exploit her. Through her various adventures—meeting a gigolo movie star and a good Samaritan who hands out staples to homeless people living in caves outside the city, attending a pilgrimage to a religious site—she whipsaws between bitter cynicism and wistful yearning, moods that Masina handles effortlessly. When she's courted by an accountant (François Périer), you can't help rooting for him to be the real deal, even as you suspect he isn't. If the plot sounds familiar, you may know it from the Broadway (and film) musical *Sweet Charity*. Be sure to get the restored edition of the film, which added seven minutes that Fellini was ordered to trim by the Catholic Church before the film could premiere in Italy.

⊙**DVD:** Includes video interview with former Fellini assistant Dominique Delouche; audio interview with producer Dino De Laurentis.

DR39

Goes well with: *La Strada*

1900

Italy/France/West Germany   1977   C   243 min.   NC-17   Drama
Dir: Bernardo Bertolucci
C: Robert De Niro, Gérard Depardieu, Donald Sutherland, Burt Lancaster, Dominique Sanda, Stefania Sandrelli, Sterling Hayden

At 243 minutes (the version currently available on VHS), Bernardo Bertolucci's epic may seem too long for even his most devoted fans, but wait: There is a 311-minute version that plays occasionally on cable/satellite channels. However, unlike lengthy panoramic historical epics like *Lawrence of Arabia* and *Napoleon,* which are best viewed on a big screen, *1900*'s more intimate settings don't require a trip to the theater, and given its length, it may be best enjoyed in increments. Two Italian boys are born at the turn of the century, and though one is a peasant and the other the son of a wealthy landowner, they grow up as best friends—until the political movements of the 1920s and 1930s tear them apart. Gérard Depardieu is the grown-up peasant with a chip on his shoulder for capitalists, and Robert De Niro is the man of means with a bit of a conscience. Sterling Hayden plays Depardieu's grandfather, who gives him his political education, and Burt Lancaster is De Niro's grandfather, who tries to give him a sense of noblesse oblige. The film's key character is De Niro's foreman, played by Donald Sutherland, whom Bertolucci uses as a symbol for the Fascist political thinking he abhors. The violence that he does to others may seem to justify a horrific end for him after Italy is liberated by the Allies, but all the same, it's a repulsive scene. *1900* is a deeply flawed but very personal work of a great filmmaker.

DR5, DR24, DR40

Goes well with: *Burn!*

NORMAL LIFE

U.S. 1996 C 102 min. R Drama

Dir: John McNaughton

C: Luke Perry, Ashley Judd, Dawn Maxey, Tom Towles, Penelope Milford

As in his previous film, the almost unbearably tense *Henry: Portrait of a Serial Killer,* director John McNaughton is fascinated with behavior that's not easily explained. A cop (Luke Perry) falls in love with a woman (Ashley Judd) who's a bit wild, but he thinks she's nothing he can't handle. Will Chris be able to pull Pam into the "normal life" of bowling games and trips to the mall, or will Pam drag him down into her erratic lifestyle? It's clear from the start who is the stronger, and *Normal Life* is like watching a car wreck unfold on the highway a hundred yards in front of you. Luke Perry is good as Chris, but the film belongs to Ashley Judd's Pam, a force of nature. When the hold-ups and shootings begin, she's the one in charge, and Chris can only meekly follow.

DR6, DR27, TH7

Goes well with: *In the Realm of the Senses*

NORTE, EL.

See *El Norte*

NOSFERATU

ESSENTIAL

Germany 1922 B&W 84 min. NR Horror

Dir: F. W. Murnau

C: Max Schreck, Alexander Granach, Gustav von Wangenheim, Greta Schroeder

The first great vampire film was also one of the last truly suggestive ones. F. W. Murnau understood the power of images, starting with the amazing appearance of Orloc (Max Schreck), with his hollowed-out eyes and foot-long fingernails. Figures emerge from shadows, the camera pans the sky for signs of bats, and everyone walks very, very slowly, as though Murnau had hypnotized the entire cast. The film had to be withdrawn in a dispute with the heirs of *Dracula* creator Bram Stoker, but, fortunately, not all the prints were destroyed. The story of the production was told in the recent *Shadow of the Vampire,* which gives in to the apocryphal story that Schreck really *was* a vampire.

⊙**DVD:** Includes audio essay by Lokke Heiss.

FA9

Goes well with: *Nosferatu the Vampyre*

NOSFERATU THE VAMPYRE

West Germany   1979   C   107 min.   PG   Horror

Dir: Werner Herzog

C: Klaus Kinski, Isabelle Adjani, Bruno Ganz, Roland Topor

Though an almost slavish remake of the Murnau film (some shots were duplicated), Werner Herzog's version stands on its own. Klaus Kinski is magnificent as the restless bloodsucker; he speaks in a very halting, weary voice that suggests he has been living for hundreds of years without a good day's sleep. Understanding the sexual dimension of the story, Herzog cast the stunning Isabelle Adjani as the object of the count's affection. Just as in the original, there is no von Helsing to stake out this vampire; the lady can handle him quite well by herself.

⊙**DVD:** Includes both German- and English-language versions, and behind-the-scenes featurette.

FA9

Goes well with: *Nosferatu*

NOTHING BUT A MAN

ESSENTIAL

U.S.   1964   B&W   92 min.   NR   Drama

Dir: Michael Roemer

C: Ivan Dixon, Abbey Lincoln, Julius Harris, Gloria Foster, Martin
   Priest, Leonard Parker, Yaphet Kotto

Nothing but a Man is a documentary disguised as a love story. That is, in this simple tale of Duff (Ivan Dixon), a black railroad worker, romancing Josie (Abbey Lincoln), a small-town preacher's daughter, director Michael Roemer (who wrote the film with Robert Young) seems to be catching a moment in history in every scene. Set in Alabama, the story is sensitive to the changing times of the 1960s; Duff is advised to "go slow" by his future father-in-law, a minister who accepts the fact that his town is about to build a school "for his people," even though Duff realizes that segregation is a thing of the past. Duff begins the story working with an all-black crew, but when he marries, he has to take a job in town in a racially mixed mill and immediately runs afoul of both white racists and his fellow black workers, who see him as a troublemaker. Dixon and Lincoln are sensational as two people working to accommodate each other and the slowly shifting social mores of the Civil Rights–era South.

DR18, DR28

Goes well with: *Mississippi Masala*

NOTTING HILL

U.K./U.S. 1999 C 123 min. PG-13 Comedy

Dir: Roger Michell

C: Julia Roberts, Hugh Grant, Hugh Bonneville, Emma Chambers, James Dreyfus, Rhys Ifans, Tim McInnerny, Gina McKee

An ingratiating star vehicle for Hugh Grant and Julia Roberts, *Notting Hill* picks up points for stepping through a minefield of clichés unscathed. It's also possible to see this story of an unlikely romance between a bookseller and an actress as a commentary on its leads' ongoing coverage in the tabloid press. Writer Richard Curtis reprises elements of his previous collaboration with Grant, *Four Weddings and a Funeral,* as our lovelorn hero, comforted and encouraged by a Greek chorus of friends, pursues the unattainable girl of his dreams. The best sequence: a skillfully edited shot of Grant walking through his neighborhood as the seasons change, one of the most imaginative passage-of-time sequences ever filmed.

⊙**DVD:** Includes "Hugh Grant's Movie Tips" featurette; deleted scenes; audio commentary by Roger Michell and Richard Curtis.

CO9, CO10, XT7

Goes well with: *Four Weddings and a Funeral*

O LUCKY MAN!
U.K./U.S.   1973   C   174 min.   R   Comedy
Dir: Lindsay Anderson
C: Malcolm McDowell, Rachel Roberts, Arthur Lowe, Ralph Richardson, Alan Price, Lindsay Anderson, Helen Mirren, Mona Washbourne

The picaresque fable is a standard literary genre, but it is rarely attempted in film. David Sherwin's screenplay, reportedly based on an idea by star Malcolm McDowell, sets up Mick as a kind of everyman whose wide-eyed gaze takes in all manner of human folly. His primary occupation as a coffee salesman lands him in hot water, as he stumbles into evil businessmen, generals, politicians, and clergymen all preying on the willingness of the masses to be duped. It's heavy-handed at times, and director Lindsay Anderson sometimes confuses the narrative by having an actor play more than one role, or even reappear as the same character when we don't expect it. What holds the film together is a terrific song score by Alan Price; Anderson occasionally interrupts his story to show Price performing his songs, like a Greek chorus of one. That Mick emerges from all his adventures unscathed and seemingly unchanged might be the ultimate cynical comment of a very skeptical movie.

CO2, CO8

Goes well with: *The Ruling Class*

ODD MAN OUT
U.K.   1947   B&W   115 min.   NR   Drama
Dir: Carol Reed

C: James Mason, Robert Newton, Kathleen Ryan, Robert Beatty, Cyril Cusack

A thriller that manages to be both realistic and allegorical, *Odd Man Out* is the story of a wounded IRA gunman (James Mason) looking for sanctuary as the police chase him about an unnamed city. Johnny McQueen has plenty of friends and supporters, but they keep missing him, and it's not long before you can see the look of doom in his eyes. So does a loony artist (Robert Newton), who wants to paint his portrait because he has never had a dying model before. Director Carol Reed plays the religious card a bit too often—okay, we get it, he's a Christ figure—but he has such a gifted performer in Mason, able to convey desperation as well as anyone who ever acted, that the distractions finally don't ruin the suspense.

⊙**DVD**

DR6

Goes well with: *The Crying Game*

OLIVER TWIST

U.K. 1948 B&W 105 min. NR Drama

Dir: David Lean

C: Alec Guinness, Robert Newton, John Howard Davies, Kay Walsh, Francis L. Sullivan, Anthony Newley

David Lean's second Dickens interpretation (after his masterful *Great Expectations*) opens, like its predecessor, with a tour-de-force scene—Oliver's mother struggling through a storm—and maintains that assured sense of purpose throughout. The script by Lean and Stanley Haynes condenses the material brilliantly; only the most ardent Dickens fans could carp about the omissions. If *Oliver Twist* is finally not up to the standards of *Great Expectations,* it has to do more with the story. Oliver's a bland character, leaving the colorful villains (Bill Sykes, played by Robert Newton, and Fagin, played by Alec Guinness) to occupy center stage. Guinness's Fagin did provoke some controversy; Jewish groups felt it leaned too heavily toward the stereotype of the hook-nosed, heartless businessman, and for years, American prints of the film had certain scenes snipped out.

⊙**DVD:** Includes interactive menu.

DR6, DR24, DR29, DR36, DR41

Goes well with: *Great Expectations*

OLYMPIA

ESSENTIAL

Germany   1936   B&W   220 min.   NR   Documentary
Dir: Leni Riefenstahl

More than sixty-five years and two dozen Olympiads later, the gold medal for documentaries about the Olympics still belongs to the very first one, Leni Riefenstahl's amazing record of the 1936 Berlin Games. Riefenstahl had already ingratiated herself with Adolf Hitler by filming *Triumph of the Will,* a record of the 1934 Nazi Party Congress in Nuremberg, so she was the logical choice to further the aims of the party with this film. Its opening section is a virtually wordless idealization of the athletes' bodies, comparing them to their ancient Greek counterparts; it's possible to read something political into it, but the point isn't obvious. Less likable are attempts to give German athletes extra credit for their accomplishments, but Riefenstahl did not make the film that Hitler expected. There is plenty of footage of non-German performers, including Jesse Owens. The filmmaker was given an immense budget and a small army of cameramen; until Kon Ichikawa's *Tokyo Olympiad,* another homegrown production, no other director was granted that kind of luxury. (It's possible that Riefenstahl's film was daunting to other filmmakers and their potential backers.) And with TV's saturation coverage and with instant highlight documentaries available on video, it's not likely we'll ever see a film as ambitious and accomplished as this one.

DO10

Goes well with: *Tokyo Olympiad*

ONCE UPON A TIME IN THE WEST

ESSENTIAL

U.S./Italy   1968   C   165 min.   PG   Action-Adventure
Dir: Sergio Leone
C: Charles Bronson, Henry Fonda, Jason Robards, Claudia Cardinale, Gabriele Ferzetti, Paolo Stoppa, Frank Wolff, Jack Elam, Woody Strode, Keenan Wynn

Director Sergio Leone had been working up to this film with his "Dollars" trilogy (*A Fistful of Dollars, For a Few Dollars More, The Good, the Bad and the Ugly*), and everything about it, from that generic title to its setting (Monument Valley, an iconic location ever since John Ford used it for *Stagecoach* in 1939) to its archetypal characters, is bigger than life. (Westerns were once derided as "horse operas"; Leone takes that label seriously.) *Once Upon a Time* isn't the ultimate Western, even for Leone (he made one more, *Duck, You Sucker*), but it feels like it. From the "Dollars" trilogy, Leone carries over the enigmatic, soft-spoken character, here called Harmonica (Charles Bronson), and surrounds him with Old West archetypes: Cheyenne (Jason Robards), the wrongly accused half-breed; Frank (Henry Fonda), the steely-eyed gunman who does the dirty business of cleaning out landowners reluctant to sell to the railroad; and Jill (Claudia Cardinale), the prostitute turned mail-order bride. Every scene, from the opening gunfight on a train station platform to the final shootout between Frank and Harmonica, is played with a marvelously theatrical deliberateness reinforced by Ennio Morricone's grand score, perhaps the best in his long career. Don't bother to watch this film if it's not a wide-screen presentation; neither of the scenes mentioned above will make any sense.

AC7, XT3, XT8

Goes well with: *The Good, the Bad and the Ugly*

ONCE WERE WARRIORS

New Zealand   1994   C   103 min.   R   Drama
Dir: Lee Tamahori
C: Rena Owen, Temuera Morrison, Mamaengoroa Kerr-Bell, Julian
  Arahanga, Taungaroa Emile

This drama of cultural assimilation opens with a shot of a beautiful New Zealand landscape—only it turns out to be an illusion, just like the idea that moving to the city from the impoverished countryside will create a better life for its main characters, Jake and Beth Hekke. They are Maori people who have all but forgotten their proud ancestry, living in an Auckland slum with their five children. Jake is occasionally employed but always ready to party; Beth is wearying, after eighteen years of marriage, of his swings from fun-loving guy to abusive drunk. Their oldest son (Julian Arahanga) joins a gang to find some stability; their next oldest is arrested, and when Beth can't appear at his trial because she is recovering from one of Jake's beatings, he is sent off to a reform school. The linchpin of the drama is the oldest daughter, Grace, a young adolescent victimized by one of Jake's drinking pals. Temuera Morrison is absolutely frightening as Jake, allowing us just enough of a glimpse of his better side before he turns into a raging and finally pathetic monster. As Beth, Rena Owen creates a believable victim of abuse, a woman determined to hold her family together, living in both fear and hope.

DR7, DR11, DR28, DR36

Goes well with: *Broken English*

ONE DAY IN SEPTEMBER

ESSENTIAL

U.S./U.K.   1999   C/B&W   92 min.   R   Documentary

Dir: Kevin MacDonald

The greatest tragedy in the history of the Olympic Games is the subject of this painstaking reconstruction, originally shown on HBO. At the 1972 Munich games, a group of Palestinian terrorists broke into the Israeli wrestling team's living quarters, and in the twenty-four hours that followed, nearly all of the principals in the drama were killed. Kevin MacDonald and his producers point the finger of blame squarely at German authorities, starting with the lax security in the Olympic Village, continuing with the botched rescue attempt at an air force base, and ending with the later release of the three surviving terrorists in a trade-off during an airliner hijacking. Although Israeli authorities have tracked down and killed two of the terrorists, one is still free, and amazingly, the filmmakers got an interview with him. The events are scrupulously recounted from news footage and through conversations with eyewitnesses and officials. The naïveté of authorities in dealing with these criminals appears appalling to us now, but at the time, the willingness of political radicals to go outside their homeland to make a violent statement was relatively new. Winner of the Academy Award for Best Documentary Feature.

⊙**DVD**

DO2, DO3, DO10

Goes well with: *4 Little Girls*

ONE FALSE MOVE

U.S.   1991   C   105 min.   R   Thriller

Dir: Carl Franklin

C: Bill Paxton, Cynda Williams, Billy Bob Thornton, Michael Beach, Jim Metzler

Fleeing a Los Angeles drug deal that ends in a bloodbath, a trio of criminals, Lila, Ray, and Pluto, think that hiding out in the small

Arkansas town where Lila grew up is their perfect cover until the heat is off. Lila (Cynda Williams) has a bit of history, though, with the local sheriff (Bill Paxton), so the plan is hardly foolproof. And Ray (Billy Bob Thornton) and Pluto (Michael Beach) don't exactly blend in with the laid-back locals. Actor-turned-director Carl Franklin's debut behind the camera is a solid one, thanks in part to the screenplay by the then-unknown Thornton. This thriller draws on the conventions of classic film noir—characters at a dead end in their lives, a past romance always creeping up to haunt somebody—with some contemporary touches: You never saw a black lead actress in any film noir in the 1940s. Williams is the real deal here, tough and tender. It's a shame the surprise popularity of this film didn't kick-start her career. Franklin won an Independent Spirit Award for his direction.

⊙**DVD:** Special Edition contains audio commentary by Carl Franklin.

DR34, TH13

Goes well with: *Sling Blade*

OPEN CITY

ESSENTIAL

Italy 1945 B&W 109 min. NR Drama

Dir: Roberto Rossellini

C: Aldo Fabrizi, Anna Magnani, Marcello Pagliero, Vito Annicchiarico, Harry Feist

Director Roberto Rossellini and his colleagues began filming this drama of occupied Rome within two months after the Allied liberation of the city, but planning had begun months before that, while the filmmakers dodged efforts by the Germans to draft them into the Fascist forces. It's a startling film, feeling immediate and yet surprisingly polished. The story concerns a resistance fighter's efforts to escape the city with the help of a priest. Although *Open City* is fondly recalled as the film that brought Anna Magnani to the attention of worldwide audiences, her role is relatively small. The last quarter of the film, involving the capture and torture of the resistance leader while the priest is forced to watch, is almost unbearably painful; you know that Rossellini and his colleagues (among them cowriter Federico Fellini) were drawing upon fresh personal recollections. Winner of the Best Foreign Language Film award from the New York Film Critics Circle. Also known as *Rome, Open City*.

⊙ **DVD**

DR36, DR38, XT7

Goes well with: *Paisan*

THE OPPOSITE OF SEX

U.S. 1998 C 105 min. R Comedy

Dir: Don Roos

C: Christina Ricci, Martin Donovan, Lisa Kudrow, Lyle Lovett, Johnny
Galecki, William Lee Scott

Dedee Truit is the youngest character in Don Roos's wicked black
comedy, but she is the one character who really knows what she
wants—and how to get it. Unfortunately for every other character in
The Opposite of Sex, Dedee's needs require stepping on a lot of toes and
fingers and backs. Christina Ricci, barely seventeen when this film was
shot, is unnervingly good as this amoral little bitch, and her victims,
played by Martin Donovan (as her gay older brother), Lisa Kudrow (as
Donovan's erstwhile girlfriend), and Lyle Lovett (as Kudrow's erstwhile
suitor), are all wonderfully thick-headed. It's like watching one of those
reality shows where you know right away which contestant is going to
survive the ordeal: You don't have to like that person, but you do have to
admire his or her focus and ambition. Lisa Kudrow's performance was
awarded Best Supporting Actress by the New York Film Critics Circle.

⊙ **DVD:** Includes audio commentary by Don Roos and deleted
scenes.

CO2, CO3, CO5

Goes well with: *Pandora's Box*

ORDET

ESSENTIAL

Denmark 1955 B&W 125 min. NR Drama

Dir: Carl Theodor Dreyer

C: Henrik Malberg, Emil Hass Christensen, Preben Lerdorff Rye, Cay
Kristiansen, Birgitte Federspiel, Ejnar Federspiel, Gerda Nielsen

What begins as a simple drama about a rural family feud over marital intentions turns into a complex inquiry into the nature of religious
faith. Writer-director Carl Dreyer is the cinema's great minimalist,
avoiding close-ups and quick cutting in favor of staying focused on the
characters' gestures and facial expressions. (It must have been exhaust-
ing for the actors who worked for him.) On Borgen's Farm in 1925, wid-

ower Morten lives with Mikkel, John, and Anders, his three sons, and Mikkel's wife, Karen, who is pregnant. Anders wants to marry the daughter of a neighbor, Peter, but Morten thinks Peter's family religion is about death, while his is about joy. The families are at an impasse when Karen becomes ill. One more fact: John, the middle son, is a religious fanatic who disappears halfway through the story to go off and preach the gospel. That's the setup, and what follows is one of the most amazing conclusions you'll ever see in any film. If you buy it, you may agree that *Ordet* is Dreyer's greatest film.

⊙**DVD**

DR11, DR30

Goes well with: *Day of Wrath*

ORPHEUS

ESSENTIAL

France 1949 B&W 95 min. NR Fantasy

Dir: Jean Cocteau

C: Jean Marais, François Périer, Maria Casarès, Marie Déa, Juliette Gréco

Writer-director Jean Cocteau continues his investigation into the process of art begun with *The Blood of a Poet*. Unlike that earlier abstract film, Cocteau works out his ideas by recasting the myth of Orpheus in modern dress. Jean Marais is the poet lured into the world of the afterlife by a seductive woman (Maria Casarès) who calls herself the Princess. Heurtebise (François Périer), her "chauffeur," returns Orpheus to his wife, Eurydice, but Orpheus can't get the experience out of his mind. "I'm on the trail of the unknown," he says, realizing that his encounter with death has revitalized his artistry. And the geometry among the four (Orpheus torn between the two women, Heurtebise falling in love with Eurydice) gets more complicated by trips back and forth through a mirror in Orpheus's house. Mirrors are the portals by which Death enters and leaves our world: "Look at yourself in mirrors all your life," Heurtebise tells Orpheus, "and you see death." The afterlife is depicted as a series of ruins; in fact, Cocteau filmed the scenes in a bombed-out military academy. A great touch: messages from the afterlife broadcast through a car radio.

⊙**DVD:** Includes Cocteau's 1950 essays on the film. Available from Criterion in "Jean Cocteau's Orphic Trilogy" with *The Blood of a Poet* and *The Testament of Orpheus*.

DR2, DR8, FA4
Goes well with: *The Blood of a Poet*

OSCAR AND LUCINDA

Australia/U.S.   1997   C   132 min.   R   Drama
Dir: Gillian Armstrong
C: Ralph Fiennes, Cate Blanchett, Ciarin Hinds, Tom Wilkinson, Josephine Byrnes, Richard Roxburgh

Gillian Armstrong's quirky and absorbing drama is ripe for rediscovery, having been ignored or dismissed when it opened in theaters. Peter Carey's novel (adapted by Laura Jones) concerns two disparate people joined in their love for gambling. He's a minister's son, raised under the tyrannical whip of old-time religion, and she's a successful businesswoman who has never met a man she would stake her fortune on. Ralph Fiennes and the sublime Cate Blanchett are both up to their roles as social misfits who decide to risk everything on a scheme to transport a glass church up an Australian river. (Carey must have seen *Fitzcarraldo* when he was writing this novel.) Armstrong is the queen of the telltale detail; every stick of furniture, every tic of a face in her films feels both well-calculated and perfectly natural.

DR13, DR18, DR21, DR29
Goes well with: *Fitzcarraldo*

OUT OF THE BLUE

Canada   1980   C   94 min.   R   Drama
Dir: Dennis Hopper
C: Linda Manz, Dennis Hopper, Sharon Farrell, Raymond Burr, Don Gordon

Eleven years after his directing debut with *Easy Rider* (and nine years after its disastrous follow-up, the almost aptly named *The Last Movie*), Dennis Hopper got his act together to make this claustrophobic drama of a family waiting to implode. Hopper plays Dad, a former truck driver who lost his license and his bearings after a horrific accident (which opens the film and sets the tone for everything to follow); Sharon Farrell is Mom, hooked on drugs, her only means of escape from a loveless marriage; and Linda Manz is Daughter, angry in the way that only teens who have had to grow up too fast can be. Manz was, pound for pound, the most intense young actor of the late 1970s, with memorable supporting performances in *Days of Heaven* and *The Wan-*

derers, and this was her moment in the sun. She seized it, turning *Out of the Blue* into the most heartbreaking portrait of adolescence since *The Four Hundred Blows.*

⊙**DVD:** Two editions. One contains only the movie; the Special Edition contains audio commentaries by Dennis Hopper, producer Paul Lewis, and distributor John Alan Simon.

DR11, DR27, DR41

Goes well with: *Ghost World*

OVER THE EDGE

U.S.   1979   C   95 min.   PG   Drama

Dir: Jonathan Kaplan

C: Michael Kramer, Pamela Ludwig, Matt Dillon, Vincent Spano, Tom Fergus, Lane Smith, Harry Northup

Coming out at the end of the 1970s, when punk music's attitude had fully infected American teens, even if they didn't quite know what to do with it, *Over the Edge,* written by Charlie Haas and Tim Hunter, is set in a planned California community whose designers threw a bone to the adolescents—look, kids, it's a cool rec center! The squares all hang out there, but the rest of the high schoolers wander around the streets, getting into trouble (most of it relatively harmless stuff—there's not a lot of drug-taking or felonious crime). The focus is on one well-meaning but confused student, played by Michael Kramer, who is genuinely alienated from his parents but afraid to take the big first step to outright rebellion. The conclusion to this story may seem tame in light of the Columbine shootings; it's also eerily prescient.

DR20, DR31, DR41

Goes well with: *if* . . .

PAISAN

ESSENTIAL

Italy 1946 B&W 115 min. NR Drama
Dir: Roberto Rossellini
C: Carmela Sazio, Gar Moore, Bill Tubbs, Harriet White, Maria Michi,
Robert van Loon, Dale Edmonds, Carlo Pisacane

Expanding on the idea he explored in *Open City* to document Italy's wartime experiences while they were still fresh, Roberto Rossellini offers six tales of the U.S. invasion of Italy. We start in Sicily and work our way up the peninsula, through Naples, Rome, Florence, the Appenines region, and the Po Valley. Every story has its powerful moments, though claims that Rossellini seamlessly blended real actors and amateur performers are slightly exaggerated. The confrontations between the harried GIs and the civilians are marked by suspicion, exploitation (going both ways), lust, and, in the film's most surprising story, a theological debate between three American chaplains (one of them Jewish) and their hosts in a monastery. Rossellini uses real locations with tremendous effectiveness, especially in the story of an American nurse ducking crossfire on the streets of Florence to be reunited with her Italian lover, a leader of the partisans. Winner of the Best Foreign Language Film award from the New York Film Critics Circle.

DR7, DR30, DR37, DR38, XT1, XT7
Goes well with: *Open City*

PANDORA'S BOX

ESSENTIAL

Germany 1928 B&W 109 min. NR Drama
Dir: G. W. Pabst

C: Louise Brooks, Fritz Kortner, Francis Lederer, Carl Goetz

It is the sexiest performance ever committed to film by an actress. Don't expect any nudity or heavy breathing; after all, this is a 1928 silent film. Louise Brooks, the girl in the black helmet, as she was famously dubbed by critic Kenneth Tynan for her bobbed hairstyle, is Lulu, the woman with an insatiable appetite for pleasure. She's the object of affection for almost every one of the film's major characters, male and female, because she radiates an enticing aura of mystery and carnality. Lulu is the mistress of a middle-aged man who is shot dead on their wedding night after assuming (understandably) that she was coming on to a former lover. A countess with designs on Lulu, together with the son of the dead man, who is also in her thrall, help her escape from custody, and after a series of misadventures she winds up a prostitute on the streets of London just in time to meet Jack the Ripper. Brooks and director G. W. Pabst understand that Lulu's sexuality is playful, not malicious, even though she causes others great pain. Other directors and actresses have tried to achieve this unique combination, but none have come close.

DR19, DR33, TH7

Goes well with: *Diary of a Lost Girl*

PARADISE LOST: THE CHILD MURDERS AT ROBIN HOOD HILLS

U.S. 1996 C 150 min. NR Documentary
Dir: Joe Berlinger and Bruce Sinofsky

At the risk of repeating themselves, documentary filmmakers Joe Berlinger and Bruce Sinofsky followed their justly acclaimed *Brother's Keeper* with another small-town murder case. This one, set in West Memphis, Arkansas, is more tangled than the alleged mercy killing in *Keeper.* Three eight-year-old boys are found dead near a wooded stream, their bodies mutilated. Circumstantial evidence points to a trio of teenagers whose main occupation seems to be sitting around listening to heavy-metal music. And because the trio talked about practicing Satanism, the assumption is that they killed the boys during some kind of ritual. When one confesses to the crime, implicating his two buddies, the case is closed. Not so fast, say Berlinger and Sinofsky; the confession is unreliable, wrung out of a mentally diminished man. The filmmakers don't offer alternative suspects, but they do present enough evidence to raise serious doubts about the guilt of Jessie Miskelly, Jr., Jason Baldwin, and Damian Wayne Echols, all awaiting appeals to their life sentences. There is a sequel, *Revelations: Paradise Lost 2,* which updates the appeals process for the three convicted killers.

DO2

Goes well with: *Brother's Keeper*

PARIS IS BURNING

U.S. 1990 C 78 min. NR Documentary

Dir: Jennie Livingston

Filmmaker Jennie Livingston attended several transvestite balls in New York's Paris Ballroom between 1985 and 1989 to record an underground phenomenon: men (mostly black and Latin) who dress up as women and compete in various contests. It's not a snickering peep show; Livingston's straightforward style quickly immerses you in this world without making any judgments. She emphasizes the competition and avoids going into much detail about the contestants' private lives until the very end, with a sad little coda. Winner of the Best Documentary award from the New York Film Critics Circle and the Grand Jury Prize at the Sundance Film Festival.

DO11

Goes well with: *Kiss of the Spider Woman*

PARTY GIRL

U.S. 1995 C 98 min. R Comedy

Dir: Daisy von Scherler Mayer

C: Parker Posey, Omar Townsend, Sasha von Scherler, Guillermo Díaz, Anthony DeSando, Liev Schreiber

Parker Posey has appeared in a score of films, both on the independent side of the street and in Hollywood productions (she was Tom Hanks's fiancée in *You've Got Mail*). Her biggest and best role to date is in this hip comedy about a downtown New Yorker and her attempts to add a little respectability to her résumé. Mary's godmother, her closest relative, is a librarian (Sasha von Scherler, the director's real-life mom) who somehow persuades this queen of late night to learn the Dewey Decimal System instead of the latest dance steps. Posey is a marvel, whether she's romancing a street vendor (Omar Townsend) or rearranging her gay DJ roommate's record collection according to her newfound template in life.

CO5, CO8, CO9, XT7

Goes well with: *The Last Days of Disco*

THE PASSION OF ANNA

Sweden 1969 C 101 min. R Drama
Dir: Ingmar Bergman
C: Liv Ullmann, Bibi Andersson, Max von Sydow, Erland Josephson

Between 1966 and 1978, director Ingmar Bergman and actress Liv Ullmann made nine films together, nearly all of them certifiably great. This drama is set on an isolated island and concerns Anna (Ullmann), a woman left crippled by an accident, her two friends (Erland Josephson and Bibi Andersson), and a loner (Max von Sydow) who lives nearby. The film begins with one character learning a terrible secret about Anna, and then withholding knowledge of that information until a stressful moment in their relationship. As a woman who has become an expert in hiding her pain, Ullmann is almost transcendent, and her three costars, all of them veterans of other Bergman films, complement her nicely.

DR18, DR27
Goes well with: *Shame*

THE PASSION OF JOAN OF ARC

ESSENTIAL

France 1928 B&W 117 min. NR Drama
Dir: Carl Theodor Dreyer
C: Renée Maria Falconetti, Eugene Sylvain, Maurice Schutz, Michel
  Simon, Antonin Artaud

It is arguably one of the greatest silent films ever made, even one of the greatest films. But it is inarguably the greatest one-shot performance ever filmed. Falconetti, a French performer of boulevard comedy, was persuaded by director Carl Dreyer to play the Maid of Orleans, and it's easy to see from the first shots of her why Dreyer took a chance on a woman in her thirties with no film experience. The film's style depends heavily on close-ups—for more than half the film, shots alternate between Joan and her prosecutors, described in the film's introduction as "a court of pious theologians and stern judges"—and Falconetti's face eloquently expresses so many emotions, you may feel exhausted by the time she's led to her death. She's almost always shot in isolation and usually from below, so that she's looking upward—at the judges or perhaps at God. Dreyer returned in two later films, *Day of Wrath* (in which an elderly woman is burned at the stake) and *Ordet,* to issues of religious faith, and a recently released DVD boxed set is a great way to see all three. The *Passion* DVD and some TV prints contain Richard Einhorn's composition "Voices of Light" on the soundtrack, and it effectively enhances Dreyer's memorable images.

⊙**DVD:** Includes separate audio track for "Voices of Light" cantata; audio essay by scholar Casper Tybjerg; audio interview with Helen Falconetti, daughter of Renée Maria Falconetti; liner notes by Carl Theodor Dreyer. Boxed set (with *Day of Wrath* and *Ordet*) also contains 1995 documentary on Dreyer.

DR17, DR30, DR39

Goes well with: *The Rapture*

PATHER PANCHALI

ESSENTIAL

India 1955 B&W 112 min. NR Drama
Dir: Satyajit Ray
C: Kanu Banerjee, Karuna Banerjee, Subir Banerjee, Runki Banerjee, Uma Das Gupta, Chunibala Devi

The first film in director Satyajit Ray's deservedly acclaimed Apu trilogy (followed by *Aparajito* and *The World of Apu*) is set in the 1920s in an impoverished household in rural India. Apu (Subir Banerjee) is oblivious to his family's struggles to make ends meet; as a child, he can create playthings out of the simplest props, and he's not at all self-conscious about his raggedy clothes. But his older sister (Uma Das Gupta) is, as is his mother (Karuna Banerjee), and when his sister steals some trinkets from a well-to-do playmate, her mother rises to her defense, even though she suspects her daughter is a thief. Father (Kanu Banerjee) is an unemployed writer, and when he goes off on a weeks-long journey, the family starts to come apart. Ray focuses on the loveliest of images in nature, reinforcing Apu's sunny view of life, but he never lets us forget how close to the edge of disaster this family is. All of the performers are wonderful, especially Karuna Banerjee, whose portrayal of a resourceful woman fighting off bitterness is a marvel.

DR11, DR41

Goes well with: *Aparajito*

PAYDAY

U.S. 1972 C 103 min. R Drama
Dir: Daryl Duke
C: Rip Torn, Ahna Capri, Elayne Heilveil, Cliff Emmich, Michael C. Gwynne

The magnificent character actor Rip Torn finally got his due with his Emmy-winning role as Artie on *The Larry Sanders Show.* But for a full dose of Rip, you have to see his amazing performance as Maury Dann. The creation of writer Don Carpenter, Maury is a country singer who's doing his best to imitate Hank Williams, and not as a singer-songwriter. Drinking, popping pills, coming on to two different ladies in the backseat of a limousine, Maury knows he'll never get out of this world alive, so he's going to live it up while he can. Some critics have compared this to *The Rose,* another film about a singer who's on a downhill slide from the first scene, but *Payday* (and Torn) never get maudlin, staying sassy and brassy until the inevitable last ride in the big Cadillac.

DR23

Goes well with: *Songwriter*

PEEPING TOM

U.K.   1960   C   101 min.   NR   Drama
Dir: Michael Powell
C: Carl Boehm, Moira Shearer, Anna Massey, Maxine Audley, Michael Powell

A mad killer films his female victims as they die and then obtains sexual pleasure from watching the playback. What kind of sick mind dreamed up this idea? Would you believe Michael Powell, the classy British filmmaker of *The Red Shoes, I Know Where I'm Going!,* and *Black Narcissus*? Coming late in his career (in fact, reaction to the film nearly finished his career), Powell's provocative study of voyeurism is a most unsettling film. It suggests that anyone who watches a film involving a murder, from a Hitchcock thriller to the creepiest slasher flick, isn't so much different from Mark Lewis (Carl Boehm), the man who hides a dagger in the tripod leg of his motion picture camera. Mark was raised by a scientist father (played by Powell) who filmed him under intensely emotional conditions, and a stepmother he calls a "surrogate female." Amazingly, this film and *Psycho,* another disturbing study of murderous voyeurism, were released within two months of each other.

⊙**DVD:** Includes British TV documentary, and audio commentary by film theorist Laura Mulvey.

DR6, DR8, DR21, DR22, TH15
Goes well with: *White of the Eye*

PELLE THE CONQUEROR

Denmark/Sweden 1988 C 150 min. PG-13 Drama
Dir: Bille August
C: Max von Sydow, Pelle Hvenegaard, Erik Paaske, Kristina Törnqvist, Morten Jørgensen

By the time *Pelle the Conqueror* ends, you may be emotionally wrung out, but you will almost surely be ready for a sequel. Bille August adapted a small portion of a four-volume novel by Martin Anderson Nexø, telling the story of a middle-aged widower and his young son emigrating from impoverished nineteenth-century Sweden to what they hope will be a better life in Denmark. Because of his age and lack of any specific job skills, Lasse (Max von Sydow) is forced to become a laborer on a farm, with his son Pelle (Pelle Hvenegaard) helping out. The two suffer great indignities—they must sleep in a former chicken coop, Pelle is bullied by kids at the local school just for being poor—but they remain devoted to each other. The film is eloquent about the cruelties and casual injustices of poverty, allowing occasional rays of hope to flicker through. Lasse woos a local woman whose husband has been lost at sea, only to have the man show up; Pelle is taken in by the farm owner's wife while he's away, but she then has to care for her bedridden husband. In the end, Pelle stops going to school, but he has learned enough to understand that the farm is no place for him. It's a sign of how involving the film is that, after more than two-and-a-half hours of Pelle's story, you want more—you have to find out what happens next. Alas, despite the film's winning both the Palme d'Or at Cannes and the Academy Award for Best Foreign Language Film, no sequel has been announced.

⊙ **DVD**
DR11, DR41
Goes well with: *The Emigrants*

PERFORMANCE

ESSENTIAL

U.K. 1970 C/B&W 105 min. R Drama
Dir: Donald Cammell and Nicolas Roeg
C: James Fox, Mick Jagger, Anita Pallenberg, Michèle Breton, Ann Sidney, Johnny Shannon

It's not a film for sissies or wimps, this directorial debut of writer Donald Cammell and cinematographer Nicolas Roeg. Half gangster melo-drama, half drug-soaked psychodrama, and 100 percent weird, the story follows the nightmarish journey of Chas Devlin (James Fox), a midlevel gangster who crosses his boss, Harry Flowers (Johnny Shannon), and takes it on the lam. He winds up taking a room with reclusive rock star Turner (Mick Jagger), whose seductive housemates (Anita Pallenberg and Michèle Breton) and magic mushrooms begin to take their toll on Chas's already loose grip on sanity. The film consciously apes Ingmar Bergman's *Persona* as Chas and Turner's personalities begin to merge. And so do their separate worlds; the film's highlight is "Memo from Turner," a fantasy production number in which Turner spits out a William Burroughs–inspired rap at Harry Flowers and his henchmen, concluding, "You gentlemen all work for me!" The music business and the world of gangsters never seemed so naturally aligned. Among the performers on the mind-blowing soundtrack: Randy Newman and Ry Cooder.

DR6, DR12, DR27

Goes well with: *Persona*

PERSONA

ESSENTIAL

Sweden 1966 B&W 81 min. NR Drama
Dir: Ingmar Bergman
C: Bibi Andersson, Liv Ullmann

Ingmar Bergman had already used the title *The Silence,* which would have worked nicely for this study of an actress who suffers a breakdown and stops talking altogether. Elisabeth Vogler (Liv Ullmann) is sent to an isolated house on the coast to recover, under the care of an unnamed nurse (Bibi Andersson). Andersson has to carry the drama with her dia-logue, while Ullmann's facial expressions do all the talking for her. As the days wear on, the nurse begins to suffer her own meltdown, relying in some ways on the complicit silence of her patient as a means of heal-ing. The two women work unexpected changes on each other, and even when you can anticipate the wrap-up, it's thrilling to watch it happen. One of Bergman's most spellbinding films, with a modest running time that's perfectly appropriate. The film suggests rather than states, the mark of any great work of art.

DR12, DR27, DR39

Goes well with: *Performance*

PI

U.S. 1998 B&W 85 min. R Drama
Dir: Darren Aronofsky
C: Sean Gullette, Mark Margolis, Ben Shenkman, Pamela Hart

You don't have to be a mathematician to understand writer-director Darren Aronofsky's spiky little thriller, but it surely helps to get some of its references. For those of us who need a calculator every time we make an entry in our checkbooks, the film still works as a study of paranoia, in part because Aronofsky has updated some elements (the Internet and e-mail should be given costar billing) while maintaining just enough ironic detachment (in the great tradition of postmodern pop culture). Max (Sean Gullette) is the guy who never has to leave his downtown New York apartment—he's wired to the world and has his food delivered. (Women are not part of the equation.) He thinks he has a way to quantify the structure of the stock market, this being a film for the Wall Street–obsessed 1990s. Ah, but we know that just when these whiz kids think they have it all figured out, the world has a way of crashing down around them. Max gets his comeuppance, and we can go back to feeling that we are indeed living in a world of random chaos, just the way we like it, right? Aronofsky won the Director's Award at the Sundance festival.

⊙**DVD:** Includes audio commentaries by Darren Aronofsky and cast; "lost" scenes; music video.

DR20, DR27, TH3, XT6
Goes well with: *American Psycho*

THE PIANO

ESSENTIAL

New Zealand/France/Australia 1993 C 121 min. R Drama
Dir: Jane Campion
C: Holly Hunter, Harvey Keitel, Sam Neill, Anna Paquin, Kerry Walker

The Piano is consistent with writer-director Jane Campion's other films about female isolation (most especially *An Angel at My Table*). Holly Hunter is the mute Ada, a Scotswoman whose joy in life is playing the piano. Widowed, with a young daughter (Anna Paquin), she decides to enter into an arranged marriage in New Zealand, but her new husband (Sam Neill) has little use for her piano. Another settler (Harvey Keitel) takes in the piano, and Ada's visits to his house to play turn into passionate romantic rendezvous. Is Ada an independent woman, or just in need of sex with a man who appreciates her love for music? Campion's allusive style, with stylized dialogue and shots of the lush New Zealand landscape, is a matter of taste. For those who get on and stay on her wavelength, *The Piano* is an intensely moving drama about unspoken needs. Oscars went to Campion for her screenplay, and to Hunter and Paquin; the latter was a bit of an upset, but her role, as the girl whose trust in her mother's judgment is broken, carries much of the film's emotional impact. The Independent Spirit Awards named it Best Foreign Film, while the New York Film Critics Circle honored Hunter, and Campion for both screenplay and direction.

⊙**DVD**

DR19, DR21, DR24, DR33, DR39, DR41

Goes well with: *An Angel at My Table*

PICKPOCKET

France   1959   B&W   75 min.   NR   Drama

Dir: Robert Bresson

C: Martin LaSalle, Marika Green, Pierre Leymarie, Jean Pélégri

Unable or unwilling to find a real job, Michel, a solitary young man (Martin LaSalle), turns to picking pockets for a living. He's arrested almost right away, but released for lack of evidence; the experience only encourages him, and soon he's devoting his life to studying the art, both in books and from other, more successful thieves. Robert Bresson's unadorned style, his intense focus on the loneliness of his character and how that feeds his sense of injustice about the world, involves us totally with Michel's limited world. Jane, his mother's lovely young neighbor, tries to reach him, but he considers her a distraction. This film was a great influence on American filmmakers such as Paul Schrader, whose loners in *Light Sleeper, Taxi Driver,* and *American Gigolo* are variations of Michel. *Gigolo*'s final scene is a copy of *Pickpocket*'s celebrated finale.

DR6, DR21

Goes well with: *A Man Escaped*

PICNIC AT HANGING ROCK

Australia   1975   C   107 min.   PG   Drama

Dir: Peter Weir

C: Rachel Roberts, Dominic Guard, Helen Morse, Jacki Weaver

In the mountains north of Sydney, Australia, during a Valentine's Day outing in 1900, three female students and a teacher mysteriously vanished near a strange volcanic formation, or so Joan Lindsay's novel would have us believe. Like *Fargo,* this is one of those fiction films that many believe was based on a true story. Given the mysteries of the Australian landscape, much of it still unexplored at the turn of the last century, any and all explanations are possible, though Peter Weir's film offers none. It's a re-creation of the Victorian era in all its splendid formality and repressed feelings. The smooth, curved rocks offering sensual shapes for exploration, the girls perspiring in their high-necked dresses, the stillness of the summer air—Weir creates an atmosphere of longing and uncertainty. It's really all the film has, but it's plenty.

⊙**DVD:** Includes liner notes by critic Vincent Canby.

DR24

Goes well with: *Walkabout*

PIERROT LE FOU

France/Italy   1965   C   110 min.   NR   Drama
Dir: Jean-Luc Godard
C: Jean-Paul Belmondo, Anna Karina, Dirk Sanders, Raymond Devos, Samuel Fuller, Jean-Pierre Léaud

Jean-Luc Godard made two great road movies, this one and *Weekend.* The latter is, at least for Godard, the more conventional film, a satire hanging its dirty laundry on the line of a weekend excursion to the country. This is a melodrama about a couple on the run, at least on the surface. Godard's screenplay combines elements of film noir—especially the "bad" woman (Anna Karina as Marianne Renoir) leading the "good" man (Jean-Paul Belmondo as Ferdinand) astray—with his own views on consumerism and his own inability to work in the classic Hollywood storytelling tradition. Marianne flees gangsters, Ferdinand flees a boring bourgeois life as a TV director, and as they drive across the south of France the bodies pile up. In a party scene, the great American director Sam Fuller is allowed to speak his famous line about the cinema being a battleground; Godard believes that, but he also can't stand how neatly ordered most films are. Marianne keeps calling Ferdinand "Pierrot," the famed character in French pantomime, as though she understands that life is nothing but role-playing. Amazingly, Godard kept right on making movies after this one, though they became increasingly fragmented and self-conscious.

⊙**DVD**

DR20, XT3, XT5

Goes well with: *Weekend*

PIXOTE

ESSENTIAL

Brazil 1981 C 127 min. NR Drama

Dir: Hector Babenco

C: Fernando Ramos da Silva, Marília Pera, Jorge Juliao, Gilberto Moura

Brazil's throwaway children are the stars of this harrowing drama. Ten-year-old Pixote (Fernando Ramos da Silva) is a virtual orphan who gets a first-class education in brutality while in reform school, then applies his lessons on the street. Director Hector Babenco, cowriting with Jorge Durán, makes Pixote a man-child with immense longing for motherly stability, and the scene in which a kindly prostitute (Marília Pera) actually breastfeeds him is both shocking and moving. Ramos da Silva, like many of the kids in the film, was the real deal, a street kid; he went straight for a time after the film became a big hit, only to return to his former life and wind up murdered. A documentary about his life is included in the DVD of *Pixote.*

⊙**DVD:** Includes documentary, "Who Killed Pixote?"

DR36, DR41

Goes well with: *Los Olvidados*

PLATOON

ESSENTIAL

U.S. 1986 C 120 min. R Drama

Dir: Oliver Stone

C: Tom Berenger, Willem Dafoe, Charlie Sheen, Forest Whitaker, Francesco Quinn, John C. McGinley, Richard Edson, Kevin Dillon, Keith David, Johnny Depp

Oliver Stone's justly acclaimed portrait of the Vietnam War through the eyes of a young, naïve soldier was one of the first independently produced films to break through to a wide audience and collect awards from both the Academy of Motion Picture Arts and Sciences and the Independent Spirits. Charlie Sheen is a stand-in for Stone and his own experiences in-country; his company's diametrically opposed officers are played by Tom Berenger (the hard-nosed, battle-scarred veteran) and Willem Dafoe (the sad-eyed sympathetic soldier). Stone leaves out the poetics of *Apocalypse Now* (though he does resort to one Christlike shot of Dafoe) in favor of a lean, mean narrative about survival in a world where everyone is an enemy of some kind.

⊙**DVD:** Includes "making of" featurette, and audio commentaries by Oliver Stone and advisor Dale Dye.

DR3, DR37

Goes well with: *Gallipoli*

THE PLAYER

ESSENTIAL

U.S. 1992 C 123 min. R Comedy

Dir: Robert Altman

C: Tim Robbins, Greta Scacchi, Fred Ward, Whoopi Goldberg, Peter Gallagher, Brion James, Cynthia Stevenson, Vincent D'Onofrio, Dean Stockwell, Richard E. Grant, Dina Merrill, Sydney Pollack, Lyle Lovett, Gina Gershon

How does any movie get made in Hollywood, let alone any good movie? You'll be asking yourself that question all the way through and far beyond a viewing of Robert Altman's brilliantly corrosive satire of moviemaking, studio-style. Griffin Mill (Tim Robbins) is a studio executive on a first-name basis with every celebrity in Hollywood (and to prove it, sixty of them turn up playing themselves here). He navigates the waters of a possible shake-up, but he is worried about anonymous messages he has been receiving from a screenwriter whose pitch he ignored. When an aspiring screenwriter (Vincent D'Onofrio) is found dead after attending a film with Mill, suspicious cops (Whoopi Goldberg, Lyle Lovett) get on his case. Once the basic theme is stated, Altman (and writer Michael Tolkin, adapting his own novel) keeps playing little riffs on it until you realize Griffin's total absence of morality is going to stand him in good stead in this little community. The opening scene, a shot that goes on for eight minutes without a break, packs in about two dozen characters and twice as many jokes. Winner of Best Picture from both the New York Film Critics Circle and the Independent Spirit Awards; the New York critics also honored Altman and cinematographer Jean Lépine.

⊙**DVD:** Special Edition contains audio commentaries by Robert Altman and Michael Tolkin; featurette by Altman; deleted scenes; menu of cameo appearances.

CO2, CO10, DR1

Goes well with: *Boogie Nights*

PLAYTIME

France 1967 C 119 min. NR Comedy
Dir: Jacques Tati
C: Jacques Tati, Barbara Dennek, Jacqueline Lecomte, Valérie Camille,
Léon Doyen

The third and most elaborate film in director Jacques Tati's series of Hulot comedies (*Mr. Hulot's Holiday* and *Mon Oncle* were the first two chapters) is a hit-and-miss satire of the contemporary urban landscape. As Terry Jones points out in the introduction to the film's DVD edition, we see none of the old world of Paris in this film; even the babbling American tourists (whose dialogue was written by Art Buchwald) catch only glimpses of the traditional sights, reflected in the glass of skyscrapers. In fact, this film could have been shot in any number of world cities, a point that has been reinforced more recently by the globalization of chain stores and restaurants, draining urban centers of their individual personalities. There's not much story here—M. Hulot is trying to keep an appointment with someone—and the film meanders along, stopping to comment on this building or that structure. The longest sequence takes place in a chic new restaurant that has opened a bit too soon—the place is falling apart, but the patrons don't seem to care, especially a Texan who's always buying the house a round of drinks and urging the band to play louder. It's pointless to watch this film if you can't see it letterboxed, because Tati masterfully uses all of the widescreen frame to set up and pay off on many of his gags. (The film is presented by "Panoramic Films.")

⊙**DVD:** Includes introduction by director/performer Terry Jones, and 1967 Tati short, "Cours du Soir."

CO4, CO8, XT8
Goes well with: *Mon Oncle*

THE PLOT AGAINST HARRY

U.S. 1989 B&W 80 min. NR Comedy-Drama
Dir: Michael Roemer
C: Martin Priest, Ben Lang, Maxine Woods, Henry Nemo

It's hard to believe that a film as striking as *The Plot Against Harry* sat on the shelf for twenty years before it was released. After all, it's not as if in 1969, when the film was shot, there were no edgy, quirky films being shown in theaters—*Midnight Cowboy* remains the only X-rated film to win a Best Picture Oscar. But Michael Roemer's film was finally rescued from oblivion, shown at festivals, and given a theatrical release—a belated happy ending. Harry Plotnick (Martin Priest) is a small-time Jewish gangster just back from a little one-year "vacation," and all hell has broken loose in his absence. Organized crime has taken over his precious turf, and there are lots of unanticipated family problems—a wayward sister, a daughter he never knew he had, a nagging wife. This is a gangster comedy-drama that prefigures some of the funniest material in *The Sopranos,* but with a Jewish twist of wry. Priest is like a character out of Saul Bellow, with a deadpan expression that would make Buster Keaton jealous.

DR6, DR36

Goes well with: *The Long Good Friday*

POINT OF ORDER!

ESSENTIAL

U.S. 1964 B&W 97 min. NR Documentary
Dir: Emile de Antonio

Emile de Antonio's distillation of hundreds of hours of TV coverage of the Army-McCarthy hearings of April–June 1954 is Exhibit A in the case against Joseph McCarthy, the Wisconsin senator who used genuine concern for Communist infiltration of the government as his meal ticket to personal glory. Under the guise of ferreting out leftists in the armed forces, McCarthy ran afoul of both Army officers and Senators when he tried to doctor evidence in a squabble over accusations that he sought preferential treatment for a newly drafted private who happened to be a friend of his chief counsel, Roy Cohn. De Antonio is not an objective historian, but there was little from these hearings that would make McCarthy look the least bit sympathetic. The army's special counsel, Joseph M. Welch, is allowed to deliver the coup de grâce when McCarthy tries to smear one of Welch's associates.

DO3, DO9

Goes well with: *Berkeley in the Sixties*

THE PORTRAIT OF A LADY

U.K./U.S. 1996 C 144 min. PG-13 Drama
Dir: Jane Campion
C: Nicole Kidman, John Malkovich, Barbara Hershey, Mary-Louise

Parker, Martin Donovan, Shelley Winters, Richard E. Grant, Shelley Duvall, Christian Bale, Viggo Mortensen, John Gielgud

Jane Campion's follow-up to her Oscar-winning *The Piano* was not nearly as successful with audiences or critics, but it deserves more attention. An adaptation of Henry James's novel (by Campion and Laura Jones), it continues Campion's fascination with stories of isolated women. Isabel Archer is an American heiress who prefers to think of herself as a romantic free agent, though she is far from promiscuous. Touring the continent (as all literary heroines of this era seemed to do), she is introduced by her mentor, Madame Merle (Barbara Hershey), to the intriguing widower Gilbert Osmond (John Malkovich). Some viewers may have been put off by Campion's stylistic flourishes, including a brave prologue: images of women, staring wordlessly at the camera. This is Nicole Kidman's real coming-out as an actress, and she's well supported by both Hershey and the ambiguous Malkovich (is he kind, creepy, or just kind of creepy?).

⊙**DVD**

DR29, DR39

Goes well with: *The Piano*

POTEMKIN.

See *Battleship Potemkin*

POWWOW HIGHWAY

U.S./U.K.   1989   C   90 min.   R   Drama

Dir: Jonathan Wacks

C: Gary Farmer, A Martinez, Amanda Wyss, Joanelle Romero, Graham Greene, Wes Studi

The buddy road movie takes a left turn with this drama about a pair of Native American pals driving from their Montana reservation to New Mexico to bail a sister out of jail. Janet Heaney and Jean Stawarz's screenplay sets up the odd couple, here a hyped-up political activist named Buddy Red Bow (A Martinez) and a phlegmatic hulk named Philbert (Gary Farmer) who's along mainly because his '64 Buick is their only means of transportation. It's a bit like *Persona* out west, with one character who does most of the talking, the other who absorbs it all. But Philbert is no dummy; when he opens his mouth, it's to offer what may sound like a non sequitur—until about fifty miles down the road, when Buddy's eyes go wide and he figures it out. By the time they make Santa Fe, after a few adventures in such exotic spots as Sheridan, Wyoming, an accommodation has been made, mostly on Buddy's part. He's still angry, but he has refined and shaped that anger. The Sundance festival gave *Powwow Highway* its Filmmaker's Trophy.

DR12, DR16, DR28, XT5

Goes well with: *Smoke Signals*

PRICK UP YOUR EARS

U.K.   1987   C   111 min.   R   Drama

Dir: Stephen Frears

C: Gary Oldman, Alfred Molina, Vanessa Redgrave, Wallace Shawn, Julie Walters

Rather than attempt a cradle-to-early-grave life of playwright Joe Orton, Stephen Frears and writer Alan Bennett concentrate on the isolation of his last days. Orton's success as a creator of outrageous comedies (*Entertaining Mr. Sloane, What the Butler Saw*) is contrasted with his miserable home life, where he remains almost literally closeted with his lover, Kenneth Halliwell. Orton only railed against Britain's repressive laws against homosexuals; he wasn't a political activist who would lend his name to attempts at reform legislation. Gary Oldman is terrific as Orton, sparking energy, vitriol, and self-loathing, often in the same sentence, and Alfred Molina as the hangdog Halliwell is the picture of a man who's defined by his association with someone more clever and handsome than he. Halliwell's "solution" to their mutual misery shouldn't come as a surprise. Vanessa Redgrave's role as Peggy Ramsey, Orton's agent, seems to be created only to get Orton out of his flat. Not that she isn't wonderful—the New York Film Critics Circle agreed, giving her their Best Supporting Actress award.

DR17, DR19, DR21

Goes well with: *Mishima*

PRIEST

U.K.   1994   C   97 min.   R   Drama

Dir: Antonia Bird

C: Linus Roache, Tom Wilkinson, Cathy Tyson, Robert Carlyle, James Ellis, Lesley Sharp

A bold attempt to deal with territory that is incognita to filmmakers both inside and outside of Hollywood, *Priest* explores the contemporary world of Catholic clergymen caught in the snare of sexual desires. Father Matthew (Tom Wilkinson) ministers to an inner-city parish that is so appreciative of his concern that rumors of his dalliance with his housekeeper (Cathy Tyson) generally go unshared. His new colleague, Father Greg (Linus Roache), is more perturbed by these arrangements—but when he slips out for an evening on the town, he heads straight for a gay bar, so there you are. The drama, written by Jimmy McGovern, turns on an adolescent girl's confessions to Father Matthew about her father, and even if a full and free exchange of theological ideas is not the result, the film does deserve points for taking the pulse of a sick patient.

⊙**DVD**

DR19, DR30

Goes well with: *Diary of a Country Priest*

THE PRIME OF MISS JEAN BRODIE

U.K.   1969   C   116 min.   PG   Drama

Dir: Ronald Neame

C: Maggie Smith, Robert Stephens, Pamela Franklin, Gordon Jackson, Celia Johnson, Jane Carr

The charismatic schoolteacher is usually seen as a heroic figure (think *Mr. Holland's Opus* or *Dead Poets Society*). The darker consequences of entrusting someone to mold young minds was provocatively explored by Muriel Spark in her novella and Jay Presson Allen in her stage adaptation, about a strong-willed teacher at the Marcia Blaine School in 1930s Edinburgh. Miss Brodie is an aesthete who hails Francisco Franco as the savior of Spain. Every year, she manages to gather a special group of students in a mutual admiration society. Allen adapted her play for this film, whose best feature is the magnificent Oscar-winner Maggie Smith as Miss Brodie, a woman of equal parts charm and spite. Robert Stephens (as her sometime lover, the art teacher), Celia Johnson (as her critical headmistress), and Pamela Franklin and Jane Carr (as two of her rebellious students) are all splendid in support. The film seems a bit claustrophobic—references to the outside world are just that, with virtually every scene played out at the school—but that reinforces the hothouse atmosphere of a private school, where deadly plants like Miss Brodie can flourish.

DR21, DR31, DR39, DR41

Goes well with: *The Loneliness of the Long Distance Runner*

PRINCESS MONONOKE

Japan   1997   C   135 min.   PG-13   Action-Adventure
Dir: Hayao Miyazaki
C: Voices of Billy Crudup, Claire Danes, Minnie Driver, Billy Bob
    Thornton, Gillian Anderson, Jada Pinkett Smith

The two adult Japanese animation features that have picked up siz-
able cult followings in the U.S. are the postapocalyptic adventure *Akira*
and this more pastoral, if no less violent, fantasy. The U.S. distributor of
this film, which set *Titanic*-like box office records in Japan, hired an
impressive crew of voice artists, but the visuals are what really count
here. It's a green fable about a warrior prince named Ashitaka (Billy
Crudup) on a quest to locate the source of the demons that are destroy-
ing his people's lands. He has been infected by one of the demons, so it
is clear that this is a one-way trip. He discovers that Irontown, a mining
village run by the iron maiden Lady Eboshi (Minnie Driver) and her
equally flinty courtesans, has been stripping the earth in search of min-
erals, angering the gods who would protect it. Things get a bit confusing with the introduction of San (Claire Danes), the title character, who
has been raised by wolves led by a big bad mother (Gillian Anderson).
San is on the side of the earth as well, but she and the gods are at odds
about how to protect it. The dazzling panoramas (see this in a letterboxed version if possible) compensate for the confusing storyline and
the one character voice that doesn't work at all: Billy Bob Thornton,
whose Arkansas twang doesn't fit his character, a comically evil monk.
    ⊙**DVD:** Includes "making of" featurette.
    AC2
Goes well with: *Crouching Tiger, Hidden Dragon*

PROMESSE, LA.

See *La Promesse*

PROOF

Australia   1992   C   91 min.   R   Drama
Dir: Jocelyn Moorhouse
C: Hugo Weaving, Geneviève Picot, Russell Crowe, Heather Mitchell

Essentially a three-character drama, *Proof* opens with the sight of a
blind man taking photographs, a sick joke that makes perfect sense
when we get to know Martin (Hugo Weaving) and his obsession with
trust. Though he can't see the world, he records his "impressions" of it

and labels them (in braille). His housekeeper, Celia (Geneviève Picot), wants to help him, but Martin correctly suspects her motives are self-ishly sexual; she's curious about what it would be like to make love to a blind man, and Martin is her experiment. The third point of this unsta-ble triangle is Andy (Russell Crowe), a likable dishwasher in whom Martin decides to put his trust. Andy's happy to help out and just as sus-picious of Celia as Martin is. The struggle among the three for some sense of control in their tiny corner of the world never descends to melodrama. Writer-director Jocelyn Moorhouse's debut is an impres-sive psychological study that will remind you of Hitchcock and Polan-ski at their best.

DR12, DR15, DR27

Goes well with: *The Servant*

PROVIDENCE

U.K. 1977 C 104 min. R Drama

Dir: Alain Resnais

C: Dirk Bogarde, John Gielgud, Ellen Burstyn, David Warner, Elaine Stritch

During a sleepless night, an elderly writer (John Gielgud) begins to create a novel starring the members of his family as characters with shifting loyalties to him and among themselves. French director Alain Resnais's first English-language film, written by David Mercer, is a first-rate exploration of the creative process and the way in which we confront our mortality. A tall order, but Resnais, Mercer, and their su-perb cast, including Dirk Bogarde, Ellen Burstyn, David Warner, and Elaine Stritch, are up to the job. Gielgud collected a Best Actor award from the New York Film Critics Circle.

DR2, DR8, DR11, DR27

Goes well with: *Wild Strawberries*

PULP FICTION

ESSENTIAL

U.S. 1994 C 154 min. R Thriller

Dir: Quentin Tarantino

C: John Travolta, Samuel L. Jackson, Uma Thurman, Harvey Keitel, Tim Roth, Amanda Plummer, Maria de Medeiros, Ving Rhames, Eric Stoltz, Rosanna Arquette, Christopher Walken, Bruce Willis, Steve Buscemi

Like *Halloween* and *Night of the Living Dead, Pulp Fiction* kicked off an unfortunate run of pale imitators, films that tried to duplicate its stylized homage to the netherworld of gangsters, hit men, drug addicts, crooked prizefighters, and the luckless dames who love 'em all. Quentin Tarantino and cowriter Roger Avary took the cliches of hundreds of films, comic books, and twenty-five-cent paperbacks and spun them into something witty and fresh, thanks in part to a brilliantly fractured narrative. *Pulp Fiction* takes the standard framing device of many films—opening and closing on the same scene—and expands the idea: What if some of the events shown between the opening and closing scene of that restaurant stick-up actually occurred later in the story? It's audacious, and it works, rewarding viewers on repeated viewings with further insights into the characters and their dilemmas. Samuel L. Jackson and John Travolta are Jules and Vincent, two hit men who think they're too cool to fool (and they are about half right); Ving Rhames is their boss, Marcellus; Uma Thurman is his dangerous mistress (wearing a Louise Brooks wig in homage to *Pandora's Box*); Bruce Willis is a palooka; and Harvey Keitel is Mr. Wolf, the enigmatic answer man. Watch for Steve Buscemi in the Buddy Holly outfit at the diner. Tarantino and Avary won awards from the Motion Picture Academy and the New York Film Critics Circle for their screenplay; Tarantino was named Best Director by the NYFCC; and the film cleaned up at the Independent Spirit Awards, winning Best Feature, Best Director, Best Male Lead (Samuel L. Jackson), and Best Screenplay.

⊙**DVD**

TH4, TH5, TH9, TH11, XT4

Goes well with: *Reservoir Dogs*

PUMP UP THE VOLUME

U.S.   1990   C   102 min.   R   Drama

Dir: Allan Moyle

C: Christian Slater, Ellen Greene, Annie Ross, Samantha Mathis, Scott Paulin

Christian Slater is a wonder to watch in this drama about the double life of a teenage disc jockey. He's a shy nerd at his new school (Hubert Humphrey High) in a bland Arizona suburb, but at night he takes to his basement to adopt his secret identity: Hard Harry, the DJ on a pirate radio station, who dispenses advice, attitude, and rock music that makes you want to get crazy. Hard Harry is Howard Stern with fewer listeners and a lot more class. His nickname derives from his alleged masturbatory activities while on the air, and that's enough to put Humphrey High's principal, a frequent target of Harry's jibes, over the edge. A student suicide gets blamed on Harry's show, so the plot against Harry intensifies. Samantha Mathis makes a strong impression in her debut as Harry's best friend. Writer-director Allan Moyle paints a convincing portrait of a teenage wasteland and the community that teens form around radio shows.

⊙**DVD**

DR31, DR41

Goes well with: *Heathers*

PURPLE NOON

France/Italy 1960 C 118 min. PG-13 Thriller
Dir: René Clément
C: Alain Delon, Marie Laforêt, Maurice Ronêt, Frank Latimore

Even if you've seen *The Talented Mr. Ripley,* you should check out the first screen version of Patricia Highsmith's creepy thriller about assumed identity. The criminally handsome Alain Delon plays Tom Ripley and Maurice Ronêt is Philippe Greenleaf, the roles played by Matt Damon and Jude Law in the remake. The setup is the same: Ripley tries to persuade Greenleaf to give up his playboy ways on the Amalfi coast of Italy and return to the loving if confining arms of his family in America. Greenleaf has no intention of surrendering *la dolce vita,* and Ripley decides to take matters into his own hands. You get the same gorgeous scenery, the same sense of moral rot among the wealthy and their hangers-on. However, in this version, the conclusion is very different, with a final shot that is one of the cinema's all-time great shockers.

⊙**DVD**

DR1, TH2, TH4

Goes well with: *Shallow Grave*

PUTNEY SWOPE

U.S. 1969 C/B&W 85 min. R Comedy
Dir: Robert Downey
C: Arnold Johnson, Pepi Hermine, Ruth Hermine, Allen Garfield, Antonio Fargas

Director Robert Downey's fame has been eclipsed for some time by the talent and off-screen antics of his actor son. The one film for which

Downey *pére* should be remembered is his satire of Madison Avenue. Arnold Johnson plays the title character, the token black man on the board of directors of a prominent ad agency. Elected chairman through a fluke in the voting procedure, he proceeds to staff the agency with black hipsters and rename it Truth and Soul, Inc. The film spoofs not only mindless ads, bottom-line corporate America, and corrupt politicians (the president of the U.S. is portrayed as a marijuana-smoking midget who is in the hip pocket of the firearms, liquor, and tobacco industries) but also the poseurs of the New Left, whom Downey sees as more dishonest than the targets of their wrath. The film is badly dated in a number of ways, but it is also an invaluable time-capsule portrait of the late 1960s.

⊙**DVD**

CO2, CO8

Goes well with: *Hollywood Shuffle*

QUADROPHENIA

U.K. 1979 C 115 min. R Drama
Dir: Franc Roddam
C: Phil Daniels, Mark Wingett, Philip Davis, Leslie Ash, Garry Cooper, Sting

The Who's follow-up concept album to *Tommy* was *Quadrophenia,* which got respectable reviews but didn't fly off the shelves. Director Ken Russell's film of *Tommy* was a wretched mess, but *Quadrophenia* was greeted more kindly by critics. Unfortunately, it didn't have the big-name stars and huge excesses of *Tommy,* and it disappeared from theaters without a trace. It's a much more coherent movie, grounded in the realities of the early 1960s clashes between mods and rockers, groups of teens who affected different dress styles and were passionate hairsplitters on the subject of what popular music was truly cool. The anguish of Jimmy, its confused hero (Phil Daniels), is lovingly detailed, as he finally decides to join the clean-cut mods, only to feel torn in more than one direction. Unlike Russell, who directed *Tommy* with both feet on the accelerator, Franc Roddam knows when to slow down and trust the more reflective ideas of Who songwriter Pete Townsend (who cowrote the screenplay with Roddam and two others). Watch for Sting as a mod who winds up with a demeaning job at a hotel.

⊙**DVD:** Includes audio commentary by Franc Roddam; animated location map; "making of" featurette; restoration demonstration; "This Is Mod Culture" fashion show.

DR21, DR24, DR41
Goes well with: *The Loneliness of the Long Distance Runner*

R

THE RAINBOW

U.K. 1989 C 104 min. R Drama
Dir: Ken Russell
C: Sammi Davis, Amanda Donohoe, Paul McGann, Christopher Gable,
David Hemmings, Glenda Jackson

Something in D. H. Lawrence must have a calming effect on Ken Russell. His breakthrough film, *Women in Love,* was a wonderfully sensual and reflective version of Lawrence's novel of the joys of friendship and the pitfalls of marriage. Over the next two decades, Russell never met a historical subject or literary work he couldn't tart up with vulgar theories and excessive stylistics. It's a joy, then, to report how modulated and affecting is *The Rainbow,* a prequel to *Women in Love,* concentrating on the character Ursula Brangwen. Glenda Jackson played Ursula in *Women;* here, she plays Ursula's mother, Anna. Sammi Davis is the young Ursula, finding her way in the world of love with the help of a very friendly swimming teacher (Amanda Donohoe) and a rough-hewn army officer (Paul McGann). Her education continues with her first job, at a school that thrives on its own rotten traditions, which include keeping a heavy thumb on its female employees.

DR19, DR29, DR39
Goes well with: *Women in Love*

RAISE THE RED LANTERN

ESSENTIAL

China/Taiwan/Hong Kong 1991 C 125 min. NR Drama
Dir: Zhang Yimou
C: Gong Li, Ma Jingwu, He Caifei, Cao Cuifen

The sexual politics of 1920s China are brilliantly dramatized in Zhang Yimou's fourth collaboration with Gong Li. She plays Songlian, a nineteen-year-old peasant girl who is persuaded to become the fourth mistress of a wealthy clan leader. Much of the drama is set in and around the central courtyard of the master's house, where a red lantern hung outside the room of a mistress indicates that she is currently top dog. While the older three women maneuver with traditional methods to gain the coveted lantern, Songlian decides to break the rules and feign pregnancy. The consequences of her rebellion are predictably disastrous. Cinematographer Zhao Fei's color schemes vie with the lovely Gong Li for our attention. Chosen Best Foreign Language Film by the New York Film Critics Circle.

DR24, DR39

Goes well with: *Ju Dou*

RAMBLING ROSE

U.S.   1991   C   112 min.   R   Drama

Dir: Martha Coolidge

C: Laura Dern, Robert Duvall, Diane Ladd, Lukas Haas, John Heard, Kevin Conway

Calder Willingham adapted his autobiographical novel about his early adolescent infatuation with his family's nineteen-year-old housekeeper. Laura Dern is the ripe and randy Rose, and director Martha Coolidge makes the most of her fluttery sensuality. Lukas Haas is Buddy, the Willingham stand-in, and Robert Duvall and Diane Ladd (Dern's real-life mom) complete the principal players as Daddy and Mother. This is no hothouse Tennessee Williams psychodrama, even if Rose does take a fancy to Daddy. Willingham is more interested in the comic possibilities of the material, and in Mother he creates an amazingly complex character who actually defends Rose's shenanigans; perhaps the young woman is enjoying the kind of youth Mother wishes she'd had. The film won Best Feature, Best Director, and Best Supporting Female (Ladd) awards from the Independent Spirit Awards.

⊙**DVD:** Includes audio commentary by Martha Coolidge; interview with Coolidge; deleted scenes.

DR3, DR11, DR39, DR41

Goes well with: *Spanking the Monkey*

RAN
ESSENTIAL

Japan/France 1985 C 161 min. R Drama
Dir: Akira Kurosawa
C: Tatsuya Nakadai, Akira Terao, Jinpachi Nezu, Daisuke Ryu, Mieko
Harada

After tackling *Macbeth* in 1957's *Throne of Blood,* Akira Kurosawa
let almost thirty years go by before turning again to the Bard. *Ran* is a
Japanese medieval version of *King Lear,* with the warlord Hidetora
Ichimonji (Tatsuya Nakadai) attempting in his old age to divvy up his
kingdom among three sons. Kurosawa has added a Lady Macbeth to the
proceedings, the manipulative Lady Kaede (Mieko Harada), but the star
of any Kurosawa production is the director's masterful control over
every detail. As in *Kagemusha,* his other great late-career spectacle,
Kurosawa offers the unbeatable blend of psychological insight into
flawed but fascinating characters (even if you're not familiar with Lear,
you know that the warlord's plan is fraught with disaster for his family
and his kingdom) and battle scenes as thrilling as any you'll ever see.
The New York Film Critics Circle tabbed *Ran* Best Foreign Language
Film, and it picked up an Oscar for its costume design.
⊙**DVD**
DR1, DR11, DR32, DR37
Goes well with: *Kagemusha*

THE RAPTURE
U.S. 1991 C 102 min. R Drama
Dir: Michael Tolkin
C: Mimi Rogers, Patrick Bauchau, David Duchovny, Kimberly Cullum,
Will Patton, James LeGros

Religion as a great comforter in people's lives has an undeniably
darker side, explored here by writer-director Michael Tolkin. Mimi
Rogers plays a phone operator whose dead-end days are relieved by her
nights of hard partying. Improbably, she meets and marries a religious
man, but when tragedy strikes their family, she becomes persuaded that
she and her children are to await further instruction from God in an isolated desert locale. It's understandable that some viewers may find this
preposterous, but the film has the courage of its convictions; it is not an
endorsement, God knows, of this woman's beliefs so much as an exploration of their benefits and inevitable shortcomings.

DR20, DR30
Goes well with: *Ordet*

RASHOMON

ESSENTIAL

Japan 1950 B&W 88 min. NR Drama
Dir: Akira Kurosawa
C: Toshiro Mifune, Machiko Kyo, Masayuki Mori, Takashi Shimura

Most Western filmgoers of a certain age can date their interest in Japanese film from exposure to Akira Kurosawa's breakthrough feature. Its concept—a story told from so many points of view that its real truth may never be known—has entered the popular culture. In twelfth-century Japan, three men gather under a huge stone gate (its name is the source of the film's title) to discuss a recent trial. The case involved a bandit (Toshiro Mifune) accosting a married couple (Machiko Kyo and Masayuki Mori) in the woods; one of them wound up dead, but the circumstances leading up to that murder are in debate. Each scenario is given its full due, and by the end of the film we're only sure of one thing: the slippery elusiveness of reality. This is no intellectual exercise, however. Both Mifune's scruffy bandit and Kyo's ambiguously seductive lady are full-blooded characters whose actions and motives change with each telling of the story.

⊙**DVD:** Special Edition includes commentary by Kurosawa scholar Donald Richie and video introduction by Robert Altman.

DR6, XT4
Goes well with: *Throne of Blood*

RED

Switzerland/France/Poland 1994 C 99 min. R Drama
Dir: Krzysztof Kieslowski
C: Irène Jacob, Jean-Louis Trintignant, Frédérique Feder, Jean-Pierre Lorit, Juliette Binoche, Julie Delpy, Benoît Régent, Zbigniew Zamachowski

The concluding segment of Krzysztof Kieslowski's Three Colors trilogy (following *Blue* and *White*) is its strongest one, detailing the interaction between Valentine (Irène Jacob), a fashion model, and a retired judge (Jean-Louis Trintignant) who has turned to eavesdropping on telephone conversations. She discovers that her well-ordered life—a sometimes absent but devoted boyfriend, a glamorous job—isn't everything she wants, while in justifying his questionable hobby to an almost perfect stranger, he finds himself admitting to failures in his own life. Kieslowski doesn't turn this into a morality play; the film has a slippery, allusive quality that gets under your skin. If you've seen the other two films in the trilogy, you'll recognize the cameos at the story's end, in a news report about a catastrophe. Winner of best foreign film prizes from the Independent Spirit Awards and the New York Film Critics Circle.

DR20

Goes well with: *Light Sleeper*

THE RED SHOES
ESSENTIAL

U.K. 1948 C 133 min. NR Drama

Dir: Michael Powell and Emeric Pressburger

C: Anton Walbrook, Marius Goring, Moira Shearer, Robert Helpmann

The tradition to which Michael Powell and Emeric Pressburger's drama belongs has all but disappeared from movie screens. To contemporary audiences, its story may seem more than a little overwrought. But that is in some ways the point: This is a very theatrical movie about the art of performing in public. It's what the misbegotten *Moulin Rouge* aspired to be, a delirious presentation of a profession that is all about artifice. Moira Shearer is the ballerina enslaved to wicked impresario Anton Walbrook until dashing composer Marius Goring comes along. She's dancing in a production of Hans Christian Andersen's *The Red Shoes,* and the conceit is that she may wind up trapped in those red shoes forever. Jack Cardiff's glorious Technicolor cinematography is the last word in using color to express mood. The DVD package is a fan's delight.

⊙**DVD:** Includes audio commentary by film historian Ian Christie, actors Marius Goring and Moira Shearer, cinematographer Jack Cardiff, composer Brian Easdale, and director Martin Scorsese; excerpts from novel read by Jeremy Irons; animated film made from storyboards.

DR4, DR18, FA4

Goes well with: *Children of Paradise*

THE REMAINS OF THE DAY
ESSENTIAL

U.K./U.S. 1993 C 135 min. PG Drama

Dir: James Ivory

C: Anthony Hopkins, Emma Thompson, James Fox, Christopher Reeve, Peter Vaughan, Hugh Grant, Michel Lonsdale

An exceptional adaptation of a book difficult to translate to another medium, *The Remains of the Day* is, with *Howards End,* the crowning achievement of the filmmaking team of producer Ismail Merchant, director James Ivory and writer Ruth Prawer Jhabvala. Kazuo Ishiguro's novel was a masterful study in narrative point of view; his Mr. Stevens, a faithful butler, offers his version of the events that lead to his downfall, and it becomes clear that Stevens is subtly and unconsciously coloring the story to his own ends. Remarkably, Jhabvala manages to retain this device without resorting to an intrusive voice-over. Anthony Hopkins brilliantly suggests how a man can unwittingly set himself up for disaster even as he is doing exactly what is expected of him. The scenes in the later part of the film between Stevens and Miss Keaton (Emma Thompson), the maid with whom he shares a torturously tangled friendship, are heartbreaking. Also superb are James Fox as Mr. Stevens's master, a man whose worst political beliefs are of no concern to Stevens (but should be), and Christopher Reeve as a key participant in a meeting that precipitates Stevens's fall from grace.

⊙**DVD:** Includes "making of" featurette and featurette on World War II–era collaborators.

DR5, DR29

Goes well with: *Howards End*

REPO MAN

U.S. 1984 C 92 min. R Comedy
Dir: Alex Cox
C: Emilio Estevez, Harry Dean Stanton, Vonetta McGee, Olivia Barash, Sy Richardson, Tracey Walter

A demented anticipation of *Wall Street, Repo Man* features Emilio Estevez, older brother of *Wall Street* star Charlie Sheen, as a young man learning the ways of the world through his new profession. Commodities trading or car repossessing: Who's to say which is the more honorable way to make a living? California punk Otto (Estevez) obtains his liberal education from the master (Harry Dean Stanton, counterpart to *Wall Street*'s Michael Douglas), but writer-director Alex Cox isn't certain that the ins and outs of sneaking up on people's cars in the middle of the night are worth a ninety-minute movie. So he tosses in a subplot about a '64 Chevy with a trunk full of cargo that interests alien hunters and squirrelly government types. It's a shaggy dog movie that chugs along like its star car and almost runs out of gas before Cox pulls a fast finish.

⊙**DVD:** Two editions. Special Edition contains audio commentary by Alex Cox. Limited Special Edition contains audio commentary by Cox; soundtrack CD; booklet including a *Repo Man* comic book.

CO2, CO8, FA1

Goes well with: *The Man Who Fell to Earth*

REPULSION
ESSENTIAL

U.K.   1965   B&W   105 min.   NR   Thriller
Dir: Roman Polanski
C: Catherine Deneuve, Ian Hendry, John Fraser, Patrick Wymark,
   Yvonne Furneaux, James Villiers

In a film era in which horrors have to be shown rather than suggested, Roman Polanski's masterpiece of a woman losing a battle with insanity, alone in her apartment over a weekend, may look quaint and almost restrained. Catherine Deneuve is Carol Ledoux, a young manicurist sharing a flat in London with her sister, Helen (Yvonne Furneaux), who has no compunction about having her married lover, Michael (Ian Hendry), spend the night. It's one thing for Carol to brush past oglers on the street as though they were carrying the plague, but her disgust and fear over the sounds of lovemaking in the next bedroom are the tip-off that her repulsion toward men (and personal contact of any kind) goes beyond shyness. When Helen and Michael go off for a weekend, the walls start closing in on Carol. Polanski leaves us little hope in this bleak tale, but he's such an imaginative filmmaker that you can't look away from the one-woman disaster unfolding before you.

DR27, TH3, TH16
Goes well with: *The Tenant*

RESERVOIR DOGS
ESSENTIAL

U.S.   1992   C   99 min.   R   Thriller
Dir: Quentin Tarantino
C: Harvey Keitel, Tim Roth, Michael Madsen, Chris Penn, Steve
   Buscemi, Lawrence Tierney, Randy Brooks, voice of Steven Wright

A warm-up exercise for *Pulp Fiction,* Quentin Tarantino's heist thriller offers the same kind of convoluted narrative and lots of tough-guy banter. The opening scene, with the principals in the crime assembled for the first time in a restaurant, is a hilarious exercise in macho one-upsmanship. Most of the action takes place after the heist is aborted by the police showing up; in an empty warehouse, several surviving members of the gang assemble to ferret out which of them was the informer. The film gradually begins to take itself more seriously (there is an unnecessarily protracted torture scene involving a cop who has been captured in the shoot-out) and begins to wear out its welcome right around the time that guns are simultaneously pulled and pointed— Tarantino's homage to Hong Kong director John Woo. Everyone in the cast is on his toes, especially Steve Buscemi (Independent Spirit Award winner for Best Supporting Male) as the unfortunately dubbed Mr. Pink and Lawrence Tierney as the big boss.
⊙**DVD**
TH5, TH13, XT4
Goes well with: *The Usual Suspects*

THE RETURN OF MARTIN GUERRE
France   1982   C   123 min.   NR   Drama
Dir: Daniel Vigne
C: Gérard Depardieu, Nathalie Baye, Roger Planchon, Maurice Jacquemont

In a sixteenth-century French village, a young man abandons his wife and farm. Nine years later he reappears, claiming he has been off fighting in the war, and that he is a changed man. There is something different about Martin, all right; for one thing, he doesn't look exactly like the old Martin. Daniel Vigne and Jean-Claude Carrière's script is a tantalizing mystery and also an inquiry into identity. It became a minor hit, got remade into an American film (*Sommersby,* set during the Civil War), and even became a musical. A concept with that many lives has something going for it, and Vigne's measured direction of his attractive stars, Gérard Depardieu and Nathalie Baye, is one of the reasons why.
⊙**DVD**
DR18, DR34
Goes well with: *Lone Star*

RETURN OF THE SECAUCUS 7

ESSENTIAL

U.S. 1980 C 106 min. R Drama

Dir: John Sayles

C: Mark Arnott, Gordon Clapp, Maggie Cousineau, Adam LeFevre, Bruce MacDonald, Jean Passanante, Maggie Renzi, David Strathairn, John Sayles

After publishing several acclaimed novels and one volume of short stories, John Sayles began a second career as a filmmaker with this comedy-drama. A ragtag group of friends assemble in rural New Hampshire for a reunion; their moniker derives from an incident in their activist past, when they were on their way to a protest in Washington but got stopped in the northern New Jersey town for a traffic violation. Sayles deftly sketches in each character, and they are all likable folks, none of them doing especially lucrative work but all reasonably happy. Still, every one of them is approaching thirty with some trepidation. Call it the Peter Pan Generation, but a certain segment of the Baby Boomers just never got over reaching the age where they weren't supposed to be trusted. Not as ambitious as *The Big Chill,* but in its own way more satisfying.

DR12

Goes well with: *Between the Lines*

RICHARD III (1955)

U.K. 1955 C 161 min. NR Drama

Dir: Laurence Olivier

C: Laurence Olivier, John Gielgud, Ralph Richardson, Claire Bloom, Alec Clunes, Cedric Hardwicke, Stanley Baker, Pamela Brown, Michael Gough

Of Laurence Olivier's three great midcareer Shakespeare films, *Henry V* is the rouser, *Hamlet* is the award winner, and *Richard III* is, appropriately, the misshapen third brother. In a way, the part is almost too juicy, and Olivier is clearly up to squeezing all he can out of the humpbacked king's machinations. With a cast of big names drawn to the Olivier flame, this is surely required viewing, though it should be said that his direction lacks the dynamism and imagination of the previous two films.

DR17, DR24, DR25, DR32

Goes well with: *Henry V* (1945)

RICHARD III (1995)

U.S./U.K.   1995   C   104 min.   R   Drama
Dir: Richard Loncraine
C: Ian McKellen, Annette Bening, Jim Broadbent, Robert Downey, Jr.,
Nigel Hawthorne, Kristin Scott Thomas, Maggie Smith, John Wood,
Adrian Dunbar, Bill Paterson

Updating Shakespeare is nothing new, and casting ringers in supporting roles is hardly novel. That's not to say that this version of the Bard's play about power politics, adapted from a successful stage presentation, is all gimmick and no roughage. In fact, Ian McKellen's Richard is arguably more malevolent, more magnetic, more *more* than Olivier's 1955 interpretation. The setting is the early part of the twentieth century, with Britain locked in some kind of civil war. There are lots of scenes involving motorized vehicles whizzing about and a fabulous set piece at London's Battersea Power Station. As for the cast, the Whitman's Sampler approach works well: Kristin Scott Thomas is a perfectly jaded Lady Anne, while Annette Bening and Robert Downey, Jr. are perfectly awful (in the best sense of that phrase) Americanized versions of the Nevilles; Jim Broadbent is the out-of-it Buckingham; and Nigel Hawthorne is the doomed Clarence. McKellen is the chocolate-covered rock in the center of this nasty box.
⊙**DVD**
DR17, DR24, DR25, DR32
Goes well with: *Hamlet* (1996)

RIDICULE

France   1996   C   102 min.   R   Drama
Dir: Patrice Leconte
C: Charles Berling, Jean Rochefort, Fanny Ardant, Judith Godrèche,
Bernard Giraudeau

In the court of Louis XVI, according to Patrice Leconte's witty take on prerevolutionary French politics, you had to talk the talk or else you'd lose your place in line to see or be seen by the king. That's what a French engineer named Ponceludon de Malavoy (Charles Berling) quickly learns when he travels from his village to Paris. His fellow citizens need a drainage project, and in the eighteenth century form of lobbying, the fastest way to get attention was not to set up a political action committee but to attend a royal event and make yourself heard with some witty and preferably withering comment about someone else. It's not like de Malavoy is selling out; he's only learning the tricks of a certain trade, and for a hydrologist he turns out to be pretty adept at sending up members of society, especially with the help of a certain lady (Fanny Ardant) who gives him pause about the woman (Judith Godrèche) he left back home. *Ridicule* took the two big César Awards, the French version of our Academy Awards, for Best Film and Best Director, and was nominated for the Best Foreign Language Film Oscar.

DR5, DR24, DR25

Goes well with: *The Four Musketeers*

RIFIFI

ESSENTIAL

France   1954   B&W   115 min.   NR   Thriller
Dir: Jules Dassin
C: Jean Servais, Carl Möhner, Magali Noël, Robert Manuel, Perlo Vita
    (Jules Dassin)

If the 1950s blacklist crippled American director Jules Dassin's career, you couldn't prove it by his first two films made in exile in Europe. After his success in Hollywood with 1948's *The Naked City,* Dassin went to England, where he made a solid film noir, *Night and the City* (1950). The best was yet to come: This caper film was so popular that its title was used for a dozen generic heist pictures, and Dassin later did his own big-budget riff on it, *Topkapi. Rififi* is a model thriller in three acts: the Setup, the Crime, and the Aftermath. Tony (Jean Servais) is an aging crook fresh out of the slammer and tempted by his younger pals into pulling off a robbery. He refuses and then reconsiders when he finds his old flame hanging out with a sleazy club owner. But Tony doesn't want to pull a smash-and-grab—he wants to break into the store's safe, which is guarded by motion detectors. Thirty-five minutes go by with no dialogue as the heist is perfectly executed—then there's the inevitable unraveling of the well-laid plans. A key moment: Each man takes a turn at what he's going to do with the money, and Tony admits he hadn't even thought about it. Now that is existential stuff, *mon ami.* Billed as Perlo Vita, Dassin plays César, the safecracker with a weakness for women.

⊙**DVD**

TH8, XT7

Goes well with: *Big Deal on Madonna Street*

RIVER'S EDGE

U.S.   1986   C   99 min.   R   Drama

Dir: Tim Hunter

C: Crispin Glover, Keanu Reeves, Ione Skye, Roxana Zal, Daniel Roebuck, Jim Metzler, Dennis Hopper

The centrifugal pull of adolescent groups, banding together against other adolescent groups, parents, school authorities, and the whole rest of the world, has never been more starkly dramatized than in this film, based on a real incident. A teen boy murders his girlfriend and shows the riverside murder scene to his friends, who then do nothing. Oh, they talk about it a lot, but only within their group. Neal Jimenez's script creates a vivid sense of doom among these small-town kids; their loyalty to one another is all they really have. You may find that Crispin Glover, as the only one of these kids who seems to have any energy, and Dennis Hopper, as the one adult contact they can trust (because he deals drugs and seems to share their dim view of the world), are from another movie (or planet). But their characters can at least articulate something; everyone else here is walking dead.

⊙**DVD**

DR20, DR34, DR41

Goes well with: *Over the Edge*

THE ROAD HOME

China   1999   C   89 min.   G   Drama

Dir: Zhang Yimou

C: Zhang Ziyi, Sun Honglei, Zheng Hao, Zhao Yuelin

Chinese director Zhang Yimou's quiet love story didn't create more than a ripple when it was released to American theaters in 2001, even if it did mark an early screen appearance by *Crouching Tiger, Hidden Dragon* star Zhang Ziyi. In extended flashbacks, she plays a young girl who's attracted to the new schoolteacher in her village and manages to attract his attention. The framing device is the present-day funeral of the schoolteacher; his now-elderly wife insists that he be buried in his original village, and while her son makes preparations, he recalls the story of his parents' courtship. The modest charms of the story are enhanced by Zhang Ziyi's touching performance; here is a face that the camera obviously adores. Winner of the Audience Award for World Cinema at Sundance.

⊙**DVD**
DR18, DR34, XT4
Goes well with: *L'Atalante*

THE ROAD WARRIOR
ESSENTIAL

Australia 1981 C 95 min. R Action-Adventure
Dir: George Miller
C: Mel Gibson, Bruce Spence, Vernon Wells, Mike Preston, Virginia
    Hey, Emil Minty, Kjell Nilsson

The second Mad Max adventure is more lavish (and comprehensible—no dubbing required this time around) than the original. Set in the familiar postapocalyptic future—although in the outback, who can really tell if civilization has vanished—the story concerns a shortage of petrol. A hardy commune is guarding its own supply against hordes of outlaws riding custom cycles and cars. They're led by Humongous, a baldie in a leather mask who is billed by one of his minions as "the Ayatollah of rock and rollah." Max (Mel Gibson) is no longer a cop, since there is nothing to police, so his only interest is in finding petrol for his own souped-up car. He throws in with the commune's desperate plan to relocate, and the chase is on. The finale is one of the great action set pieces in all of movies, with a score of vehicles trying to keep up with a huge tanker truck driven by Max. The vehicular choreography would have done Busby Berkeley proud, and whatever the stuntmen made on this picture, they were underpaid. A movie that set the bar for dozens of lesser imitators to aspire to, *The Road Warrior* is tops in its class.

⊙**DVD**
AC2, AC4, AC5
Goes well with: *Mad Max*

ROADIE
U.S. 1980 C 105 min. PG Comedy
Dir: Alan Rudolph
C: Meat Loaf, Kaki Hunter, Art Carney, Gailard Sartain, Alice Cooper,
    Blondie, Roy Orbison, Hank Williams, Jr., Ramblin' Jack Elliot,
    Asleep at the Wheel

Rationally defending *Roadie* against the slings and arrows of outraged critics (in other words, anyone who ever reviewed it) is a tough job, but someone has to do it. First off, it is the best film ever to star Meat Loaf, who plays Travis W. Redfish, a Texas beer-truck driver whose real ambition in life is to travel that rock-and-roll highway of life with his idol, Alice Cooper. Travis is no singer (and you thought Meat Loaf was going to do a few tunes!), but he is an electronics whiz who will make sure Alice's (or is that Mr. Cooper's?) equipment is in tiptop shape. Travis sets out to make his fortune, encountering lots of other traveling bands, including Asleep at the Wheel, Blondie, Hank Williams, Jr., and the sublime Roy Orbison. The screenplay, by Texas legend Big Boy Medlin (try to find him in a film encyclopedia) and Michael Ventura, crams enough redneck jokes into the opening fifteen minutes to fill up fifty films set in the Lone Star State, but the movie is best when it hits the road.

CO10, XT5

Goes well with: *Songwriter*

ROCCO AND HIS BROTHERS

Italy 1960 B&W 180 min. NR Drama
Dir: Luchino Visconti
C: Alain Delon, Renato Salvatori, Annie Girardot, Katina Paxinou, Claudia Cardinale, Roger Hanin

Described as "the last gasp of the neo-realist spirit," *Rocco and His Brothers* does hearken back to the Italian films of the immediate post-war period in its story of urban survival. But by the late 1950s, Milan was no longer struggling to recover from the ravages of war, so the wounds inflicted on the Parondi family, as they move from the country-side to the big city, are self-inflicted. Luchino Visconti and four cowriters adapted Giovanni Testore's novel of family disintegration, as the five Parondi men drift in and out of jobs, stints in the boxing ring and the military, and marriages, with Rocco (Alain Delon) the lone hope of his widowed mother (Katina Paxinou). For many years, American audiences, exposed only to a 144-minute version of this film, couldn't understand what the fuss was about. The full-length version is now available on both tape and DVD.

⊙**DVD**

DR11, DR36

Goes well with: *Once Were Warriors*

ROGER & ME

ESSENTIAL

U.S. 1989 C 87 min. R Documentary
Dir: Michael Moore

Michael Moore is a self-styled pain in the ass of corporate America, and his mission—to expose greed and heartlessness in the halls of big business—is admirable, even if you may find his methods inspired more by David Letterman than Ralph Nader. Moore knows how to work the media by staging events that are likely to wind up on the nightly TV news programs. His target here is Roger Smith, then the chairman of General Motors, a company whose decision to close an assembly plant in Flint, Michigan (not coincidentally Moore's hometown), put thousands of workers on the streets. The chronology of Moore's three-year odyssey to explore the reactions of the town's citizens and to confront Smith face to face with the consequences of his company's actions is confusing. This is, according to Moore, a "docu-comedy," which presumably means part truth and part entertainment. In spite of Moore's label, the New York Film Critics Circle declared *Roger & Me* the Best Documentary of 1989.

DO1

Goes well with: *American Dream*

ROME, OPEN CITY.

See *Open City*

RONDE, LA.

See *La Ronde*

ROOM AT THE TOP

U.K. 1959 B&W 118 min. NR Drama
Dir: Jack Clayton
C: Laurence Harvey, Simone Signoret, Heather Sears, Hermione Baddeley, Donald Wolfit

Laurence Harvey's charming sneer was put to most effective use in this adaptation of John Braine's novel about blind ambition. Joe Lampton is a British version of Theodore Dreiser's Clyde Griffiths, a man on the make caught between two women. Alice (Simone Signoret), the unhappily married older woman, is whom Joe is most comfortable with, but it's Susan (Heather Sears), the daughter of his boss at the factory, who will ensure his future. The film racked up six Oscar nominations, including Best Picture and Best Director. Harvey lost to *Ben-Hur*'s Charlton Heston for Best Actor, but Signoret's indelible portrait of a woman willing to settle for less was a winner with Academy voters. The film spawned two sequels, *Life at the Top* and *Man at the Top,* neither of them graced with Harvey's brittle charm.

⊙**DVD**

DR1, DR18

Goes well with: *This Sporting Life*

A ROOM WITH A VIEW

U.K.   1986   C   115 min.   NR   Drama
Dir: James Ivory
C: Maggie Smith, Helena Bonham Carter, Denholm Elliott, Julian Sands, Daniel Day-Lewis, Simon Callow, Judi Dench, Rupert Graves

The miniboom of E. M. Forster screen adaptations that began with 1984's *A Passage to India* got a big boost with the unexpected popularity of this film. The filmmaking team of producer Ismail Merchant, director James Ivory, and screenwriter Ruth Prawer Jhabvala don't try to inflate Forster the way Lean did, and there's a lovely intimacy to this drama of a young woman's education in love. Lucy (Helena Bonham Carter) is awakened to the possibilities of romance on a trip to Florence and the Tuscan countryside, and now her attention is divided between the dashing George Emerson (Julian Sands) and the prissy Cecil Vyse (Daniel Day-Lewis). We know what's best for Lucy, as do a half-dozen characters in the film, but it comes down to making a wrong choice before you understand which one is right. Tony Pierce-Roberts's cinematography (a winner with the New York Film Critics Circle) may have you booking the next plane to Italy. *Room* picked up Oscars for Best Adapted Screenplay, Art Direction, and Costume Design, and a Special Distinction Award from the Independent Spirits; Daniel Day-Lewis won a Best Supporting Actor award from the New York Film Critics Circle.

⊙**DVD**

DR5, DR18, DR29, XT7

Goes well with: *The Wings of the Dove*

'ROUND MIDNIGHT

U.S./France   1986   C   131 min.   R   Drama
Dir: Bertrand Tavernier
C: Dexter Gordon, François Cluzet, Gabrielle Haker, Sandra Reaves-

Phillips, Lonette McKee, Herbie Hancock, Bobby Hutcherson, Wayne Shorter, John Berry, Martin Scorsese, Philippe Noiret

Appropriately, it took a French filmmaker to tell the story of American jazz artists who felt more at home in Europe than in their own country. American screenwriter David Rayfiel's perceptive script was brought to the screen in the loving hands of Bertrand Tavernier, with a surprisingly effective performance by tenor saxophonist Dexter Gordon in his first acting role. His Dale Turner is reportedly an amalgam of pianist Bud Powell and sax man Lester Young, both masters of their instruments who never felt fully appreciated in the States. François Cluzet plays Francis, Dale's biggest fan, who discovers him at low ebb and carefully works to get his life and career back in order. Gordon, with his hulking presence and gruff line readings, perfectly plays off the shorter and voluble Cluzet; shuffling from club to club, Dale and Francis become the Mutt and Jeff of the Paris jazz scene. Herbie Hancock's Oscar-winning musical score deserves high praise; he assembled an all-star lineup of musicians to support Gordon's fine work on the soundtrack.

⊙**DVD**

DR12, DR23, XT7

Goes well with: *Stormy Monday*

RUBY IN PARADISE

U.S. 1993 C 115 min. R Drama

Dir: Victor Nunez

C: Ashley Judd, Todd Field, Bentley Mitchum, Allison Dean, Dorothy Lyman

The runaway woman finding a new life for herself: a familiar story given a fresh kick by writer-director Victor Nunez and newcomer Ashley Judd. Ruby flees her Tennessee home after her mother's death, looking for a home by the ocean, sensing that she can draw strength from the rhythm of the tides. Panama City, Florida, seems her idea of paradise, and a job in a souvenir store will do for the moment, especially since her boss (Dorothy Lyman) seems generous. Soon enough, there are two men in her life, and although Ruby stupidly succumbs to a fling with one (the no-good son of her boss), she's smart enough to cut her losses and keep on pushing. Nunez neither patronizes nor sanctifies Ruby, and the story's version of a happy ending isn't the expected one. Judd was named Best Female Lead by the Independent Spirit Awards, and the film took home the Grand Jury prize at Sundance.

DR16, DR34, DR39
Goes well with: *The Naked Kiss*

RULES OF THE GAME
ESSENTIAL

France 1939 B&W 110 min. NR Comedy-Drama
Dir: Jean Renoir
C: Marcel Dalio, Nora Gregor, Mila Parély, Jean Renoir, Gaston
  Modot, Roland Toutain

It's generally regarded as Jean Renoir's greatest film, though some prefer *Grand Illusion.* On the eve of World War II, a French aviator, André Jurieu (Roland Toutain) lands in Paris after a record-setting transatlantic flight, and his only concern is that his mistress isn't there to greet him. It's the first of many amusing moments in this comedy that almost imperceptibly turns serious. The bulk of the action takes place over a long weekend at a country estate, hosted by the Count de la Chesnaye (Marcel Dalio) and his wife, Christine (Nora Gregor), Jurieu's missing lover. Naturally, Jurieu is there, along with his pal Octave (Renoir). There is a long hunting scene (clearly not shot under the auspices of the Humane Society), there is staged entertainment by some of the guests, there is much drinking, and there are inevitable romantic entanglements and misunderstandings involving both the guests and the servants. Some prints of the film begin with the disclaimer that what follows is only for entertainment and not intended as social criticism. Ri-i-ight. Upon its original release *Rules of the Game* was correctly condemned by those whose behavior it satirizes; it was severely edited and not restored to its original length until the 1950s. The film ends on a suitably melancholy note with one of the guests commenting on their host, "Le Chesnaye has class, and believe me, his race is dying out."
  CO7, DR5
Goes well with: *Gosford Park*

THE RULING CLASS
U.K. 1972 C 154 min. PG Comedy
Dir: Peter Medak
C: Peter O'Toole, Alastair Sim, Arthur Lowe, Harry Andrews, Coral
  Browne, Michael Bryant, Carolyn Seymour

As a portrait of British eccentrics, *The Ruling Class* is hard to beat. Its main character, the fourteenth Earl of Gurney (Peter O'Toole), has just inherited the title (and a tidy fortune) from his late father (Harry Andrews), but the new Earl is too busy thinking he's Jesus Christ—or is it Jack the Ripper? The rest of his family despairs of his ever regaining his marbles, but they can't decide whether to have him committed or just killed. Peter Barnes's adaptation of his play does go on a bit, with fully orchestrated production numbers that look like rejects from *Springtime for Hitler.* But one of the world's great indoor sports is watching the British make fun of their own institutions, and *The Ruling Class* is jolly good fun for fans of that pastime.

⊙**DVD:** Includes audio commentaries by Peter O'Toole, Peter Medak, and Peter Barnes, and Medak's on-the-set home movies.

CO2, CO3, CO7

Goes well with: *Life Is Sweet*

SAFE

ESSENTIAL

U.S. 1995 C 119 min. R Drama
Dir: Todd Haynes
C: Julianne Moore, Xander Berkeley, Peter Friedman, James LeGros, Mary Carver, Jessica Harper, Brandon Cruz

Is it just me, or is it the air I'm breathing, the chemicals in my water, the perfumes in those magazine ads, the strange hum I feel whenever I drive by a power plant? Todd Haynes's film poses the delicate question, Can a person have a mental breakdown these days and blame it on the environment? This is not a spurious issue, since many cases have been reported of allergies to a wide variety of elements that most of us take for granted. Carol White (Julianne Moore), a San Fernando Valley housewife, could be having more than just a bad day or week, in her lovely home equipped with all the modern appliances and conveniences. Keeping his camera at a long arm's length from Moore, who's framed in mostly medium and long shots, Haynes emphasizes her sense of isolation. Her retreat to a holistic healing center in the New Mexico desert invites stinging shots at New Age quackery, but again, the film makes no firm commitment. After all, Carol is feeling better in her new digs with her new friends, isn't she, and isn't that what we're all concerned about, feeling that we're really safe?

⊙**DVD**
DR20, DR21
Goes well with: *Happiness*

SALESMAN

ESSENTIAL

U.S. 1969 B&W 90 min. G Documentary
Dir: Albert Maysles, David Maysles, and Charlotte Zwerin

Following a group of door-to-door Bible salesmen on their rounds may not sound like your idea of a good time, but in the hands of brother documentarians Albert and David Maysles (and their associate, Charlotte Zwerin), it's a thought-provoking and even humorous experience. The Maysles were among the pioneers of the cinema verité movement, which strove to capture a sense of everyday reality with as little mediation (narration, off-camera interviewer) as possible. *Salesman* was the first verité film to get a relatively substantial theatrical release. Its four salesmen, working for the Mid-American Bible Company, ply their trade in the neighborhoods of Boston and Opa-Lock, Florida, and attend a sales meeting in Chicago. Paul Brennan, nicknamed the Badger, is the film's star, though not because he's the star salesman—far from it. The Maysles and Zwerin capture so many heartbreaking moments, as Brennan struggles to make even one sale a day and keep his spirits up, that you may find yourself looking away from the screen in sympathy for him.

⊙**DVD:** Includes audio commentaries by David Maysles and Charlotte Zwerin, and a 1968 TV interview with the Maysles brothers.

DO7, DO11

Goes well with: *American Dream*

SALVADOR

ESSENTIAL

U.S. 1986 C 123 min. R Drama
Dir: Oliver Stone
C: James Woods, James Belushi, Michael Murphy, John Savage, Elpidia Carillo, Cynthia Gibb, John Doe

Writer-director Oliver Stone had his coming-out party in 1986 with the release of *Platoon* and this film, both nominated for original screenplay Oscars. *Salvador*'s screenplay is cocredited to Richard Boyle, a photojournalist whose experiences formed the basis for this descent into Latin American hell, circa 1980 to 81. James Woods, making a big jump from who's-that-character-actor to leading man, is the intense Boyle, who clearly modeled his lifestyle after that of Hunter S. Thompson. Boyle even has a traveling companion, à la *Fear and Loathing in*

Las Vegas; he's played by James Belushi, who spends most of the film screaming at Woods to stop driving so fast or muttering, "We gotta get out of here, man." Boyle gets to see the fruits of CIA meddling in foreign affairs up close and personal, and it starts to wear on his sense of objectivity—as if you couldn't guess from the start that the film is an indictment of U.S. policy south of the border. The highlight: Boyle's first trip to confession in thirty-two years. Woods's performance won Best Male Lead at the Independent Spirit Awards.

⊙**DVD:** Includes audio commentary by Oliver Stone; "making of" documentary; twenty-five minutes of footage that was cut to get the film an R rating.

DR25, DR38

Goes well with: *Welcome to Sarajevo*

SATURDAY NIGHT AND SUNDAY MORNING
U.K.   1960   B&W   90 min.   NR   Drama
Dir: Karel Reisz
C: Albert Finney, Shirley Ann Field, Rachel Roberts, Norman Rossington

"All I'm out for is a good time—the rest is propaganda." So says Arthur Seaton, the antihero of Alan Sillitoe's excellent screen version of his novel. Arthur works in a machine shop, and he's smart enough to know that he's got a brain-dead job but not clever enough to better himself. Albert Finney, coming off his debut earlier the same year in *The Entertainer,* plays Arthur as all smiles and winks, and he's a regular twentieth-century Tom Jones with the ladies, too. Brenda (Rachel Roberts) is his married lover, but then there's Doreen (the ravishing Shirley Ann Field), a single girl who lives at home with a watchful mum. The inevitable complications drag the prankish Arthur kicking and screaming into adulthood. "There's easier ways of getting things than lashin' out," Brenda tells him in the final scene, but you can tell by the mischievous look on Arthur's face that his lashin' days are far from over.

⊙**DVD**

DR19, DR21

Goes well with: *Look Back in Anger*

SCANDAL
U.K./U.S.   1989   C   106 min.   R   Drama
Dir: Michael Caton-Jones

C: John Hurt, Joanne Whalley, Bridget Fonda, Ian McKellen, Leslie Phillips, Britt Ekland, Deborah Grant, Daniel Massey, Jeroen Krabbé

Britain's Profumo affair, recalled here in a surprising mix of low drama and high comedy, should put to shame any opinion that the Lewinsky-Clinton clinches endangered anything more than the dignity of both principals. In 1963, John Profumo, the married war minister, unwittingly shared a lover named Christine Keeler with a Russian naval attaché who also happened to be a known spy. The fascinating character in all of this muck, on whom the movie rightly focuses, is an osteopath named Stephen Ward, who introduced Christine (and her pal Mandy Rice-Davies, and many more girls) to men in high places as a way of currying favor. John Hurt is Ward, one moment urbanely dropping the names of his very best friends and the next moment panic-stricken at how his neatly constructed house of cards is about to collapse. Joanne Whalley (billed as Joanne Whalley-Kilmer) is a wonderfully saucy Keeler, and Ian McKellen plays Profumo as the kind of man who could marry a movie star (Valerie Hobson, played here by Deborah Grant) and still think he was entitled to shag a twenty-one-year-old call girl.

⊙**DVD**

DR1, DR17, DR19, DR25

Goes well with: *O Lucky Man!*

SCANNERS

Canada   1981   C   102 min.   R   Horror

Dir: David Cronenberg

C: Jennifer O'Neill, Stephen Lack, Patrick McGoohan, Michael Ironside

It may have been the movie that inspired the sketch on the late, beloved *SCTV* in which Joe Flaherty and John Candy starred in "The Farm Film Report," a rural parody of Siskel and Ebert's film review show. Sitting in bib overalls, the two mumbled through a recitation of a film's story, keying its success on whether something or someone "blowed up real good" in the course of the story. (And since *Scanners* writer-director David Cronenberg is, like the *SCTV* cast, a Canadian, well, you figure it out.) Yes, *Scanners* is that movie you may have heard of, the one where several heads explode, courtesy of the title characters, who can use their telepathic powers for good or evil. Cronenberg loves to delve into government or corporate conspiracies (he's the Oliver

Stone of the Great White North), and here the evil scanners are doing the bidding of some shadowy nexus of intelligence agencies and multinational corporations. The film presents a believably generic-looking world in which telling friend from foe is nearly impossible.

⊙**DVD**

FA2, FA8

Goes well with: *Videodrome*

SCHOOL DAZE

U.S.   1988   C   121 min.   R   Comedy

Dir: Spike Lee

C: Laurence Fishburne, Giancarlo Esposito, Tisha Campbell, Kyme, Joe Seneca, Art Evans, Ellen Holly, Ossie Davis, Bill Nunn, Branford Marsalis, Kadeem Hardison, Spike Lee, Tyra Ferrell, Jasmine Guy, Kasi Lemmons, Samuel L. Jackson, Phyllis Hyman

Spike Lee's encore to his debut feature, the ingratiating comedy *She's Gotta Have It,* is a much more ambitious film that left most audiences wondering if Lee was a one-film wonder. They were wrong; *School Daze* offers a unique and very funny take on black-on-black prejudice. It's set in a historically black institution of higher learning where the Jigaboos (hip, happenin' brothers and sisters) compete with the Wannabes (conservative assimilators) for the soul of the campus. There isn't much of a plot, just a series of running skirmishes between the respective fraternities and sororities of the two factions. The cast, full of up-and-coming stars (look fast for Samuel L. Jackson), is energetic, there are several solid production numbers, and the film ends on a typical Lee note: a wake-up call for all African Americans to work together for the cause of eliminating a much more insidious form of prejudice.

⊙**DVD**

CO5, CO8, DR28

Goes well with: *Get on the Bus*

SECRET HONOR

U.S.   1984   C   90 min.   NR   Drama

Dir: Robert Altman

C: Philip Baker Hall

Sometimes less is more. With all due respect to Oliver Stone and Anthony Hopkins and their lavishly produced film about the only president to resign his office, the honor of the best movie about Richard Nixon goes to this one-man show featuring Philip Baker Hall. Robert Altman respects the conceit of this stage piece by Donald Freed and Arnold M. Stone—Nixon prowling the Oval Office during a restless night—and doesn't try to open things up with other characters and locales. But he takes full advantage of the mobility of the motion picture camera to offer angles, close-ups, and lighting variations that weren't available to theater audiences. As expected, Nixon, fueled by Chivas Regal, is in full rant, and given all we've learned in the quarter century since he left office, none of his expletive-undeleted thoughts about those who would destroy him seem improbable. Hall gets it all down, from full-blown arrogance to weeping insecurity.

DR17, DR25, DR27

Goes well with: *The Madness of King George*

THE SECRET OF ROAN INISH

U.S.   1994   C   102 min.   PG   Fantasy

Dir: John Sayles

C: Jeni Courtney, Eileen Colgan, Mick Lally, Richard Sheridan, John Lynch

A change of pace for John Sayles: his first film set outside the United States, and moreover an adaptation (of a novel by Rosalie K. Fry) by a writer-director who usually writes his screenplays from scratch. In 1940s Ireland, Fiona (Jeni Courtney), a ten-year-old girl, comes to live with her grandparents in a remote Irish fishing village and becomes fascinated, as all children are, by the myths and legends associated with this remote locale. Working more as fabulist than social realist, Sayles proves his versatility by weaving an enchanting spell of mystery. Like Fiona, we are new to this place (the film was shot in County Donegal), so we see everything through her eyes; it's Sayles's way of turning us all into ten-year-olds again, and it works splendidly.

⊙**DVD**

DR16, DR41, FA4, FA6

Goes well with: *Cold Comfort Farm*

SECRETS & LIES

ESSENTIAL

France/U.K.   1996   C   142 min.   R   Drama

Dir: Mike Leigh

C: Brenda Blethyn, Marianne Jean-Baptiste, Timothy Spall, Phyllis

Logan, Claire Rushbrook, Elizabeth Berrington, Michele Austin, Alison Steadman

It has the makings of a soap opera—adopted daughter seeks out birth mother after her stepparents' deaths—but Mike Leigh's drama of family ties is more sophisticated and affecting than any daytime serial. Hortense (Marianne Jean-Baptiste) is a young, successful black woman who manages to track down her birth mother, Cynthia (Brenda Blethyn), a white working-class woman who had given up Hortense for adoption before raising two other children by her long-gone husband. With some gentle prodding from Hortense, the two women strike up a friendship, but there are the other offspring to deal with: Roxanne (Claire Rushbrook), a street sweeper with a queen-size chip on her shoulder for Cynthia, and Maurice (Timothy Spall), a successful portrait photographer who mediates the brawls between his sister and mother. As in the best films of Jean Renoir, Leigh allows us to understand and sympathize with each character's motives, leading up to an inevitable revelation scene that's both cathartic and almost too painful to watch. The Independent Spirit Awards gave *Secrets & Lies* their Best Foreign Film prize.

DR5, DR11, DR28

Goes well with: *High Hopes*

THE SERVANT

U.K.   1963   B&W   115 min.   NR   Drama

Dir: Joseph Losey

C: Dirk Bogarde, James Fox, Sarah Miles, Wendy Craig, Catherine Lacey, Patrick Magee

Joseph Losey's first collaboration with writer Harold Pinter (followed by *Accident* and *The Go-Between*) is an adaptation of a novel by Robin Maugham, though the subject matter, a psychological tug-of-war exposing the vanities of class distinctions, is grade-A Pinter. James Fox is Tony, the wealthy and indolent master, and Dirk Bogarde is Hugo, his putative servant. From the start, Hugo is clearly in charge of the house, though he allows Tony the illusion that he's still the boss. Tony's girlfriend, Susan (Wendy Craig), rightly suspects Hugo's motives, so the servant hires a maid (Sarah Miles), whom he claims to be his sister, to seduce Tony. *The Remains of the Day* it's not; cutting social satire it is. Pinter's screenplay was honored by the New York Film Critics Circle.

⊙**DVD:** Available separately or as part of the Dirk Bogarde Collection, which includes *Accident* and *The Mind-Benders*.

DR5, DR19, DR27

Goes well with: *The Remains of the Day*

SEVEN BEAUTIES

ESSENTIAL

Italy 1976 C 115 min. R Comedy

Dir: Lina Wertmüller

C: Giancarlo Giannini, Fernando Rey, Shirley Stoler, Elena Fiore

Lina Wertmüller became the first woman director to be nominated for an Academy Award with this film, which remains her most enduring achievement. Giancarlo Giannini is Pasqualino, a wartime hood who does what he can to support his seven ugly sisters (the source of the title). His misadventures land him in a German prison camp, where, after a lifetime of having his way with women (shown in flashback), he is put to the ultimate test: Will he submit to the advances of a hefty woman guard (Shirley Stoler) to save his own skin? At the time of its release, *Beauties* inspired more hype than any film in recent memory, with Wertmüller compared to Orson Welles and Ingmar Bergman. She never fulfilled that kind of buildup, and some critics find this film in retrospect to be "fifth-rate slapstick" and "an obnoxious misogynistic freak show." To these eyes, it's a brilliant satire on the Italian male ego, comparable to *Divorce—Italian Style*.

⊙**DVD**

CO2, DR26

Goes well with: *Life Is Beautiful*

THE SEVEN SAMURAI

ESSENTIAL

Japan 1954 B&W 208 min. NR Action-Adventure

Dir: Akira Kurosawa

C: Toshiro Mifune, Takashi Shimura, Yoshio Inaba, Ko Kimura, Seiji Miyaguchi, Minoru Chiaki

Not only the greatest action film ever made, *The Seven Samurai* is also a meditation on the code of honor that all soldiers must follow when they agree to fight for a cause, no matter how great the odds against them are. The samurai in question are a group of warriors hand picked by Kambei

(Takashi Shimura), who has been hired by a village of farmers seeking relief from the bandits that regularly raid their stores of food. The farmers are appalled when Kambei returns to the village with only a paltry force (five other samurai, plus a warrior wannabe played with ferocious energy and humor by Toshiro Mifune), but he reminds them that they can fight for themselves as well—he and his men will train them. The full-length version of the film—accept nothing less—may seem slow going to fans of contemporary action films made for limited attention spans, but its rewards are many. Kurosawa fills his frame with movement: galloping horses, men running at world-class sprinter speeds, arrows whizzing back and forth, lance poles swung furiously. The dynamic final battle, shot in a rainstorm (the vertical sheets of water contrasting with the horizontal movement of men, animals, and weapons), is exhilarating moviemaking.

⊙**DVD:** Includes audio commentary by film historian Michael Jeck. AC4, AC8

Goes well with: *Yojimbo*

THE SEVENTH SEAL

ESSENTIAL

Sweden 1957 B&W 96 min. NR Drama
Dir: Ingmar Bergman
C: Max von Sydow, Gunnar Björnstrand, Nils Poppe, Bibi Andersson, Bengt Ekerot

One of the landmark Ingmar Bergman movies is this saga set in the plague-ravaged fourteenth century. A knight (Max von Sydow) returning from the Crusades to be reunited with his wife after ten years meets a traveling company of performers along the way. He also is tracked by a chess-playing black-robed figure symbolizing death. The knight has lost his faith in the blood and gore of the battlefield, and making his way through a countryside where people are dying of disease and starvation and being burned as witches isn't exactly improving his disposition. The performers, including a happy juggler, his wife, and their infant, offer another view. Though it is Bergman's best-known film (thanks to parodies and references in works by filmmakers from Woody Allen to Barry Levinson), its abstractions and discursive dialogue make it a matter of taste for some viewers.

⊙**DVD:** Includes audio commentary by film historian Peter Cowie. DR8, DR30

Goes well with: *The Burmese Harp*

SEX, LIES, AND VIDEOTAPE

ESSENTIAL

U.S.   1989   C   100 min.   R   Drama

Dir: Steven Soderbergh

C: James Spader, Andie MacDowell, Peter Gallagher, Laura San Giacomo

Independent filmmaking got a huge boost with the success of Steven Soderbergh's debut film, first at the Cannes Film Festival (where it won the Palme d'Or) and then with American audiences, critics, and award givers. James Spader plays Graham, the man with a video camera, intent on recording the sexual musings of young women. He drifts into a reunion with John (Peter Gallagher), a slick lawyer whose wife, Ann (Andie MacDowell), rightly suspects him of infidelity but doesn't know it's with her sister (Laura San Giacomo). The story boils down to a cat-and-mouse game between the impotent Graham and the repressed Ann as they try to strip one another, not of clothes but of pretensions. It's the kind of filmmaking the French thrive on but few American filmmakers seem to have the talent for. Soderbergh is a happy exception, and as his mostly brilliant career has proven, *sex, lies, and videotape* was no shallow come-on. The Independent Spirits awarded it Best Feature, Best Director, Best Female Lead, and Best Supporting Female; it also won the Audience Award at Sundance.

⊙**DVD:** Includes audio commentaries by Steven Soderbergh and filmmaker Neil LaBute.

DR18, DR20, DR21

Goes well with: *My Night at Maud's*

SEXY BEAST

U.K./Spain   2000   C   88 min.   R   Thriller

Dir: Jonathan Glazer

C: Ray Winstone, Ben Kingsley, Ian McShane, Amanda Redman, Cavan Kendall, Julianne White, Álvaro Monje, James Fox

Just when it seemed that the jokey *Lock, Stock and Two Smoking Barrels* had finished off the British crime film, along came this little gem. Gal (Ray Winstone) is a retired gangster, sunning himself poolside at his villa in Spain, when two unannounced visitors arrive. The first is an omen; the second is Don Logan (Ben Kingsley), an emissary from Gal's old boss, bearing an invitation to participate in an unusual heist back in dear ol' Blighty. The film is divided into two acts: Gal and Don's tug-of-war over the invitation, and Gal's inevitable return to London. Winstone, tousle-haired and laid back, and Kingsley, his head shaved and his attitude in full don't-mess-with-me mode, make great sparring partners, and the heist, which requires tunneling from a spa swimming pool into a neighboring bank vault, is staged with verve. Louis Mellis and David Scinto's script percolates with mannered tough-guy talk; it's like a collaboration between Harold Pinter and David Mamet.

⊙DVD

DR27, TH8

Goes well with: *Mona Lisa*

SHADOW OF THE VAMPIRE

U.S./U.K./Luxembourg   2000   C   93 min.   R   Drama

Dir: E. Elias Merhige

C: John Malkovich, Willem Dafoe, Cary Elwes, John Aden Gillet, Eddie Izzard, Udo Kier, Catherine McCormack

Working under the assumption that it isn't enough merely to dramatize the difficulties any film faces in getting made, or how a great film can flourish under the chaotic conditions of film production, *Shadow of the Vampire* poses a simple question: What if the actor hired to play Dracula in a film really was a vampire? And this is not just any Dracula film but the first great one, *Nosferatu,* the 1922 classic directed by F. W. Murnau. John Malkovich plays Murnau as the typically distracted artiste, more concerned with getting the light right than worrying about whether his leading man, Max Schreck (Willem Dafoe), is getting into the part a little too enthusiastically. It's a marvelous re-creation of silent film production methods, highly recommended for anyone interested in film history, with the caveat that it's tongue-in-cheek speculation.

⊙**DVD:** Special Edition contains audio commentary by E. Elias Merhige; "making of" featurette; interviews with cast and crew.

DR17, DR22

Goes well with: *Nosferatu*

SHADOWS

ESSENTIAL

U.S.   1960   B&W   87 min.   PG   Drama

Dir: John Cassavetes

C: Hugh Hurd, Lelia Goldoni, Ben Carruthers, Anthony Ray, Rupert Crosse

Actor John Cassavetes shot this film, his first venture as a director, for a reported $40,000 from earnings he made acting in a long-forgotten TV series, *Johnny Stacatto.* As in all Cassavetes films, a script of sorts existed, but the director urged his actors to improvise around their characters and the situations he had outlined for them. Those situations revolve around a light-skinned black woman (Lelia Goldoni) and her relationships with a white lover (Anthony Ray) and her two less-than-approving brothers (Ben Carruthers and Hugh Hurd). It's a wonderful snapshot of late-1950s New York and the era's new attitudes toward race and sex. Don't expect polished cinematography or clearly recorded dialogue; the unpolished presentation matches the messiness of these characters' lives.

⊙**DVD**

DR28, DR36

Goes well with: *Nothing But a Man*

SHAKESPEARE IN LOVE

ESSENTIAL

U.S./U.K.　1998　C　122 min.　R　Comedy

Dir: John Madden

C: Joseph Fiennes, Gwyneth Paltrow, Geoffrey Rush, Judi Dench, Simon Callow, Colin Firth, Imelda Staunton, Ben Affleck, Tom Wilkinson, Antony Sher

Leaving aside the question of Oscar justice and whether it is possible to compare any comedy with any drama in competition for an award, *Shakespeare in Love* is a total delight. Writers Marc Norman and Tom Stoppard's lovely conceit, that the Bard (Joseph Fiennes) required some real-life romance to be able to complete *Romeo and Juliet,* is perfectly realized by a talented cast and nimble direction by John Madden. The film is sexy, wise about love, knowing about what it takes to produce any stage show, and very twentieth century in its attitude toward the central female character, played by Gwyneth Paltrow. She's a woman promised in marriage to a fop who will whisk her away to his new plantation in some place called Virginia, but in the meantime she's determined to make a brief run at acting, even if that means disguising herself as a man to play a woman. For the record, yes, the film did win seven Oscars, among them Best Picture (over *Saving Private Ryan*) and awards for Paltrow (on whom so much depends, and she delivers), Judi Dench (for an amusing if brief turn as Queen Elizabeth), original screenplay, art direction, score, and costume design. The New York Film Critics Circle also recognized Norman and Stoppard's screenplay.

⊙**DVD:** Includes featurette, "Shakespeare in Love and on Film"; audio commentaries by John Madden, cast, and crew; deleted scenes.

CO6, CO9, CO10

Goes well with: *Tom Jones*

SHALL WE DANCE?

Japan 1996 C 118 min. PG Drama

Dir: Masayuki Suo

C: Koji Yakusho, Tamiyo Kusakari, Naoto Takenaka, Eriko Watanabe

Daring to borrow the title of an Astaire-Rogers classic, this Japanese comedy also dares to imagine that its two attractive central characters can have a relationship that is chaste. Sugiyama (Koji Yakusho) is locked into the world of the Japanese salaryman (think Jack Lemmon in *The Apartment*), with a neatly ordered existence. On his way home one night, he glances from his train into the window of a dance instruction studio and spots a particularly attractive instructor (played by former ballerina Tamiyo Kusakari). It turns out that Sugiyama is in need not of love (he has a wife and children at home) but of some meaning in his life. He becomes a dancer accomplished enough to enter a ballroom competition, and he and his instructor twirl their way to glory. Writer-director Masayuki Suo knows how to push the buttons that are standard equipment in the "Life's Lessons" subgenre, and the film's saving grace is that it avoids the easy out of cheapening an essentially spiritual quest with dirty dancing between the sheets.

DR4, DR16

Goes well with: *The Eel*

SHALLOW GRAVE

U.K. 1994 C 94 min. R Thriller

Dir: Danny Boyle

C: Kerry Fox, Christopher Eccleston, Ewan McGregor, Ken Stott, Keith Allen

Getting rich quickly and easily is the international mania, with lotteries, game shows, reality programs, and sure-fire stock buys all encouraging us to think that big money can be ours with very little effort. That's what makes the premise of *Shallow Grave*—three Scottish flatmates discover a suitcase full of money and decide to keep it—so easy to swallow. Juliet (Kerry Fox), David (Christopher Eccleston), and Alex (Ewan MacGregor) inhabit a crueler version of the *Seinfeld* world of in-jokes and putdowns of everyone not in the group. Were they less cynical, they also might be less suspicious of one another when things heat up. Writer John Hodge keeps turning up that thermostat, and director Danny Boyle offers distorting wide-angle camera angles to ratchet up the tension. *Shallow Grave* falls a hair short of being a bit too smart for its own good; Hodge, Boyle, and producer Andrew MacDonald made an even better film next time out, *Trainspotting*.

⊙**DVD**

TH4, TH5

Goes well with: *Blood Simple*

SHAME

ESSENTIAL

Sweden 1968 B&W 103 min. R Drama

Dir: Ingmar Bergman

C: Liv Ullmann, Max von Sydow, Gunnar Björnstrand, Sigge Furst, Birgitta Valberg

Ingmar Bergman's closest brush with making a war film is this masterpiece, about the effects a civil conflict have on a pair of married violinists. Jan and Eva Rosenberg (Max von Sydow and Liv Ullmann) have fled to an island, believing their location will insulate them from the reality raging on the mainland. Like Hoefgen, the actor in *Mephisto,* the Rosenbergs are convinced that being an artist inoculates you from the messier things in life. Denial leads to panic and then to near-despair, as they are forced out of their comfortable surroundings and must face the awful democracy of being war refugees. Arrests for collaboration, bribery, sexual compromise, and murder quickly follow, and in the end even their escape route is blocked by the war's victims. It's a staggering ground-level view of war that's more powerful than nearly any combat film.

DR38

Goes well with: *The Night of the Shooting Stars*

SHANGHAI TRIAD

China/France 1995 C 109 min. R Drama

Dir: Zhang Yimou

C: Gong Li, Li Baotian, Xiaoxiao Wang, Li Xuejian, Chun Sun

A fourteen-year-old boy, Shuisheng (Xiaxiao Wang), comes to 1930s Shanghai at the behest of his uncle, who works for the crime lord Tang (Li Baotian). In one week, this naïve boy witnesses a bloody gang war, is packed off to a secluded getaway with the boss and his mistress, and is drawn into further intrigue among the city's gangsters. This is a coming-of-age story with a vengeance that may remind some viewers of the E. L. Doctorow novel (and film) *Billy Bathgate*. In that story, however, the boy was an admirer of the criminal Dutch Schultz; Shuisheng is more a passive observer, though he eventually bonds with Bijou (Gong Li), the pampered mistress, for whom he performs menial chores. The most striking feature of Zhang Yimou's seventh film with Gong Li is Lu Yue's brilliant cinematography, recognized by the New York Film Critics Circle. In the film's third act, set on an island hide-out, color filters are employed to match the darkening mood of the story.

⊙**DVD**

DR6, DR24, DR41

Goes well with: *The Go-Between*

SHERMAN'S MARCH

ESSENTIAL

U.S.   1986   C   157 min.   NR   Documentary

Dir: Ross McElwee

It has nothing to do with the Civil War but everything to do with the South and one man's journey through its verdant landscape. Ross McElwee claims he set out to make a documentary about the far-reaching effects of Union General William Sherman's devastating 1864–65 sweep from Atlanta to the sea and then northward toward Richmond. A native southerner, McElwee begins his one-man odyssey in his adopted home in the North, filming himself making preparations to leave and admitting that he may look up a few old girlfriends along the way. He's easily diverted, and the film becomes a hilarious account of his love life, past and present, as he encounters, identifies, and tags species after species of southern womanhood. If McElwee weren't so lovelorn and generally distracted, you'd want to slap him for toting his camera everywhere, making people talk on the record about their feelings. But this is the modern age, after all, and most people, as we have learned from countless hours of TV news and talk shows (not to mention the recent rash of reality programs), have no compunction about "sharing" when a camera is pointed their way. McElwee also counts on the garrulousness of his subjects, and they all come through for him, especially an old teacher friend, Charleen, who is just sure she knows the right girl for him. The Sundance Film Festival gave *Sherman's March* its Grand Jury Prize for Documentary.

DO7, XT5

Goes well with: *The Tao of Steve*

SHE'S GOTTA HAVE IT

ESSENTIAL

U.S.   1986   C/B&W   84 min.   R   Comedy
Dir: Spike Lee
C: Tracy Camilla Johns, Tommy Redmond Hicks, John Canada Terrell, Spike Lee

In another time, Nola Darling would have been called promiscuous, but in the sexually liberated, women-on-top 1980s, Nola, the cheerful heroine played by Tracy Camilla Johns in Spike Lee's debut feature, is just indecisive. She's sleeping with three men: the sincere if a bit square Jamie (Tommy Redmond Hicks), the handsome but full of himself Greer (John Canada Terrell), and the hip-hopping bike messenger Mars Blackmon (Lee). You want great psychological insight? Baby baby baby (to quote Mars), you have got the wrong movie. You want comic riffing on the supersize male id from three different perspectives (I can take care of you, You can take care of me, and Take care of yourself and I'll do the same over here)? You've come to the right place. Lee has made better movies than this one, but he has never made one this relaxed or funny. The film won the Best First Feature award from the Independent Spirit Awards.

CO8, CO9

Goes well with: *Party Girl*

SHOAH

France   1985   C   566 min.   NR   Documentary
Dir: Claude Lanzmann

Claude Lanzmann's massive documentary strives to be the definitive film record of the Holocaust, and if it falls short (though it's difficult to think of another film that deserves that accolade), it's worth viewing for its many stunning images and moving interviews. Lanzmann does not use archival footage; he intends this to be a present-day record of his subject, so he tracks down survivors of the death camps, former guards, and, perhaps most revealing, ordinary citizens who lived near the camps. Some of those subjects are remarkably candid in justifying or minimizing the extermination policies of the Nazis. His camera takes us on tours of the camps as they exist today, allowing us to imagine the horrors that went on inside these walls. The length of the film and its tendency to go off on long tangents work against its impact. Still, the home viewing experience is the way to see a film of this length, especially if you can rent it for a week or two. Named Best Documentary by the New York Film Critics Circle.

DO3, DO9

Goes well with: *The Sorrow and the Pity*

SHOOT THE PIANO PLAYER

ESSENTIAL

France   1960   B&W   92 min.   NR   Drama
Dir: François Truffaut
C: Charles Aznavour, Marie Dubois, Nicole Berger, Michèle Mercier, Albert Rémy

What can you do for an encore when your first film is one of the cinema's great autobiographical works? François Truffaut did not make *Four Hundred More Blows;* instead he shifted gears to adapt David Goodis's moody novel *Down There,* about a former concert pianist reduced to working in a seedy cafe. Sad-eyed Charles Aznavour is perfectly cast as Charlie, the man with a bitter past (his wife committed suicide in a dispute over his career) who's trying to just get by. Charlie falls in love with Lena, a waitress at the café; his kid brother, Fido, is kidnapped by gangsters; Lena persuades him to return to the concert stage, and. . . . There is more, but a recitation of the plot can't convey the mood, a unique combination of energy and melancholy, and the amazing number of pop culture sources Truffaut drew on to make this deceptively simple film. Like all the best Truffaut, it is exceptionally generous to nearly all its characters.

⊙**DVD**

DR6, DR21, XT7

Goes well with: *Ulee's Gold*

SHORT CUTS
ESSENTIAL

U.S. 1993 C 189 min. R Drama
Dir: Robert Altman
C: Andie MacDowell, Bruce Davison, Jack Lemmon, Julianne Moore, Matthew Modine, Anne Archer, Fred Ward, Jennifer Jason Leigh, Chris Penn, Lili Taylor, Robert Downey, Jr., Madeleine Stowe, Tim Robbins, Lily Tomlin, Tom Waits, Frances McDormand, Peter Gallagher, Annie Ross, Lori Singer, Lyle Lovett, Buck Henry, Huey Lewis, Robert Doqui

Working from a set of eight short stories and a poem by Raymond Carver, Robert Altman (who scripted with Frank Barhydt) chose not to produce a series of vignettes but to interweave some of the characters from those stories. This technique works well with a writer like Carver, who carved out a certain turf, mostly on the lower-middle-class side of the tracks, among people with muffled hopes and ambitions. Carver evoked the quiet desperation that Thoreau first touched upon, and Altman illustrates that to shattering effect. Most of the California couples shown here are teetering on the edge of disaster, and the film's final-scene earthquake is enough to produce more than just property damage. There is, for all the indecent behavior shown here, an enormous amount of compassion for characters who practice phone sex, who cruise a family picnic ground for babes, who go right on fishing after they discover a dead body in the stream, who make threatening phone calls over a birthday cake delivery. For all the accolades that *Nashville* (a film with a heart hard as stone) has gathered, this is the epic film for which Altman will ultimately be remembered. The Independent Spirit Awards honored it with Best Feature, Best Director, and Best Screenplay awards.

DR20, DR29
Goes well with: *Happiness*

SHORT EYES

U.S. 1977 C 104 min. R Drama
Dir: Robert M. Young
C: Bruce Davison, José Pérez, Nathan George, Don Blakely, Shawn Elliott, Curtis Mayfield, Freddy Fender, Miguel Piñero

The title is prison slang for the lowest of the low, the child molester, and this adaptation of Miguel Piñero's play doesn't sugarcoat the treatment a short eyes can expect from his fellow cons. Bruce Davison isn't just one of the few white men in his cell block; he's also in for the crime that no one can excuse. Filmed on location in an abandoned New York City prison, *Short Eyes* is a showcase for Piñero's ear for the way men behind bars establish and maintain turf. Watch for music stars Curtis Mayfield and Freddy Fender among the cast. Piñero's short life was the subject of a recent film, starring Benjamin Bratt.

DR26, DR32

Goes well with: *Kiss of the Spider Woman*

SID AND NANCY

U.S./U.K.   1986   C   111 min.   R   Drama

Dir: Alex Cox

C: Gary Oldman, Chloe Webb, Drew Schofield, David Hayman, Debby Bishop, Courtney Love

Sid Vicious, bass player for the seminal British punk band the Sex Pistols, and Nancy Spungen, his American girlfriend, died ignoble deaths in May 1979, less than two years after the band's debut recordings. Vicious was no Kurt Cobain (and Spungen, basically a groupie, was certainly no Courtney Love), and as writer-director Alex Cox freely admits, this is not a movie about the music but about their love. Gary Oldman and Chloe Webb give their all in the lead performances and do persuade us that, through all the drug-fueled madness that ended with murder and a drug overdose in New York's Chelsea Hotel, these two kids were crazy about each other. They needed each other, they fed off each other's weaknesses, and rock and roll made it all possible.

⊙**DVD:** Includes audio commentary; documentary, "England's Glory"; audio interview with Sid Vicious; Sid and Nancy Spungen interviews from *D.O.A.: A Right of Passage.*

DR10, DR17, DR23

Goes well with: *The Filth and the Fury*

SIRENS

Australia/U.K.   1994   C   94 min.   R   Drama

Dir: John Duigan

C: Hugh Grant, Tara Fitzgerald, Sam Neill, Elle MacPherson, Portia de Rossi, Kate Fischer

It's such an obvious setup that you may find yourself groaning just reading about it. Uptight minister visits liberated painter, famed for his erotic religious works, to try to persuade him to cease and desist, while said minister's wife discovers the joys of romping nude with said artist's models. Two aspects make writer-director John Duigan's film an easy pill to swallow: It is based on fact, the painter being Australian Norman Lindsey, whose work in the early decades of the twentieth century was considered somewhat scandalous (he's now considered a national treasure down under); and the performers throw themselves into this essentially silly story with abandon. Hugh Grant, stuttering like he's a reincarnation of Jimmy Stewart, is the allegedly progressive Anglican, Tara Fitzgerald his buttoned-up wife, Sam Neill is Lindsey, and among the three sirens is the striking Elle MacPherson, she of a dozen or more *Sports Illustrated* swimsuit issues. If you can't afford a trip to Australia's breathtaking Blue Mountains (described by one visitor as "the Grand Canyon with trees"), *Sirens* will take you there, which makes one more reason to see this charming comedy.

⊙**DVD**

DR2, DR16, DR17

Goes well with: *La Belle Noiseuse*

SLACKER

ESSENTIAL

U.S.   1991   C   97 min.   R   Comedy

Dir: Richard Linklater

C: Richard Linklater, Rudy Basquez, Jean Caffeine, Jan Hockey, Stephan Hockey, Mark James, Bob Boyd

Richard Linklater's debut feature is a series of vignettes, set in the Austin neighborhood known as the Drag, a six-block stretch of Guadalupe Street that borders the campus of the University of Texas. The general consensus among the self-styled philosophers who practice the fine art of creative indolence in the coffee shops, bars, bookstores, and clubs of this mecca for moderns seems to be, This country is going to hell, but hey man, don't get too upset about it, just have another beer/toke. Linklater's pseudodocumentary approach is not some festival of talking heads staring directly at the camera; the gliding camerawork (by Lee Daniel) eases us in and out of conversations as though we were at a party, dropping by various points of the room to eavesdrop. It's a unique comedy that deserves multiple viewings. That is Linklater as the cab passenger in the opening scene.

CO8, CO11
Goes well with: *Dazed and Confused*

SLAM

U.S.   1998   C   103 min.   R   Drama
Dir: Marc Levin
C: Saul Williams, Sonja Sohn, Bonz Malone, Marion Barry, Jr.

The best movie about prison life since *Short Eyes, Slam* is also a drama about an unusual form of redemption. Raymond Joshua (Saul Williams) is a low-level Washington, D.C., drug dealer caught in the aftermath of a shooting with a small amount of marijuana. In D.C. Jail, he becomes a target for a gang of inmates convinced he set up the victim— his own boss—for a double-cross; but in the film's best scene, he literally raps his way out of a jailyard assault. Ray is a street poet, and his talent comes to the attention of Hopha, a veteran inmate (Bonz Malone), and Lauren, a creative writing teacher (Sonja Sohn). Freed on bail, Ray returns to the streets with a new message for his wounded pal and homeys. This Grand Jury Prize winner at Sundance has the authenticity of an postwar Italian neorealist film and none of the bluster of so many commercial films of the 1980s and 1990s that offer mixed messages about the glamour of street life. And yes, that's former D.C. mayor Marion Barry, Jr., as the judge who sentences Ray to prison with the admonition, "These drugs are ruining our community."

⊙**DVD:** Includes audio commentaries by Marc Levin and Bonz Malone.

DR2, DR6, DR16, DR26, DR28, DR36
Goes well with: *Menace II Society*

SLING BLADE

ESSENTIAL

U.S.   1996   C   134 min.   R   Drama
Dir: Billy Bob Thornton
C: Billy Bob Thornton, Dwight Yoakam, J. T. Walsh, John Ritter, Lucas Black, Natalie Canerday, James Hampton, Robert Duvall, Jim Jarmusch

Billy Bob Thornton's contributions as cowriter and actor in the surprise independent hit *One False Move* were lost in the excitement over director Carl Franklin and female lead Cynda Williams. Flash forward four years, and it's Billy Bob's coming-out party, an expansion of a short film he wrote but did not star in. This time Thornton made sure all eyes would be on him, as he nabbed the juicy role of Karl Childers, the mentally impaired man-child. Just released from an institution, where he has spent most of his life for committing a horrific murder when he was literally a child, Karl's adjustment to a world he never made is slow and sometimes painful. His friendships with a young boy, Frank Wheatley (Lucas Black), and his boss (John Ritter) are offset by the menace of Doyle (Dwight Yoakam), the abusive boyfriend of Frank's mom (Natalie Canerday). You can see almost immediately where all this is headed, and *Sling Blade*'s only defect is how long it takes to get there. The narrative pace is pitched at a clip to match Karl's drawn-out drawl, and that eventually diminishes the impact of the drama. Thornton's screenplay won an Oscar, and the film was honored at the Independent Spirit Awards as Best First Feature.

⊙**DVD**

DR21, DR34, DR41

Goes well with: *Cockfighter*

SLUMS OF BEVERLY HILLS

U.S.   1998   C   91 min.   R   Comedy

Dir: Tamara Jenkins

C: Natasha Lyonne, Alan Arkin, Marisa Tomei, Kevin Corrigan, Jessica Walter, Carl Reiner, Rita Moreno, Eli Marienthal, David Krumholz, Mena Suvari

Writer-director Tamara Jenkins's debut film is that rare coming-of-age comedy produced in the last twenty-five years that is spunky, sassy, and above all sensitive about the way teenagers deal with problems like embarrassing parental behavior and breasts that are too big. Vivian Abromowitz (Natasha Lyonne, who's wonderful) has two problems: her well-developed breasts and her peripatetic family, led by a single dad, Murray (Alan Arkin), with limited means but a determination that his kids attend the best schools in the Los Angeles area. That means temporarily renting apartments in less desirable neighborhoods that happen to be within first-rate school districts. Vivian's cup runneth over with other problems: a cute neighbor (Kevin Corrigan) who is just the far side of weird, and a ditsy cousin (Marisa Tomei) fleeing her wealthy parents to share quarters with the already strapped Abromowitz clan (there are an older and younger brother, too). Jenkins creates a half-dozen memorable characters but keeps our eyes on Vivian, a girl looking for some stability in her life but not so desperate that she'll make a big mistake to get it.

⊙ **DVD**

CO3, CO4, CO5

Goes well with: *A Soldier's Daughter Never Cries*

SMOKE

U.S./Germany 1995 C 112 min. R Drama

Dir: Wayne Wang

C: William Hurt, Harvey Keitel, Stockard Channing, Harold Perrineau, Jr., Forest Whitaker, Victor Argo, Giancarlo Esposito, Ashley Judd

A drama that centers on a Brooklyn smoke shop, *Smoke*'s script, by novelist Paul Auster, feels like something for a French or Italian film in which characters drift in and out of a neighborhood café, sharing their problems with the owner or simply commenting on life. Harvey Keitel plays Augie Wren, the shop owner, whose biggest problem is a flood that cost him a shipment of Cuban cigars. His favorite customer, a writer named Paul Benjamin (William Hurt), is grieving over the loss of his wife; Thomas "Rashid" Cole (Harold Perrineau, Jr.) is a troubled young black man whom Benjamin befriends. In smaller roles are Forest Whitaker as Cole's estranged father, Stockard Channing as Wren's ex-wife, and Ashley Judd as her junkie daughter. The tone is one of gentle ruefulness, the narrative pace leisurely, and the rewards modestly satisfying. Auster was honored by the Independent Spirit Awards as Best First Screenplay.

DR11, DR36

Goes well with: *Wings of Desire*

SMOKE SIGNALS

U.S. 1998 C 88 min. PG-13 Drama

Dir: Chris Eyre

C: Adam Beach, Evan Adams, Irene Bedard, Gary Farmer, Tantoo Cardinal, Cody Lightning, Tom Skerritt

If it weren't for *Powwow Highway, Smoke Signals* would earn the distinction of being the first Native American road movie. The films beat a similar path, from a reservation in the north (here the Coeur d'Alene community in Idaho) to the southwest (Phoenix); the not-so-easy riders in both films are odd couples (here, Evan Adams as the nerdy Thomas-

Builds-the-Fire and Adam Beach as the angry Victor Joseph); and the mission is similar (to deal with family business). The films even share an actor, Gary Farmer, the laconic hulk of *Powwow Highway,* here playing Victor's estranged father. The film gets off to a wonderful start with a witty introduction to life on the Rez through a voice-over originating from its radio station (shades of *Northern Exposure*'s "Chris in the Morning" program). Sherman Alexie adapted this amiable comedy-drama from a story in his wonderfully titled collection *The Lone Ranger and Tonto Fistfight in Heaven,* and the film picked up a rare double at Sundance, the Filmmaker's Trophy and the Audience Award.

⊙**DVD**

DR12, DR16, DR28, XT5

Goes well with: *Powwow Highway*

SMOOTH TALK

U.S. 1985 C 92 min. PG-13 Drama

Dir: Joyce Chopra

C: Treat Williams, Laura Dern, Mary Kay Place, Levon Helm, Elizabeth Berridge

Based on a short story by Joyce Carol Oates, *Smooth Talk* captures that author's feel for the uncertainties of sexual awakening. Laura Dern is a teenager with a feisty attitude toward her parents (Mary Kay Place and Levon Helm), which goes with the territory. When she finds herself the object of attention from a handsome older man (Treat Williams), she's both flattered and not a little confused. And when he happens to drop by her house while her parents are away, the stage is set for a life-turning experience. Or is it? The film's tantalizing ambiguities almost demand a second viewing. A Grand Jury Prize winner at Sundance, this film was originally shown on PBS's *American Playhouse* series.

DR41

Goes well with: *Rambling Rose*

A SOLDIER'S DAUGHTER NEVER CRIES

U.S. 1998 C 127 min. R Drama

Dir: James Ivory

C: Kris Kristofferson, Barbara Hershey, Leelee Sobieski, Jesse Bradford, Anthony Roth Constanzo, Dominique Blanc, Jane Birkin

At first, this product of the Merchant-Ivory team (producer Ismail Merchant and director James Ivory, plus writer Ruth Prawer Jhabvala, here writing in collaboration with Ivory) doesn't seem to fit their résumé, which consists largely of adaptations of distinguished literary works (*Room with a View, Howards End, The Remains of the Day*). It is, however, concerned at least tangentially with the literary life, in this case that of author James Jones. His daughter, Kaylie, is the film's focus; her autobiographical novel (which allows for name changes and other acts of poetic license) is the basis for the story of a successful writer who decamps from America in the 1950s for Paris, where he and his wife raise his daughter and son, only to return to America when the kids are teens. Not really a "My Dad Was a Celebrity" story, this is a tale of cultural adjustment doubled. Leelee Sobieski is Channe, the girl who learns to *parle français* only to have to switch gears and learn the social mores of a Long Island high school just as she's awash in hormonal changes. The film carefully tracks the way she compensates for always being (or feeling like) an outsider. Kris Kristofferson is Bill, the stand-in for Jones, and Barbara Hershey is Marcella, stand-in for Gloria Jones; they're both excellent at playing loving but distracted parents.

⊙**DVD**

DR7, DR11, DR17, DR41

Goes well with: *Slums of Beverly Hills*

SONGWRITER

U.S.   1984   C   94 min.   R   Comedy

Dir: Alan Rudolph

C: Willie Nelson, Kris Kristofferson, Melinda Dillon, Rip Torn, Lesley Ann Warren, Mickey Raphael, Richard C. Sarafian

It may seem like an amiable companion piece to *Roadie,* director Alan Rudolph's other comedy about the business of making music, but it should be noted that Rudolph was reportedly asked to step in and direct this film about country singers only three days before shooting began. Working from a script by Bud Schrake, Rudolph basically stayed out of the way of his two charismatic stars, Willie Nelson and Kris Kristofferson, for this tale of backstabbing promoters (Richard C. Sarafian), honky-tonk women (Lesley Ann Warren), and other assorted music-biz types. The story, about the good ol' boys getting something back from the music people whose only talent lies in ripping off the creative types, is just a way of filling time between the numerous songs, including "Who'll Buy My Memories," one of Nelson's most haunting compositions.

CO10
Goes well with: *Roadie*

THE SORROW AND THE PITY

ESSENTIAL

Switzerland/France/West Germany 1970 B&W 260 min. PG Documentary

Dir: Marcel Ophüls

In France, they would never be called the greatest generation, the ordinary citizens who lived under the Nazi Occupation and either did nothing to fight their oppressors or collaborated with them. Marcel Ophüls's landmark documentary was the first film to extensively record the first-hand memories of that shameful chapter in French history. He concentrates on one town, Clermont-Ferrand, to present a story that is by turns heartbreaking and maddening. Ophüls's film also raises troubling questions about human behavior; who's to say that any one of us wouldn't make the same choices if it meant our survival? That's the source of the film's compassionate title. For those who have noted the Academy's obsession with recognizing nearly any film about World War II and in particular the Holocaust, it's astounding to recall that this masterwork lost the Oscar to an all-but-forgotten documentary called *The Hellstrom Chronicle;* the New York Film Critics Circle got it right.

⊙**DVD**
DO3, DO9
Goes well with: *Au Revoir, les Enfants*

SOUND AND FURY

U.S./U.K. 2000 C 80 min. NR Documentary
Dir: Josh Aronson

The ability of medical science to overcome a handicap runs into a surprising obstacle in this compact and emotionally riveting exploration of the deaf community's resistance to cochlear ear implants. The Artinian brothers—Peter is deaf, Chris is not—are faced with the same decision over one of their children. Peter is married to Nita, a deaf woman, and all three of their kids are deaf; the oldest, an amazingly bright five-year-old, Heather, decides she wants the operation, but her parents are torn. They love the nurturing environment that the deaf community has provided them and are afraid that if their daughter can hear and speak, she'll want little to do with them. Chris's decision is easier; he and his hearing wife, Mari, have three children, and only one—an infant twin— can't hear. The debates between the brothers and with their parents (who can both hear and want the implants for both children) are almost too painful to watch at times. The film is more even-handed than you might expect, though the filmmakers might have offered more evidence to support Peter and Nita's claims.

⊙**DVD:** Includes deleted scenes.

DO7, DO11

Goes well with: *Careful, He Might Hear You*

THE SPANISH PRISONER

U.S.   1998   C   112 min.   PG   Thriller

Dir: David Mamet

C: Campbell Scott, Steve Martin, Rebecca Pidgeon, Ben Gazzara, Ricky Jay, Felicity Huffman, Ed O'Neill

Returning to the world of con games that was the focus of *House of Games,* his debut as a director, David Mamet's film about a disaffected high-tech systems developer fools us even as we know the scam is on. Mamet's sleight-of-hand, at least for viewers who choose not to try to second-guess everything in the story, is amazing. He's like the talented magician whose little bits of business are always masking his true intentions. Campbell Scott is effectively nerdy and sincere as the mark, a man who thinks his company is going to rip him off, so he turns to suave stranger Steve Martin (who hardly ever blinks) for a better offer. Rebecca Pidgeon is the suspicious secretary who fuels Scott's paranoia about nearly everyone but the key person. The film brilliantly captures how the contemporary business world, in which everything is caused to move at the speed of light, is ripe for this kind of shenanigans; the scam is over and done before you can send a confirming fax or leave a message on someone's pager.

⊙**DVD**

TH2, TH5

Goes well with: *House of Games*

SPANKING THE MONKEY

U.S.   1994   C   100 min.   NR   Comedy-Drama

Dir: David O. Russell

C: Jeremy Davies, Alberta Watson, Benjamin Hendrickson, Carla Gallo

Spanking the Monkey has picked up a reputation as a comedy about incest. That's not exactly true; *Spanking* is a very funny movie, and it does contain a close encounter between a teenage son and his bedridden mom (kids, don't try this at home), but that scene is definitely not played for laughs. Ray Abelli (Jeremy Davies) is in that twilight zone between high school and a premed education at MIT. Instead of working an internship in Washington, D.C., he's confined to his suburban New York home with his mother (Alberta Watson), suffering from a broken leg, while his salesman father (Benjamin Hendrickson) is off on an extended business trip. Ray seems ill at ease everywhere, in part because he has lived so long with two people whose marriage is an extended screaming match. He's awkwardly inept with a high school girl with a crush on him, and clearly out of step with his putative high school buddies, who aren't that impressed that he's going to MIT in the fall. The one person who can offer him comfort is both the right and the wrong person for the job. Writer-director David O. Russell creates a hothouse atmosphere here, but he doesn't push the envelope into full-blown decadence. Winner of Independent Spirit Awards for Best First Feature and Best First Screenplay, and of the Audience Award at Sundance.

DR11, DR19, DR41
Goes well with: *Ghost World*

STANLEY KUBRICK: A LIFE IN PICTURES

ESSENTIAL

U.S. 2001 C 142 min. NR Documentary
Dir: Jan Harlan
C: Tom Cruise (narrator), Woody Allen, Alex Cox, Nicole Kidman, Malcolm McDowell, Matthew Modine, Jack Nicholson, Alan Parker, Sydney Pollack, Martin Scorsese, Steven Spielberg, Peter Ustinov

Perhaps the ultimate independent filmmaker, Stanley Kubrick took his own sweet time to make films his own way. Except for his earliest films, Kubrick's work was financed and distributed by major Hollywood studios, but he enjoyed a rare autonomy over his work. After Kubrick died in 1999, his brother-in-law, Jan Harlan, who was also credited as producer on several of his films, assembled this documentary about the filmmaker whose work proved a lightning rod for critics and audiences. There are generous clips from all of his features and interviews with key collaborators (including a rare documentary appearance by Jack Nicholson), as well as his wife and one of his daughters. There are also home movies of Kubrick and his family, who sometimes looked like reluctant performers. It's an authorized film, so there is little negative space here, though in one moment from the filming of *The Shining* Kubrick appears to be bullying actress Shelley Duvall, who confirms our impression with her interview. But this is likely to remain the most complete screen portrait we'll have of Kubrick for many years. (For the record, the best Kubrick films are *The Killing, Spartacus, Dr. Strangelove, 2001: A Space Odyssey, Barry Lyndon,* and *Full Metal Jacket.*)

⊙**DVD:** Available only in the Stanley Kubrick Collection, which includes remastered prints of *2001: A Space Odyssey, Barry Lyndon, A Clockwork Orange, Dr. Strangelove, Full Metal Jacket, Lolita, The Shining,* and *Eyes Wide Shut.*

DO4, DO5

Goes well with: *Wild Man Blues*

STARTUP.COM

U.S. 2001 C 103 min. R Documentary

Dir: Chris Hegedus and Jehane Noujaim

The swift rise and fall of companies in the digital age is, by nature of the ever-shifting landscape, tough to document. *Startup.com* succeeds admirably in capturing the high expectations and low returns of an Internet website that sounded like a good idea at the time. Former high school buddies Kaleil Isaza Tuzman (the salesman of the pair) and Tom Herman (the techie) intend to provide citizens of the Net with a site where they can do business with their local government and pay a parking ticket online. Tuzman is Mr. Outside, always on his way to or from a meeting, his cell phone glued to his ear; Herman is Mr. Inside, the guy who dreams in HTML. They should complement each other, and they do, for a time. But when the going gets tough, Herman requires more quality time with his daughter (he's divorced), while Tuzman plows ahead with a little coup d'état. In the spirit of the cinema verité approach of Hegedus's husband and frequent collaborator D. A. Pennebaker (*Dont Look Back, The War Room*), the style of the film is more show than tell. Not all relationships are fully explained, and chronology is a bit hard to follow, though you can tell time has elapsed if Herman's facial hair has changed. (It does so at least three times over the course of recorded events.) Codirector Jehane Noujaim's relationship with Tuzman (they were former platonic roommates) allowed her and Hegedus extensive access to him, and he is not exactly a wallflower when the camera is on.

⊙**DVD:** Includes audio commentaries by Chris Hegedus and Jehane Noujaim, and "Documentarians on Documentary" featurette.

DO1, DO7

Goes well with: *Pi*

STATE AND MAIN

U.S./France   2000   C   105 min.   R   Comedy
Dir: David Mamet
C: Alec Baldwin, William H. Macy, Philip Seymour Hoffman, Sarah Jessica Parker, Rebecca Pidgeon, Charles Durning, Patti LuPone, David Paymer, Julia Stiles, Ricky Jay

Perennial tough guy David Mamet (*House of Games, The Spanish Prisoner*) exposes his lighter side in this comedy about a Hollywood film crew invading a small New England town. The characters are familiar types—the randy male star (Alec Baldwin), his insecure female costar (Sarah Jessica Parker), the timid screenwriter (Philip Seymour Hoffman), the harassed director (William H. Macy), the obnoxious producer (David Paymer), the thick-headed mayor (Charles Durning) and his social climber wife (Patti LuPone)—but Mamet gives them all a fresh coat of paint, and the skilled cast makes them as funny as in any previous films of this subgenre. In particular, Hoffman is allowed to show a previously untapped talent for romantic moves as he courts a local bookstore owner (Rebecca Pidgeon).

⊙**DVD:** Includes audio commentaries by Sarah Jessica Parker, William H. Macy, David Paymer, and Patti LuPone.

CO10, CO11

Goes well with: *Living in Oblivion*

STATE OF SIEGE

France/Italy/West Germany   1973   C   120 min.   NR   Thriller
Dir: Costa-Gavras
C: Yves Montand, Renato Salvatori, O. E. Hasse, Jacques Weber

As a political thriller, *State of Siege* isn't in the same league as Costa-Gavras's big hit, *Z,* but then few films in that genre are. What *State of*

THE STORY OF ADELE H / 375

Siege lacks in sheer excitement it makes up for in the courage of its conviction that U.S. involvement in the politics of Latin America is meddling of the worst kind in the affairs of sovereign nations. Yves Montand plays Philip Santore, a semifictional version of Daniel Mitrone, an employee of the U.S. Agency for International Development who was assassinated by Uruguayan dissidents in the 1960s. *State of Siege,* which caused a major political flap when it was denied a screening in Washington's Kennedy Center, hasn't dated much, with reports still coming out of Latin America of the heavy hand of America working to protect its vital interests.

DR25, TH1

Goes well with: *Z*

STORMY MONDAY

U.K./U.S.   1988   C   93 min.   R   Drama

Dir: Mike Figgis

C: Melanie Griffith, Tommy Lee Jones, Sting, Sean Bean, James Cosmo

Taking its title from the great blues song by T-Bone Walker, *Stormy Monday* also borrows the rueful mood of that tune for its story of a jazz club owner fighting to keep developers from bulldozing the character right out of his town. That town is Newcastle, England, a resort in bad need of a makeover, if you believe American businessman Cosmo (Tommy Lee Jones at his oiliest). Sting plays Finney, the club owner who won't sell out, Melanie Griffith is his star waitress, and Sean Bean is Brendan, the club janitor with other talents than just sweeping floors. The movie lays on the smoky atmosphere and sinuous music—it's hard to recall any scenes taking place during the day—for a timely look at Yankee corporate imperialism and a romantic view of those who stand up to it.

DR23, DR36

Goes well with: *'Round Midnight*

THE STORY OF ADELE H

France   1975   C   97 min.   PG   Drama

Dir: François Truffaut

C: Isabelle Adjani, Bruce Robinson, Sylvia Marriott, Reubin Dorey

The teenage Isabelle Adjani reportedly broke a contract with the Comédie-Française to make her breakthrough film with François Truffaut. Parisian theatergoers' loss was international filmgoers' gain, as Adjani offered a stunning interpretation of a woman obsessed by love. Adele H was Adele Hugo, daughter of the French literary lion, whose fixation on an English soldier swept her along to his various postings in France, Canada, and Barbados. Adjani's face was not just camera-friendly; she was capable of expressing a sea-change in emotion without any obvious effort. She was nominated for an Academy Award for her performance, losing to Louise Fletcher in *One Flew Over the Cuckoo's Nest*'s sweep of the major Oscars. She did win the New York Film Critics Circle prize; the critics also gave the Best Screenplay award to Jean Gruault, Suzanne Schiffman, and Truffaut.

⊙**DVD**

DR17, DR18

Goes well with: *Two English Girls*

THE STORY OF WOMEN

France 1988 C 110 min. NR Drama

Dir: Claude Chabrol

C: Isabelle Huppert, François Cluzet, Marie Trintignant, Nils Tavernier

Isabelle Huppert stars in this fact-based tale of a woman who provided abortions in occupied France and was guillotined for her services. In the current highly charged atmosphere, in which the debate over freedom of choice and right to life often operates on a level of malevolent threat or high-flown rhetoric, it's fascinating to watch the same topic in a totally different context. Huppert's Marie Latour is only trying to get by; her fairly useless husband cannot support her, and she takes a lover as much out of spite as need. The opportunity to help women who have nowhere else to turn appeals to her, even though she's aware that the Vichy government has declared abortions a crime against humanity and the state. Claude Chabrol's restrained approach to the material muffles any melodramatics but not the emotional impact of Latour's decision. Winner of the Best Foreign Language Film award from the New York Film Critics Circle.

DR24, DR38, DR39

Goes well with: *The Marriage of Maria Braun*

STRADA, LA.

See *La Strada*

STRANGER THAN PARADISE

ESSENTIAL

U.S./West Germany   1984   B&W   90 min.   R   Comedy
Dir: Jim Jarmusch
C: John Lurie, Eszter Balint, Richard Edson, Cecillia Stark

Stranger Than Paradise opens in New York, with its trio of nearly somnambulant characters offering variations on the "Whadya doin' tonight?" theme of at least half the beer commercials currently shown on TV. Willie (John Lurie) is entertaining his cousin Eva (Eszter Balint), who's visiting from Hungary, while his pal Eddie (Richard Edson) hangs out. They move on to Cleveland to check in on Willie and Eva's relatives, and then on to Florida, if only to escape the monotony of the Ohio winterscape, well known to director Jim Jarmusch, a native of nearby Akron. (The slow black-and-white pan across wintertime Lake Erie, where sky and water are an indistinguishable gray, is the funniest shot in the film.) Anyone who claims that *Seinfeld* is the great contemporary comedy in which nothing happens has never seen *Stranger Than Paradise.* Jarmusch's debut feature mixes two camps of deadpan humor: midwestern normal and Manhattan hip. It gets funnier every time you see it or think about it. The U.S. Film Festival (Sundance) gave it a Special Jury award.

⊙**DVD**

CO2, XT5

Goes well with: *Powwow Highway*

STRAWBERRY AND CHOCOLATE

Cuba   1994   C   110 min.   R   Drama
Dir: Tomás Gutiérrez Alea and Juan Carlos Tabío
C: Jorge Perugorría, Vladimir Cruz, Mirta Ibarra, Francisco Gattorono

Havana, 1979: a bad time and place to be gay. Diego (Jorge Perugorría) knows that, and he lives a semicloseted life, keeping his enthusiasm under wraps or carefully contained in his apartment. An encounter with David (Vladimir Cruz), a student committed to Marxist politics and as straight as they come, offers Diego a challenge. If he can't seduce this lovely young man, he can offer friendship and perhaps a little perspective on the government David so blindly supports. *Strawberry and Chocolate* keeps its odd-couple premise from degenerating into a gay version of *The Defiant Ones* by tamping down the political speeches and concentrating on each man's need: Diego's to be a teacher (he's always offering David books to read) and David's to get some perspective on his life. Winner of a Special Jury Prize at Sundance.

DR12, DR19, DR25

Goes well with: *Kiss of the Spider Woman*

STREETWISE

ESSENTIAL

U.S. 1984 C 92 min. NR Documentary

Dir: Martin Bell

The presence in the streets of prosperous cities, like Seattle, of hundreds of homeless children is the subject of Martin Bell's searing documentary. There are no sociologists or caseworkers interviewed here, just the street kids telling their stories, mostly of how they get through a day, sometimes making vague reference to how they wound up where they are. It's an utterly unsentimental look at a serious problem that most TV news shows would layer over with insipid music and portentous narration. It's also a harrowing companion piece to Bell's next film, *American Heart,* also shot in Seattle, whose (fictional) story took an occasional dip into these murky waters. Winner of a Special Jury Prize at the U.S. Film Festival (Sundance).

DO1, DO7

Goes well with: *American Heart*

SUBURBIA

U.S. 1996 C 118 min. R Drama

Dir: Richard Linklater

C: Giovanni Ribisi, Steve Zahn, Amie Carey, Samia Shoaib, Ajay Naidu, Nicky Katt, Parker Posey

Do you really need to see a film about bored suburban white kids who hang out at all-night convenience stores? You do if it's directed by Richard Linklater, the man behind *Slacker* and *Dazed and Confused,* the man who put the fun back in ennui (it's in there somewhere; just keep looking). Linklater, working from a play by Eric Bogosian, charts the comings and goings of a posse of get-a-lifes who are waiting not for Godot but for a former high school classmate who hit it big as a rock star. He is expected to cruise by his old hangout any moment now. Bogosian's script may seem a little tidy, but it also contains plenty of snarky little surprises; just when you think you have someone figured out, they go and do or say something to change your mind. Think *Clerks* without the extreme alpha-male attitude.

DR20, DR32, DR41

Goes well with: *Dazed and Confused*

SUNDAY, BLOODY SUNDAY

U.K. 1971 C 110 min. R Drama

Dir: John Schlesinger

C: Glenda Jackson, Peter Finch, Murray Head, Peggy Ashcroft, Tony Britton

One of the first mainstream films to deal honestly with a bisexual character caught in a romantic triangle, *Sunday, Bloody Sunday* offers two powerful performances at different points of that triangle. (And, as the Meat Loaf song says, two out of three ain't bad.) Peter Finch and Glenda Jackson are at their fearsome best, delivering Penelope Gilliat's lines with intelligence and intensity. Murray Head (as the object of affection for both Finch and Jackson) isn't up to the level of his costars, in part because his role seems undernourished. John Schlesinger, coming off his Oscar-winning effort in *Midnight Cowboy,* scales back his flashy direction here, to good effect. Gilliat's screenplay won an award from the New York Film Critics Circle.

DR19

Goes well with: *Strawberry and Chocolate*

A SUNDAY IN THE COUNTRY

France 1984 C 94 min. G Drama

Dir: Bertrand Tavernier

C: Louis Ducreux, Sabine Azéma, Michel Aumont, Geneviève Mnich, Monique Chaumette

An elderly widowed painter asks his married son and his family, along with his single daughter, to spend a summer's day at the longtime family home. Ladmiral (Louis Ducreux) is a painter entering the twilight of a career in which he defied the Impressionist movement to paint in his own style. (The film is set in the World War I era.) His son, Gonzague (Michel Aumont), is a stuffy banker who had aspirations to become a painter but not the nerve to follow his father's act. The daughter, Irene (Sabine Azéma), shows up in a spiffy motorcar (Gonzague and his family arrived by train), and it's clear that her energy will shake up things for the rest of the afternoon. There are no emotional confrontations or deep dark secrets revealed in this drama, but it's a deceptively simple story about family dynamics and how an artist transmutes his vision to canvas. By the end of the day, Ladmiral is alone and about to begin a new painting; we're sorry to see the story end, because we won't get a look at the finished product. Winner of the Best Foreign Language Film award from the New York Film Critics Circle.

⊙**DVD:** Includes audio commentary by Bertrand Tavernier.

DR11

Goes well with: *Ma Saison Préférée*

SUNSHINE

Hungary/Austria/Germany/Canada   1999   C   182 min.   R   Drama
Dir: István Szabó
C: Ralph Fiennes, Rosemary Harris, Rachel Weisz, Jennifer Ehle, Molly Parker, Deborah Kara Unger, James Frain, John Neville, Miriam Margolyes, William Hurt, Bill Paterson

A multigenerational epic of Hungarian history, reflected in the experiences of one Jewish family, *Sunshine* almost lets its reach exceed its grasp. Ralph Fiennes plays characters in each of the three generations covered by the story; it's a stunt that works in principle (it's amazing more directors haven't tried it), though Fiennes's restrained approach is not quite what a sprawling epic requires. István Szabó and cowriter Israel Horovitz are intent on showing not only how Jews suffered under succeeding forms of government, but how all Hungarians were afflicted with rulers—the oligarchy of the Austro-Hungarian Empire, the cruelties of the Nazis, and the tyrannies of the Communists—that were largely indifferent to the wishes of the citizens, Gentiles and Jews alike. That is the ultimate value of *Sunshine* as an ambitious historical document that should inspire further inquiry into this country's sad history.

⊙**DVD**

DR11, DR24, DR25, DR28, DR38

Goes well with: *My Family (Mi Familia)*

SURVIVING PICASSO

U.S.   1996   C   125 min.   R   Drama
Dir: James Ivory
C: Anthony Hopkins, Natascha McElhone, Julianne Moore, Joss Ackland, Joan Plowright

Pablo Picasso has amazingly drawn few filmmakers to the flame of his genius. Producer Ismail Merchant (here working with David Wolper), director James Ivory, and writer Ruth Prawer Jhabvala don't attempt a full-scale biography; they concentrate on 1943–53, when Picasso (Anthony Hopkins) took a mistress, Françoise Gilot (Natasha McElhone), who was almost forty years his junior. She bore him several children and accepted that his protean personality was by its nature not monogamous. That is, she accepted it for a time, then departed, and as the film slides toward that moment, it becomes clear that this story is more about Gilot than Picasso. As magnetic as Anthony Hopkins is (compare this performance with his repressed Stevens in Merchant-Ivory's *The Remains of the Day*), the tall, dark, and handsomely composed McElhone is the best reason to see this film. It's based on a 1988 book, *Picasso: Creator and Destroyer* by Arianna Stassinopoulos, who is now known as Arianna Huffington.

DR17, DR39

Goes well with: *Sirens*

THE SWEET HEREAFTER

ESSENTIAL

Canada   1997   C   110 min.   R   Drama

Dir: Atom Egoyan

C: Ian Holm, Sarah Polley, Bruce Greenwood, Tom McCamus, Arsinée Khanjian, Alberta Watson, Gabrielle Rose, Maury Chaykin

The devastating effect of a catastrophe on a small town is only one of the subjects of Atom Egoyan's adaptation of Russell Banks's novel. A school bus full of a Canadian village's children slides off a wintry road and into a lake, leaving only one teenage survivor (Sarah Polley). Mitchell Stephens (Ian Holm), an attorney, shows up in town looking to initiate a lawsuit, but he's hardly a shark swimming in for the kill, as we see in a moving scene on his plane ride in. Stephens's house calls on the citizens of the village allow us to see the diversity of reactions to the tragedy, as well as some secrets that deepen the sorrow we feel for these people. Holm is magnificent as a man carrying too much emotional baggage, and Polley is unforgettable as the teenager whose life was troubled even before the accident. Egoyan and Banks understand the essential loneliness of the human condition, and this film is as eloquent an expression of that idea as any ever made. Winner of Best Foreign Film at the Independent Spirit Awards.

⊙**DVD:** Includes audio commentaries by Atom Egoyan and Russell Banks; video discussion of book and film; interviews with cast; Charlie Rose interview with Egoyan.

DR8, DR11, DR29, DR34

Goes well with: *Exotica*

SWINGERS

U.S. 1996 C 96 min. R Comedy

Dir: Doug Liman

C: Jon Favreau, Vince Vaughn, Ron Livingston, Patrick Van Horn, Alex Désert, Deena Martin, Katherine Kendall, Heather Graham

Any film that creates its own language (here, giving new spin to common words like "babies" and "money") runs the risk of coming off as smug, but *Swingers* has a sweet soul beneath its hip exterior. For that, thank writer Jon Favreau, who also stars as Mike, your basic Hollywood wannabe: an actor who can't catch a professional break and a young single who's just as unlucky in love. Enter Trent (Vince Vaughn) and his pals, who can't help Mike get a gig but can teach him the ways of the world of romance. Kind of. It's clear right away, after a disastrous road trip to Vegas, that if Mike is a kindergartener in the ways of love, Trent is barely out of the first grade. They are a hilarious team, but this is more a knowing comedy than something derived from a lame *Saturday Night Live* skit. A highlight: the answering machine gag.

⊙**DVD**

CO9

Goes well with: *The Tao of Steve*

SWOON

U.S. 1992 B&W 95 min. NR Drama

Dir: Tom Kalin

C: Daniel Schlachet, Craig Chester, Ron Vawter, Michael Kirby, Michael Stumm

The crime of the century, pre–O. J. Simpson, was the Leopold-Loeb murder of Bobby Franks in Chicago in 1924. The story has already been told for the movies in *Compulsion,* which hinted at the twisted relationship between the murderers but eventually seemed more interested in the lawyer (Orson Welles as a fictionalized Clarence Darrow) who brilliantly argued that the killers be judged insane. *Swoon* writer-director Tom Kalin is more fascinated by the possibility that Nathan Leopold and Richard Loeb were gay lovers, shunting to the side the theory that they concocted the crime only as a way of demonstrating their superior intellect. The film's stylization may prove annoying to some viewers, as it cuts the story into bite-size fragments and then tosses chronology out the window for at least the first half, but Kalin's artful use of the trial transcripts suggests that the racist, homophobic society judging these young men was as sick as they were. Ellen Kuras's cinematography won an award at Sundance.

DR17, DR19, DR27, XT4, XT6

Goes well with: *Heavenly Creatures*

T

TAMPOPO

Japan 1986 C 114 min. NR Comedy
Dir: Juzo Itami
C: Ken Watanabe, Tsutomu Yamazaki, Nobuko Miyamoto, Koji Yakusho

Food as a metaphor for life? You can do much worse—any sport, for starters—and *Tampopo* offers this proposition with a twinkle in its eye. Juzo Itami's story, about a noodle-shop owner (Tsutomu Yamazaki), her truck driver pal (Ken Watanabe), and their search for the perfect chef and recipes to save her business, is a shaggy-dog tale that's naturally more digressive than focused. Most of the stories are about the intimate relationship between food and sex or food and love, and *Tampopo* is much more playful on that subject than *Like Water for Chocolate,* which took itself as seriously as a flourless chocolate torte with buttercream icing. Itami clearly has seen a lot of films produced in the West, as *Tampopo*'s plate is filled with references to them.

⊙**DVD**
DR36, XT2
Goes well with: *Big Night*

THE TAO OF STEVE

U.S. 2000 C 90 min. R Comedy
Dir: Jenniphr Goodman
C: Donal Logue, Greer Goodman, Kimo Wills, Ayelet Kaznelson, David Aaron Baker, Nina Jaroslaw

A comedy with modest and surprising charms to match those of its lead character, *The Tao of Steve* gently lets the air of out of the hot-air balloon that is Don Juanism. Dex (Donal Logue) is fat, rumpled, and immensely appealing to the ladies of Santa Fe. The setting of this film is no accident; Santa Fe has long nurtured self-styled philosophers like Dex, guys who actually read Nietzsche and Lao-tzu for pleasure and then select passages to support their babe-a-day habit. The "Steve" of the title is Steve McQueen (and also TV characters Steve McGarrett and Steve Austin), described by Dex and his housemates as the prototypical American male. At a college reunion (which suggests that ten years after graduation Dex is still matriculating), he meets Sid (Greer Goodman), another woman on whom he can practice his wisdom. The cat-and-mouse game that ensues is more economically satisfying than those in attenuated Hollywood comedies like *When Harry Met Sally* and *You've Got Mail*. (Goodman and the director are sisters, and they co-authored the screenplay with Duncan North, who, the closing credits suggest, is the basis for Dex's character.) Donal Logue's performance won a Special Jury Prize at Sundance.

⊙**DVD:** Includes audio commentaries by cast and crew; "The Steve Test."

CO9, DR16

Goes well with: *Swingers*

A TASTE OF CHERRY

Iran   1997   C   95 min.   NR   Drama

Dir: Abbas Kiarostami

C: Homayon Ershadi, Abdolrahman Bagheri, Afshin Khorshid Bakhtiari

The premise of this drama, a surprise winner of the Palme d'Or at the 1996 Cannes Film Festival, is simple: A man wants to commit suicide, but he requires the help of one other man. That the setting is Muslim-dominated Iran, which forbids suicide, complicates his mission, as he drives around the outskirts of Tehran, chatting with men who expect to be asked to do day labor. The reasons for his despair are never made clear, and that's all for the better, because it allows filmmaker Abbas Kiarostami to keep our attention on his dilemma, the need for simple human contact that will allow him to end his life. *A Taste of Cherry* isn't interested in the narrative necessities; it creates a mood of foreboding and longing. Kiarostami's ending is ambiguity with a capital A, seeming to undercut everything we've already witnessed but actually offering an ironic commentary on it.

⊙**DVD:** Includes interview with Abbas Kiarostami.

DR8, DR16, DR21

Goes well with: *Ikiru*

A TAXING WOMAN

Japan 1987 C 127 min. NR Comedy-Drama

Dir: Juzo Itami

C: Nobuko Miyamoto, Tsutomu Yamazaki, Hideo Murota, Shuji Otaki

As in his genre-bending film *The Funeral,* Juzo Itami blends social satire with drama. Here he adds a generous helping of the police procedural, though the cops are tax inspectors honing in on a crooked businessman. The director's wife, Nobuko Miyamoto, plays Rytoko Itakura, an unflappable single mother who is promoted from tax collector to the all-male inspector unit. With her freckled face, large glasses, and persistent cowlick, Itakura at first comes on as a comical figure, but as she pursues Gondo (Tsutomu Yanazaki, her *Funeral* costar), a businessman who specializes in adult hotels, the mood of the story shifts. Tax rates in Japan, we are told in the film's prologue, run as high as 80 percent, and cheating has been raised to an art form; Gondo is the Picasso of tax evaders, but the script doesn't make him a total monster. Itami's film was so popular that he and Miyamoto collaborated on a sequel, *A Taxing Woman's Return.*

⊙**DVD**

CO8, DR6, DR39

Goes well with: *The Funeral*

TELLING LIES IN AMERICA

U.S. 1997 C 101 min. PG-13 Drama

Dir: Guy Ferland

C: Kevin Bacon, Brad Renfro, Maximilian Schell, Calista Flockhart, Paul Dooley, Jonathan Rhys-Meyers, Luke Wilson

What sins writer Joe Eszterhas committed on Hollywood films like *Basic Instinct* and *Showgirls,* he atoned for (a few of them, anyway) with this off-Hollywood piece of autobiography. It's set in the 1950s Cleveland of his youth, focusing on a high school kid (Brad Renfro) caught between an Old World widower of a father (Maximilian Schell) and a charismatic local disc jockey (Kevin Bacon), who is his entrée to the world of show biz. Bacon, playing a character named Billy Magic, has enough energy to light up all of downtown Cleveland, bopping from his studio to recording sessions to clubs, one hand always out to accept little "gifts" from record promoters eager to have their platters spun on his top-rated show. The Rock & Roll Hall of Fame wound up in Cleveland because of guys like Magic, who is a fascinating mix of questionable ethics and solid appreciation for the burgeoning rhythm-and-blues sounds of the day. As a result, Billy's ultimate unmasking (for the benefit of his protégé's education) has a bittersweet taste.

⊙**DVD**

DR3, DR11, DR23, DR41

Goes well with: *Repo Man*

THE TENANT

France/U.S.　1976　C　125 min.　R　Drama

Dir: Roman Polanski

C: Roman Polanski, Isabelle Adjani, Melvyn Douglas, Shelley Winters, Jo Van Fleet, Bernard Fresson, Lila Kedrova

Reversing the genders, Roman Polanski offers a variation of the story he told in *Repulsion.* Catherine Deneuve was the paranoid tenant in that film; here Polanski takes on the role himself, as Trelkovsky, an office worker who moves into a run-down Paris apartment building, only to learn that the previous occupant of his flat committed suicide by throwing herself out the window. Anyone else would shudder and get on with his life, but Trelkovsky even starts dressing up in the clothes left behind by the dead woman. And any other guy would pick up on the aggressive sexual signals broadcast by an attractive coworker (Isabelle Adjani), but Trelkovsky remains fixated on his identity crisis. *The Tenant* shows Polanski still at the top of his game, even after his exile from Hollywood, though his subsequent career has not yielded a film this powerful and disturbing.

DR27, TH3

Goes well with: *Repulsion*

THE TEXAS CHAINSAW MASSACRE

ESSENTIAL

U.S.　1974　C　83 min.　R　Horror

Dir: Tobe Hooper

C: Marilyn Burns, Gunnar Hansen, Edwin Neal, Allen Danzinger, Paul A. Partain

The unholy trinity of independently produced horror films of the late 1960s and 1970s is *Night of the Living Dead, Halloween,* and this film.

Chainsaw offers the least accomplished filmmaking of the three, but it's an undeniably effective exercise in eliciting primal fear. Five young Texans, three men and two women, stumble onto a rural farmhouse occupied by a family that slaughters humans for their own consumption. News stories of this kind of gruesome behavior pop up occasionally, but they're usually about a lone killer; in *Chainsaw,* if you get away from one member of this murderous clan, there's another one lurking around the corner to get you. Should it be surprising that fans of this film tend to be devotees of those reality TV series like *Survivor*?

⊙**DVD:** Includes audio commentaries by Tobe Hooper, Gunnar Hansen, and cinematographer Daniel Pearl; deleted scenes and alternate footage; blooper reel.

FA7

Goes well with: *Halloween*

THEREMIN: AN ELECTRONIC ODYSSEY
U.S./U.K.   1993   C/B&W   104 min.   PG   Documentary
Dir: Steven Martin

What do the science-fiction film *The Day the Earth Stood Still* and the Beach Boys song "Good Vibrations" have in common? They both use the electronic musical instrument developed by Russian scientist Leon Theremin. The eerie sounds it makes are nothing compared to the long and strange life of its creator, who was ninety-five years old in 1991 when filmmaker Steven Martin tracked him down in Moscow to tell his story. Theremin died two years later, but not before Martin was able to film his recollections and a reunion with his protégée, Clara Rockmore (who died in 2001). Theremin's story, featuring a politically incorrect marriage to a ballerina star, abduction by Soviet agents, imprisonment, and neglect while inventors like Robert Moog were getting credit for their synthesizer inventions, is fascinating stuff. It's heartening to see that he lived long enough to know that Martin's film would commemorate his achievements.

⊙**DVD**

DO5

Goes well with: *Fast, Cheap & Out of Control*

THE THIN BLUE LINE
ESSENTIAL

U.S.   1988   C   101 min.   NR   Documentary
Dir: Errol Morris

It may be the only documentary that ever freed a man from death row. Errol Morris's stunning study of injustice Texas-style focuses on Randall Adams, a man wrongly accused of murdering a cop during a routine traffic stop in 1976. Circumstantial evidence and faulty testimony put Adams behind bars, and the nature of his alleged crime, as well as the state in which it was committed, assured he was going to die for it. Morris does in this film what Truman Capote did in *In Cold Blood*, bringing some of the techniques of fiction filmmaking to bear to tell a true story. He repeats reenactments of the crime and surrounding events, varying details slightly to raise doubts, while mixing in compelling interview footage with Adams and David Harris, the real killer. Harris was serving time for another crime when Morris was making this film, but he would not confess to the murder in question. Unusual for a documentary, the musical score by Philip Glass is a major contributor to the film's impact. Winner of the Best Documentary prize from the New York Film Critics Circle; unaccountably, it wasn't even nominated for an Academy Award.
DO2

Goes well with: *Brother's Keeper*

THINGS CHANGE

U.S.   1988   C   100 min.   PG   Comedy
Dir: David Mamet
C: Don Ameche, Joe Mantegna, Robert Prosky, J. J. Johnston, Ricky Jay, J. T. Walsh

David Mamet's second film as a director offers a clue in the screenwriting credits that this will not be a reprise of *House of Games*'s nasty little con games. Mamet's cowriter is none other than Shel Silverstein, the whimsical song lyricist and children's book author, and the two seem to split the difference in terms of sensibility here. Mamet gets the setting—the Mob, setting up a guy to take a fall—while Silverstein gets the tone—playful and rueful. Gino (Don Ameche) is a shoemaker with an unfortunate resemblance to a Mob boss about to go on trial for charges he can't beat. The Mob persuades the aging Gino to sit in for the Don at the trial, make a confession, and serve the time, assuring Gino he'll be well-treated on the inside. Jerry (Joe Mantegna) is assigned to watch Gino in the few days before the trial starts, and soon the two guys are off to Lake Tahoe for a little R&R "on the company's nickel," of course. This cannot end well, but it does not end violently, either. A sweet comedy that never overplays its hand.

⊙**DVD**

CO1, DR12, DR14

Goes well with: *'Round Midnight*

THINGS YOU CAN TELL JUST BY LOOKING AT HER

U.S. 2001 C 109 min. PG-13 Drama

Dir: Rodrigo García

C: Glenn Close, Cameron Diaz, Calista Flockhart, Kathy Baker, Amy Brenneman, Valeria Golino, Holly Hunter, Matt Craven, Noah Fleiss, Miguel Sandoval, Gregory Hines, Danny Woodburn

Originally made as a theatrical feature by a Hollywood studio, *Things* became an orphan when the studio pulled the plug on distributing it, and it wound up premiering on a cable/satellite movie channel. It's hard to believe that a film with this cast would get that kind of disrespect, but clearly the bean counters at the studio didn't see much profit in a five-part anthology of stories about women in crisis. The stories overlap slightly, with some recurring characters; this is not as ambitious or edgy a film as *Short Cuts,* but it has its own pleasures. In "This Is Dr. Keener," Glenn Close plays a single woman who is a successful physician trying to deal with a live-in invalid mother and a luckless love life. She consults a fortune teller (Calista Flockhart), who reappears in the fourth story, "Good Night Lilly, Good Night Christine," as a lesbian dealing with the fatal illness of her lover (Valeria Golino). "Fantasies About Rebecca" is about a bank manager (Holly Hunter) involved with a married man (Gregory Hines) and an unwanted pregnancy. "Someone for Rose," the drollest story, traces a romantic fixation by a single mom (Kathy Baker) on her new neighbor, a dwarf (Danny Woodburn). "Love Waits for Kathy" brings the opening scene of the film, in which police investigate a woman's suicide, full circle with the story of two sisters, a police detective (Amy Brenneman) and her blind sibling (Cameron Diaz) and their different approaches to love. The film ends on an unexpectedly whimsical and satisfying note, with a totally unexpected scene in a bar. Writer-director Rodrigo García, a cinematographer, comes honestly by his ability to tell a story; he is the son of noted novelist Gabriel García Márquez.

⊙**DVD**

DR18, DR19, DR39

Goes well with: *Short Cuts*

THE THIRD MAN

ESSENTIAL

U.K. 1949 B&W 104 min. NR Thriller
Dir: Carol Reed
C: Orson Welles, Joseph Cotten, Alida Valli, Trevor Howard, Bernard Lee, Wilfred Hyde-White

Adapting his own novel, Graham Greene (with some assistance from Carol Reed and Orson Welles) created an instant classic of postwar intrigue that was such a staple on late-night TV in the pre-VHS/DVD era that you may feel you've seen bits and pieces of it dozens of times. Joseph Cotten plays a pulp fiction writer with the unlikely name of Holly Martins; he arrives in occupied Vienna to look up an old pal, Harry Lime (Welles), for a job. Reports of Lime's demise are premature, but stories that he was involved in black-market activities that led to the death of innocent children are unfortunately fact. The British (and their temporary allies the Russians) hire Martins to flush Lime out—literally, because he's hiding in Vienna's vast sewer system. Nearly all of the action takes place at night on rain-slicked streets, and Reed, perhaps nudged by the presence of Welles, offers delirious camera angles to capture the action. The zither music was by Anton Karas; his version of the film's theme sold two million copies and was one of six different recordings of the music to appear on the pop charts in 1950.

⊙**DVD:** Includes introduction by Peter Bogdanovich; radio production of story; Joseph Cotten's voice-over introduction; restoration demonstration.

DR6, DR12, DR36
Goes well with: *Odd Man Out*

35 UP

ESSENTIAL

U.K. 1991 C/B&W 122 min. NR Documentary
Dir: Michael Apted

In 1963, Michael Apted began a most ambitious ongoing film series, assisting director Paul Almord in interviewing thirteen British schoolchildren, then seven years old. Apted then returned every seven years to see how they were progressing in life. The series is now at *42 Up;* the only entries available on video are *28 Up, 35 Up,* and *42 Up,* and only *42 Up* is available on DVD. The later chapters do a good job of catching up viewers who may have come late to the series, showing clips from previous films and offering a quick voice-over perspective on the subjects. Through the years, subjects have dropped out and then returned to the series, but Apted has been able to maintain contact with a high percentage of his subjects. At thirty-five, most have settled down and are raising families (a common thread: moving to the country to escape the hazards of urban life). Several of the women (but none of the men) have divorced. The series' most compelling character is saved for last in this entry: Neil, a college dropout who was homeless in *28 Up* but is now living in subsidized housing in the Shetland Islands, working in local theater and writing. He is also on medication for a variety of ailments, and he is certain that he suffers from a chemical imbalance that has limited his ability to function well—so certain that he has no plans to marry or have children. This is engrossing stuff that doesn't feel voyeuristic at all.

DO7

Goes well with: *42 Up*

THE 39 STEPS

ESSENTIAL

U.K. 1935 B&W 87 min. NR Thriller

Dir: Alfred Hitchcock

C: Robert Donat, Madeleine Carroll, Lucie Mannheim, Godfrey Tearle, Peggy Ashcroft, John Laurie, Wylie Watson

It's generally regarded as the first film in which Alfred Hitchcock put it all together, a peerless blend of romance and intrigue. And it hasn't aged one bit. Robert Hannay (Robert Donat) is accused of murdering a woman in his London apartment, and he flees the city with both the police and a ring of spies on his tail. On the way into northern England, he picks up a traveling companion (Madeleine Carroll), to whom he becomes handcuffed. They're in search of the elusive Mr. Memory, a stage performer who holds the key to the mystery (and an explanation of the title). By the story's end, we don't really care what the spies are after or that the cops have the right man; we only know that Hannay and his new companion are in love. Among the film's many clever touches is the eerie resemblance of the spy ring's chief to Franklin Roosevelt. Along with *The Lady Vanishes,* the best of the pre-Hollywood Hitchcock films.

⊙**DVD:** Two editions. Laserlight contains introduction by Tony Curtis. Criterion has audio commentary by Hitchcock scholar Marian

Keene; 1937 radio adaptation; documentary on Hitchcock's British films.

TH6, TH11, TH17, XT5

Goes well with: *The Man Who Knew Too Much*

THIRTY TWO SHORT FILMS ABOUT GLENN GOULD

Canada/Finland/Netherlands/Portugal   1993   C   93 min.   NR
  Drama/Documentary

Dir: François Girard

C: Colm Feore

The Canadian pianist Glenn Gould was almost as famous a recluse as he was a musician. In 1964, at the relatively tender age of thirty-two, he refused to venture again onto the concert stage, claiming he could only be satisfied in the perfectible world of recording studios. (He died in 1982, at the age of fifty.) François Girard's fragmented semidocumentary reflects the structure of Gould's most famous recording, his 1955 debut of Bach's thirty-two *Goldberg Variations.* (He reprised the recording in 1981, the last one made at CBS's famed 30th Street studios in Manhattan.) Re-created scenes from Gould's life (in which he is played by Colm Feore) mix with recordings of his frequent radio appearances, animation sequences, and abstractions set to his music. (Gould himself is only glimpsed.) The film is, despite the pitfalls of this sideways approach, more provocative than precious, suggesting that the standard tack taken by programs like A&E's *Biography* isn't always the best way to capture the spirit of a difficult subject.

⊙**DVD**

DO4, XT6

Goes well with: *Hilary and Jackie*

THIS SPORTING LIFE

ESSENTIAL

U.K.   1963   B&W   134 min.   NR   Drama

Dir: Lindsay Anderson

C: Richard Harris, Rachel Roberts, Alan Badel, William Hartnell,
  Colin Blakely, Arthur Lowe

The most enduring of the new wave of British films from the late 1950s and early 1960s, *This Sporting Life* is also among the best films to present the popularity of sports as a two-edged sword. Richard Harris is Frank Machin, a coal miner in Britain's north country who's convinced that his skill at rugby is his ticket out of the mines. As he rises to professional stardom, he also pursues his widowed landlady, Mrs. Hammond (Rachel Roberts), who is reluctant at first to give way to Frank's advances. Frank's motto—"You see something you want, and you go out and get it"—serves him well on both fronts, but his victories prove hollow. David Storey's adaptation of his own novel makes its points with grace and subtlety, and both leads were never better: Harris as a brute blinded by ambition, Roberts as a woman clawing for a second chance at happiness and realizing she's not going to get it.

⊙**DVD:** Includes essay by Adrian Turner.

DR1, DR21, DR35, DR40

Goes well with: *The Loneliness of the Long Distance Runner*

THE THREE MUSKETEERS

U.S. 1973 C 105 min. PG Action-Adventure

Dir: Richard Lester

C: Oliver Reed, Raquel Welch, Richard Chamberlain, Michael York, Frank Finlay, Christopher Lee, Geraldine Chaplin, Faye Dunaway, Charlton Heston, Jean-Pierre Cassel, Roy Kinnear, Spike Milligan

The best version of Dumas's oft-filmed adventure tale is a skillful blend of action, adventure, political intrigue, and humor. It's the perfect collaboration among a writer (George MacDonald Fraser) with respect for the material, a director (Richard Lester) with a great flair for physical action and comedy, and a well-chosen cast that brings depth and in some cases unexpected shadings to their characters. Oliver Reed makes a wonderfully brooding Athos, and his performance anchors both this film and especially the sequel, *The Four Musketeers.* Michael York is a splendidly naïve D'Artagnan; Frank Finlay and Richard Chamberlain round out the troupe of swordsmen. The supporting cast is just as wonderful, especially Raquel Welch and Roy Kinnear as fumbling servants, Christopher Lee as Rochefort, and Charlton Heston as Richelieu. The producers provided their cast and director with a script long enough for two films, and then they neatly divided the story into two parts, releasing them one year apart. Lawsuits ensued, but the happy outcome for audiences was a thrilling pair of adventure films.

⊙**DVD**

AC8, CO6, DR24, DR25

Goes well with: *The Four Musketeers*

THRONE OF BLOOD

ESSENTIAL

Japan 1957 B&W 108 min. NR Drama
Dir: Akira Kurosawa
C: Toshiro Mifune, Isuzu Yamada, Takashi Shimura, Minoru Chiaki

Akira Kurosawa's first Shakespeare film is among the best adaptations ever of the Bard, with the Macbeth tale translated to medieval Japan. Toshiro Mifune and Isuzu Yamada are the lord and lady who push each other's buttons to make the ultimate power play. Kurosawa trims the play down (nothing important is gone) and comes up with one stunning visual after another to illustrate and elaborate on the text. The moving forest is one highlight, and the finale, with Mifune set upon by his own men and turned into a human pincushion who refuses to die, is breathtaking in both concept and execution. When critics talk about Kurosawa's unrivaled stature among the world's great directors, this is one of the films they use for proof.

DR1, DR25, DR32

Goes well with: *Ran*

TIME BANDITS

U.K. 1981 C 116 min. PG Fantasy
Dir: Terry Gilliam
C: Sean Connery, Shelley Duvall, John Cleese, Katherine Helmond, Ian Holm, Michael Palin, Ralph Richardson, Peter Vaughan, David Warner, Kenny Baker, David Rappaport, Craig Warnock

Terry Gilliam, the lone American among Monty Python's Flying Circus, headed for the director's chair after the troupe broke up. (He was the one who provided the wonderfully absurd animation inserts for the TV show and occasionally acted as well.) This is his first film away from the Pythons, though it does feature several of his old mates, and it's a preview of greater things to come (*Brazil, The Adventures of Baron Munchausen, 12 Monkeys*). Six pugnacious dwarves show up one night in the bedroom of a little boy and promise to take him on adventures through time. It's the classic children's fantasy of being guided through a strange and mysterious world; think *The Wizard of Oz* with more wit and less music. Craig Warnock is the time traveler, and among his celebrity sightings are Napoleon (Ian Holm), Agamemnon (Sean Connery), and Robin Hood (John Cleese). Ralph Richardson plays the

Supreme Being, David Warner the man they just call Evil; it's their lit-tle spat that sets the whole adventure in motion. Gilliam set out to make a story more in line with the spirit of the Brothers Grimm, so there are occasionally dark moments that may frighten younger children.

⊙**DVD:** Includes audio commentaries by Terry Gilliam, Michael Palin, John Cleese, David Warner, and Craig Warnock.

FA4, FA6

Goes well with: *The Secret of Roan Inish*

THE TIMES OF HARVEY MILK

ESSENTIAL

U.S.   1984   C   87 min.   NR   Documentary

Dir: Robert Epstein

C: Harvey Fierstein (narrator)

America's first openly gay politician, San Francisco Board of Super-visors member Harvey Milk, was also America's first gay political mar-tyr. In 1978, a year after he was elected, Milk and San Francisco Mayor George Moscone were murdered by disgruntled politician Dan White. The act itself sparked sorrow in that city's gay community, and when White was given an incredibly lenient sentence (the insanity defense at its most perverted), that grief turned to outrage. Robert Epstein's film records the whole sad story here in admirably restrained fashion. Mark Isham's melancholy score adds immeasurably to the mood of this fea-ture, which won Best Documentary awards from both the Academy and the New York Film Critics Circle, as well as a Special Jury Prize at the U.S. Film Festival (forerunner of Sundance).

DO4

Goes well with: *Boys Don't Cry*

THE TIN DRUM

ESSENTIAL

Poland/West Germany/Yugoslavia/France   1979   C   142   min.   R
  Drama

Dir: Volker Schlöndorff

C: David Bennent, Mario Adorf, Angela Winkler, Daniel Olbrychski,
  Charles Aznavour

Gunther Grass's allegedly unfilmable novel became a celebrated film in 1979, sharing the Palme D'Or with *Apocalypse Now* at the

Cannes Film Festival and later winning the Oscar for Best Foreign Language Film. Grass's literary conceit was that the history of Germany from World War I through the rise of the Nazis could be told through the eyes of a child who refuses to grow up—the point being that little Oskar understands better than anyone around him what the chaos of the 1920s will give way to. Oskar has two means of expressing his outrage: pounding on his toy drum, and screaming with window-shattering force. Volker Schlöndorff (who cowrote the script with Jean-Claude Carrière and Franz Seitz) found a way to compress Grass's sprawling novel and present its fantastical imagery without losing its power. In David Bennent, the filmmaker also found an actor capable of persuasively playing an adult locked inside a child's body.

⊙**DVD:** Includes audio commentary by Volker Schlöndorff and video essay.

DR21, DR24, DR29, DR38, DR41
Goes well with: *Sunshine*

TO DIE FOR

U.S./U.K.   1995   C   107 min.   R   Comedy
Dir: Gus Van Sant
C: Nicole Kidman, Matt Dillon, Joaquin Phoenix, Illeana Douglas, Casey Affleck, Alison Folland, Dan Hedaya, Wayne Knight, Kurtwood Smith, David Cronenberg

Making a bid for her fifteen minutes of fame, small-town New Hampshire TV weathergirl Suzanne Stone (Nicole Kidman) knows that as soon as the networks get a look at tapes of her winter storm warnings, she'll be on her way to becoming the next Jane Pauley or Lesley Stahl. There's only one problem: her loving husband, Larry (Matt Dillon), who's happy to be a small-town guy with lots of children to take care of. Children are not part of Suzanne's plan, a plan that, as Buck Henry's barbed screenplay demonstrates, can include murder if necessary. Kidman gives such a riveting performance as the self-centered Suzanne that you may overlook how good the supporting cast of this delicious satire is, especially Joaquin Phoenix and Alison Folland as Suzanne's spacey young acolytes-turned-accomplices and Illeana Douglas as Larry's suspicious sister. And yes, fans of director David Cronenberg, that is your man in the penultimate scene. As they say in New England, this is wicked good fun.

⊙**DVD**

CO2, CO8, CO11, DR1, TH7

Goes well with: *Normal Life*

TOKYO OLYMPIAD

ESSENTIAL

Japan 1966 C/B&W 170 min. NR Documentary

Dir: Kon Ichikawa

Though not as inherently dramatic as Leni Riefenstahl's standard-bearer *Olympia,* Japanese director Kon Ichikawa's chronicle of the eighteenth Olympiad is a solid silver medalist in the competition for best Olympics documentary. Shamefully cut in half when it was released theatrically in the United States in 1966, the film is now available in its full-length glory and, just as essential, in a wide-screen format. (Some events, especially track races, wouldn't make sense with a cropped image.) Tokyo did not produce many dramatic moments, either in competition or out of it (as Munich most tragically did eight years later). But it was Asia's first Olympiad—Japan had been slated to host the 1940 games, which were called off due to a little aggressive behavior on the part of Japan and the previous host nation—and the first one since World War II in which Germany entered a united team. The film's most striking image comes right at the beginning: a gorgeous shot of Mt. Fuji, with a little traveling plume of smoke moving along a road in the foreground—the runner with the Olympic torch making his way to the stadium. Ichikawa makes artful use of sound, from the grunts and shouts of the athletes to the distant cheers of the crowd to the plopping of raindrops on soggy athletes (it appears that at least three or four days were hampered by precipitation) to the thuds of women volleyball players hitting the floor. The last twenty minutes follow the progress of the marathon through the streets of Tokyo, with Ethiopia's Abebe Bikila effortlessly cruising to a second straight gold medal, leaving everyone gasping in his wake.

⊙**DVD**

DO10

Goes well with: *Olympia*

TOKYO STORY

ESSENTIAL

Japan 1953 B&W 134 min. NR Drama

Dir: Yasujiro Ozu

C: Chishu Ryu, Chieko Higashiyama, So Yamamura, Setsuko Hara, Kyoko Kagawa, Shiro Osaka, Eijiro Tono, Kuniko Miyake

Generally regarded as Yasujiro Ozu's masterwork—and one of the greatest films made by any director—*Tokyo Story* unfolds so slowly and casually that you may wonder for a while what all the fuss is about. Ozu regular Chishu Ryu and Chieko Higashiyama play a married couple in their sixties who have raised their five children in a small coastal town in southern Japan. They decide to visit two of the grown children, a son and daughter, in Tokyo; on the return trip, the wife falls ill, and they lay over in Osaka to see a second son. (Another son died eight years ago, leaving a widow in Tokyo, and the youngest daughter still lives at home.) The wife recovers long enough to return home, where she becomes critically ill and dies. Out of these simple events, Ozu (and his cowriter, Kogo Nada) fashion an amazingly evocative story. The midpoint of the story is where Ozu's concerns over family relations really take shape. The couple split up for one night in Tokyo, the mother to visit her widowed daughter-in-law (played by the amazing Setsuko Hara), the father to go drinking with two old buddies. While the men express disappointment over how their children have turned out, the mother's obvious affection for her daughter-in-law suggests a closeness she doesn't enjoy with her own children.

DR8, DR11, DR14

Goes well with: *An Autumn Afternoon*

TOM JONES

ESSENTIAL

U.K. 1963 C 129 min. NR Comedy

Dir: Tony Richardson

C: Albert Finney, Susannah York, Hugh Griffith, Edith Evans, Joyce Redman, Diane Cilento, Joan Greenwood, David Tomlinson, Peter Bull, David Warner, Lynn Redgrave, Micheál MacLiammóir (narrator)

It may be fashionable to look back in anger at what the success of *Tom Jones* allegedly did to the British film scene, jerking it away from the socially conscious dramas of the five or so years prior to the film's 1963 release and into an era of lighter entertainment. (And after all, wasn't that Tony Richardson, producer and director of some of those dramas, at the helm of *Tom Jones?*) In fact, *Tom Jones,* with Albert Finney as Henry Fielding's eighteenth-century rake, inspired no run of bawdy takes on the classics. It did, however, give British film the world-wide visibility that respectable but relatively low-impact films like *This Sporting Life* and *Saturday Night and Sunday Morning* couldn't. Had someone given Fielding's massive novel a go-round ten years earlier, you might not be reading an entry for it; Richardson seized on the new freedom in movies to suggest—after all, nudity in films was still a few years off—randy behavior that could only offend the most puritanical viewers. Everyone on screen, especially the Western family—Hugh Griffith's bibulous Squire, Susannah York's creamy Sophie, and Edith Evans's prim Miss Western—is having such a good time that it would take an act of high curmudgeonliness not to join in. *Tom Jones* won the Academy Awards for Best Picture and Best Director, as well as for John Osborne's screenplay and John Addison's musical score. Richardson, Finney, and the film won the favor of the New York Film Critics Circle.

⊙**DVD:** Two editions. MGM version restores seven minutes of footage edited for 1989 theatrical rerelease.

CO6, CO9, DR29

Goes well with: *Shakespeare in Love*

TOPSY-TURVY
ESSENTIAL

U.K. 1999 C 160 min. R Drama
Dir: Mike Leigh
C: Jim Broadbent, Allan Corduner, Lesley Manville, Eleanor David, Ron Cook, Kevin McKidd, Timothy Spall, Martin Savage, Shirley Henderson, Alison Steadman

Between his film debut in 1971 and his return to features in 1987, director Mike Leigh worked in theater and television, and his affection for the world of the former is evident in every frame of this magnificent portrait of W. S. Gilbert (Jim Broadbent) and Arthur Sullivan (Allan Corduner). Leigh wisely compresses his story into one behind-the-scenes tale, the making of *The Mikado*. It came at a critical time for the team, who were coming off a rare flop. Gilbert in particular was feeling tapped out by the experience and threatening to retire, until he attended a museum exhibit on Japanese culture. Fascinated by cultural rituals that seem so rigid, even to a Victorian, Gilbert managed to persuade Sullivan to renew their partnership. Leigh takes us through every stage of planning the show, and he strikes the perfect balance between explicating history and making it dramatic. You are not likely ever to see a more detailed and entertaining film about what goes into a live production. The New York Film Critics Circle awarded it Best Film and Best Director; it also won Oscars for costume design and make-up.

⊙**DVD:** Includes "making of" featurette.

DR2, DR4, DR17, DR24

Goes well with: *Cradle Will Rock*

TOUGH GUYS DON'T DANCE

U.S. 1987 C 110 min. R Comedy-Thriller

Dir: Norman Mailer

C: Ryan O'Neal, Isabella Rossellini, Debra Sandlund, Wings Hauser, Lawrence Tierney, Penn Jillette, Frances Fisher, John Bedford Lloyd, Clarence Williams III

Norman Mailer dabbled in film directing in the 1960s with a pair of what were essentially home movies, then wisely withdrew to his literary endeavors, with some detours into screenwriting, until this adaptation of his own detective novel. Of course, Mailer could never write a novel in any genre without trying to rearrange the rules a bit, so his characters were almost self-consciously pulpy, his plot almost incomprehensible. The film actually improves on the book—consider it a better draft—in part because it takes itself far less seriously. Tim Madden (Ryan O'Neal) is an ex–drug dealer who wakes up from a hangover in his blood-spattered car with no idea what that head is doing in the back seat. His father (film noir icon Lawrence Tierney) is of little help, and a local cop (Wings Hauser) is out to send him away. O'Neal is perfect as the onetime golden boy gone to seed, and the film's location, wintertime Provincetown, full of people waiting out the winter with nothing to do but get into trouble, is his strongest costar.

CO2, TH13, TH17

Goes well with: *Blood and Wine*

TRAINSPOTTING

ESSENTIAL

U.K. 1996 C 94 min. R Comedy

Dir: Danny Boyle

C: Ewan McGregor, Ewen Bremner, Jonny Lee Miller, Kevin McKidd, Robert Carlyle, Kelly Macdonald

The daily routine of a serious drug addict makes for boring dramatic material: (1) get high, (2) come down, (3) look for money to buy another fix, (4) repeat steps 1, 2, and 3. Some filmmakers, like Darren Aronofksy (*Requiem for a Dream*), try to solve the problem with visual fireworks but fall short of engaging our sympathies or interest. Gus Van Sant (*Drugstore Cowboy*) added humor to make his junkies more charming than alarming. Then there's the approach adopted by Danny Boyle and writer John Hodge: a combination of visual pyrotechnics (the unforgettable Toilet Cam sequence) and huge dollops of black humor (a breakfast table scene that would do the Monty Python chaps proud). Adapted from Irvine Welch's caustic novel about the misadventures of an Edinburgh enclave of heroin addicts, *Trainspotting* provided break-through roles for Ewan McGregor (as Renton, our friendly guide) and Robert Carlyle (as Begbie, the scariest of the lot). Renton rants to the camera and on the soundtrack about the emptiness of bourgeois values, coming on like the reincarnation of Jimmy Porter from *Look Back in Anger,* though in Renton's case it sounds like he's justifying his exis-tence as a layabout. The title is explained in a scene that involves two characters doing spot-on impressions of Sean Connery.

⊙**DVD**

CO2, CO8, DR10, DR16

Goes well with: *Drugstore Cowboy*

TRAVIATA, LA.

See *La Traviata*

TREES LOUNGE

U.S.   1996   C   94 min.   R   Drama

Dir: Steve Buscemi

C: Steve Buscemi, Mark Boone, Jr., Chloë Sevigny, Michael Buscemi, Anthony LaPaglia, Elizabeth Bracco, Daniel Baldwin, Carol Kane, Debi Mazar, Michael Imperioli, Samuel L. Jackson, Seymour Cas-sel, Mimi Rogers, Rockets Redglare

Character actor Steve Buscemi moves center stage for this film, his directorial debut (which he also wrote), in which he plays yet another sad-sack character, this one a habitué of a suburban Long Island bar (the title establishment). Like Cliff and Norm from *Cheers,* Tommy Basilio is a lovable loser whose philosophical rantings are greeted with a lot of eye-rolling by his fellow drinkers. He's in debt to a garage owner (An-thony LaPaglia) who has stolen his girlfriend (Elizabeth Bracco), and he's in dutch with another buddy (Daniel Baldwin) for hanging around with his teenage daughter (Chloë Sevigny). This drama would be even funnier if it weren't so determinedly downbeat about Tommy's inability to master even the simple task of driving an ice cream van.

⊙**DVD:** Includes audio commentary by Steve Buscemi.

DR9, DR11, DR34

Goes well with: *Affliction*

TRIUMPH OF THE WILL
ESSENTIAL

Germany   1935   B&W   110 min.   NR   Documentary
Dir: Leni Riefenstahl

The most notorious documentary ever made, *Triumph of the Will* is an undeniable triumph of technique over content. To defend this stunningly shot, edited, and presented record of the Sixth Nazi Congress at Nuremberg in 1934 on purely aesthetic grounds is not to ignore its celebration of a morally repugnant ideology. Leni Riefenstahl has backtracked for much of her life on how much she supported Hitler's aims, wrapping herself in the cloak of the artist. However you view that claim, it is possible to watch this film as a great work of cinematic art. Riefenstahl understood the power of imagery: massed crowds, all perfectly lined up in nearly endless rows, set against heroic-looking architecture. And she edited speeches to their essence, intercutting shots of the crowd and other images to emphasize certain points. It is, finally, propaganda of the highest order, and because what it helped unleash has informed so many lives for the last seventy years, it cannot be ignored.

⊙**DVD:** Includes Leni Riefenstahl's 1935 documentary short "Day of Freedom," about the German Army.

DO3, DO9

Goes well with: *Olympia*

TROUBLE IN MIND
ESSENTIAL

U.S.   1985   C   111 min.   R   Drama
Dir: Alan Rudolph
C: Kris Kristofferson, Keith Carradine, Lori Singer, Genevieve Bujold, Joe Morton, Divine, George Kirby, John Considine

A companion piece to Alan Rudolph's *Choose Me, Trouble in Mind* offers an ensemble cast playing urban types looking for love. It's set in Rain City, clearly a stand-in for Seattle, and much of the action revolves around a café run by Wanda (Genevieve Bujold). She serves up cups of joe to ex-cops like Hawk (Kris Kristofferson) and blondes (Lori Singer) who fairly scream, "I'm big trouble—so why don't you fall in love with me anyway?" Keith Carradine, the mysterious Romeo of *Choose Me,* is in full comic mode as the blonde's fast-talking husband, who sports increasingly bizarre hair styles that look like they came out of a machine at a Dairy Queen. Divine, the transvestite star of many John Waters films, makes his male debut here as Hilly, the big boss of the town's underworld. (Unfortunately, it was also his last film; he died of a heart attack after filming was completed.) *Trouble* takes itself just seriously enough to be genuinely moving, but there's a strong sense of playfulness here, too. The Independent Spirit Awards honored Toyomichi Kurita's cinematography.

DR18, DR36, TH13

Goes well with: *Choose Me*

TRULY MADLY DEEPLY

U.K. 1991 C 107 min. PG Drama
Dir: Anthony Minghella
C: Juliet Stevenson, Alan Rickman, Bill Paterson, Michael Maloney, Christopher Rozycki

It's the movie that *Ghost* could have been but simply wasn't. Anthony Minghella's script is about a woman communing with her dead lover—he actually appears to her at odd moments. Juliet Stevenson is such a gifted actress, you can instantly see why Minghella wrote the screenplay with her in mind. Alan Rickman, usually encouraged to overact when he plays sneering villains, is endearingly low-key as the spirit who shows up with some of his pals from the great beyond to watch Woody Allen movies on the telly in the wee small hours. There are no wacky psychics, no threats to the heroine's life, and no faux sex scenes over a potter's wheel, just an honestly felt character study of how one woman deals with her grief.

⊙**DVD:** Includes audio commentary by Anthony Minghella and interview with Minghella.

DR8, DR18, FA9

Goes well with: *Wings of Desire*

TRUST

U.S./U.K. 1990 C 105 min. R Drama
Dir: Hal Hartley

C: Adrienne Shelly, Martin Donovan, Merritt Nelson, John McKay, Edie Falco

Hal Hartley revisits some of the themes he explored in his debut film, *The Unbelievable Truth*. Adrienne Shelley and Martin Donovan are once again the stars; she plays Maria, a high school student who becomes a pariah to her family when she announces she is pregnant by her jock boyfriend. She's taken in by Martin, a man with his own family issues, involving a domineering father. In Hartley's world (which is located on Long Island, not too far east of the city), misfits gravitate toward one another, but because they are misfits, the issues of trust never go away. Their struggle toward accommodation with each other and the rest of the world is both funny and painful to watch. Not surprisingly, Hartley's films are much admired but little seen. *Trust* won the Waldo Salt Screenwriting Award at the Sundance festival.

DR12, DR21

Goes well with: *The Unbelievable Truth*

TWIN FALLS, IDAHO

U.S.   1999   C   110 min.   R   Drama
Dir: Michael Polish
C: Michael Polish, Mark Polish, Michele Hicks, Jon Gries, Patrick Bauchau, Lesley Ann Warren, Garrett Morris, William Katt, Holly Woodlawn

Conjoined, or Siamese, twins have been featured in several horror or suspense films (*Freaks, Sisters, Basket Case*), but it took a pair of real (though not conjoined) twins to come up with a more respectful approach to this physical abnormality. Mark and Michael Polish wrote the screenplay, Mark directed, and they costar as Francis (Michael) and Blake Falls (Mark). The two are living in a seedy hotel on Idaho Street in an unnamed town, and for their birthday, Blake decides to give his brother the gift of a session with a prostitute (Michele Hicks). This setup evolves slowly into an improbable love story, laced with the approach of death for one of the twins. Though *Twin Falls* owes something to the films of David Lynch, it never descends into the darker areas his work explores. It's a bittersweet love story with surprising resonance.

⊙**DVD:** Special Edition contains audio commentary by Polish brothers.

DR8, DR15, DR27, TH3
Goes well with: *Dead Ringers*

TWO ENGLISH GIRLS

ESSENTIAL

France 1971 C 132 min. R Drama

Dir: François Truffaut

C: Jean-Pierre Léaud, Kika Markham, Stacey Tendeter, Sylvia Marriott

Among the most sadly neglected of François Truffaut's films is this contemplation on the vagaries of romance. Set during the World War I era, the story involves Claude Roc (Jean-Pierre Léaud), a Frenchman captivated by the two contrasting Brown sisters, sculptress Anne (Kika Markham) and teacher Muriel (Stacey Tendeter), who live on the coast of Wales. There are many emotional handicaps (and at least one physical one) for these characters to overcome, and to list them here would spoil the pleasure of discovery for a first-time viewer. Just know that this film deserves to be placed among the very best of Truffaut's work, including *Jules and Jim*—both films were based on source novels by Henri-Pierre Roché. It also features lovely color cinematography by Néstor Almendros. Originally released at 97 minutes, Truffaut made the restoration of the film to its original length of 132 minutes one of his final projects before he died in 1984. That version is the one that matters.

⊙**DVD**

DR18, DR29

Goes well with: *Jules and Jim*

U

ULEE'S GOLD

ESSENTIAL

U.S.   1997   C   111 min.   R   Drama

Dir: Victor Nunez

C: Peter Fonda, Patricia Richardson, Jessica Biel, J. Kenneth Campbell,
Christine Dunford, Steve Flynn, Dewey Weber

Peter Fonda saw his acting career get a jump start when he hooked up
with independent filmmaker Victor Nunez for this moving portrait of a
Florida beekeeper drawn into family troubles against his better instincts. Ulysses Jackson is a widower taking care of two granddaughters
whose daddy, Jimmy (Ulee's son-in-law), is doing time in the state pen
for a robbery and whose momma, Helen (Ulee's daughter), is doing
drugs anywhere she can find them. Ulee tries to keep his life as simple
as possible, but that's not possible when two of Jimmy's confederates in
the robbery who slipped away from the law find out that the stolen
money is hidden on Ulee's land. Fonda's restraint is eloquent testimony
to his character's survival instincts, to shut off as much emotion as possible to protect himself from further harm in his life. It's a performance
his old man would have been proud to see—or give.

⊙**DVD**

DR6, DR11, DR21

Goes well with: *Shoot the Piano Player*

UN COEUR EN HIVER

France   1992   C   105 min.   NR   Drama

Dir: Claude Sautet

C: Daniel Auteuil, Emmanuelle Béart, André Dussollier

Maurice Ravel's chamber music is not as well-known or celebrated as his orchestral compositions, so it's refreshing to see a filmmaker use several pieces (a trio and two sonatas) as the emotional coloring behind a story set in (surprise!) the world of classical music. Stéphane (Daniel Auteuil) and Maxime (André Dussollier) are partners in a violin-making business. Camille (Emmanuelle Béart) is a violinist and Maxime's lover; she becomes the object of Stéphane's desire as well. Director and cowriter Claude Sautet has said that Ravel's Trio set the mood for this melancholy story of love, and one of the sonatas, influenced by Ravel's post–World War I fascination with American jazz, underscores Camille's tumult as she faces an emotional entanglement with two men. It's a rare and nearly perfect blend of music and story; the recordings used in the film are available on compact disc under the film's title.

DR18, DR23

Goes well with: *Meeting Venus*

THE UNBEARABLE LIGHTNESS OF BEING

U.S. 1988 C 172 min. R Drama

Dir: Philip Kaufman

C: Daniel Day-Lewis, Juliette Binoche, Lena Olin, Derek de Lint, Erland Josephson, Pavel Landovský, Donald Moffat

Sex and politics aren't necessarily strange bedfellows, though they're too often associated with scandalous behavior by politicians. This adaptation of Milan Kundera's novel (by Philip Kaufman and Jean-Claude Carrière) marries the Prague Spring of 1968 and its disheartening aftermath with the romantic conquests of a young doctor named Tomas (Daniel Day-Lewis). As the story opens, Tomas and his current lover, Sabina (Lena Olin), feed off the energy of Czechoslovakia's newfound freedoms. Then Tomas meets Teresa (Juliette Binoche), who is as withdrawn and modest as Sabina is flamboyant and uninhibited. The three characters dance around each other for nearly three hours, a length that allows for elaboration of Kundera's ideas regarding isolation and responsibility. (Naysayers would claim the film's length only allows for repetition of these notions.) Day-Lewis and Olin are superb, and even if you can sense the film's inevitable conclusion coming, it won't lessen its impact. Sven Nykvist's cinematography was honored at the Independent Spirit Awards.

⊙**DVD:** Includes audio commentaries by Philip Kaufman, Lena Olin, Jean-Claude Carrière, and editor Walter Murch.

DR19, DR20, DR29, DR33
Goes well with: *Red*

THE UNBELIEVABLE TRUTH
ESSENTIAL

U.S. 1990 C 90 min. R Comedy
Dir: Hal Hartley
C: Adrienne Shelly, Robert Burke, Chris Cooke, Julia McNeal

Hal Hartley's debut is a dark comedy about dislocation in the suburbs of Long Island. Audry (the magnetic Adrienne Shelly) is a teen adrift in the impossibly not-there world of school and homework and stupid boys. When she meets the older Josh (Robert Burke), she's intrigued, especially after the rumors start flying: Is he an ex-con or an ex-priest? Either possibility is tantalizing to Audry, who's just desperate enough to think that anything attached to danger is better than the hand she's been dealt. Hartley keeps our sympathies for Audry at arm's length; she has a right to rebel, but the film suggests the limits of that rebellion as well.

CO2, CO11
Goes well with: *Trust*

UNDER THE SAND
France 2000 C 96 min. NR Drama
Dir: François Ozon
C: Charlotte Rampling, Bruno Cremer, Jacques Nolot, Alexandra
  Stewart, Pierre Vernier

On vacation, Jean and Marie Drillon go to the beach. Jean goes for a swim while Marie reads, and Jean disappears. Did he drown, did he walk off? No body is found, and Marie returns to their flat in Paris and carries on with her life, assuming that Jean is still around, not as a ghost but as a presence of some kind. She speaks of him as though he were alive, but she is sometimes reminded of his disappearance, as when she spots a student in her class at the university who was a lifeguard at the beach. Charlotte Rampling gives a brilliantly understated performance in this quietly observed film about two important subjects: dealing with death, and what we don't know about those we love dearly. The film's pivotal scene is Marie's visit with Jean's mother in a nursing home; as the two women wrestle over the nature of Jean's fate, you can sense Marie beginning to question assumptions about her husband.

⊙**DVD:** Includes audio commentary by François Ozon and interview with Charlotte Rampling.

DR8

Goes well with: *Truly Madly Deeply*

THE UNDERNEATH

U.S. 1994 C 99 min. R Thriller

Dir: Steven Soderbergh

C: Peter Gallagher, Alison Elliott, William Fichtner, Adam Trese, Joe Don Baker, Paul Dooley, Elisabeth Shue, Anjanette Comer, Shelley Duvall

Remaking a classic film noir is tricky business, counting on either a lapse of memory among the moviegoing public (haven't I seen this somewhere before?) or indulgence from the completists (not as good as the original, but not bad, either). Steven Soderbergh's heist melodrama, a redo of 1949's *Criss Cross,* borrows that film's story and emotional geometry but offers so many new takes on the material that in some ways a comparison between the two is of the apples-oranges variety. *Criss Cross* was melodramatic, *Underneath* (taking off from its title) is subdued, starting with its low-key trio of stars (Peter Gallagher, Alison Elliott, and William Fichtner). The story—a gambler returns to his hometown, finds his old flame taken up with a gangster, decides to pull a heist that will net enough money to get her and himself away—is almost secondary to a mood of foreboding. And Soderbergh once again exhibits his love for fractured narrative by stuffing this film full of flashbacks; as in *The Limey,* these are not digressions but elaborations.

⊙**DVD**

TH8, TH13, XT4

Goes well with: *The Limey*

THE USUAL SUSPECTS

ESSENTIAL

U.S. 1995 C 105 min. R Thriller

Dir: Bryan Singer

C: Stephen Baldwin, Gabriel Byrne, Chazz Palminteri, Kevin Pollak, Pete Postlethwaite, Kevin Spacey, Suzy Amis, Benicio Del Toro, Giancarlo Esposito, Dan Hedaya, Paul Bartel

A film that managed the unusual feat of pleasing the public, the critics, the members of the Motion Picture Academy and most of the film purists for whom any contemporary voyage into the waters of film noir is a journey likely to end up with a shipwreck of a film. Christopher McQuarrie's Oscar-winning screenplay is about a heist involving five disparate lowlifes, one of whom, a smooth-talking cripple named Verbal (Oscar winner Kevin Spacey), is only too happy to pass on what he knows about the botched affair. As he spins his yarn to a police detective (Chazz Palminteri), it becomes clear that the mastermind behind this whole show is a criminal named Keyser Soze. And to release any more information to a first-time viewer of this film (assuming there are any left) would be criminal. Bryan Singer's smooth direction, skillful playing by all (the other five suspects are Gabriel Byrne, Stephen Baldwin, Kevin Pollak, and Benicio Del Toro), and a knockout ending that may have you rewinding for another look are three more good reasons to check this thriller out. Spacey won Best Supporting Actor accolades from the New York Film Critics Circle for his performances in this and three other films; the Independent Spirit Awards honored Benicio Del Toro's supporting performance and McQuarrie's screenplay.

⊙**DVD:** Special Edition includes audio commentary by Bryan Singer and Christopher McQuarrie; deleted scenes; four featurettes; gag reel.

TH5, TH8, TH12, TH13, TH17, XT4

Goes well with: *Reservoir Dogs*

V

VAGABOND

France/U.K.   1985   C   105 min.   NR   Drama
Dir: Agnès Varda
C: Sandrine Bonnaire, Macha Méril, Stéphane Freiss, Laurence Cortadellas

The life of a teenager who chooses life on the road over any kind of conventional bourgeois existence is told in flashback by Agnes Varda. Sandrine Bonnaire fulfills the promise of her debut in *A Nos Amours* with a stunning performance as Mona, a young woman whose fiercely unconventional ways are never explained. Varda allows Mona's encounters with various people she meets in her travels to inform the viewer's opinion of her. Should we envy her freedom from responsibility or condemn it as an act of selfishness? You may find yourself changing your mind several times during the film. It's the strongest film of Varda's long career, accessible without conceding to popular convention, lyrical without being sentimental.
⊙**DVD**
DR21, DR39, XT4
Goes well with: *La Cérémonie*

VALLEY GIRL

U.S.   1983   C   95 min.   R   Comedy
Dir: Martha Coolidge
C: Nicolas Cage, Deborah Foreman, Colleen Camp, Frederic Forrest, Elizabeth Daily

In the fall of 1982, Frank Zappa released his only single to make the pop charts, "Valley Girl," a spoof of the cultural hot-button topic of that moment, the teenage airheads of California's San Fernando Valley. Then came the movie, which had no right to be anything more than a feeble attempt to cash in on the whole craze of kids who use "like" at least four times in every sentence and think trips to the mall are cultural experiences of the highest order. In fact, the film was more than a cut above the teen comedies that have, in the last twenty-five years, generally defined the lowest common denominator in American moviemaking. *Valley's* clever script made its heroine (played by Deborah Foreman) brighter and sassier than the stereotype Zappa riffed on, and it cleverly turned her parents (Colleen Camp and Frederic Forrest) into 1960s alums who are dismayed at their daughter's rebellion against their sold-out lives. Throw in a young Nicolas Cage as the VG's love interest, smart direction by Martha Coolidge, and, like, we have a winner.

CO5, CO8

Goes well with: *Slums of Beverly Hills*

VAMPIRES, LES.

See *Les Vampires*

THE VANISHING

France/Netherlands 1988 C 102 min. NR Thriller
Dir: George Sluizer
C: Bernard-Pierre Donnadieu, Gene Bervoets, Johanna Ter Steege

It's the kind of movie that creeps up on you years after you've seen it. George Sluizer, working from a script by Tim Krabbé (who adapted his own novel, *The Golden Egg*), fashions a setup that is absolutely elemental to contemporary life: the unexplained disappearance of a loved one. In this case, it happens during a rest stop along a busy highway, where Saskia (Johanna Ter Steege) walks into a store and leaves her lover, Rex (Gene Bervoets), waiting . . . and waiting . . . and waiting. No one has seen her get into another vehicle, and for years he's left to track down tiny leads that wind up dead ends. Then mysterious postcards begin appearing in his mailbox, sent by a stranger (Bernard-Pierre Donnadieu) who finally contacts him and makes an offer Rex cannot refuse. Rex is like of any of us—he has to know, and his quest for knowledge leads to a stunning climax.

⊙**DVD**

DR27, TH1, TH16

Goes well with: *With a Friend Like Harry*

VANYA ON 42ND STREET

U.S. 1994 C 120 min. PG Drama

Dir: Louis Malle

C: Wallace Shawn, Phoebe Brand, George Gaynes, Jerry Mayer, Andre Gregory, Julianne Moore, Larry Pine, Brooke Smith, Lynn Cohen, Madhur Jaffrey

Louis Malle's final film is also one of his strongest—and for how many directors can you make that claim? It's a new way of seeing Anton Chekhov's play *Uncle Vanya,* adapted by David Mamet and Andre Gregory. The play's (and film's) cast gathers in Manhattan's decrepit New Amsterdam Theatre for a workshop, a sort of rehearsal in street clothes under the guidance of their director (Andre Gregory). After some fits and starts, the performers proceed to "do" the play while seated. Malle is playing here with the delicate illusions of the theater and the limitations of film in sustaining that. If you have ever seen a filmed performance of a play, you know there is something missing; you're two steps removed from the players and the scenery, and the illusion can't hold that kind of distance. Only a gifted cast (led by Wallace Shawn as Vanya, Julianne Moore as Yelena, and George Gaynes as the Professor) could pull this off.

DR4

Goes well with: *Topsy-Turvy*

VIDEODROME

Canada/U.S. 1983 C 87 min. R Science Fiction

Dir: David Cronenberg

C: James Woods, Sonja Smits, Deborah Harry, Peter Dvorsky, Les Carlson

It may not convert you to the Church of David Cronenberg, where bodies turn into machines and there's no distinction between "live" and "on tape." For the more adventurous and those with strong stomachs, Cronenberg's little fables of technology slowly devouring mankind are the kind of stories that put the pulp back into pulp fiction. James Woods is well cast here as a cable TV programmer with a yen for a satellite channel that seems to be showing films featuring hardcore sex and actual murders. He takes it on himself to investigate this phenomenon and discovers a cult that can help him become the programmer he always wanted to be. Rock singer Deborah Harry is his girlfriend, more than ready for a little adventure of her own.

⊙**DVD**

FA2, FA8

Goes well with: *Scanners*

THE VIRGIN SUICIDES

U.S. 2000 C 97 min. R Drama

Dir: Sofia Coppola

C: James Woods, Kathleen Turner, Kirsten Dunst, Hannah Hall, Chelse Swain, A. J. Cook, Leslie Hayman, Josh Hartnett, Michael Paré, Scott Glenn, Danny DeVito, Hayden Christensen, Giovanni Ribisi (narrator)

The debut of writer-director Sofia Coppola did her famous father Francis proud. In adapting Jeffrey Eugenides's novel of five suburban midwestern sisters headed for doom, Coppola understands that atmosphere counts for more than narrative drive or depth of character. The film creates a world that is almost suffocating in repression and longing; this may be the *Citizen Kane* of overheated teen lust movies. An unseen narrator makes it clear that the story, set in the 1970s, is being recounted by its grown male characters, a group of teen boys understandably smitten by the Lisbon girls, so what we get are the impressions of memory rather than the details of the here and now. (Several inserts of Michael Paré as the adult version of one of the boys, Trip Fontaine, overplay the film's hand.) Kirsten Dunst, as Lux Lisbon, the fourth-oldest but most mature sister, makes you wish that some filmmaker would take yet another stab at *Lolita*. As her parents, James Woods and Kathleen Turner play admirably against nearly every role in their respective filmographies: He is the distracted math teacher oblivious to any nuance of human behavior, and she is the tight-lipped mother using the Catholic Church as a cudgel to beat her girls into submission. And for a film with that gloomy title, this is a movie that is very funny on the details of teen courtship in a time that seems much longer ago than twenty-five years.

⊙**DVD:** Includes "making of" featurette.

DR8, DR11, DR29, DR41

Goes well with: *Heavenly Creatures*

VIRIDIANA

ESSENTIAL

Spain/Mexico 1961 B&W 90 min. NR Drama

Dir: Luis Buñuel

C: Francisco Rabal, Silvia Pinal, Fernando Rey, Margarita Lozano

When Luis Buñuel left Spain in the late 1930s, Francisco Franco was about to seize power. After twenty years in exile in the United States and Mexico, Buñuel returned to his native country. Franco was still in power, but Buñuel was allowed to make this film under the watchful eye of the state censors. Make that the semiwatchful eye, for Buñuel pulled a fast one, creating a superbly dark-hearted drama about the inability of the Catholic Church to deal with the realities of the world. (The film was banned in Spain and honored at Cannes as the 1961 festival's best film, and Buñuel was once again a man in exile.) Viridiana is the name of a novitiate (Silvia Pinal) who is assigned to visit her widowed uncle (Fernando Rey) on his farm just before taking her final vows. He sees her as the reincarnation of his bride, who died thirty years ago on their wedding night, and he asks her to don her aunt's wedding dress, after which he drugs her. Viridiana winds up sharing ownership of the farm with her uncle's illegitimate son, and she attempts to make it a haven for homeless beggars, who turn it into their private clubhouse. You don't have to be a lapsed Catholic to love Buñuel's willingness to challenge the strictures of organized religion. Viridiana is a woman of virtue but little experience in the ways of the world; Buñuel clearly sees religion as irrelevant to those most in need of its charitable aims.

DR21, DR30

Goes well with: *Belle de Jour*

VISIONS OF LIGHT: THE ART OF CINEMATOGRAPHY

ESSENTIAL

U.S./Japan   1993   C/B&W   90 min.   NR   Documentary

Dir: Arnold Glassman, Todd McCarthy, and Stuart Samuels

The visuals in any film are its most important component, but it's not enough to exclaim how "beautiful" the cinematography is without understanding the way an image is lit and framed (and in some cases not framed) to realize the measure of that importance. *Visions of Light* is a tantalizing tutorial in the way shadows on a screen, whether in the theater or on TV, speak to us so eloquently. Made with the cooperation of the American Society of Cinematographers, this documentary contains images from over 125 films, ranging from *The Birth of a Nation* (shot by pioneering cameraman Billy Bitzer) to *Goodfellas* (photographed by Michael Ballhaus). All of the interviewees, who include Gordon Willis (*The God-*

father), Caleb Deschanel (*The Black Stallion*), Michael Chapman (*Raging Bull*), and Néstor Almendros (*Days of Heaven*), add invaluable insights about their work and the films that influenced their careers. Best story: William A. Fraker describing how Roman Polanski anticipated audience reaction to an unusual shot in *Rosemary's Baby.* A must-see on DVD. Voted Best Documentary of 1993 by the New York Film Critics Circle.

⊙**DVD**

DO5

Goes well with: *Stanley Kubrick: A Life in Pictures*

W

THE WAGES OF FEAR

ESSENTIAL

France/Italy 1952 B&W 148 min. NR Action-Adventure
Dir: Henri-Georges Clouzot
C: Yves Montand, Charles Vanel, Peter Van Eyck, Vera Clouzot, Folco Lulli, William Tubbs

Four European men, adrift and nearly penniless in a squalid Latin American village, are lured by the promise of a big payday for a dangerous job: An oil company needs a load of nitroglycerin to be delivered to a remote well fire burning out of control. The route is through jungle and over mountains, and these men are just desperate enough to take the chance. That's the setup for one of the greatest adventure films of them all, though some viewers may not appreciate its dim view of humanity. None of these men (Yves Montand, Folco Lulli, Peter Van Eyck, Charles Vanel) is particularly heroic or generous; they're in it for the money. But, as he did in *Diabolique,* Henri-Georges Clouzot finds a way to make you care about less-than-honorable people, if only because their survival is at stake every minute. Beware of versions of this film running as short as 105 minutes; a 156-minute version exists, but no sources consulted indicate it is available on video. The DVD on Criterion runs 148 min.

⊙**DVD**

AC2, AC4

Goes well with: *Mountains of the Moon*

WAITING FOR GUFFMAN

ESSENTIAL

U.S.   1997   C   84 min.   R   Comedy
Dir: Christopher Guest
C: Christopher Guest, Eugene Levy, Fred Willard, Catherine O'Hara, Parker Posey, Lewis Arquette, Matt Keeslar, Bob Balaban, Paul Dooley, Paul Benedict, Larry Miller, Brian Doyle-Murray

Christopher Guest and cowriter Eugene Levy have created a premise, the attempts by residents of Blaine, a small Missouri town, to put on a special stage show commemorating the town's sesquicentennial, that is both promising comic material and a minefield of condescending potshots at those pathetic folks out there in the flyover states. The genius of *Guffman*'s comedy is in its two directors—Guest, who tiptoes past the land mines to get the honest laughs, and the character he plays, Corky St. Clair. Corky is a New York "artiste of the theatre" who has agreed to helm *Red, White and Blaine,* and his self-delusions of grandeur infect everyone involved, save the town council, which won't grant him $100,000 for his budget. (For a moment Corky considers packing it in and heading back east, but fortunately for us, he sticks it out.) Corky's cast, including a married pair of travel agents (Fred Willard and Catherine O'Hara), a Dairy Queen server (Parker Posey), and a dentist (Levy), are all as talented as he, which is to say, not at all.

⊙**DVD:** Special Edition contains audio commentaries by Christopher Guest and Eugene Levy, and deleted scenes with commentary.

CO10, CO11, CO12

Goes well with: *Who Am I This Time?*

WALKABOUT

Australia   1971   C   100 min.   NR   Action-Adventure
Dir: Nicolas Roeg
C: Jenny Agutter, Lucien John, David Gulpilil, John Meillon

Cinematographer-turned-director Nicolas Roeg made his first solo effort a ravishing adventure set in the Australian outback, where a teenage girl (Jenny Agutter) and her little brother (Lucien John) are stranded after their father goes mad. Edward Bond's script, an adaptation of a novel by James Vance Marshall, explores the cross-cultural problems that crop up when the pair meet an aborigine (David Gulpilil) who is alone but not without resources of his own. He has been deserted, too, but deliberately, to do his "walkabout," or rite of passage into manhood. The sexual tension between the two adolescents is palpable, and Roeg's imagery of nature (water, smooth tree limbs) reinforces the mood. But the girl can't (and won't) understand her savior, though her brother has no qualms about a black man leading them to safety. It's a great adventure and coming-of-age story that takes full advantage of the striking Australian landscape. The running time and rating reflect the 1996 reissue; tapes running 95 minutes and rated PG may still be in circulation.

⊙**DVD:** Unrated director's cut; includes audio commentary by Nicolas Roeg and Jenny Agutter; liner notes by Roger Ebert.

AC2, DR7, DR41

Goes well with: *Burke and Wills*

THE WAR ROOM

U.S.   1993   C   96 min.   PG   Documentary
Dir: D. A. Pennebaker and Chris Hegedus

Striking while the iron was still red-hot, D. A. Pennebaker and Chris Hegedus anticipated the Clinton victory in 1992 and got permission to hang out with some of his key campaign staffers in the titular location, command central for the Man from Hope's bid for the White House. The stars of this film, and a lovely mismatched pair they are, are James Carville and George Stephanopoulos. Carville is reptilian in both appearance and manner, a man who eats, breathes, and sleeps politics, relishing every battle, no matter how small. Stephanopoulos is idealistic, well-meaning, boyishly charming, and clearly a foil for Carville's aggressive machismo. If Billy Wilder were making a film about them, he would cast Walter Matthau and Jack Lemmon in the roles.

⊙**DVD**

DO9

Goes well with: *Feed*

THE WATERDANCE

U.S.   1992   C   106 min.   R   Drama
Dir: Neal Jimenez and Michael Steinberg
C: Eric Stoltz, Wesley Snipes, William Forsyth, Helen Hunt, Elizabeth Peña, Grace Zabriskie

In 1985, Neal Jimenez was left paralyzed from the waist down by a fall, and he went on to write and codirect a good movie about his rehabilitation experiences. Joel Garcia is his screen name, and Eric Stoltz plays him with a ferocity he's not always allowed to show in his other film roles. Most of the action takes place in a rehab hospital, where you might get a sense of déjà vu if you recall Marlon Brando's screen debut, *The Men,* about World War II vets in the same setting. Garcia's two best buddies (played with great relish by Wesley Snipes and William Forsyth) aren't a perfect fit for him or each other, and his love life (with his married girlfriend, played by Helen Hunt) is hardly the model of domestic tranquility. To the film's great credit, none of these loose ends is neatly tied up in the end. Jimenez's screenplay won an Independent Spirit Award (which also honored the film as Best First Feature) and an Audience Award at Sundance.

⊙**DVD**

DR3, DR15, DR16

Goes well with: *My Left Foot*

THE WEAVERS: WASN'T THAT A TIME!

U.S. 1982 C 78 min. PG Documentary
Dir: Jim Brown

Lee Hays, Fred Hillerman, Ronnie Gilbert, and Pete Seeger—"two low baritones, one brilliant alto, and a split tenor," in Seeger's words—comprised America's seminal folk-song group. They topped the charts for thirteen weeks in 1950 with their recording of "Goodnight Irene," only to wind up on the blacklist a few years later for their fidelity to union and leftist activities. This documentary tribute, including archival footage and current-day interviews (Hays is definitely the comedian of the group), is such a joyful experience that you almost forget its reason for being. Hays was ill when the film was shot, and he died before its release. (At his request, friends put his ashes on his compost heap.) The group had disbanded and re-formed with different members a number of times over the years, and filming was the occasion for two last shows at Carnegie Hall, which are only briefly excerpted here. This is a film that begs for a DVD release with additional footage of those shows and, really, everything the filmmakers gathered.

DO5

Goes well with: *The Buena Vista Social Club*

THE WEDDING BANQUET

U.S./Taiwan 1993 C 111 min. R Comedy
Dir: Ang Lee

C: Winston Chao, May Chin, Mitchell Lichtenstein, Sihung Lung

The marriage of convenience, a staple of screwball comedies of the 1930s and 1940s, gets a witty update in Taiwanese director Ang Lee's first English-language film. Wai-Tung (Winston Chao) is a successful Taiwanese-American living with his gay lover (Mitchell Lichtenstein) in New York. Back home, his parents still can't understand why their attractive son hasn't married, and their trip to Manhattan prompts swift action: Wai-Tung proposes to his tenant Wei-Wei (May Chin), a native of mainland China in need of a green card, that they marry— strictly for show. Lee and cowriters Neil Feng and James Schamus wring expected laughs out of all the possible situations, and the film goes deeper than a Hollywood hack job would to suggest the sad desperation of a man who has it all, except a pact of mutual trust with his parents.

CO3, CO9, DR7, DR11, DR19

Goes well with: *Eat Drink Man Woman*

WEEKEND
ESSENTIAL

France/Italy   1967   C   103 min.   NR   Comedy-Drama
Dir: Jean-Luc Godard
C: Mireille Darc, Jean Yanne, Jean-Pierre Kalfon, Valérie Lagrange, Jean-Pierre Léaud

Jean-Luc Godard's social comedy is an unusually ingratiating mix of satire and polemics. The wafer-thin story is of a bourgeois couple's weekend outing to the countryside, where they encounter the longest traffic jam in the history of the movies, detailed in one long breathtaking shot by cinematographer Raoul Coutard. Their off-road adventures prove to be even more harrowing, as they stumble onto a cell of Maoist revolutionaries living off the land, hoping to foment their own apocalypse now rather than later. Characters speak directly to the camera, and those viewers of a certain age and political stripe may suffer from flashbacks to their more politicized youth of this era. Godard is serious enough to include this material in his film, but you don't have to take it seriously. The message that the couple, with their pathetic addiction to name-brand material goods, sends is powerful enough on its own.

CO8, DR20, XT5

Goes well with: *Pierrot le Fou*

WELCOME TO SARAJEVO

U.K./U.S. 1997 C 101 min. R Drama
Dir: Michael Winterbottom
C: Stephen Dillane, Woody Harrelson, Emira Nusevic, Marisa Tomei,
Kerry Fox, Goran Višnjic, Emily Lloyd

The story of journalists under fire in a modern war of attrition is given a new spin in this affecting drama from Michael Winterbottom and writer Frank Cottrell-Boyce. They've based their film on the real experiences of British TV journalist Michael Nicholson (here named Michael Henderson and played by Stephen Dillane), who crossed the line from objective observer to involved activist in his reporting on the plight of children orphaned during the 1992–93 siege of Sarajevo. Henderson pledges to a little girl named Emira (Emira Nusevic) that he will get her to a safe place, and then makes good on that promise by taking her back with him to England. All this happens in the first seventy minutes of the film, so you know there will be complications. The film skillfully blends dramatic footage and news images, condemning the inaction of the international community on humanitarian matters. The most wrenching moment: A bus of children escaping the country is stopped by a force of Serbs.
DR38
Goes well with: *Salvador*

WELCOME TO THE DOLLHOUSE

U.S. 1995 C 87 min. R Comedy
Dir: Todd Solondz
C: Heather Matarazzo, Brendan Sexton III, Daria Kalinina, Matthew
Faber, Angela Pietropinto, Eric Mabius

Junior high is one of the great neglected subjects of filmmaking, and this film demonstrates why. It's one thing to relive your carefree grade-school days or fast times at high school, but those limbo years of confusing hormonal shifts and sadistic social cruelty as an art form are best left undisturbed. Todd Solondz remembers, and he insists we watch poor Dawn Wiener (imagine the taunting such a name would produce— I can) stumble through the gauntlet of a school cafeteria packed with would-be comics. At home, Dawn (the affectingly homely Heather Matarazzo) is hammocked between an older brother whose rock band practices in their garage, and an insufferable little sister who gets whatever attention their parents don't lavish on their son. The hell of adoles-

cence was never funnier or more painful. Matarazzo won the Debut Performance Award from the Independent Spirit Awards, while the film
picked up the Grand Jury Prize at Sundance.

⊙**DVD**

DR11, DR21, DR31, DR41

Goes well with: *Slums of Beverly Hills*

WHEN WE WERE KINGS

ESSENTIAL

U.S. 1996 C 92 min. PG Documentary
Dir: Leon Gast

The 1974 Muhammad Ali–George Foreman heavyweight fight, the
so-called "Rumble in the Jungle," was preceded by so many astonishing
events that the fight itself seemed almost anticlimactic. This was the
first title bout fought in Africa, and the first appearance on the world
stage of promoter Don King. An accompanying music festival (featuring James Brown and B. B. King) added to the hype, which hardly
needed anything more than the presence of Ali, itching to get back the
crown he'd lost when he refused induction into the military eight years
before. Foreman was big and bad (not the cuddly pitchman he is today),
and Ali played on that image, just as he'd taunted Sonny Liston and Joe
Frazier earlier in his career. A Foreman injury only delayed the anticipation of Ali getting slaughtered. Director Leon Gast spent many years
assembling the footage he needed to make this comprehensive record,
and his use of writers Norman Mailer and George Plimpton, both of
whom were ringside at the fight, for their recollections gives the film
class and perspective. The film won best documentary awards from the
Academy, the New York Film Critics Circle, and the Independent Spirits; it also was given a Special Recognition award at Sundance.

⊙**DVD**

DO4, DO10

Goes well with: *Fallen Champ: The Untold Story of Mike Tyson*

WHERE ANGELS FEAR TO TREAD

U.K. 1991 C 112 min. PG Drama
Dir: Charles Sturridge
C: Helena Bonham Carter, Judy Davis, Rupert Graves, Giovanni
Guidelli, Barbara Jefford, Helen Mirren, Thomas Wheatley

The miniboom in the late 1980s and early 1990s of E. M. Forster adaptations (*A Room with a View, Howards End*) ended not with a thud but a hearty and unexpected chuckle with this adaptation of his first novel. Lilia Heriton (Helen Mirren), a widow approaching middle age, upsets her uptight in-laws by marrying a younger man, an Italian she met on a tour of the continent. Her brother-in-law (Rupert Graves) is dispatched to put an end to this madness, and when he can't, he and his prissy sister (Judy Davis) are forced to return to try to retrieve Lilia's orphaned baby. It's a drama embroidered with many amusing moments, and the always marvelous Mirren and equally splendid Davis carry the film as a kind of relay team, since they share few scenes together. And the Tuscany locations are a soothing background to the social madness in the forefront.

DR7, DR11, DR29

Goes well with: *A Room with a View*

WHITE OF THE EYE

U.K. 1987 C 110 min. R Thriller
Dir: Donald Cammell
C: David Keith, Cathy Moriarty, Art Evans, Alan Rosenberg, Alberta Watson

If it were only for its story—happily married woman discovers that her husband is a serial killer who targets females—*White of the Eye* would be nothing more than your ordinary woman-in-jeopardy time-waster. The key name here is writer-director Donald Cammell. His blighted career, which ended in suicide, produced only a handful of films; this one is his best solo work (he also codirected the similarly disturbing *Performance* with cinematographer Nicolas Roeg). Cammell can't tell a story straight—he's always digressing to offer up bizarre imagery—and that works well for freshening up well-worn material like this. Set in an Arizona mining town, *White of the Eye* offers desert vistas, Indian mysticism, and a killer (played by David Keith) who has come unhinged so quietly that even the woman he sleeps with (Cathy Moriarty) has no clue what he's up to. In a way, Cammell's technique is a reflection of the killer's own mind, racing at warp speed to justify his twisted view of the world.

TH15, TH16

Goes well with: *Peeping Tom*

WHO AM I THIS TIME?

U.S. 1982 C 60 min. PG Comedy
Dir: Jonathan Demme

C: Susan Sarandon, Christopher Walken, Robert Ridgley, Dorothy Paterson

A whimsical take on the world of amateur theater, *Who Am I This Time?* is an adaptation of a Kurt Vonnegut story about a timid hardware clerk (Christopher Walken) who inhabits the stage characters he's asked to play in convincing fashion. Susan Sarandon is the new thespian in town who doesn't get this fact at first, and she's instantly attracted to her costar's brawling turn as Stanley Kowalski. Back in the plumbing aisle, this would-be Brando has, to her dismay, turned into Wally Cox. Jonathan Demme took a break from his budding career in films to direct this totally charming comedy for public television.

CO9, CO10, CO11

Goes well with: *Waiting for Guffman*

THE WHOLE WIDE WORLD

U.S.   1996   C   111 min.   PG   Drama
Dir: Dan Ireland
C: Vincent D'Onofrio, Renée Zellweger, Ann Wedgeworth, Harve Presnell

The tiny world of writer Robert E. Howard was a small town in Texas, where he lived with his parents and cranked out pulp fiction starring Conan the Barbarian and other less enduring heroes. This quietly observed drama details his brief relationship with Novalyne Price Ellis, a local schoolteacher and aspiring writer who asked for an introduction to the reclusive Howard. Vincent D'Onofrio, brooding but tender, makes Howard a believably arrested adolescent struggling to walk and talk like a man. Renée Zellweger is the impressionable but hardly retiring Novalyne. Her interest in Howard is both professional and personal, but the two never became lovers. Howard committed suicide in 1936 at the age of thirty. The script, cowritten by Ellis and Michael Scott Myers, is based on her memoir.

DR2, DR17, DR18, DR21

Goes well with: *Surviving Picasso*

WHO'S THAT KNOCKING AT MY DOOR

U.S.   1968   B&W   90 min.   R   Drama
Dir: Martin Scorsese
C: Zina Bethune, Harvey Keitel, Anne Collette, Lennard Kuras, Michael Scala, Harry Northup

Martin Scorsese's first feature was a warm-up for his breakthrough third film, *Mean Streets*. Harvey Keitel appeared in both as a young Italian American living what might be termed a 1960s slacker lifestyle, which consists of a lot of hanging out at a Little Italy "social club" with his pals. The presence of the Mob is only obliquely referenced here; the story concentrates on J.R.'s attraction to a young woman (Zina Bethune) and his dismay at learning about a tragedy in her past. Scorsese packs his soundtrack with rock and roll—the title tune and "I've Had It" are standouts—from the prepsychedelic and British Invasion era, when songs on the radio sounded just like the music those goombahs down on the street corner were making every night. Scorsese could only get a distributor after he agreed to shoot J.R.'s sexual fantasy, which meant a minute or two of female nudity.

DR18, DR36, XT7
Goes well with: *Household Saints*

THE WILD CHILD

France   1969   B&W   85 min.   G   Drama
Dir: François Truffaut
C: François Truffaut, Jean-Pierre Cargol, Jean Dasté, Paul Villé

Among François Truffaut's most elegant and underrated films, *The Wild Child* tells the true story of a young boy found living in the forest outside a village in late-eighteenth-century France. It was a time when Rousseau's theory of the noble savage would butt heads with rational scientific thinking, here represented by Itard (Truffaut), a physician who takes the boy in and tries to teach him the ways of civilization. Truffaut narrates the story in an almost passionless voice that contrasts with Itard's growing emotional involvement with Victor (as he comes to call the boy, who is played by Jean-Pierre Cargol). It's a provocative and moving story of the power and limitations of education, with splendid use of Vivaldi on the soundtrack. Néstor Almendros's black-and-white camerawork, and the artful employment of irises as transitions between scenes, give the film the feel of a drama from the silent era.

⊙**DVD**
DR16, DR17, DR21, DR24, DR41
Goes well with: *Every Man for Himself and God Against All*

WILD MAN BLUES

U.S.   1998   C   105 min.   PG   Documentary
Dir: Barbara Kopple

Woody Allen's post–Mia Farrow career resuscitation took a big leap sideways with the release of Barbara Kopple's documentary. This is not about the Wood-man as film auteur; this is about his moonlighting job as a jazz clarinetist, and how he took his act on the road to Europe with a band of Dixieland jazz veterans. Of course, the real interest here is the dynamic between Woody and his wife and former stepdaughter, Soon-Yi Previn, and the film makes it clear that she's no submissive Mrs. in this domestic arrangement. If you feel like Kopple is spending too much time on the live performances, that may be an indication you don't care for Dixieland, or that you care too much to listen to Woody go at it. Ah well, neither Artie Shaw nor Benny Goodman ever made a movie as good as *Annie Hall*. Tom Hurwitz's cinematography won a prize at Sundance.

DO4

Goes well with: *Stanley Kubrick: A Life in Pictures*

WILD REEDS

ESSENTIAL

France   1994   C   110 min.   NR   Drama

Dir: André Téchiné

C: Elodie Bouchez, Gaël Morel, Stéphane Rideau, Frédéric Gorny, Michèle Moretti

The teenagers in André Téchiné's drama have the usual assortment of problems that adolescents of any era deal with, so it's the time and setting—the south of France in 1962—that gives this film an extra dimension. Henri (Frédéric Gorny) is an Algerian immigrant who is opposed to his home country's then-current fight for independence from its colonial master. François (Gaël Morel) is dealing with his budding homosexuality in a repressive era, while the object of his affection is in turn attracted to his best gal pal, Maite (Elodie Bouchez). The daily shifts in these high school crushes, romances, and friendships are charted with delicacy and just the right helping of humor. Winner of the Best Foreign Language Film prize from the New York Film Critics Circle.

⊙**DVD**

DR19, DR31, DR41

Goes well with: *Flirting*

WILD STRAWBERRIES

ESSENTIAL

Sweden   1957   B&W   90 min.   NR   Drama

Dir: Ingmar Bergman

C: Victor Sjöstrom, Ingrid Thulin, Bibi Andersson, Gunnar Björn-strand, Folke Sundquist, Gertrud Fridh, Max von Sydow

Ingmar Bergman's study of a man looking back on a life of disappointments is remarkably light on its feet. Isak Borg (the great silent-film director Victor Sjöstrom) is a seventy-eight-year-old widowed physician about to return to his hometown to receive an honor. On the car journey there, accompanied by his daughter-in-law, Marianne (Ingrid Thulin), he reminisces (both consciously and in dreams) about his life, most of it involving disappointments in love. His fiancée (Bibi Andersson) married his brother, and his wife (Gertrud Fridh) betrayed him with another man. When Marianne lowers the boom with a revelation about her marriage to his cold-hearted son, Evald, the elder Borg begins to understand how his own chilly demeanor has not served him well. The film is no dreary trudge, thanks to Gunnar Fischer's sparkling cinematography and Bergman's nimble mixing of the conscious and unconscious, the past and present. And there's some amusing interplay between Borg and his longtime housekeeper, who are in essence married and in fact may enjoy a more loving relationship than he had with his wife.

⊙**DVD** Special Edition on Criterion includes audio commentary by film historian Peter Cowie and a feature-length documentary on Ingmar Bergman.

DR14, DR16, XT4

Goes well with: *Providence*

WINGS OF DESIRE

ESSENTIAL

West Germany/France   1988   C/B&W   130 min.   PG-13   Drama
Dir: Wim Wenders
C: Bruno Ganz, Solveig Dommartin, Otto Sander, Curt Bois, Peter Falk

Arguably Wim Wenders's greatest film, *Wings of Desire* achieves a kind of ethereal quality appropriate to its protagonists. Bruno Ganz and Otto Sander play two angels who hover over Berlin, listening to the thoughts of its citizens, attempting to guide them gently through the shoals of contemporary life. Thanks to amazingly evocative black-and-white cinematography by Henri Alekan, the film never seems to touch the ground, sometimes soaring hundreds of feet above the city that would soon be united (a development Wenders clearly anticipated), sometimes dropping to ground level but never feeling grounded in the mundane. Eventually, Ganz's angel falls in love with a lovely trapeze artist (Solveig Dommartin), and he has to admit that he longs to be mortal and experience the true joys (and risk the pain) of love. Peter Falk plays himself in the film's most amusing sequences. It's a brilliant and daringly conceived meditation that offers great rewards on repeat viewings. The Independent Spirit Awards named it Best Foreign Film, and the New York Film Critics Circle bestowed a prize on Alekan's camerawork.

DR8, DR36, XT7

Goes well with: *Truly Madly Deeply*

THE WINGS OF THE DOVE

U.K./U.S.   1997   C   101 min.   R   Drama

Dir: Iain Softley

C: Helena Bonham Carter, Linus Roache, Alison Elliott, Charlotte Rampling, Elizabeth McGovern, Michael Gambon

Henry James's novel of opportunism, set in England and Venice, could easily be the blueprint for a film noir. Kate (Helena Bonham Carter) loves Merton (Linus Roache), but he puts his principles as a crusading journalist above making money. Kate's aunt (Charlotte Rampling), on whom she depends, is opposed to any marriage that won't mean financial independence for her niece. Enter American heiress Molly (Alison Elliott), a woman of great fortune but poor health, and Kate is soon arranging for Merton to court her, figuring that the dying woman's fortune will eventually fall to him. The setup is well played out, and when the scene shifts to Venice, that city's damp mystery seems to infect the characters with a severe case of dread and foreboding. Bonham Carter's hard-edged beauty has never been better used. The final confrontation between Kate and Merton is one of the saddest scenes of lovemaking ever filmed.

⊙**DVD**

DR5, DR18, DR29, XT7

Goes well with: *A Room with a View*

THE WINSLOW BOY

U.S.   1999   C   104 min.   G   Drama

Dir: David Mamet

C: Nigel Hawthorne, Rebecca Pidgeon, Jeremy Northam, Gemma Jones, Guy Edwards, Matthew Pidgeon, Colin Stinton

Terrence Rattigan's 1946 play, based on a true court case in Edwardian England, has found an unlikely adaptor in American playwright David Mamet, whose other films, set in present-day America, have been derived from his stage work or from original screenplays. Mamet proves adept at entering Rattigan's world, in which a thirteen-year-old boy, Ronnie Winslow, is accused of a small theft and expelled from a prestigious naval academy. His father (Nigel Hawthorne) and older sister (Rebecca Pidgeon) mount a crusade to restore the boy's (and their family's) good name, and Mamet skillfully portrays the effect their singlemindedness has on everyone inside the family and associated with it, including a suave barrister, Sir Robert Morton (Jeremy Northam), who agrees to take the case to court. Mamet confounds our expectations by not showing any scenes inside the courtroom, keeping our focus on the characters rather than the trial. Hawthorne and Northam are superb in portraying two men of great determination.

⊙**DVD:** Special Edition contains audio commentaries by David Mamet and cast, and "making of" featurette.

DR11, DR24, DR32

Goes well with: *Howards End*

WITH A FRIEND LIKE HARRY

France   2000   C   117 min.   R   Thriller
Dir: Dominik Moll
C: Laurent Lucas, Sergi López, Mathilde Seigner, Sophie Guillemin

A chance meeting with a casual acquaintance, the guest who overstays his welcome, the old friend who can't let go of the past—these seemingly ordinary elements are the foundation for an ingeniously constructed psychological thriller. Michel (Laurent Lucas), a married man with two daughters, is on his way to a country house he has been fixing up when he runs into Harry (Sergi López), a high school classmate he barely remembers. Ah, but Harry remembers Michel very, very well, and he slowly ingratiates himself into Michel's life. As in a good Hitchcock thriller, we are one step ahead of Michel in learning the method to Harry's madness; director Dominik Moll and cowriter Gilles Marchand are very clever about giving away information. By the time the first corpse appears, you may find yourself screaming at Michel to gather up his family and flee for his life, but the filmmakers won't let us off that easy. López's performance is right up there with Robert Walker's great turn in Hitchcock's *Strangers on a Train*.

⊙**DVD**
DR12, DR27
Goes well with: *La Cérémonie*

WITHNAIL AND I

U.K. 1987 C 105 min. R Comedy
Dir: Bruce Robinson
C: Richard E. Grant, Paul McGann, Richard Griffiths, Ralph Brown

In the last days of the 1960s, a pair of unemployed, underfed, and overboozed actors, Withnail (Richard E. Grant) and "I" (Paul McGann), are just barely getting by in their London flat, which they share with a small army of cockroaches. Then Withnail's uncle offers them the use of a country cottage, and the boys feel a sojourn to the rural districts would improve their outlook on life. Then the uncle (Richard Griffiths), roly-poly and full of affection for his nephew's pal, shows up. Actor turned writer-director Bruce Robinson based his screenplay on his own autobiographical novel; it is clear that McGann is Robinson, but Withnail's real-life counterpart is unknown, not that it matters much. Grant is sensationally funny as a man who will never admit how desperate he really is, all the while shifting the blame for his misfortunes onto anyone else available. The film captures the helter-skelter mood of the era in quick glimpses and astutely chosen tunes on the soundtrack.

⊙**DVD:** Includes limited edition Ralph Steadman poster of original film art; "Withnail & Us" documentary on the film.

CO2, DR12
Goes well with: *Cold Comfort Farm*

WOMAN IN THE DUNES

Japan 1964 B&W 123 min. NR Drama
Dir: Hiroshi Teshigahara
C: Eiji Okada, Kyoko Kishida, Koji Mitsui, Hiroko Ito

A young entomologist, engrossed in study at a beach, misses his bus back home, and the people of a nearby village offer him accommodation in the home of a widow who lives in a nearby sand pit. The catch is that they won't let him escape the pit, where the woman labors to extract sand that threatens to engulf the village. As the fates of the two captives become intertwined, the film takes on an otherworldly quality, thanks to the black-and-white images of cinematographer Hiroshi Segawa and the masterful direction of Hiroshi Teshigahara, who was nominated for an Oscar, as was the film.

⊙**DVD**

DR26, DR27

Goes well with: *The Music of Chance*

THE WOMAN NEXT DOOR

France 1981 C 106 min. R Drama

Dir: François Truffaut

C: Gérard Depardieu, Fanny Ardant, Henri Garcin, Michele Baumgartner, Veronique Silver

François Truffaut's penultimate film continues his investigation of the power of love to enrich and sometimes destroy, begun with his third feature, *Jules and Jim.* The premise is simple: Bernard (Gérard Depardieu), a happily married man with a young son living in the postcard-pretty village of Grenoble, discovers that the wife of the childless couple who has just moved in next door, Mathilde (Fanny Ardant), is a former lover. As the two begin an affair, the details of their former romance are carefully revealed, and it soon becomes clear that this is no light look at the dilemmas of love. Giving this story an added dimension is the narrator, Madame Jouve (Veronique Silver), who manages a tennis club and has her own history of thwarted romance. Depardieu and Ardant (appearing in her first Truffaut film—she became his last love offscreen) are sensational, both as a romantic team and as actors who portray with heartbreaking conviction a pair of characters unwilling to let go of their unresolved past.

⊙**DVD**

DR19

Goes well with: *The Last Metro*

A WOMAN UNDER THE INFLUENCE

U.S. 1974 C 155 min. R Drama

Dir: John Cassavetes

C: Peter Falk, Gena Rowlands, Katherine Cassavetes, Lady Rowlands, Fred Draper

Mabel Longhetti, the title character of John Cassavetes's best film, is clearly not doing well. Her husband, Nick, has been up all night working on a sewer repair job and has brought his crew home for a big breakfast.

And Mabel, who starts the meal in full Martha Stewart mode, soon begins talking like English is a second language to her. Gena Rowlands, working under the direction of her husband and frequent collaborator, creates in Mabel a character of rich ambiguity. She is ill, but how much do her loving husband (Peter Falk) and both sets of parents contribute to her feelings of helplessness? They're all trying to help her, but the script suggests they've been hurting her for so long that they can't tell the difference. In some of his films, Cassavetes can be too generous with his actors, allowing scenes to play beyond the point of audience exhaustion, but here that technique works superbly to explore the nuances of Mabel's behavior. Both Cassavetes and Rowlands were nominated for Oscars. That's Rowlands's mother playing Mabel's mom and Cassavetes's mother as Nick's.

⊙**DVD**

DR11, DR27, DR39

Goes well with: *Faces*

A WOMAN'S TALE

Australia 1991 C 93 min. PG-13 Drama

Dir: Paul Cox

C: Sheila Florance, Gosia Dobrowolska, Norman Kaye, Chris Haywood

Australian actress Sheila Florance was literally dying to play the lead in Paul Cox's moving film about an elderly woman's last days. Florance did die shortly after the film was completed, but you'd never know that she (or Martha) was suffering from cancer. Yes, this is a positive film about living one's life to the fullest, but it skips blithely past the mushy sentiments. Defying her son, who wants to move her to a nursing home, Martha intends to die in her own cozy apartment, attended by a young nurse (Gosia Dobrowolska), while she makes the rounds of her neighbors and friends until she's immobilized by her illness. Director Paul Cox, who scripted with Barry Dickins, refuses, like Martha, to give in to false piety, so it's impossible to be depressed by the certain ending.

DR8, DR14, DR16, DR39

Goes well with: *Ikiru*

WOMEN IN LOVE

ESSENTIAL

U.K. 1969 C 129 min. R Drama

Dir: Ken Russell

C: Alan Bates, Oliver Reed, Glenda Jackson, Eleanor Bron, Jennie Linden, Alan Webb

After a tempestuous career in British TV, where he turned out a series of flamboyantly stylized "biographies" of artists ranging from Isadora Duncan to Richard Strauss, director Ken Russell broke through to film audiences with his third feature, an adaptation of D. H. Lawrence's novel. Two sisters, Gudrun (Glenda Jackson) and Ursula (Jennie Linden), are attracted to two male friends, Gerald (Oliver Reed) and Birkin (Alan Bates). It's an honest depiction of Lawrence's struggle to understand the nature of the two genders and how they play off one another. Gudrun and Gerald are the "smart" couple who are inevitably involved in wrestling matches that are more mental than physical (like the famous nude one between the two male leads). Russell is relatively restrained here, as though working with Lawrence brought out his contemplative side; further proof of that lies in *The Rainbow,* a prequel to this story, which he made twenty years later. Jackson won an Oscar for her performance.

DR12, DR18, DR29, DR39

Goes well with: *The Rainbow*

WOMEN ON THE VERGE OF A NERVOUS BREAKDOWN

ESSENTIAL

Spain   1988   C   88 min.   R   Comedy
Dir: Pedro Almodóvar
C: Carmen Maura, Antonio Banderas, Julieta Serrano, María Barranco, Rossy De Palma

The film that made Spanish director Pedro Almodóvar an international star is still his funniest comedy. It's as if Almodóvar saw the comic possibilities in John Cassavetes's *A Woman Under the Influence;* Pepa (Carmen Maura) is slowly coming unraveled, thanks to her faithless boyfriend, his new girlfriend, his son, his son's girlfriend. . . . Almodóvar keeps piling on subplots and introducing new characters (she's a friend of a friend of his brother's wife) until we start to feel like we're the ones having a breakdown, only all the comings and goings and explosions and fires and screaming fits and hysterical collapses are played for hard laughs. The comic-book-colored décors are a visual clue that we're in for a campy good time, and Almodóvar and his finely tuned cast don't disappoint. The New York Film Critics Circle bestowed Best Foreign Language Film honors on *Women.*

⊙**DVD**
CO9
Goes well with: *All About My Mother*

A WORLD APART
U.S./Zimbabwe   1988   C   112 min.   PG   Drama
Dir: Chris Menges
C: Barbara Hershey, David Suchet, Jeroen Krabbé, Jodhi May, Rosalie
    Crutchley, Tim Roth, Adrian Dunbar

The fact that it takes on a rarely explored subject—a child's-eye view
of having parents whose political activities put them in grave physical
danger—might be enough to recommend this film. Fortunately, *A World
Apart* doesn't try to cheapen the true story of Shawn Slovo's childhood
in South Africa, where her white parents' antiapartheid stance fractured
their family life. Molly (Jodhi May) is a thirteen-year-old who just
wants some sense of stability at home, but she can't have it with Dad
(Jeroen Krabbé) on the run because of his Communist affiliation and
Mom (Barbara Hershey) writing scathing columns about the government's racist policies. Mom's arrest during the ninety-day crackdown of
1963 turns Molly into the kid everyone avoids at school, and things get
worse. Cinematographer Chris Menges (*The Killing Fields, The Mission*), working from a script by Slovo, makes an impressive directorial
debut. He may back the cause Molly's parents are fighting for, but his
real sympathies lie with the girl who becomes a victim of her parents'
own idealism. Menges was awarded Best Director by the New York
Film Critics Circle.

DR11, DR17, DR25, DR41
Goes well with: *King of the Hill*

THE WORLD OF APU
ESSENTIAL
India   1959   B&W   106 min.   NR   Drama
Dir: Satyajit Ray
C: Soumitra Chatterjee, Sharmila Tagore, Alok Chakravarty, Swapan
    Mukherjee

The final chapter in Satyajit Ray's masterful Apu trilogy finds Apu a
grown man, recently graduated from university and ready to take his
place in the adult world. Through a bizarre set of circumstances, he

agrees to marry the fiancée of a friend, and their postmarital courtship blossoms into love. Each of the previous two chapters contained the death of a key character, but Ray saves the most shocking one for this film. How Apu deals with this tragedy is the true test of his maturity. There is no way that these films can be overrated, and it's important to see the trilogy from the beginning, starting with *Pather Panchali* and continuing with *Aparajito,* to feel the cumulative power of Ray's story-telling.

DR8, DR11, DR16

Goes well with: *Aparajito*

THE YEAR MY VOICE BROKE
Australia 1987 C 103 min. PG-13 Drama
Dir: John Duigan
C: Noah Taylor, Loene Carmen, Ben Mendelsohn, Graeme Blundell,
Lynette Curran, Bruce Spence

Danny (Noah Taylor) is a young teen living in a small isolated town in Australia's New South Wales in 1962. His interest in mental telepathy and hypnosis is augmented by an ongoing fascination with Freya (Loene Carmen), a slightly older girl who was Danny's childhood friend; she still thinks of them as pals, but his hormones are sending his brain a different message. Writer-director John Duigan fills in this familiar coming-of-age story with nice flourishes, including the characters of Trevor (Ben Mendelsohn), a charismatic jock whom Freya is attracted to, and Jonah (Bruce Spence), a railroad worker and frustrated writer whom Danny sees as a mentor. There's also a good feel for the frustrations of life in a small town, where conformity exacts a terrible price on some citizens. Duigan continued Danny's story in *Flirting.*
⊙**DVD**
DR31, DR34, DR41
Goes well with: *Flirting*

THE YEAR OF LIVING DANGEROUSLY
Australia 1983 C 115 min. PG Drama
Dir: Peter Weir
C: Mel Gibson, Sigourney Weaver, Linda Hunt, Michael Murphy, Bill
Kerr

The political thriller laced with romance runs the risk of satisfying fans of neither. Peter Weir directed and cowrote (with three credited scripters) this fairly satisfying hybrid, set during the 1965 coup of President Sukarno's government. It was a time of homegrown political movements that rejected any foreigners, like Mel Gibson's Aussie journalist, and diplomatic personnel, like Sigourney Weaver's assistant to the British military attaché. But the show belongs to Linda Hunt's gender-bending turn as a Chinese-Australian cameraman. It's not just a remarkable physical feat but a superb character study of a jaded onlooker who figures that one form of corruption is about to replace another. Hunt won best supporting actress prizes from both the Academy and the New York Film Critics Circle.

⊙**DVD**

DR18, DR25, DR38

Goes well with: *Welcome to Sarajevo*

YI YI (A ONE AND A TWO)

ESSENTIAL

Taiwan/Japan   2000   C   173 min.   NR   Drama

Dir: Edward Yang

C: Nien-Jen Wu, Elaine Jin, Issey Ogata, Kelly Lee, Jonathan Chang, Hsi-Sheng Chen

Edward Yang's chronicle of a Taiwanese family is the kind of film that restores your faith in the ability of film to tell stories simply and most affectingly. The film begins with a wedding and ends with a funeral, and it spans only a few months in the lives of N.J. (Nien-Jen Wu), his wife, Min-Min (Elaine Jin), their teenage daughter, Ting-Ting (Kelly Lee), and their young son, Yang-Yang (Jonathan Chang). Yang effortlessly moves among the four characters and their concerns: N.J. sees his high-tech company in real peril and on a business trip hooks up with an old flame, while Min-Min succumbs to the strain of her job and her live-in mother's poor health and goes off on a religious retreat, Ting-Ting goes through the usual adolescent awakenings of love, and Yang-Yang discovers the joys of taking photographs. Yang pulls no stylistic tricks here, but he is wonderfully discreet, shooting many conversations through windows or glass partitions. Named Best Foreign Language Film by the New York Film Critics Circle.

⊙**DVD**

DR8, DR11

Goes well with: *Eat Drink Man Woman*

YOJIMBO

ESSENTIAL

Japan 1961 B&W 110 min. NR Action-Adventure
Dir: Akira Kurosawa
C: Toshiro Mifune, Eijiro Tono, Seizaburo Kawazu, Isuzu Yamada, Hi-roshi Tachikawa

On its own, *Yojimbo* is yet another exciting collaboration between Akira Kurosawa and Toshiro Mifune, the story of a samurai with his own code of ethics, which amount to Me First. He enters a village wracked by a violent feud; both clans make him offers, and he accepts both, then watches the two sides destroy each other. If this sounds familiar, you've probably seen its Western reincarnation, *A Fistful of Dollars,* the first of three collaborations between another great filmmaker and star, Sergio Leone and Clint Eastwood. Kurosawa's film plays the situation more for laughs than Leone's, though it can be argued that all of the spaghetti westerns had a certain tongue-in-cheek quality. The story continues in *Sanjuro.*
⊙**DVD**
AC5, AC8, XT3
Goes well with: *A Fistful of Dollars*

YOU CAN COUNT ON ME

ESSENTIAL

U.S. 2000 C 111 min. R Drama
Dir: Kenneth Lonergan
C: Laura Linney, Mark Ruffalo, Matthew Broderick, Rory Culkin, Jon Tenney, Gaby Hoffmann, Kenneth Lonergan

In the impoverished movie year 2000, Kenneth Lonergan's modestly mounted and immensely rewarding drama was a sparkling gem. Laura Linney plays a small-town bank manager and single mom whose life is shaken up by the appearance of her wayward brother, played with a peculiar intensity by Mark Ruffalo. Lonergan packs their restaurant reunion scene with an immense amount of information that is subtly imparted, a sign of faith that the viewer doesn't need everything spelled out. Both leads are terrific, as is Matthew Broderick as Linney's married boss and lover, in a variant of the character he played in *Election*. Lonergan even gives himself a choice part as a priest who advises Linney on her love life. Lonergan's screenplay won Independent Spirit, New York Film Critics Circle, and Sundance Film Festival awards; the film was also judged Best First Feature by the Independent Spirit Awards and won the Grand Jury Prize at Sundance. Linney's performance was honored by the New York critics.

⊙**DVD:** Special Edition contains audio commentary by Kenneth Lonergan and cast and crew interviews.

DR11, DR34

Goes well with: *Ma Saison Préférée*

THE YOUNG POISONER'S HANDBOOK

U.K./France/Germany   1995   C   99 min.   NR   Comedy
Dir: Benjamin Ross
C: Hugh O'Conor, Antony Sher, Ruth Sheen, Roger Lloyd-Pack, Charlotte Coleman

Every young man should have a hobby, and Graham Young's is mixing chemicals. Every young man should have a goal in life, and Mr. Young's is to become the greatest poisoner in history, with his family as his first victims. Benjamin Ross and cowriter Jeff Rawle based their screenplay on a true case, and they've given the facts a macabre spin. Graham (Hugh O'Conor) is a wide-eyed kid, isolated from his snobbish classmates and ignored at home, who has substituted ambition for morality. You have to laugh at his focus, even if that chuckle occasionally catches in your throat.

CO1, CO2, CO5

Goes well with: *The Butcher Boy*

<h1 style="text-align:center">Z</h1>

Z

France/Algeria   1969   C   127 min.   PG   Thriller
Dir: Costa-Gavras
C: Yves Montand, Irene Papas, Jean-Louis Trintignant, Charles Denner, Georges Géret, Jacques Perrin, François Périer, Marcel Bozzufi

Costa-Gavras's exciting political thriller suggests how an immense conspiracy of government agents, hired thugs, and corrupt politicians can attempt to disguise a murder as an accident. Amazingly, even six years after John F. Kennedy's assassination and the attendant speculation over its perpetrators, few films had suggested this possibility. The film is based on the 1965 murder of a Greek physician and activist, though it was shot in Algeria, since Greece was still under the thumb of a military dictatorship in 1969. Yves Montand plays the victim; Jean-Louis Trintignant plays the magistrate hired by the government to take a cursory look into the affair—and winds up playing hardball with his bosses. This is a kinetic film; characters always seem to be running down a street or arriving breathlessly at a meeting. Costa-Gavras plays the murder scene over and over from different angles, anticipating the TV sports obsession with instant replay. *Z* was a huge hit in the U.S., breaking box-office records for foreign-language films and reaping several Oscar nominations, including Best Picture. It did win Oscars for Best Foreign Language Film and for Film Editing; the New York Film Critics Circle gave it their Best Film and Best Director prizes.

⊙**DVD**
DR25, TH4, XT4
Goes well with: *State of Siege*

ZERO FOR CONDUCT

France 1933 B&W 44 min. NR Drama
Dir: Jean Vigo
C: Jean Dasté, Robert le Flon, Louis Lefebvre, Constantin Kelber

After nearly seventy years, it's still the king of boarding-school movies. This minimovie is a dreamlike exploration of the world of repressive rules, nighttime pillow fights, and finally a full-scale revolt in which a group of visiting VIPs are greeted with a fusillade of garbage. Jean Vigo completed only two features, a documentary, and a short film before his untimely death in 1934 at the age of twenty-nine. Vigo was clearly influenced by the Surrealists (the headmaster is a bearded dwarf whose imperious strut is hilariously pompous), though his film is firmly grounded in the realities that he experienced as an unhappy child whose father died when Jean was twelve. The film was greeted on its release in France with dismay and official condemnation and was banned from exhibition for eleven years, a tribute to its effective lampooning of authority. Its echoes would find their way into many films, most notably *The Four Hundred Blows* and *if . . .*

DR3, DR7, DR31, DR41
Goes well with: *if . . .*

KEY TO SUBGENRES

ACTION-ADVENTURE-WESTERNS
AC1: COPS AND GANGS
AC2: MAN VS. NATURE
AC3: MARTIAL ARTS
AC4: MISSION IMPOSSIBLE
AC5: ONE-MAN ARMIES
AC6: OUTLAWS
AC7: REVENGE, GETTING
AC8: SWORDS AND SORCERY

COMEDY
CO1: AMATEUR CROOKS
CO2: DARK COMEDY
CO3: FAMILY MIRTH
CO4: FISH OUT OF WATER
CO5: GROW UP!
CO6: HISTORICAL HIJINKS
CO7: MANNERS, COMEDIES OF
CO8: MODERN TIMES
CO9: ROMANCE CAN BE FUN
CO10: SHOW-BIZ, EVERYONE'S IN
CO11: SMALL-TOWN ODDITIES
CO12: SPOOFS

DOCUMENTARIES
*DO1: CONTEMPORARY SOCIETY
AND ITS DISCONTENTS*
*DO2: CRIME AND ITS
AFTERMATH*

DO3: HISTORICAL RECORD
DO4: LIVES OF THE FAMOUS
*DO5: MOVIES ABOUT MOVIES,
MUSIC, AND THE ARTS*
DO6: PERFORMANCE FILMS
DO7: PERSONAL STORIES
DO8: THE PLACE AND TIME
DO9: POLITICS AS USUAL
DO10: SPORTS WORLD
DO11: SUBCULTURES

DRAMA
DR1: AMBITION, BLIND
DR2: ARTIST AT WORK
DR3: AUTOBIOGRAPHY
DR4: BACKSTAGE PASSES
*DR5: CLASS DISTINCTIONS
AND RITUALS*
DR6: CRIME, LIVES OF
DR7: CULTURE CLASHES
DR8: DEATH, DEALING WITH
DR9: DRINKING DAYS
*DR10: DRUGS AS A WAY
OF LIFE*
DR11: FAMILY STRIFE
DR12: FRIENDSHIPS
DR13: GAMBLING FEVER
DR14: GOLDEN OLDSTERS
*DR15: HANDICAPS,
OVERCOMING*

DR16: LIFE LESSONS
DR17: LIVES OF REAL PEOPLE
DR18: LOVE STORIES
DR19: LOVE, FORBIDDEN
VARIETIES
DR20: MALAISE, MODERN
DR21: MISFITS AND NONCON-
FORMISTS
DR22: MOVIES, MAKING
DR23: THE MUSIC SCENE
DR24: OUT OF THE PAST
DR25: POLITICS, ANYONE?
DR26: PRISONERS—CRIMINAL,
POLITICAL, AND OTHERS
DR27: PSYCHODRAMA
DR28: RACIAL AND ETHNIC
MATTERS
DR29: READ THE BOOK?
DR30: RELIGION AND FAITH
DR31: SCHOOL DAYS
DR32: SEEN THE PLAY?
DR33: SEX SEX SEX
DR34: SMALL TOWN BLUES
DR35: SPORTS STORIES
DR36: URBAN SCENE
DR37: WAR IS HELL: SOLDIERS'
STORIES
DR38: WAR IS HELL II: CIVILIAN
CASUALTIES
DR39: WOMEN'S ISSUES
DR40: WORKING-CLASS
TROUBLES
DR41: YOUTH, TROUBLED

FANTASY/HORROR/SCIENCE FICTION
FA1: ALIEN VISITORS
FA2: CULTS
FA3: DYSTOPIAS

FA4: FAIRY TALES AND LEGENDS
FA5: FANTASTIC SETTINGS
FA6: IN THE MIND OF A CHILD
FA7: MAD KILLERS
FA8: SCIENCE RUN AMOK
FA9: THE UNDEAD

MUSICALS
MU1: OPERAS
MU2: SHOW-BIZ TALES

THRILLERS
TH1: BLACKMAIL/HOSTAGES
TH2: CON GAMES
TH3: CRACKING UP
TH4: CRIME COVERUPS
TH5: DOUBLECROSSES
TH6: ESPIONAGE
TH7: FEMMES FATALES
TH8: HEISTS
TH9: HIRED KILLERS
TH10: KILLING FOR LOVE
TH11: LAUGHS AND THRILLS
TH12: MASTER CRIMINALS
TH13: NEO-NOIR
TH14: REVENGE IS MINE
TH15: SERIAL KILLERS
TH16: WOMEN IN DANGER
TH17: THE WRONG MAN

VIDEO EXTRA
XT1: ANTHOLOGY FILMS
XT2: FOOD ON THE MENU
XT3: HOMAGES TO AMERICAN
FILMS
XT4: PLAYING WITH TIME: FLASH-
BACKS, FLASH FORWARDS
XT5: ROAD TRIPS

SUBGENRES INDEX

DR12: FRIENDSHIPS

DR25: POLITICS, ANYONE?

FANTASY/HORROR/SCIENCE FICTION
FA1: ALIEN VISITORS

FA2: CULTS

FA3: DYSTOPIAS

PEDRO ALMODÓVAR
All About My Mother
Live Flesh
Women on the Verge of a
Nervous Breakdown

ROBERT ALTMAN
Cookie's Fortune
Gosford Park
The Player
Secret Honor
Short Cuts

ALLISON ANDERS
Gas Food Lodging
Mi Vida Loca

LINDSAY ANDERSON
if...
O Lucky Man!
This Sporting Life

PAUL THOMAS ANDERSON
Boogie Nights
Hard Eight

WES ANDERSON
Bottle Rocket

MICHELANGELO ANTONIONI
Blowup
L'Avventura

MICHAEL APTED
42 Up
35 Up

ALFONSO ARAU
Like Water for Chocolate

GILLIAN ARMSTRONG
High Tide
The Last Days of Chez Nous
My Brilliant Career
Oscar and Lucinda

MORTEN ARNFRED
The Kingdom

DARREN ARONOFSKY
Pi

JOSH ARONSON
Sound and Fury

RICHARD ATTENBOROUGH
Chaplin

BILLE AUGUST
Pelle the Conqueror

GABRIEL AXEL
Babette's Feast

ROGER MICHELL
Notting Hill

NIKITA MIKHALKOV
Burnt by the Sun

GEORGE MILLER
Mad Max
The Road Warrior

ANTHONY MINGHELLA
The English Patient
Truly Madly Deeply

JOHN CAMERON MITCHELL
Hedwig and the Angry Inch

HAYAO MIYAZAKI
Princess Mononoke

FREIDA LEE MOCK
Maya Lin: A Strong Clear
Vision

DOMINIK MOLL
With a Friend Like Harry

JAMES MOLL
The Last Days

MARIO MONICELLI
Big Deal on Madonna Street

MICHAEL MOORE
Roger & Me

JOCELYN MOORHOUSE
Proof

ERROL MORRIS
Fast, Cheap & Out of Control
Gates of Heaven
Mr. Death: The Rise and Fall of
Fred A. Leuchter, Jr.
The Thin Blue Line

ALLAN MOYLE
Pump Up the Volume

CHRISTOPHER MÜNCH
The Hours and Times

F. W. MURNAU
The Last Laugh
Nosferatu

MIRA NAIR
Kama Sutra: A Tale of Love
Mississippi Masala

SILVIO NARIZZANO
Georgy Girl

GREGORY NAVA
El Norte
My Family (Mi Familia)

RONALD NEAME
The Prime of Miss Jean Brodie

TIM BLAKE NELSON
Eye of God

MIKE NEWELL
Dance with a Stranger
Four Weddings and a Funeral

STÉPHANE AUDRAN (B. 1932)
Babette's Feast
Coup de Torchon
The Discreet Charm of the
Bourgeoisie

DANIEL AUTEUIL (B. 1950)
Girl on the Bridge
Jean de Florette
Ma Saison Préférée
Manon of the Spring
Un Coeur en Hiver

BOB BALABAN (B. 1945)
Best in Show
Ghost World
Gosford Park
Waiting for Guffman

CHRISTIAN BALE (B. 1974)
American Psycho
Henry V (1989)
The Portrait of a Lady

JEAN-MARC BARR (B. 1960)
Breaking the Waves
Dancer in the Dark
Hope and Glory

PAUL BARTEL (1938–2000)
Basquiat

Eating Raoul
The Usual Suspects

ALAN BATES (B. 1934)
The Entertainer
Far from the Madding Crowd
Georgy Girl
The Go-Between
Gosford Park
Women in Love

PATRICK BAUCHAU (B. 1938)
Choose Me
Entre Nous
The Rapture
Twin Falls, Idaho

EMMANUELLE BÉART (B. 1965)
La Belle Noiseuse
Manon of the Spring
Nelly and Monsieur Arnaud
Un Coeur en Hiver

KATE BECKINSALE (B. 1974)
Cold Comfort Farm
The Last Days of Disco
Much Ado About Nothing

**JEAN-PAUL BELMONDO
(B. 1933)**
Breathless
Pierrot le Fou

JULIETTE BINOCHE (B. 1964)
The English Patient
Red
The Unbearable Lightness of
Being

JANE BIRKIN (B. 1946)
Blowup
La Belle Noiseuse
A Soldier's Daughter Never
Cries

**GUNNAR BJÖRNSTRAND
(1909–1986)**
The Seventh Seal
Shame
Wild Strawberries

CATE BLANCHETT (B. 1969)
Elizabeth
Oscar and Lucinda

BRIAN BLESSED (B. 1937)
Hamlet (1996)
Henry V (1989)
Much Ado About Nothing

DIRK BOGARDE (1921–1999)
Accident
Darling
Providence
The Servant

SANDRINE BONNAIRE (B. 1967)
A Nos Amours
La Cérémonie
Vagabond

DAVID BOWIE (B. 1947)
Absolute Beginners
Basquiat
The Man Who Fell to Earth
Merry Christmas, Mr.
Lawrence

KENNETH BRANAGH (B. 1960)
Hamlet (1996)
Henry V (1989)
Much Ado About Nothing

RICHARD BRIERS (B. 1934)
Hamlet (1996)
Henry V (1989)
Much Ado About Nothing

JIM BROADBENT (B. 1949)
Bridget Jones's Diary
The Crying Game
Life Is Sweet
Richard III (1995)
Topsy-Turvy

**MATTHEW BRODERICK
(B. 1962)**
Election
Mrs. Parker and the Vicious
Circle
You Can Count on Me

ELEANOR BRON (B. 1934)
Help!
The House of Mirth
Women in Love

RALPH BROWN (B. 1960)
The Crying Game
Impromptu
Withnail and I

ADRIAN DUNBAR (B. 1958)
The Crying Game
The General
Hear My Song
My Left Foot
Richard III (1995)
A World Apart

CHARLES S. DUTTON (B. 1951)
Cookie's Fortune
Get on the Bus
Menace II Society
Mississippi Masala

ROBERT DUVALL (B. 1931)
The Apostle
Rambling Rose
Sling Blade

CLINT EASTWOOD (B. 1930)
A Fistful of Dollars
For a Few Dollars More
The Good, the Bad and the
Ugly

**CHRISTOPHER ECCLESTON
(B. 1964)**
Elizabeth
Let Him Have It
Shallow Grave

CHRIS EIGEMAN (B. 1965)
Barcelona
Kicking and Screaming
The Last Days of Disco
Metropolitan

GIANCARLO ESPOSITO (B. 1958)
The Usual Suspects
Night on Earth

School Daze
Smoke

**SHIRLEY ANN(E) FIELD
(B. 1936)**
The Entertainer
Hear My Song
My Beautiful Laundrette
Saturday Night and Sunday
Morning

RALPH FIENNES (B. 1962)
The End of the Affair
The English Patient
Oscar and Lucinda
Sunshine

ALBERT FINNEY (B. 1936)
The Duellists
The Entertainer
Saturday Night and Sunday
Morning
Tom Jones

COLIN FIRTH (B. 1960)
Apartment Zero
Bridget Jones's Diary
The English Patient
Shakespeare in Love

PETER FONDA (B. 1939)
Easy Rider
The Limey
Ulee's Gold

EDWARD FOX (B. 1937)
The Day of the Jackal
The Duellists
The Go-Between

Prick Up Your Ears
Sid and Nancy

LAURENCE OLIVIER
(1907–1989)
The Entertainer
Hamlet (1948)
Henry V (1945)
Richard III (1955)

MICHAEL PALIN (B. 1943)
And Now for Something
Completely Different
Monty Python and the Holy Grail
Monty Python's Life of Brian
Monty Python's The Meaning
of Life
Time Bandits

GWYNETH PALTROW (B. 1973)
Hard Eight
Mrs. Parker and the Vicious
Circle
Shakespeare in Love

MARY-LOUISE PARKER (B. 1964)
The Five Senses
Longtime Companion
The Portrait of a Lady

BILL PATERSON (B. 1945)
Comfort and Joy
The Killing Fields
Richard III (1995)
Sunshine
Truly Madly Deeply

MICHEL PICCOLI (B. 1925)
Belle de Jour

Contempt
The Discreet Charm of the
Bourgeoisie
La Belle Noiseuse

REBECCA PIDGEON (B. 1963)
The Spanish Prisoner
State and Main
The Winslow Boy

MARY KAY PLACE (B. 1947)
Citizen Ruth
Eye of God
Smooth Talk

MARTHA PLIMPTON (B. 1970)
Eye of God
I Shot Andy Warhol
Mrs. Parker and the Vicious
Circle

SARAH POLLEY (B. 1979)
Exotica
Go
The Sweet Hereafter

PARKER POSEY (B. 1968)
Basquiat
Best in Show
Dazed and Confused
Henry Fool
Kicking and Screaming
Party Girl
subUrbia
Waiting for Guffman

KELLY PRESTON (B. 1963)
Citizen Ruth
Drugstore Cowboy
From Dusk till Dawn

**CHARLOTTE RAMPLING
(B. 1945)**
Georgy Girl
Under the Sand
The Wings of the Dove

STEPHEN REA (B. 1946)
The Butcher Boy
The Crying Game
The End of the Affair
Life Is Sweet

**MICHAEL REDGRAVE
(1908–1985)**
Dead of Night
The Go-Between
The Innocents
The Lady Vanishes
The Loneliness of the Long
Distance Runner

VANESSA REDGRAVE (B. 1937)
Blowup
Cradle Will Rock
Howards End
Isadora
A Man for All Seasons
Mrs. Dalloway
Prick Up Your Ears

CORIN REDGRAVE (B. 1939)
Excalibur
Four Weddings and a Funeral
In the Name of the Father

LYNN REDGRAVE (B. 1943)
Georgy Girl
Gods and Monsters
Tom Jones

OLIVER REED (1938–1999)
The Four Musketeers
Funny Bones
The Three Musketeers
Women in Love

KEANU REEVES (B. 1964)
Much Ado About Nothing
My Own Private Idaho
River's Edge

ALBERT RÉMY (1911–1967)
Children of Paradise
The Four Hundred Blows
Shoot the Piano Player

MAGGIE RENZI
Eight Men Out
Matewan
Return of the Secaucus 7

FERNANDO REY (1915–1994)
The Discreet Charm of the
Bourgeoisie
Seven Beauties
Viridiana

**MIRANDA RICHARDSON
(B. 1958)**
The Apostle
The Crying Game
Dance with a Stranger

**RALPH RICHARDSON
(1902–1983)**
The Fallen Idol
O Lucky Man!
Richard III (1955)
Time Bandits

Note: Films are indexed here by the primary country or countries of origin. Filming location and nationality of director and cast are the main determining factors.

Films listed in this index were available on DVD as this guide went to press. A + symbol next to a title indicates that the DVD contains extra features beyond the standard cast and crew biographies and trailers. For details on those features, consult the entry for each title. For further updates on DVD availability, use the websites referenced in the Resource Directory.

TOM WIENER has been writing about films, TV, and popular culture for twenty-five years at publications such as *American Film* magazine and *Satellite Direct.* His previous film guide, *The Book of Video Lists,* went through five updated versions. He is a book reviewer for *USA Today* and *The Washington Post Book World.*